D1242089

Immigrant Youth in Cultural Transition

Acculturation, Identity, and Adaptation Across National Contexts

Immigrant Youth in Cultural Transition

Acculturation, Identity, and Adaptation Across National Contexts

Edited by

John W. Berry
Queen's University, Canada
Jean S. Phinney
California State University, Los Angeles
David L. Sam
University of Bergen, Norway
Paul Vedder
Leiden University, The Netherlands

 LAWRENCE ERLBAUM ASSOCIATES, PUBLISHERS
2006   Mahwah, New Jersey   London

Lawrence Erlbaum Associates, Inc., Publishers
10 Industrial Avenue
Mahwah, New Jersey 07430
www.erlbaum.com

Cover art provided by Peter Phinney

Cover design by Tomai Maridou

Library of Congress Cataloging-in-Publication Data

Immigrant youth in cultural transition : acculturation, identity, and
adaptation across national contexts / by John W. Berry ... [et al.].
    p. cm.
Includes bibliographical references and index.
ISBN 0-8058-5156-9 (cloth : alk. paper)
1. Immigrants—Cultural assimilation—Cross-cultural studies. 2. Teenage immigrants—Social conditions—Cross-cultural studies. 3. Acculturation—Cross-cultural studies.   I. Berry, John W.
JV6342.I46   2006
305.235—dc22   2005049511
                                          CIP

Printed in the United States of America
10 9 8 7 6 5 4 3 2 1

*To the many young people and their parents
who generously gave their time to take part in our study,
and to youth everywhere as they navigate
their own cultural transitions.*

Contents

Foreword

Karen Phalet[1]

In Europe, as in classic immigration countries outside Europe, the children of post-1965 immigrants are now leaving school and entering the labor market in increasing numbers. How this "new second generation" makes the transition to adult life, and how it is able to negotiate multiple cultures and identities, is crucial for the success or failure of immigrant integration in our societies. At the same time, old as well as new societies of immigration are receiving an increasingly diversified inflow of new immigrants, who often bring their families and children. They enter the country as asylum seekers or refugees, through marriage with settled immigrants, or as undocumented workers. As a consequence, ethnocultural diversity is the rule rather than the exception in today's cities, schools, and work places. Especially in new societies of immigration, the diversification of ethnic languages, religions, cultures, and identities is upsetting commonsense notions of national culture, identity, and values (Phalet & Kosic, 2006).

While I am writing this foreword, hundreds of young people of immigrant origin in the French *banlieues* are out on the streets, challenging the police and setting fire to cars and schools. Although the scale of the riots is unprecedented, the incident in itself is by no means a novelty. Local clashes of ethnic youth with the police do not usually make it into the national, let alone the international, press. Thus, Le Monde (November 8, 2005) reported no less than 28,000 registered incidents of ritual car burnings in the *banlieues* this year alone, preceding the nationwide riots. From a European perspective, media images of torched cars have come to symbol-

[1]Karen Phalet is Professor at the Faculty of Social Sciences of the Universities of Utrecht and Nijmegen. As a senior research fellow of the European Research Centre On Migration and Ethnic Relations (Ercomer) at Utrecht University, she is doing cross-cultural and acculturation research in European cities and in multi-ethnic schools. She publishes regularly in edited volumes and in international journals. She is Associate Editor of the *Journal of Cross-Cultural Psychology.*

ize a growing public and political concern with the acculturation and adaptation of ethnic youth.

Since the late 1990s, unemployment rates among school leavers without or with lower qualifications have been on the rise (OECD, 2003). Moreover, there is hard evidence of ethnic discrimination in the labor market so that ethnic youth are even less likely to find stable and well-paid jobs (Heath & Cheung, in press). Finally, in some countries like France or the Netherlands, recent government policies reducing public investment in disadvantaged groups and neighborhoods, along with an exclusionary public discourse rejecting cultural difference, have fueled feelings of anger and resentment among many young people (Body-Gendrot, 2003).

But economic restructuring and ethnopolitical tension are only one side of the broader picture. Optimists see good reasons why the experiences of today's ethnic youth may be more positive than those of earlier immigrants. Most countries have extended civil and social rights to immigrants and adopted effective antidiscrimination legislation, in line with European Union directives. In many countries, immigrant communities have built their own associations, with a view to provide social support, preserve their culture, and protect their rights. Interestingly, pessimists and optimists alike tend to overgeneralize their opposite—problematic or positive—views of the futures of ethnic youth in our societies. To date, public debates and policies targeted at ethnic youth have not usually been informed by scientific research findings (Bonifazi & Strozza, 2003). For the purpose of monitoring ethnic diversity or disadvantage, however, more and more countries have started generating national data on the origins and careers of immigrant groups. Still, official data sources are largely descriptive and most often limited to aggregate-level statistics on the main populations of foreign nationality and their school-aged children. Typically, migration studies and policies tend to overlook or underestimate the great diversity of acculturation strategies and experiences at the individual level of ethnic youth and their families. Indeed, cross-cultural, social, and developmental psychologists are only beginning to develop their own comparative research agenda by studying the varying fates of ethnic youth across ethnic and national contexts.

This book puts psychological acculturation research firmly on the map. Drawing on the International Comparative Study of Ethnocultural Youth, John Berry, Jean Phinney, David Sam, Paul Vedder and others bring together new comparative findings on the psychological acculturation and adaptation of ethnic youth. The most notable feature of the ICSEY project is undoubtedly its wide comparative scope, which offers unique insights into the varying experiences of ethnic youth across ethnic and national cultural contexts. Since the mid 1990s, participants of immigrant and national (i.e., nonimmigrant) origin from 13 receiving societies have been involved in the study. Specifically, the study compares settler societies with a long history of immigration (e.g., Canada) with former colonial societies in the northwest of Europe (e.g., France) and with more recent societies of immigration in the north (e.g., Norway) and south of Europe (e.g., Portugal). In addition, some immigrant groups (i.e., Vietnamese and Turkish) were studied across several receiving societies, whereas other groups were present in only one society (e.g., Mexicans in the United States). In addition to immigrant youth proper, the study also includes samples of second-generation youth and national youth in the same countries as comparison groups. Participants are not representative of the ethnic and national populations under study, and they are not necessarily selected using comparable procedures in each participating country. Hence, variations in acculturation, identification, and adaptation across cultures should be interpreted with due caution. Still, the cross-cultural pattern of associations reveals common psychological processes underlying more or less favorable intercultural relations and cross-cultural adaptation.

In particular, the study adds to the state of the art in psychological acculturation research in at least two major ways. First of all, the comparative approach of the ICSEY study is an unprecedented and impressive example of coordinated cross-cultural research on the key questions of intercultural relations and immigrant adaptation. For instance, the *Journal of Cross-Cultural Psychology* has published a wealth of single-country studies of acculturation. Until recently, however, truly comparative research efforts across national boundaries have been rare (e.g., Deaux, 2000). One obvious reason for the scarcity of cross-national acculturation research is that in most countries, issues of migration and cultural diversity are politically sensitive and closely entwined with distinct national histories, identities, and vocabularies. Therefore, the meanings of key concepts such as *integration, assimilation*, and *multiculturalism* differ considerably between Canada, Australia, Israel, the United States, and most European countries. As Reicher and Hopkins (2001) observed in their introduction to their book *Self and Nation* (p. vii), national preconceptions are most often buttressed by considerable political and personal investments, which make them hard to challenge. In the area of acculturation research, such preconceptions have complicated the development of a balanced "derived etics" approach to the experiences of immigrant families and children (Phalet & Kosic, 2006). Looking beyond national terminologies and understandings, the ICSEY project goes a long way to developing a much needed "derived-etics" approach of psychological acculturation. Clearly, the main aim and strength of the study is its articulation of the "etics" of acculturation. Thus, the way the study was set up couples considerable flexibility in the stage of nationally organized data collection with a rather stringent—given the great diversity of countries, groups, and data sources—approach to cross-cultural measurement and hypothesis testing (Van de Vijver & Leung, 1997). As a result, the authors were mostly successful in developing and documenting common concepts and measures of acculturation that are valid across a wide range of cultural groups and societies. This makes the book a valuable resource for cross-cultural psychological assessment in increasingly diverse societies.

Last but not least, the study brings together three different subdisciplines within psychology, which have developed strong but mostly separate research traditions examining the cultures and identities of ethnic youth: cross-cultural, developmental, and social psychology. Building on the seminal cross-cultural work of John Berry and others in Canada, the study replicates first of all a great number of studies that have used attitude-type measures of acculturation strategies to predict immigrant adaptation. Thus, across immigrant groups and countries, what has been called the integration strategy, combining positive attitudes toward ethnic and national cultures, is most often related to psychological well-being and smooth sociocultural adaptation. At the same time, the findings reveal significant variation across cultural contexts: For example, among Turkish youth in Europe, a popular separation strategy—rather than integration—seems most psychologically rewarding. But the study goes beyond cross-cultural acculturation studies in the narrow sense, and makes good use of relevant theories, concepts, and measures from social and developmental psychology. Importantly, by bringing together different strands of research on ethnic youth, much researched attitudinal measures of acculturation are complemented with self-reported behaviors, values, and self-identifications. Despite the well-known discrepancies between various aspects of acculturation, the analysis suggests the existence of coherent acculturation profiles across cultures, which closely reflect Berry's original acculturation strategies. In addition, the unique comparative design combines the social-psychological study of intercultural relations between immigrant and national origin groups with the study of intergenerational relations between immigrant parents and their children in cross-cultural developmental psychology. By bringing together different perspectives and theories on intercultural and intergenerational relations, the study gives a dynamic account of acculturation experiences as they are jointly shaped by developmental processes within the family and by group processes within the wider society. Together, the findings document the diverse and changing cultures, identities, and values in immigrant families and youth. Thus, they are challenging overly general and most often problematic public images of migration and cultural difference.

Preface

Immigration is a worldwide phenomenon, both in countries that have been built on the flow of people to develop their societies and in countries that are relatively new to the immigration experience. There is now a vast literature on the psychological and social changes that take place among immigrants and their descendants in the societies that are long-standing receivers of immigrants. Most of these studies focus on one or a few groups that are starting their new lives in one society of settlement. On the basis of these single-country studies, it has proved very difficult to discern any general principles about how the process of acculturation takes place or how well people adapt to their new settings. What has been missing are comparative studies that seek to understand whether acculturation and adaptation take place in similar ways across immigrant groups and across differing societies of settlement. Also missing are studies that seek to identify the features of the immigrant and receiving people and settings that may support or undermine these processes. Are there some general principles that operate to allow researchers to make sense of this vast literature? And could such general principles serve as a basis for the development and implementation of policies and programs in the numerous countries that are now experiencing immigration and settlement issues, some for the first time?

These questions have interested the group of researchers involved in this project for a number of years. Termed the "International Comparative Study of Ethnocultural Youth" (known by its acronym ICSEY), we came together to build a team of like-minded colleagues in 13 countries (see list of team members at the end of the preface). A comparative study of acculturation and adaptation was proposed by one of us (John Berry) in an article in 1987, in which a matrix was presented that listed societies of settlement on one axis and immigrant groups on the other axis (Berry, Kim, Minde, & Mok, 1987). The proposal included suggestions for a common set of psychological and social variables that would be investigated in a sample of individuals in all societies and all immigrant groups in the framework. The proposal emphasized that individuals from both the immigrant and receiving groups should be included in the research. The ICSEY project can be seen as one outcome of these ideas. Moreover, to optimize the possibility of making controlled comparisons, the ICSEY group decided to sample at least one common immigrant group in as many countries as possible. The first immigrant group we included was Vietnamese, and the second was Turks.

The focus on youth became a central part of the project when colleagues with interests in developmental issues (Jean Phinney, Colette Sabatier, & David Sam) joined together with John Berry to form the core team in 1992. This group of four researchers brought together interests in acculturation, identity, and development. To better explore these combined interests, the decision was made to include a sample of parents; this allowed the examination of generational questions and family relationships that may be important in acculturation and adaptation.

In 1994, other colleagues joined the first four members of the team, adding interests in other aspects of immigration and the opportunity to expand the range of countries in the project. These new colleagues—Karmela Liebkind, Kyunghwa Kwak, Paul Schmitz, Erkki Virta, and Charles Westin—participated in the further development and refinement of the research instrument. The inclusion of new members in any research project raises new issues. For ICSEY, these issues were dealt with by adopting an arrangement in which members were independent, maintaining their own research programs while contributing to the common goal of creating the conditions for good-quality research. Moreover, all ICSEY members profited from the initial decision that participating countries could add questions or scales to the common questionnaire. This allowed team members to study topics that were of particular interest to their own society and to the ethnic groups living there. In short, participation in ICSEY clearly had added value to members of the group.

This stage of the project lasted until the data were collected. This costly effort could not be realized without financial support. However, finding such support for conducting the study in all of the various countries was deemed too difficult to pursue. It was decided that research funding was to be a national responsibility. This was the first time that synchronization of project activities could no longer be seen as a common responsibility of all participating researchers. The support programs of national research funding bodies were decisive. Availability of funding determined when data collection started. The first countries started collecting data in 1995. The final data were included in the comparative data set in 2002. That the completion of the data set took so long was due not only to funding problems but also to the fact that the ICSEY team aimed at extending the number of participating countries so that the range of immigration experiences and of cultural diversity would be enlarged.

In cross-cultural psychology, a widely accepted principle is that societies should be selected for comparison for theoretically relevant reasons. Two aspects of societies were considered as potentially important in how, and how well, immigrants would settle into their new societies. We thus decided to include countries that ranged from those that were experienced in immigration to those that were not so experienced. A related decision was to include countries that promoted cultural diversity (pluralism) as a matter of national policy and those that were interested in promoting a more uniform national culture. This decision required the expansion of the project to include countries that varied on these two dimensions.

The wish to expand the number of countries included in the project, and hence the number and variety of researchers, was a source of both stimulation and difficulty. The challenges of this expansion were mainly overcome by creating opportunities to meet frequently and to discuss matters openly. We also relied on modern technology such as e-mail and telephone conferencing. Over the years we also had research meetings at various locations, usually associated with international conferences. In the later stages of the project, symposia were presented at these conferences to report on progress. These meetings took place in Amsterdam (1994), Stockholm (1995), Montreal (1996) Los Angeles (1998), San Francisco (1998), Leiden, the Netherlands (1999), Pultusk, Poland (2000), Yogyakarta, Indonesia (2002), and Xi'an, China (2004).

ICSEY is an interesting case of international research collaboration. From conception to completion, the ICSEY team has taken 12 years to publish this book. We experienced a number of circumstances that have played a role in both sustaining the effort and in presenting the problems and pitfalls that we had to deal with. Reflecting on the processes that were essential to completing this project is important at a time when scholars all over the world are increasingly expected to collaborate (Martin, Craft, & Tillema, 2002). Key to its success were (a) a common interest in comparative acculturation research, (b) assurance that each participant could easily identify a common and a personal value and could experience support in realizing these values, (c) sufficiently frequent and clear communications with regular opportunities for personal contact either with the whole team or with subgroups of the team, and (d) an opportunity to do good research with a competitive edge. Many pitfalls mentioned by Martin et al. (2002), such as language and cultural differences among researchers and a lack of shared commitment to a common methodological approach, were experienced in the ICSEY project, but these were overcome. The fact that many participants were cross-cultural psychologists, or were experienced comparative researchers, was helpful in this respect. So, too, was the fact that all participants respected and enjoyed the expertise and comradeship of the other participants.

In this book you will find an overview of the main findings from the ICSEY project. These chapters are supplemented by more specific journal articles and book chapters, some of which have already been published. A list of these publications, as well as other information about the ICSEY project, can be found on our Web site: http://www.ceifo.su.se/icsey/icsey.html. This Web site was developed and is maintained by Erkki Virta at the University of Stockholm. Readers should note that many of these specific publications present partial findings (e.g., based on data from a few countries or with only some of the variables). Hence, there are likely to be some discrepancies between results and interpretations in these other publications and those reported in this book.

The present book contains nine chapters, each co-authored by those who contributed to the writing of the chapter. Other members of the ICSEY team, who are listed at the end of the preface, contributed to the international data set and provided information about the societies of settlement and immigrant groups with which they worked.

To introduce the project, chapter 1 presents the main research questions guiding the study and lays out a general conceptual framework for the project. Chapter 2 provides information on the design of the study and presents profiles of the 13 societies of settlement and the participating immigrant groups. Chapter 3 describes the participants and the methods of data collection and data analyses employed. Chapter 4, the first chapter to present results, provides information on the acculturation experience of immigrant youth, including attitudes, identity, behaviors, values, and perceived discrimination. A second set of results in chapter 5 reveals the ways immigrant youth are adapting, both psychologically and socioculturally. In chapter 6, the information from chapters 2, 4, and 5 is brought together to evaluate the general research framework presented in chapter 1, using structural equation modeling. Chapters 7 and 8 then take a closer look at two specific issues. In chapter 7, we examine the values regarding family relationships held by adolescents and their parents, their differences over values, and how such differences affect the adaptation of the youth. In chapter 8, the two immigrant groups for which we have multiple samples (Vietnamese and Turks) are examined in much detail. This allows us to evaluate the general model from chapter 6 while holding the background of the immigrant group constant. Finally, in chapter 9 we present a summary of our main findings, with some conclusions and implications. These pertain to current issues in the research literature on immigration, acculturation, and adaptation, and to issues of immigration and settlement policies and programs in immigrant-receiving countries.

—John W. Berry
Jean S. Phinney
David L. Sam
Paul Vedder

Members of ICSEY Team

Australia
Cynthia Leung, Department of Psychology, Victoria University, Melbourne
Rogelia Pe-Pua, School of Social Science and Policy, University of New South Wales, Sydney
Rosanna Rooney, School of Psychology, Curtin University, Perth
David Sang, Department of Psychology, University of Western Australia, Perth

Canada
John Berry, Department of Psychology, Queen's University, Kingston
Kyunghwa Kwak, Department of Psychology, Queen's University, Kingston

Finland
Karmela Liebkind, Department of Social Psychology, University of Helsinki, Helsinki

France
Colette Sabatier, Department of Psychology, Université Victor Segalen, Bordeaux

Germany
Paul Schmitz, Institute of Psychology, University of Bonn, Bonn

Israel
Gabriel Horenczyk, School of Education, Hebrew University of Jerusalem, Jerusalem

The Netherlands
Paul Vedder, Center for the Study of Education and Instruction, Leiden University, Leiden
Fons J. R. van de Vijver, Department of Psychology, Tilburg University, Tilburg

New Zealand
Colleen Ward, School of Psychology, Victoria University of Wellington, Wellington

Norway
David Sam, Department of Psychosocial Science, University of Bergen, Bergen

Portugal
Felix Neto, Faculty of Psychology, University of Porto, Porto

Sweden

Charles Westin, Center for Research in International Migration and Ethnic Relations, Stockholm University, Stockholm

Erkki Virta, Center for Research in International Migration and Ethnic Relations, Stockholm University, Stockholm

United Kingdom

Lena Robinson, School of Social Sciences, University of Paisley, Glasgow

United States

Jean Phinney, Department of Psychology, California State University, Los Angeles

Acknowledgments

This project has taken more than a decade to develop and carry out. During this period, we have received support, both financial and research assistance, from many sources. We are pleased to thank the following agencies and individuals.

Research Grants

Australia
    Faculty of Arts Quantum Grant, Victoria University
    Psychology Department Special Grant, Victoria University, Australian Research Council
    Curtin University of Technology School of Psychology (RECAP)
    Professor Charles Watson (Dean of Division of Health Sciences)
Canada
    Canadian Ethnic Studies Research Committee, Ministry of Multiculturalism
    Social Sciences and Humanities Research Council of Canada
Finland
    The Academy of Finland
New Zealand
    School of Psychology, Victoria University of Wellington
    Royal Society of New Zealand, James Cook Fellowship
Norway
    The Research Council of Norway, Project 107361/330
    The Johann Jacobs Foundation of Switzerland
Portugal
    Fundacao para a Ciencia e a Tecnologia
Sweden
    Swedish Council of Social Research

United Kingdom
British Academy, Grant SG 32453
United States
Grant S06 GM-08101 from the Minority Biomedical Research Support Program of the National Institutes of Health

Research Assistance

Australia
Faculty of Arts and the Department of Psychology, Victoria University
School of Social Science and Policy, University of New South Wales
Rooty Hill High School
Plumpton High School
Helen Lardizabal
School of Psychology, University of Western Australia, Nguyen Minh Khoi
Canada
In each of the cultural groups included in the Canadian sample, we worked with an assistant who is a member of the community. We are pleased to thank: K. Nguyen, D. Kim, M. Danaher, and T. Purohit.
Finland
Translation to Finnish of the questionnaire was carried out by Karmela Liebkind and Erkki Virta. Erkki Virta conducted the study under the supervision of Karmela Liebkind. Two assistants, who did all the practical work, provided invaluable help: Eira Pohjanvaara and Kaisa Ranta-aho. Inga Jasinskaja-Lahti applied ICSEY instruments in her studies on Russian youth for her PhD thesis, and her data on Russians and Finns have been used as part of the Finnish ICSEY data.
Israel
Valuable help was provided by Dr. Zvi Bekerman.
Norway
Graduate student Bodil Bjelland was primarily responsible for the translation of the questionnaire into Norwegian. Huan N. Nguyen and Helge Molde (graduate students) voluntarily saw to the data collection. Invaluable help and support were obtained from school teachers in the cities of Bergen, Drammen, Oslo, Stavanger, and Trondheim and are gratefully acknowledged.
New Zealand
We thank Jo Kleeb for data collection and library research and Elsie Ho and Cynthia Cheung for support with data collection in the Chinese community.
Sweden
Translation of the questionnaire into Swedish was carried out by Erkki Virta and Catarina Nyberg, who also was an invaluable help to Erkki Virta in conducting the pilot study. In the main study, Erkki was supported by Anna Andersson (now Anna Enwall). Many others contributed to the pilot study and/or the main study: Helena Bohm, Ulla Böhme, Helena Kivisaari, Eira Pohjanvaara, Kaisa Ranta-aho, Sofia

Wikner, Eva Åhs, and several members of CEIFO staff. Invaluable help was received from headmasters and teachers in many Stockholm schools. The study would not have succeeded without the active and enthusiastic participation of the pupils in those schools.

The Netherlands
Professor Lotty Eldering (Leiden University) took the initiative for the Dutch participation in ICSEY.

Of great help were the undergraduate and graduate students who, as members of their community and proficient in the languages of their community, collected the data. Coen Kouwenhoven patiently and conscientiously assisted in data handling and data analyses

United Kingdom
Research support was provided by one research assistant and school teachers in Leicester.

United States
Numerous undergraduate and graduate students took part in the project as research assistants; their participation was essential to the successful completion of the study. Many of them were supported by Grant S06 GM-08101 from the Minority Biomedical Research Support (MBRS) Program or by Grant R25 GM-61331 from the MBRS RISE Program, of the U.S. National Institutes of Health.

Overall Editorial Assistance

We very much appreciate the editorial assistance of Susan Lloyd in formatting, referencing, and indexing the book.

List of Figures

Chapter 5

List of Tables

Chapter 8

List of Appendixes

1 Introduction: Goals and Research Framework for Studying Immigrant Youth

John W. Berry
Queen's University

Jean S. Phinney
California State University, Los Angeles

Kyunghwa Kwak
Queen's University

David L. Sam
University of Bergen

BACKGROUND TO THE STUDY

Migration is a worldwide phenomenon, one that poses both opportunities and challenges for migrants and those in receiving societies alike. At the present time (United Nations Population Division, 2002), there are 175 million people living in countries in which they were not born, a level that has doubled in the past 25 years. Although this figure includes those who have moved from one country to another, and hence are officially "migrant," it ignores almost equal numbers of children of these immigrants who are often perceived as immigrants despite having been born in their country of residence. In this project, we take an inclusive approach to understanding immigration issues facing young people; this requires incorporating both immigrant children and the later offspring of adult immigrants into the category of *immigrant youth*.

The long-term outcome of migration is the formation of culturally diverse populations, all attempting to live together within nation states. Such culturally plural societies are composed not only of these first- and second-generation immigrants but also of the numerous ethnocultural communities that persist for many generations following migration. As a consequence, most contemporary societies now face questions about how to manage their immigration flows and the resulting cultural pluralism (Appleyard, 2001; Baubock, Heller & Zolberg, 1996; Kymlicka, 1995). Research that has addressed this domain (e.g., Berry, 1997; Portes & Rumbaut, 2001) makes it very clear that nation states, immigrant and ethnocultural groups within them, and their individual members do not all respond to these complex situations in the same way. There are vast national differences in policies, with some countries seeking homogenization, and others seeking cultural pluralism. There are also variations in the positions taken by ethnocultural organizations and communities with respect to how they prefer to live in the new society. For individuals in all these communities, there are important differences among them with respect to the strategies used by families and their members to engage the society in which they live. These variations in intercultural preferences contribute to *how*, and *how well*, immigrants (as groups and as individuals) adapt to the larger society.

This book reports on a large international study that seeks to answer three questions that are rooted in these phenomena:

1. *How* do immigrant youth live within and between two cultures? These cultures are usually those of their immigrant parents, families, and communities (their *heritage* culture) on the one hand, and those of their peers and the larger society on the other. We refer to this as the *intercultural* question.

2. *How well* (in personal, social, and academic areas of their lives) do immigrant youth deal with their intercultural situation? We refer to this as the *adaptation* question.

3. We expect that there will be variations (across individuals, ethnocultural groups, and societies of settlement) in the answers to these first two questions. Therefore, the third goal is to discover the patterns of relationships between how adolescents engage in their intercultural relations and how well they adapt. We believe that there are many possible patterns in these relationships, with variations that depend on three set of factors: (a) personal and demographic factors (including age, gender, and length of residence), (b) factors that are external to individuals and their communities (such as the cultural diversity of the society of settlement and their policies with respect to such diversity), and (c) differences between the immigrant groups and the larger society (such as differences in values, and religion). We refer to this as the *cross-cultural* question.

Although much of the early research on immigration and settlement was carried out in the social science disciplines of economics, sociology, anthropology, and demography (e.g., Portes, 1995), there is an obvious role for psychology and the other behavioral sciences (Berry, 2001). Clearly, the social, political and economic contexts need to be studied (as indeed they are in this project). However, our core interest is in individual young people (including relationships among them and their families) as they seek to (re)establish their lives in complex intercultural situations. This focus on individuals in context is the core feature of our project, one that distinguishes us from studies that have been carried out in the anthropological and sociological traditions. To address our questions, we draw on various branches of psychology (cross-cultural, developmental, and social) for concepts and tools (including assessment and statistical procedures).

Over the past 9 years, a group of psychologists from 13 countries has developed and carried out this International Comparative Study of Ethnocultural Youth (the ICSEY project). This project began as a sequel to studies then being carried out in Canada, Norway, and the United States. It expanded to include a wide range of countries, all of which are experiencing immigration to varying extents. It has involved research with more than 5,000 immigrant youth from 32 ethnocultural groups and smaller samples of their parents and their national peers (i.e., those native to the society of settlement).

In its broadest terms, this project can be seen as a converging of interests. From cross-cultural psychology we have adopted the concept of *acculturation* (Berry, 1990; Berry & Sam, 1997; Ward, 1996; Ward, Bochner, & Furnham, 2001), and from developmental and social psychology we have adopted the concept of *cultural identity* (Liebkind, 1992a; Phinney, 1990). The former refers to the cultural and psychological changes that result from the contact between cultural groups, including the attitudes and behaviors that are generated. The latter refers to the sense of attachment a person has to a particular group, including beliefs and feelings linking him or her to these groups. Although these two approaches have long and relatively independent traditions in psychology, we believe that they are conceptually and empirically related (Liebkind, 2001) and that together they can help us to better understand how, and how well, immigrant youth live in their intercultural worlds.

We are not the first to raise these questions, or to draw on the social and behavioral sciences to answer them. As the references at the end of this book show, there was much groundwork on which to lay the foundations for this project. However, we are among the first to ask these questions explicitly using the comparative method. In this study we make four kinds of comparisons by sampling across: (a) 13 countries of settlement, (b) 32 immigrant groups, (c) both youth and parents, and (d) both the immigrant and national populations. With comparisons across countries and across immigrant groups, we can search for commonalities and variations; with comparisons between parents and youth, we can examine convergence or divergence in intercultural adaptation within immigrant families (Foner, 1997); and with comparisons among ethnocultural groups (both immigrant and nonimmigrant) in the larger society, we can search for consensus about how all peoples might live together in culturally diverse societies (Bourhis, Moïse, Perreault & Senécal, 1997).

Given the dramatic increase in immigration to many countries and the changing policy and attitudinal responses to immigration in these countries (Dacyl & Westin, 2000; Kymlicka, 1995; Simon & Lynch, 1999), our study has also been driven by concerns with public policy and practical program development. Is there a way to develop policies and programs in areas such as immigration, settlement, community relations, and schooling so that the contemporary flow of people is both seen as, and actually becomes, advantageous to both the immigrant population and those already settled? Our study was designed to provide some insights into to these issues.

IMMIGRATION AND DIVERSITY

People have been on the move from the beginning of human existence: moving from Africa to Asia and Europe; from Asia and Africa to the Americas; then from Europe, Asia, and Africa to much of the world. Many serious problems have attended most of these movements, including warfare, slavery, colonization, and domination. New societies were created from this flux, some with continuing conflicts but also some with innovative social arrangements to deal with the reality that there are now virtually no societies that are culturally homogeneous. The contemporary world is facing this reality, often viewed as involving two separate issues: (a) the *immigration flow* (the arrival and settlement of the first generation) and (b) *ethnocultural diversity* (the longer term presence of numerous cultural communities, based in the second and subsequent generations).

For some researchers (those dealing only recently with immigrants arriving in relatively uniform societies), the main concern is with the arrival and settlement of immigrants. Research on immigration has been characterized by numerous empirical studies of specific groups, resulting in a massive array of findings but little in the way of theory (Portes, 1997). According to Portes (1997), there is, at present, no overarching, widely accepted theoretical approach to understanding immigration phenomena, nor is one likely to be developed anytime soon. However, there are a few themes within the broad domain of immigration that may yield theoretical advances. One of these themes is "the new second generation" (Portes, 1997; Zhou, 1997b), where the focus has come to bear on the children of immigrants. These studies are providing opportunities for theoretical development on the adaptation of immigrants and the impact of immigrants (of all generations) on the receiving society. A second theme is the movement away from single-country studies toward comparative research and analyses (e.g., Ghuman, 1994, 2003). The present study incorporates both of these themes, allowing for the possibility of theoretical advance.

For other researchers, the main concern is with the second issue: understanding and managing intercultural relations that follow immigration (e.g., Dacyl & Westin, 2000; Kymlicka, 1995). Much of the interest in this area has come about because the descendants of immigrants do not inevitably become absorbed or assimilate, as many earlier commentators had assumed. They take variable courses or pathways: Some do become indistinguishable from the majority in the larger society; some remain culturally vital while achieving full and equitable participation, creating a society made up of many and diverse cultural communities; others also remain culturally vital but stay largely outside the life of the larger society; still others are alienated from their cultures, becoming enmeshed in difficult social situations that are problematic for themselves and the larger society.

These variable outcomes have come to be recognized more over the past 25 years. One approach to studying them, which is used in this project, proposes that there are many different ways to live in intercultural arenas and to settle into daily life in culturally plural settings. One way to identify these variations in acculturation (Berry, 1980, 1984a) has been to distinguish among four *acculturation strategies: integration, assimilation, separation,* and *marginalization.* These different ways of acculturating are described fully in chapter 4. Other researchers (Rumbaut & Portes, 2001; Zhou, 1997b) have proposed a process of acculturation that they call *segmented assimilation*; they distinguish four varieties of acculturation: *consonant acculturation, consonant resistance to acculturation, selective acculturation,* and *dissonant acculturation.* All these concepts recognize the existence of diverse patterns of acculturation and adaptation to life in the new society. They challenge the assumption that acculturation inevitably leads to cultural and psychological loss by immigrant peoples and to the homogenization of the larger society.

A second approach to understanding how people come to live within and between the two societies is through the examination of their cultural identity. Immigrants arrive in a new country with a clear sense of their identity as members of their country of origin, for example, as Vietnamese or Turkish. Over time, their sense of self typically evolves (Phinney, 2003). As they learn the language and customs of the new society, they begin to identify with it to varying degrees. If they can become citizens, the identification is probably strengthened. At the same time, their sense of their cultural group membership changes, as they see themselves as part of an ethnocultural group, in a larger context. They may take on a double ethnic label, such as Vietnamese American, and begin to think of themselves as part of two cultures (their ethnic culture and the national culture). The ways in which immigrants' cultural identities change over time in a society of settlement is influenced both by their ethnic community and by the larger society, and the character of the relationships between them.

For adolescents, the development of these identities is part of the larger developmental task of identity formation. Young people who come to a new country as children, or who are born to immigrants, face the challenge of developing a cultural identity based on both their family's culture of origin and the culture of the society in which they reside. Outcomes of this process mirror the acculturation attitudes discussed earlier. One's cultural identity can be primarily *ethnic,* based in one's ethnic group, primarily *national,* based in the national society, or *bicultural,* based on a balancing or blending of the two cultures (Phinney & Devich-Navarro, 1997). If youth are unable to resolve the cultural identity issues that they face, they may exhibit identity *diffusion* (Marcia, 1994).

In both the acculturation and identity approaches, there is a set of common features that we consider in this project: For immigrant youth, we examine their intercultural contacts, their language, their identifications with the national society and ethnic communities, and the quality of their lives (both their personal and sociocultural well-being) as they live in these culturally diverse societies.

Because so much human migration has been attended by intergroup conflict and personal distress, there has been a tendency to view immigration and ethno-cultural group relations as problematic. Although most of the world's current antagonisms and overt conflicts have intercultural elements (including conflicts of language and religion), we believe that such difficulties are not inevitable. In contrast to this view of immigration as problematic, it is clear to us that people in most societies, even while experiencing the challenges of immigration and diversity, live in relative peace and have a good quality of life. Indeed, these issues appear to play no critical role in the development of societies: Of the four countries near the top of the United Nations Human Development Index, two (Norway and Japan) have little immigration and diversity, whereas two others (Australia and Canada) are countries that are high in (and even cherish) both immigration and diversity. We examine the nature of cultural diversity and the role that it may play in the acculturation and adaptation of immigrant youth in this book (in chapters 2 and 6).

A related issue concerns the quality of lives of the first (immigrant) generation and subsequent generations. As we have noted, for a long time immigration was seen as a negative experience, with problematic outcomes among immigrants. This view was possibly the result of research carried out largely by individuals concerned with personal problems (psychiatrists and clinical psychologists) and with social problems (sociologists and social workers). However, it is now abundantly clear that although such problems do exist, many immigrants settle into their new societies rather well, attaining educational, occupational, and social standings comparable to those in the larger society (e.g., Beiser, 1999; Fuligni, 1998a; Scott & Scott, 1989). Thus, we may conclude that problematic settlement and adaptation are not inevitable. By examining the range of successes and the factors associated with them, we may be in a position to assist in the promotion of policies and practices that can shift the balance away from the negative, and toward the positive, outcomes to which all people aspire.

If the evidence now points to first-generation immigration as having a generally positive and successful long-term outcome, what can be said about the second generation? This issue has recently come to the fore (Ghuman, 1994, 2003; Portes & Zhou, 1993; Rumbaut & Portes, 2001), raising the question of whether the problems once assumed to be present in the immigrants are now found among the second-generation youth, who experience a double transition. As for youth everywhere, immigrant youth must deal with the transition between childhood and adulthood. Although this transition is culturally variable (Dasen, 2000; Schlegel, 2003), it is present for virtually all young people (Scott & Scott, 1998). In addition, like the original migrants, second-generation youth must deal with the two cultural worlds of their own families and cultural communities, and of their peers, schools, and the larger society. Furthermore, peers are often drawn from a large variety of immigrant cultures. Although there is a smaller body of research with youth, the existing evidence (e.g., Aronowitz, 1992; Sam & Berry, 1995; Portes & Rumbaut, 2001) suggests equally high variability in the quality of their lives as that found for their parents. Once again, if there is substantial variation in how and how well immigrant youth are living, can such variability help us to understand the factors that promote their eventual successful adaptation and well-being? This question is central to our project.

DEVELOPMENTAL ISSUES

Because of the complexity of the interactions among developmental and acculturative changes, formulating comprehensive theories of immigration for developing individuals has been difficult. An understanding of the role of development in the adaptation of immigrant youth requires consideration of both developmental and acculturative changes. While young people are adapting to a new culture, they are also undergoing developmental changes (Schönpflug, 1997). Several models have been suggested to explain the differing outcomes for immigrant youth, based on work with particular groups of adolescents, but research does not provide clear support for a single model.

There are likely to be variations in the acculturation experience and adaptation of ethnocultural groups, depending on three factors: voluntariness of contact, mobility (migrant or sedentary), and permanence (Berry & Kim, 1988). For example, Ogbu (1991) emphasized differences between those who came to a new society voluntarily and those who came involuntarily. Involuntary migrants, for example, African Americans in the United States, are expected to fare worse than those who came by choice to improve their situation. Although this perspective may apply to African Americans, its application to current immigrants from other backgrounds is not clear. One might expect that refugees like Southeast Asians, forced from their countries by war, would show poor adaptation. However, research shows largely positive outcomes among adolescents from these groups (e.g., Beiser, 1999; Rumbaut, 1994; Zhou & Bankston, 1998), based on many factors besides their involuntary status. Other models emphasize the ways immigrants' cultural values contribute to the adaptation of youth (Fuligni & Tseng, 1999; Fuligni, Tseng, & Lam, 1999; Gibson, 1995) or the importance of developing bicultural competence (LaFromboise, Coleman, & Gerton, 1993). Clearly, more research is needed to advance our theoretical understanding of this process. Longitudinal studies are needed to disentangle the interactive effects of development and acculturation (Fuligni, 2001). Large-scale studies, such as the current one, that examine a range of demographic and contextual factors can provide a basis for theory building.

From a developmental perspective, immigration should be thought of as occurring among people across the life span, from infancy to old age. Among the many factors that influence the process and outcomes of immigration, age is one of the most important. To understand the impact of immigration, it is essential to consider the age at the time of migration, the length of time since migration, and the particular developmental tasks the immigrant is dealing with. Adaptation outcomes have often been studied by dividing children and youth in immigrant families on the basis of generation or place of birth, that is, first generation (born in country of origin) and second generation (born in country of settlement). How-ever, this practice does not take into account adaptation differences based on age of immigration or length of residence in a new society. In the ICSEY data, we use two variables, length of residence and proportion of life in the country of settlement, to explore changes over time. Chapters 4 and 5 examine differences in intercultural variables and adaptation in relation to time since immigration.

Our focus is on adolescence, a period when developmental issues raised by im-migration are of particular salience. The experiences of adolescents during and af-ter immigration fall within a developmental period characterized by changes marking the transition from childhood to adulthood. Key developmental processes of this period are a changing balance of autonomy and relatedness in the family and the increasing importance of peers. For adolescents in immigrant families, these processes are influenced by the varied cultural frameworks in which they are growing up (Garcia Coll & Magnusson, 1997).

During the transition from childhood to adulthood, young people make impor-tant decisions about who they are and who they hope to be in the future; that is, they form an identity. Immigrant adolescents develop an identity as a member of their own group (Phinney, 1990) and, to varying degrees, as a member of the larger soci-ety (Phinney & Devich-Navarro, 1997). The extent to which they develop a prefer-ence for either the ethnic or national group or combine them into a bicultural identity has implications for their psychological adjustment (LaFromboise et al., 1993; Phinney, Dupont, Espinosa, Revill, & Sanders, 1994; Phinney, Horenczyk, Liebkind, & Vedder, 2001). In chapter 4, we examine the strength of adolescents' identities with respect to both their ethnic group and the larger society. The impact of these identities on adaptation is explored in chapter 5.

By socializing within the family and the community, adolescents learn the values, traditions, and practices of their culture. In many immigrant families, these values typically emphasize interdependence among family members (Fuligni, 1998b; Phinney, Ong, & Madden, 2000), including the expectation of mutual support within the family. With increased age, there are countervailing pressures for greater autonomy; peers from other groups provide models of alter-native ways of interacting with parents and others. A strong sense of obligation to the family may benefit immigrant youth by providing clear roles and a sense of direction (Fuligni, 1998a), but it may also create conflicts, as adolescents strive for more autonomy in their own lives. The role of differences between adoles-cents and parents in family obligations and the implications of such differences are explored in chapter 7 and 8.

As they get older, adolescents are more oriented toward peers generally and to-ward members of the opposite sex in particular. Immigrant parents are often stricter than other parents in Western societies in regulating social behaviors like dating. In some cases they try to limit social contacts to peers from the same ethnic group. As immigrant youth make friends across ethnic group lines, conflicting pressures from parents and peers regarding social contacts can pose a challenge for these adolescents.

In each of these cases, adolescents are faced with decisions as to the extent to which they retain the values and behaviors of their family and community and adopt those of the larger society. Because of the varying influences and opportunities they face in making choices on these issues, immigrant adolescents take many different developmental pathways toward adulthood in a new society. The study of the complex interaction of factors that influence these developmental pathways can contribute to an understanding of adjustment of adolescents from immigrant families. The kinds of choices that adolescents make and the experiences they have in dealing with life in their host society are examined in chapter 4, and their impact is explored in chapters 5 and 6.

FAMILY RELATIONSHIPS

One of the main goals of the ICSEY project is to understand how immigrant youth manage to live in two cultures. A key aspect of this process is the values and attitudes within the adolescents' families and the extent to which adolescents accept these values and attitudes. Adolescents acquire within the family the adaptive patterns of behavior, personal characteristics, values, and social responses expected of them in their heritage culture. Once the family has migrated, parents cannot rely on the new society to assist in the cultural transmission of their own groups' values. Rather, adolescents are increasingly exposed to the values of their new society through peers and schooling.

Within the literature on immigrant adolescent adaptation, family relations have been explored through two major issues: Do immigrant adolescents undergo a more problematic period of development with their family than their counterparts from nonimmigrant families? To what extent do family relations affect their individual well-being and psychosocial adaptation? Keeping these two broad research questions in mind, our project examines family relations between adolescents and their parents, and the influence of discrepancies in family relationship values on adolescent adaptation. In the case of immigrant families confronted with adaptation to other cultures, it is likely that adolescents adapt more quickly than their parents. Parents and their children undergo different rates of acculturation, resulting in intergenerational differences (e.g., Chung & Okazaki, 1991; Kurian, 1986; Matsuoka, 1990; Nguyen & Williams, 1989; Rosenthal, Ranieri, & Klimidis, 1996; Szapocznik & Kurtines, 1993). For example, the acculturation attitudes of adolescents generally favor integration whereas their parents may favor separation (Berry & Sam, 1997), resulting in dissonant acculturation (Portes, 1997). For immigrant families, dissonant acculturation can easily lead to more serious family difficulties than for nonimmigrant families in general, although it does not necessarily do so (Phinney & Ong, 2002; Phinney et al., 2000).

Some research (e.g., Rosenthal et al., 1996; Stewart et al., 1998) suggests that conflicts with parents affect adolescents' adaptation adversely; other studies have not shown that family relationships influence adolescents' adaptation outside the home. Fuligni et al. (1999), for example, found that although endorsement of family obligations by adolescents was associated with positive relationships with family members, the cohesiveness of family relations did not extend its effect to relationships of adolescents with their peers or to their adaptation at school.

In summary, to answer the two broad research questions stated earlier, this project examines relationships between adolescents and their parents and the influence of these relationships on adolescent adaptation. We examine intergenerational disagreements on autonomy and family obligations across immigrant and nonimmigrant families and across ethnocultural groups from different national societies, as well as the influence of intergenerational discrepancies on adolescents' well-being and social adjustment. These results are presented in chapter 7.

TERMINOLOGY

The study of immigration and adaptation is complex and has been examined by many researchers from many disciplines. This has resulted in a plethora of concepts and terms, often with overlapping, and sometimes contradictory, meanings. To assist the reader, we present explicit definitions of the terms we use in this volume:

Immigrants–persons who have moved from one society to another and settled into their new society. These are also referred to as *first-generation* immigrants (except, in this study, for those who arrived in the society of settlement before age 7).

Second-generation immigrants–persons born in the society to first-generation immigrants or who arrived in the society of settlement after age 7.

Nonimmigrants–persons who were born in the society in which they now live. They are descended from earlier immigrants to the countries in which we carried out our research. We generally use the term *national* to identify this group, which excludes second-generation immigrants for the purposes of this study.

Youth–persons between ages 13 and 18, both immigrant and nonimmigrant. The term *adolescents* is used interchangeably.

Immigrant youth–an inclusive term that refers both to immigrant children and to children of immigrants. It thus incorporates both first- and second-generation youth.

Ethnocultural–an adjective used to describe the ethnic and cultural qualities that are characteristic of every group living together in a society. It is an inclusive term that incorporates both immigrants and nonimmigrants. Specific names are used to refer to each group.

Larger society–the overall society that incorporates all ethnocultural groups, including both immigrants and nationals.

Society of settlement–the society into which immigrants arrive and settle.

By using these terms in these ways, we seek to avoid the extra baggage that often accompanies terms such as *mainstream, majority, dominant, minority, nondominant,* and *host society.*

RESEARCH FRAMEWORK

To guide our approach to these questions, we developed a research framework that incorporates four sets of variables (see Fig. 1.1): at the group level, *context* variables; at the individual level, *intercultural, adaptation,* and *demographic* variables. The main direction of relationships among these sets of variables is from the group context variables that describe some features of the populations and contexts in the project, to the variables that describe the individuals who are sampled.

As in all behavioral science research that seeks to understand people in their social and cultural settings, we begin with the broader set of information about the societies of settlement, the ethnocultural groups, and the relationships among them. Without such information, we would lack sufficient means to interpret similarities and differences in the individual-level psychological data. These context variables include the *immigration* climate (which has contributed to the actual degree of diversity in the society) and the *pluralism* climate (the policy orientation to diversity adopted by the larger society) that immigrants experience.

Group differences refer to the degree of dissimilarity in cultural values, religion, and visibility between each immigrant group and the society into which it have become settled. These context variables are presented more fully in chapter 2, and their role in acculturation and adaptation are evaluated in chapter 6.

Intercultural variables describe the way individuals view and feel about relationships among groups and behave in multicultural settings. These are considered to be a function of many features of their groups' context, including their historic, demographic, economic, and political situation. The process of acculturation takes place following the contact between cultural groups and involves changes in both groups. Psychological acculturation takes place in individuals and includes the acculturation attitudes that people have toward the process.

In this study, we distinguish among views regarding four ways of acculturating. As noted earlier, we assess participants' orientation toward assimilation, integration, separation, and marginalization. Similarly, cultural identity refers to an individual orientation that arises when people live interculturally. Although there are many aspects to a person's identity (e.g., class, gender), *cultural identity* refers to thoughts and feelings about belonging to one's ethnocultural group (*ethnic identity*) and to the larger society (*national identity*). It is, in essence, a sense of belonging to, or attachment with, either or both these cultural groupings. Language issues (including language proficiency and use) also arise during intercultural living: Which languages are learned, and which are used in which kinds of interactions, are all decisions that are made daily, particularly by those in immigrant groups. Similarly, it is important to examine the pattern of social contacts with members of ones own group, and with others (especially with those representing the established national society).

12

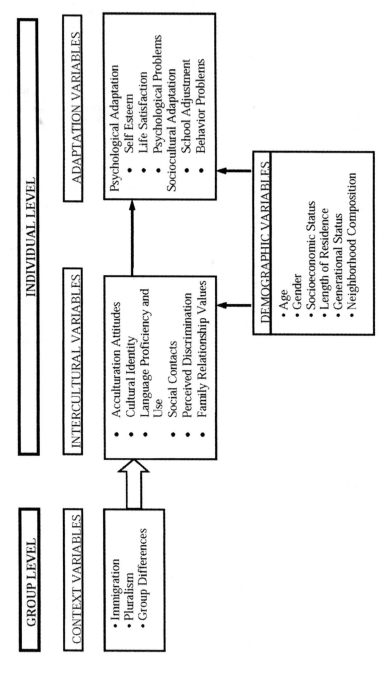

FIG. 1.1. International comparative study of Ethnocultural Youth framework for studying acculturation and adaptation.

Discrimination against immigrant individuals and groups is a common feature of intercultural relations. While objective assessments are possible (e.g., evidence of differential income, education, housing), it is how people perceive their differential treatment that is thought to be psychologically important to the quality of intercultural life. Finally, when the focus is on youth, there is inevitably a concern with their relationships with parents; hence, we include an examination of the values regarding parent–child relationships held by both adolescents and parents. Each of these intercultural variables is defined more fully, and the background literature is reviewed, in chapter 4.

The adaptation variables describe the outcomes for ethnocultural youth. These are seen to flow from both their groups' context and their intercultural relations. Although adaptation is both a process and a longer term outcome, an understanding of the process can be attained only when assessments are made at more than one point in time. In the present study there is only one assessment; hence, the adaptation variables are viewed as a kind of snapshot of how well youth are doing. A distinction has been made between two kinds of adaptation identified by Ward (1996): psychological and sociocultural. *Psychological adaptation* refers to characteristics that are internal to the individual: good mental health (i.e., few psychological problems of anxiety, depression, and psychosomatic symptoms) and a high sense of well-being (i.e., self-esteem and life satisfaction). *Sociocultural adaptation* refers to the quality of the relationships between individuals and their sociocultural contexts. Among youth, this form of adaptation is often examined in terms of their attitudes toward and success in school, and lack of problem behaviors in their community.

Comparative research is rooted in the study of group similarities and differences. As we have noted, we believe that by examining several ethnocultural groups that are settled in a variety of societies, we can understand the roots of positive intercultural relations and successful adaptation. This research is also rooted in the study of individual differences, as is most behavioral science research. Hence, several demographic features of individuals in our samples are assumed to contribute to variation in intercultural relations and adaptation, and perhaps moderate the relationship between these two sets of variables. Most obviously, the age and gender of our participants are likely to be important. The socioeconomic status (SES) of one's family also has an obvious role in how, and how well, a young person will live in his or her intercultural situation. As in any study of immigration, length of residence (ranging from recent arrival to having been born in the country) and generational status (first or second) are likely to be very important individual characteristics. Finally, a local context variable (neighborhood composition) is examined. This variable ranges from neighborhoods that are almost culturally homogeneous (where either all residents are members of the youth's ethnocultural group or entirely of other groups) to mixed neighborhoods.

Although the study was not designed for analyzing developmental aspects of acculturation and adaptation, we are able to use a cross-sectional approach to acculturation and adaptation processes by including background variables such as age, length of residence, and generational status.

RESEARCH QUESTIONS

In this project we ask some fundamental questions regarding how and how well immigrant youth live in the intercultural situation in which they find themselves. We have chosen to emphasize some aspects and thus have had to ignore others. As behavioral scientists, we have focused on individuals; however, because of our concern for cultural factors in human behavior, we have also chosen to emphasize the cultural (and intercultural) contexts in which individuals live and act.

In this project we attempt to address some of the most fundamental questions facing immigrants and the societies that receive them. First, are there some basic and coherent ways immigrants seek to live in their new societies? That is, are there systematic patterns in the ways that individuals go about their intercultural living following their immigration? We have termed this question the *how* issue. Second, can we assess *how well* individuals are adapting to their new life circumstances? In particular, for youth, are there problems or successes in their personal sense of well-being and in their school and community endeavors? Third, can we discern any systematic relationships between how and how well youth are establishing their new lives? Finally, if there are substantive answers to the first three questions, we may be able to provide proposals for policy and program development that will assist immigrant groups and individuals, as well as the larger society, in achieving a more positive outcome for this massive contemporary flow of peoples across international borders.

2 Design of the Study: Selecting Societies of Settlement and Immigrant Groups

John W. Berry
Queen's University

Charles Westin
Erkki Virta
Stockholm University

Paul Vedder
Leiden University

Rosanna Rooney
Curtin University

David Sang
University of Western Australia

In this chapter, we describe the design and the contextual backgrounds of the societies of settlement and the immigrant groups involved in the ICSEY project. This entails first a discussion of some principles that underlie the design of comparative studies of acculturation. We then present descriptions of some of the core features of the 13 societies of settlement that are theoretically relevant to the project. Finally, we outline some of the important features of the immigrant groups we studied, including information that is necessary for understanding the processes of acculturation and adaptation that occur as they interact with others in their societies of settlement.

DESIGN OF THE COMPARATIVE STUDY OF IMMIGRANT YOUTH

There are two basic principles offered by cross-cultural psychology (Berry, Poortinga, Segall, & Dasen, 2002) that should be taken into account when designing a culture-comparative study. One (called the *cultural principle*) is that all hu-

15

man behavior develops, and is exhibited, in the context of culture; hence, no individual can be understood unless that person's cultural background is first understood. The other (called the *comparative principle*) is that when doing studies of human behavior across cultures, we should not use just any society but should instead select those that will provide some theoretical basis for explaining the similarities and differences in behaviors that may be found. These two principles have been employed in the design of this project. The cultural principle requires the elaboration of some features of the societies of settlement, and of the immigrant groups that have come to settle in them, and an account of the nature of their intercultural relationships. This cultural principle also requires that we identify some features of the societies that, on theoretical grounds, are likely to be important for pursuing the main research questions in the study.

In dealing with the comparative principle, we selected societies in which there are sufficient numbers of immigrants to provide samples of immigrant youth. This means focusing on societies that have had a substantial involvement with immigration. It also means that we exclude societies where there are relatively few immigrants (such as Japan) or where there are large numbers, but the immigrants are there only temporarily (such as refugees in Pakistan). We also need to select societies that exhibit some variation in their immigration pattern, for without such variation, we would simply be doing a series of replications and miss out on the power of the comparative method.

In selecting societies of settlement, we began with a three-fold classification of countries based on their immigration history. First, we focused on societies that have been largely built using a deliberate process of immigration (sometimes called *settler societies*). These are societies that have actively sought immigrants, have policies and programs to attract them, and have explicit criteria for their selection. They are also usually the societies with the largest percentage of immigrants and relatively positive public attitudes toward immigration. Included in this group are Australia, Canada, Israel, New Zealand, and the United States.

Second, we chose societies that have been involved in immigration but historically were the source of immigrants rather than the destination. We call these *former colonial societies*. In this second group are countries that have been receiving relatively large numbers of immigrants (mainly formerly colonized populations) over the past 50 years but that do not have explicit policies that seek immigrants. Despite this, these countries tend to have moderate levels of immigration. Included here are France, Germany, the Netherlands, and the United Kingdom.

A third group of countries have also been the source of immigrants, and do not seek immigration, but have more recently been receiving immigrants (usually in smaller numbers). We call these societies *recent receiving societies*. Included here are Finland, Norway, Portugal, and Sweden (although Portugal is a former colonial society, compared with others, it has only recently begun to receive immigrants in large numbers).

This three-fold categorization served as an initial sampling frame for selecting the 13 societies of settlement in our project. In using these categories we believe there are important differences between the categories with respect to the extent of immigration and their policies. We further explored these differences using two indicators that are theoretically important for this project: the actual degree of cultural diversity found in a society and the national policy orientation toward such diversity (hereafter called *cultural diversity* and *diversity policy*, respectively).

Our interest in these dimensions of diversity (both cultural diversity and diversity policy) is based on the work of Murphy (1965), who hypothesized that immigrants will adapt better when cultural communities provide support for immigrants during acculturation and when there is public support for cultural diversity. Murphy found evidence for this proposal using indicators of mental health among immigrants to pluralistic societies (Canada and Singapore) compared with societies lower in cultural pluralism. In keeping with this line of reasoning, we expect that immigrant youth will have more positive intercultural relations, and more positive psychological and sociocultural adaptation, in societies that have relatively large numbers of immigrants, that have established cultural communities, and that promote immigration and diversity as a national goal.

Some features related to cultural diversity and diversity policy of the 13 societies in our study are presented in Table 2.1. The 13 societies are listed alphabetically within the three types of societies mentioned earlier, based on their immigration history and background. The first column is the percentage of immigrants in each society (all those who were born outside the country). Generally, the initial categorization in terms of the three types of societies is supported by the percentage of immigrants now in the population: Settler societies have the highest percentage of immigrants, whereas recent societies have fewest, with Sweden being the main exception. The second column is an index of actual diversity (described later). The third column provides a classification of the societies according to their degree of support for cultural diversity (also described below).

Although the percentage of immigrants residing in a society is one indicator of cultural diversity, other indicators are available in the literature. To produce the index of cultural diversity, we used three other indicators The first is an index of cultural homogeneity developed by Kurian (2001). It is based on demographic factors (such as variation in ethnic origin) and ranges from 4 to 100. The second indicator is an index of ethnolinguistic fractionalisation (Inglehart 1997; Taylor & Jodice, 1983): This is the probability that two randomly selected persons from one country will not speak the same language. The third indicator is one of ethnic diversity (Sterling, 1974), scored on a five-point scale ranging from nations with nearly homogeneous ethnic composition to heterogeneous nations with many small ethnic groups. These three indicators, together with the percentages of immigrants in a country, were standardized across the 13 countries and combined to create the cultural diversity scores in the second column of Table 2.1. These scores range from a high of 1.42 and 0.65 for Canada and Israel, respectively, to a low of −0.97 and −1.11 for Norway and Portugal, respectively. These cultural diversity scores are used in later chapters when we assess whether such cultural diversity is related to how, and how well, immigrant youth acculturate in their society of settlement.

TABLE 2.1
Immigration and Cultural Diversity Characteristics
of 13 Societies of Settlement

Society of Settlement	Percentage of Immigrants	Actual Diversity Index	Policy Diversity Classification
Settler societies			
Australia	24.6	–0.08	High
Canada	18.9	1.42	High
Israel	37.4	0.65	Low
New Zealand	22.5	0.04	High
United States	12.4	0.10	Medium
Former colonial societies			
France	10.6	–0.51	Low
Germany	9.0	–0.85	Low
Netherlands	9.9	–0.78	Medium
United Kingdom	6.8	–0.21	Medium
Recent receiving societies			
Finland	2.6	–0.65	Low
Norway	6.7	–0.97	Low
Portugal	2.3	–1.11	Medium
Sweden	11.2	–0.59	Medium

It is important to note that the index of cultural diversity is determined not only by the presence of immigrants in a country. Many countries are multiethnic and multilingual as a historical fact of co-existence of ethnic and linguistic communities within the borders of the country. The values presented in Table 2.1 reflect immigration-related ethnic diversity in most countries. As is pointed out in chapter 6, the four indicators that are included in the cultural diversity index are all moderately to highly positively correlated. We thus think it is justified to claim that this index of cultural diversity portrays the degree of cultural pluralism present in a society and reflects the potential for (and probably the actual degree of) interethnic and interlinguistic contacts that people experience in a particular society.

In this project we selected societies that also vary in their policies with respect to cultural diversity. Diversity policy refers to the degree to which governments and other administrative bodies promote cultural diversity as a national goal. Policies and practices that promote the maintenance of heritage cultures, and that facilitate contacts among different ethnocultural groups in society, are considered to be supportive of cultural pluralism. Some of the 13 countries selected are explicitly multicultural in public policy and have supportive public attitudes (such as Australia, Canada, and New Zealand); some reject cultural diversity as a way of living together, preferring to achieve a culturally homogeneous society (such as Finland, France, Germany, Israel, and Norway); and some are intermediate in their acceptance of pluralism (such as the Netherlands, Portugal, Sweden, the United Kingdom, and the United States). These are identified as high, medium, or low, respectively, in Table 2.1.

Our placement of societies on the dimension of diversity policy was based on a classification available in the political science literature (Banting & Kymlicka, 2004). Banting and Kymlicka (2004) proposed 9 criteria with which to place societies on a dimension of acceptance of multiculturalism. These are the existence of: a government policy promoting multiculturalism, a multicultural ministry or secretariat, adoption of multiculturalism in the school curriculum, ethnic representation in the media, exemptions of cultural groups from codes that are rooted in the dominant society (e.g., Sunday closing), allowing dual citizenship, funding of ethnocultural organizations, funding of bilingual or heritage language instruction, and affirmative action for disadvantaged immigrant groups.

It should be noted, however, that this classification of societies on diversity policy may be misleading in specific cases. For example, the fact that a country is officially bilingual may not be indicative of acceptance of immigrants, as such a bilingual policy may be the result of historical necessity. This is the case, for example, in Finland, where this country's official bilingualism is less the result of the recognition of an ethnolinguistic minority (the Swedish-speaking Finns) than of the historical fact that Finland had belonged to Sweden for more than 600 years. As a consequence, Swedish and Finnish are both the national languages of Finland; however, such official bilingualism may have little bearing on the immigration policies of the country or the acceptance of immigrants by the population in the larger society (McRae, 1997).

SOCIETIES OF SETTLEMENT

Table 2.2 presents a listing of the 13 societies of settlement and the specific immigrant groups from which we drew samples. The actual numbers in these samples, and other details, are provided in chapter 3.

The following profiles of the societies of settlement, and of the immigrant groups, were developed from information compiled and initially drafted by the researchers working in each of the societies of settlement. These colleagues are identified in the preface and are here acknowledged as contributors to these sections.

Beyond these two features of the cultural diversity of the 13 societies of settlement, there are other qualities that may affect how well immigrant youth are doing in their new societies. Following are narrative portrayals of each of the 13 societies, which provide contextual information that is important in our later interpretation of the findings. These portraits are attempts to meet the requirements of the cultural principle (mentioned in the previous section), which provides some context for understanding the behavioral data reported in subsequent chapters.

TABLE 2.2
Societies of Settlement, and Groups in the Study

Settler Societies		Recent Receiving Societies	
Australia	Vietnamese	Finland	Vietnamese
	Chinese		Turks
	Filippino		Russians
	Nationals		Nationals
Canada	Vietnamese	Norway	Vietnamese
	Koreans		Pakistani
	South Asians (Indians)		Turks
	Nationals		Chilean
Israel	Russians		Nationals
	Ethiopians	Portugal	Cape Verdeans
	Nationals		Angolans
New Zealand	Chinese		South Asians (Indians)
	Pacific Islanders		Mozambicans
	Nationals		Timorese
United States	Vietnamese		Nationals
	Armenians	Sweden	Vietnamese
	Mexicans		Turks
	Nationals		Kurds
			Chileans and Central Americans
Former Colonial Societies			Finns
France	Vietnamese		Nationals
	Turks		
	Maghrebians		
	Portuguese		
	Nationals		
Germany	Turks		
	Portuguese		
	Aussiedler		
	Nationals		
Netherlands	Turks		
	Antilleans		
	South Asians (Surinamese)		
	Nationals		
United Kingdom	South Asians (Indians)		
	Nationals		

Settler Societies

Australia

Australia has a high level of immigration, with 24.6% of the population of nearly 20 million not born in the country. In the three cities where ICSEY data were collected, the percentage of immigrants varied from 33.4% in Sydney and 33.2% in Melbourne to 23.1% in Perth. Australia is moderate on actual cultural diversity in Table 2.1.

The ethnic origin of the population is 92% European, 7% Asian, and 1% Aboriginal and other. The origin of the immigrant groups is 1.95% Chinese, .08% Vietnamese, .07% Filippino. Nearly 200 countries have been identified as sources of immigrants, with the United Kingdom/Ireland, New Zealand, Italy, former Yugoslavia, and Vietnam as main source countries in 1996. Among the main Asian source countries are Vietnam, China, the Philippines, and Malaysia. Compared with nonimmigrants, the overseas-born immigrants are much more concentrated in the urban areas.

The unemployment rate overall in Australia was 8.1% in 1998. For the research samples, unemployment varied from 5.2% for those from Hong Kong to 27% for those from Taiwan. Unemployment rate, however, is related to length of residence. More young immigrants than older immigrants attend educational institutions.

The Migration Act of 1958 granted citizenship rights to non-Europeans and avoided references to "race." In 1973 the former "White Australian Policy" was also formally abolished: Race was disregarded in the selection of immigrants, and citizenship rights became available for all immigrants after 3 years of permanent residency. Australia now has a nondiscriminatory immigration policy, which means that anyone from any country can apply to immigrate. There are two major immigration programs: the migration program and the humanitarian program. First, the migration program consists of: (a) the skilled stream, selected on the basis of particular work and business skills, nomination by particular employers in Australia, or possession of significant capital to establish a business of benefit to Australia—a points test applies; and (b) the family stream, selected on the basis of family relationship to a sponsor in Australia. Second, the humanitarian program consists of: (a) refugee, which is based on the United Nations definition; (b) special humanitarian, for people who are not refugees but have suffered gross violations of their human rights; and (c) special assistance category for displaced people. All applicants need to meet health and good character standards.

Australia is listed as high with respect to diversity policy in Table 2.1. A multiculturalism policy was introduced in 1975, in which programs related to access and equity were established. Over the years, there has been a policy shift from assimilation (1947–1964) to integration (1964–1972), to cultural pluralism (1972–1975), then to multiculturalism (1975). This last policy has been defined in 1989 as made up of three dimensions: cultural identity (the right to express and share immigrants' individual cultural heritage, including their language and religion), social justice (equality of treatment and opportunity, removal of barriers of race, ethnicity, culture, religion, language, gender, or place of birth), and economic efficiency (the need to maintain, develop, and use effectively the skills and talents of all Australians, regardless of background). More recently (1999), the government defined the multicultural policy as following four principles: civic duty, cultural respect, social equity, and productive diversity. Strategies that are designed to optimize the benefits of cultural diversity for all Australians were also proposed.

Opinion polls carried out between 1943 and 1998 found widespread support in Australia for the government's nondiscriminatory immigration policy and endorsement for multiculturalism. There was some resistance to the level of Asian migration, primarily due to a false perception about the number of Asian immigrants in the country. However, trends in unemployment appeared to be a strong determinant of public support for immigration and multiculturalism. A nationwide survey was conducted at a time (1988) when immigration and multiculturalism were the focus of debates within various circles in the society. Among the key findings was wide support for higher immigration levels or at least maintaining the existing levels, a finding that applied to all immigrant groups mentioned in the survey. However respondents found "Australian people" and "British people" as most acceptable, and "Muslim people" as least acceptable.

Canada

Canada has the highest score on the actual diversity index in Table 2.1. This is due in part to the relatively large proportion of immigrants but also to other features of the society, such as the presence of two large ethnolinguistic groups (French and English). It has a high level of immigration, with 18.9% of its 31 million population not born in the country. In Toronto, where the ICSEY data were collected, 44.0% of the population are immigrants, the highest of all cities in our study. Immigration has transformed the city over the past 50 years: Between 1951 and 2001, the percentage of the population with origins in the U.K. declined from 73% to 27%, and the most frequent names in the Toronto phone book changed from Smith and Brown to Smith, Lee, Wong, Brown, Singh, Kim, Mohammed, and Patel. Within Canada, Toronto is the most diverse city in the country, with almost 30% of all immigrants settling there.

The ethnic origins for the country as a whole are: British Isles, 40%; French, 27%; other European, 20%; Aboriginal, 1.5%; and other (mostly Asians), 11.5%. In Toronto, of the total population, 1.8 million were not born in Canada. The largest groups are from China (11%: 5% People's Republic of China and 6% Hong Kong), Great Britain (10%, United Kingdom and Ireland), Italy (8%), Jamaica (5%), the Philippines (5%), Portugal (5%), Vietnam (3.5%), India (2.4%), and Korea (1.4%). In recent years, around two thirds of the annual flow of 250,000 to 300,000 immigrants have come from Asia, including independent (selected) immigrants, refugees and those who come under the family reunification program.

The overall population growth rate is 1.06%, and the fertility rate is 1.65. However, for the Aboriginal population, the fertility rate is more than double the overall rate. The economy is characterized by relatively high affluence (US$26,474 per capita), and immigrants have slightly higher incomes than the average. First-generation immigrants on average have a slightly higher educational qualification than the overall population. The unemployment rate has been in the 7% to 8% range for the past few years, with some variation around this figure according to immigration status and ethnic origin.

The goal of Canada's immigration policy is to take in 1% of the population each year (around 300,000 people). There are four categories of immigrants: (a) independent class for individuals who meet certain criteria, (e.g., age, education, needed job skills) who receive points for each criterion, and are admitted if they pass a certain threshold; (b) family reunification class to admit designated family members; (c) entrepreneurial class, to encourage investment for job creation; and (d) an asylum seeker/refugee class for those who meet Geneva Convention or other humanitarian criteria.

Canada is listed among the highest on policy diversity in Table 2.1. In 1972, Canada introduced a policy of multiculturalism. This policy has four goals. First, it seeks to avoid assimilation by encouraging ethnic groups to maintain and develop themselves as distinctive groups within Canadian society; this element has been termed the "own group maintenance and development" goal of the policy (Berry, 1984b). Second, a fundamental purpose of the policy is to increase intergroup harmony and the mutual acceptance of all groups that wish to maintain and develop themselves; this has been termed the "other group acceptance and tolerance" goal. Third, the policy argues that cultural group development by itself is not sufficient to lead to group acceptance; "intergroup contact and sharing" is also required. Fourth, full participation in Canadian society by groups cannot be achieved if some common language is not learned; thus, the "learning of official languages" (English and French) is also encouraged by the policy.

In national surveys (e.g., Berry & Kalin, 1995; Berry, Kalin, & Taylor, 1977), Canadians generally support integration and reject assimilation and segregation. as ways for immigrants to live in their new country. There is also a rather high level of acceptance of multicultural ideology, which is an indicator of a positive value placed on cultural diversity. Canadians are also generally tolerant rather than prejudiced. Intergroup attitudes are generally positive, although they are somewhat less positive among French-origin respondents. Attitudes also vary in degree of acceptance of particular groups: peoples of North and West European origin are most highly evaluated, followed by those from East and South Europe, East Asia, the Caribbean, and South Asia.

Israel

Israel is a country of high immigration, with 37.4% of its population of almost 6 million having been born abroad. Israel is thus high on actual diversity in Table

2.1. The government department that assists immigrants upon arrival refers to its work as that of "immigrant absorption." This policy has resulted in Israel being listed as low on diversity policy. However, there is currently a debate about whether to accommodate cultural diversity to a greater extent, prompted largely by the arrival of many immigrants from Ethiopia and Russia.

With respect to ethnic background, 81% are Jews and 19% are Arabs. Among the Jewish population, the largest origin groups are Russian (12%) and Ethiopian (3%).

The 1950 "Law of Return" grants every Jew the right to immigrate to Israel and to become a citizen. The net migration rate is 4.42 immigrants per 1,000 population. Since 1990, 700,000 immigrants from the former Soviet Union have arrived. And since 1984, 22,000 Ethiopian Jews have settled. The population growth rate is 1.81%, and the fertility rate is 2.6%. The average per capita income is US$14,603.

Schooling is compulsory from 5 to 15 years of age, during a 6-day school week; education is free. There are three types of education: state (68.4% of primary education), state/religious (21.3%), and independent religious education (10.3%). There are Hebrew language classes for newcomers. Most Arab students are in separate schools under the auspices of state education. Religious students are separated from nonreligious students, and Jewish students are separated from Arab peers.

Special measures are taken to facilitate the economic, occupational, social, and cultural inclusion of immigrants during their first 3 years in Israel. Immigrants are granted special benefits during this period, including a generous sum of money for initial adjustment, tax reduction, assistance in rent and mortgage, and scholarships for university studies. The government also encourages others (such as public institutions, volunteer organizations, schoolchildren, and university students) to promote immigrant absorption. Earlier, there was a housing dispersal policy, but it is no longer implemented.

The attitudes of the national (majority) population toward the different acculturating groups are influenced by socioeconomic factors, political circumstances, and ideological considerations. As a result, the Israeli public seems to hold differential attitudes toward the various acculturating groups. A recent study (Canetti-Nisim & Pedahzur, 2003) found that 37.3% of the Israeli respondents show negative ("xenophobic") attitudes toward immigrants from the former Soviet Union, 43.2% toward Palestinian citizens of Israel, and 78.7% toward foreign workers.

New Zealand

In 2003 the New Zealand population reached 4 million. On the basis of its 2001 census, the ethnic origin of the population was recorded as: 80% European, 14.6% Maori, 6.5 Pacific (3.2% Samoan), 6.6% Asian (2.8% Chinese), and 6.9% other. New Zealand is high on the immigration dimension, with 19.5% of its population being born overseas. New Zealand falls just on the positive side of the actual diversity index in Table 2.1, but it is classified as high on the index of policy pluralism, due to some extent to a formal recognition of its bicultural character.

Most immigrants (53%) settle in Auckland. The overseas-born proportion of the population in the regions where the New Zealand data were collected (Auckland, Waikato, Wellington, Hawkes Bay, and Christchurch) ranged from 1% (Hawkes Bay) to 31% (Auckland). Wellington, the national capital and largest data collection site, has 20% overseas-born residents, which approximates the national average.

New Zealand has a long history of immigration, and some regard the Treaty of Waitangi, signed in 1840 between Maori, the indigenous people of Aotearoa/New Zealand, and the British Crown, as the country's earliest immigration document. In recent times, New Zealand has seen several changes in its immigration policy. In 1991 the country radically altered its approach to immigration and engaged in the active recruitment of skilled and entrepreneurial immigrants. As this was preceded by the 1986 changes that opened the doors to nontraditional sources of migration, the country has seen a dramatic shift in the pattern of immigration, with recent immigrants now coming primarily from Asia.

Migrants are currently admitted in several categories, the most common of which is the general skills classification, where residence is obtained by reaching a specified number of points based on factors such as age, language fluency, and employment potential. Admission as a permanent resident is also available through business, family reunification, and humanitarian categories. Quotas exist for Samoan immigration (1,100 per annum) and United Nations–mandated refugees (750 per annum).

Although overseas-born residents are more likely to hold educational qualifications than native-born residents (81% vs. 70%, respectively), they are less likely to be employed. Sixty-seven percent of the total New Zealand population participate in the labor force; this compares with 75% of New Zealand–born Chinese, 45% of overseas-born Chinese, 66% Pasifika, and 56% Maori. The median New Zealand income is $18,500, but this varies significantly across ethnic groups. The median New Zealand European income is $19,800 compared with median Maori and Pacific incomes of $14,800. The median Chinese income is lower at $10,800; however, this is due to large differentials between New Zealand-born ($20,200) and overseas-born ($7,900) residents.

The New Zealand government has recently identified settlement issues as a key aspect of a successful immigration plan, but at present there are limited programs in place to facilitate immigrant integration and adaptation. One of the few areas where support is widely available is in education. Education is free for New Zealand nationals and residents (age 5 to 19), and schooling is compulsory from ages 6 to 16.

After obtaining a residence permit, migrants are permitted to vote in New Zealand elections. After having resided in the country for 3 years, an application for citizenship may be lodged. New Zealand permits dual citizenship, and naturalized New Zealand citizens are entitled to all of the rights afforded to native-born citizens.

For the most part, New Zealanders support a multicultural ideology, and in a recent household survey of 500 residents, 88% agreed that it is a good thing for New

Zealand to be made up of different races, religions, and cultures (Ward & Masgoret, 2004). This compared favorably with research in Australia (85% endorsement; Dunn, 2003) and in the European Union (36%–75% endorsement) in the Eurobarometer (2000) study. However, it should be noted that New Zealand maintains an official policy of biculturalism based on the Treaty of Waitangi, and research by Ward (2004) has shown that 49% of the New Zealand European youth and 47% of the Maori maintain that New Zealand culture is defined by both European and Maori traditions.

United States

The United States is a country of moderate immigration, with 11.7% of its total population of around 296 million having been born in another country. On the actual pluralism index in Table 2.1, the United States falls slightly above the midpoint of the dimension, and on the diversity policy dimension, it is also moderate. However, in Los Angeles, where the ICSEY data were collected, the percentage of immigrants is 35.1%.

Ethnic origins of the U.S. population are approximately 73% from Europe, 13% from Latin America, 12% from Africa, and 4% from Asia. California receives around one third of all arriving immigrants. About 40% of all illegal immigrants in the United States reside in California. A change in immigration law in 1965 dramatically increased the numbers of non-European immigrants. A majority of immigrants now come from Asia, Latin America, and other non-European regions.

Average per capita income is $43,318. European Americans and Asian Americans are above the average: $48,000 and $55,000, respectively. African Americans and Latinos are considerably below average: $30,000 and $33,000, respectively. According to the 2000 census, the overall unemployment rate for those over 16 years is 3.7%. For the four ethnocultural groups, the percentages are: European Americans, 3.0%; Asians, 3.2%; Latinos, 5.7%; and African Americans, 6.7%.

Education is a state responsibility. It includes 1 year of kindergarten, 6 years of primary education, 2 or 3 years of middle school, and 3 or 4 years of high school. Educational attainment is generally high for Asian Americans; 49.8% of those over age 25 have a college degree. Among European Americans, the figure is 30%. Far fewer African Americans (17.3%) and Latinos (11.4%) have college degrees.

A preference system operates in the selection of immigrants: family reunification, employment criteria, refugee status, and diversity. Recently, 67% were family reunification, 12% were employment based, and 16% were refugees.

Two thirds of the U.S. population believe that rates of immigration should be reduced. In California, 59% of the voters endorsed a proposition aimed at denying access to health and welfare benefits for illegal immigrants. However, this has not been implemented. Incidents of racial or ethnic violence occur periodically and are reported in the newspapers. Nevertheless, in Los Angeles, most individuals encounter people from a wide range of backgrounds on a daily basis and interact comfortably with them in a variety of settings, including school, work, and leisure activities.

Former Colonial Societies

France

France is a country of moderate immigration, with 10.6% of its population of 60 million having been born outside the country. In the cities, the percentage is higher, with 37% immigrants in the Paris region. This moderate level of immigrants, the second highest in Europe, contributes to the moderate score on the index of actual diversity in Table 2.1. In contrast, France is rated low on diversity policy, which reflects a widespread and historically rooted view of France as a unified and unitary country.

The ethnic origins of the population are mainly French. The largest immigrant groups are from Portugal (570,000), Spain (320,000), Tunisia (200,000), Morocco (530,000), Algeria (570,000), and Vietnam (75,000). It has been estimated that in 1997 about 300,000 illegal immigrants lived in France, mostly from Asia, Sub-Saharan Africa, and Latin America.

From 1990 to 1993, the immigration flow was stable at about 100,000 per year, but it has since then decreased to about 65,000 per year. Between 1990 and 1999, the proportion of immigrants from European countries declined, but the proportion from the Maghreb (Algeria, Tunisia, Morocco) and Turkey, Asia, and Sub-Saharan Africa regions increased.

Immigrants are found more in unskilled employment and often have temporary and part-time work. Their wage level is therefore low. The average salary of immigrant men working full-time is 89.9% of the average salary of all men in France working full-time; for women, this proportion is 87.3%. The overall unemployment rate in France is 11%. Immigrants run a higher risk of unemployment given equivalent age, sex, and qualifications, but there are large differences among immigrants.

The educational qualification of immigrants reflects largely that of the country of origin. Before 1975 adult migrants often were illiterate; for example, 50% of the immigrants from Morocco and Algeria never went to school, and those coming from Portugal had very little education. After 1975 the general level rose, in part because many came as students. Statistics indicate that children born in France within an immigrant family do better at school than French children. From ages 6 to 16, school is mandatory; it is free of charge for all children, including those of illegal immigrants. At all levels, children of immigrants are admitted either to a regular class, if necessary with supplemental teaching or help in French, or to a class in which they learn French. Mother tongue lessons are available, and lessons outside regular school hours are sometimes available.

With respect to diversity policy, France was founded on the belief that abolishing recognition of social and cultural origins will result in equality for all. No group has special rights, and assimilation has been France's response to immigrants since the 19th century. Assimilation does not mean giving up one's religion, ethnic identity, or language (the private sphere), but it does mean accepting French ways in the public sphere. From 1974 on, in the context of a shrinking labor market, immigration came to be seen as a problem by many. In 1999, 61% of French thought there were too many foreigners living in France (mainly Arabs) and 27% said they have problems in daily life because of foreigners; 50% saw immigration as a source of insecurity, and 50% saw it as a source of cultural enrichment. Algerians are ranked as the most rejected group in France on all attitude surveys. Portuguese are well accepted; they are seen as hard workers.

In a survey by the European Commission, respondents were asked whether they personally find the presence of people of another nationality, race, or religion disturbing. In France, 17% said "yes"; the average of the 15 European Union countries was 15%. The percentage in France for race was 19% (European average 15%), it was 17% for religion (European average 14%). Thus, French respondents are slightly less accepting of immigrants than other Europeans in general. The French also appeared to be less willing than the European average to accept people from countries south of the Mediterranean and from central and eastern Europe.

Germany

Germany has a moderate level of immigration, with immigrants constituting 9% of its 83 million inhabitants. However, this percentage must be seen in the context of the absolute number of immigrants; around 650,000 immigrants arrive each year. Despite this large number, Germany rates relatively low on the actual diversity index and rates just as low on diversity policy in Table 2.1. Immigration to Germany started in the 1950s, when Germany was rebuilt with great intensity after the war. The need for labor led to the recruitment of "guest workers" mainly from Mediterranean countries. This form of immigration was stopped in the 1970s when the economy began to stagnate. In North Rhine Westphalia, where the ICSEY data were collected, 11.1% of the population is immigrant, but in the main cities this proportion is double.

Immigration rates to Germany were among the highest in Europe during the last two decades of the 20th century. The estimated net migration rate for 2001 was 4.0 migrants per 1, 000 population, resulting from family reunification (mainly of Turks), high rates of asylum seekers, and the return of ethnic Germans or Aussiedler. Of the 9% of Germany's population who are immigrants, one fourth come from other European Union countries, (mainly Italy, Greece, Austria, Spain, and Portugal). The largest groups of non-E.U. immigrants were Turks (29%) and former Yugoslavs (10%). About 15% were asylum seekers. The overall fertility rate is 1.38 children, but it is on average twice as high in immigrant groups. The overall population growth rate is 0.27%.

The large refugee flow into Germany reached its peak in 1992 with 438,000 requests for asylum, which represented 80% of all asylum requests in Europe in that year. This stimulated policymakers to change legislation. While maintaining the general right to asylum, asylum now can be denied to those who come from safe regions or travel through safe countries to Germany.

At the beginning of the 1980s, the first ethnic Germans (Aussiedler) also came as refugees from behind the "Iron Curtain," the old frontier between East and West Europe. Their numbers were initially low, but the fall of the Berlin Wall gave impetus to the idea of the German State for all Germans. Most of them came from Russia, Kazakhstan, Romania, and Poland. Since 1990 some 200,000 have returned each year.

For decades the German government has maintained that Germany is not a country of immigration and that immigrants would eventually return to their countries of origin. As a consequence, little was done to support immigrant integration. Another consequence of this legal system is a relatively low proportion of naturalization of immigrants and a high percentage of noncitizen residents. For example, only around 10% of Turks have become German citizens.

Until 1994 the educational participation of immigrant students increased both in number and level relative to the participation of national students. Since then, however, participation has declined. Children may attend Kindergarten when they are 4, but compulsory schooling starts at 6, when most children go to a four-grade elementary school. From there, depending on individual abilities, they can continue in three different school types or streams, depending on academic and vocational goals.

In 1998 about 20% of all legally employable immigrants and 10% of all nationals were registered as unemployed.

Germany's immigrant policy can be characterized on the one hand as an attempt to treat all residents (independent of their country of origin) as equal in terms of salaries and social security, but on the other hand there are strong incentives to return to their countries of origin. These two characteristics have been termed *temporary integration* (Broeders, 2001). Thus, segregation, rather than full integration, is the implicitly suggested acculturation outcome (Brubaker, 2001; Yildirim, 1997).

The Netherlands

The Netherlands is moderate on the immigration dimension, with 9.9% of its total population of 16 million born elsewhere. In the cities where the data were collected, the percentage of immigrants was higher. Including both first- and second-generation immigrants, these cities had 24% to 44% immigrants. In Table 2.1, the Netherlands is placed relatively low on the actual diversity index but is classified as moderate on the diversity policy index.

The ethnic origin of the population is 94% Dutch, which includes about 100,000 immigrants from the Antilles and Aruba, who have Dutch citizenship (because these are dependent overseas regions), as well as an unknown portion of 295,000 immigrants from Surinam (which is a former overseas region). The main origins of immigrants are Morocco, Turkey, and the former Yugoslavia.

The net migration rate is 1.99 migrants per 1,000 population, resulting from family reunification and asylum seekers. Family formation is important in the Turkish and Moroccan groups. The overall fertility rate is 1.49 children, but it is much higher in ethnocultural groups, particularly Moroccan (4 children per woman) and Turkish (3 children per woman). The overall population growth rate is 0.47%.

Average gross income for employed males is about US$26,900, but for employed females it is about US$14,950. The average yearly income of ethnocultural group members is about US$3,000 less. The unemployment rate is 6.2% for men and 11.1% for women. The unemployment rate for ethnocultural groups was 3 to 5 times higher, and they were unemployed for much longer periods. The participation rate of Moroccan and Turkish women in the labor market is very low.

Medical and educational services are generally accessible to all persons living in the Netherlands.

Primary schooling is 8 years (ages 4–12), and secondary school is 4 to 6 years (vocational and academic streams). The compulsory school age is from 5 to 15 years of age. Parents do not have to pay fees for their 4- to 15-year-old children. All schools are fully state funded. Until 2004 a cultural policy was pursued, consisting of lessons in the (official) language and culture of the original country of students of Mediterranean origin for 2.5 hours per week during school hours (monocultural courses) and intercultural education for all students (multicultural courses). More than three fourths of the Moroccan and Turkish students at primary schools took lessons in their original language.

The government officially tries to maintain a two-track immigrant policy, aiming at integrating immigrants into Dutch society and preserving cultural identity. Two values guide this policy: equality of opportunity and equivalence of cultures. The government currently invests in compulsory introductory courses (Dutch language, and orientation to Dutch society and to the labor market) for newcomers, and in adult education for older immigrants. Surinamese, Antilleans, Moroccans, Turks, and refugees are the main target groups for this part of the integration policy.

Support for home language lessons for immigrant children (until 2004) and intercultural courses for all students are a means to guarantee cultural equivalence. Also, financial support to immigrant organizations contributes to this aim, as does the right to establish fully state-funded denominational schools. About two thirds of the primary schools in the Netherlands are Protestant or Catholic. These schools are fully funded by the government. Muslims and Hindus also have the constitutional right to establish their own schools, provided they meet the national standards. About 30 Muslim schools are currently in operation, constituting 4% of the total Muslim student population.

Since 1973, the Netherlands, like many other northwest European countries, has pursued a restrictive immigration policy, which makes it difficult to immigrate as a foreign laborer. Economic immigration has changed into family reunification immigration. More than 90% of the Mediterranean laborers today have their families in the Netherlands

Several surveys show that the attitudes of the Dutch towards immigrant and asylum seekers have become more negative in recent years (Arends-Tóth & van de Vijver, 2003; Verkuyten & Thijs, 2002; Zegers de Beijl, 1999).

United Kingdom

The United Kingdom has a moderate level of immigration, with 6.8% of its total population of 60 million not born in the country. In Leicester, where the ICSEY sample was drawn, 36% are immigrants, and the majority of these (26%) were immigrants from India. The United Kingdom is also moderate on both actual and policy diversity in Table 2.1.

Most immigrant communities have proportionately more young people and fewer older people than those born in Britain. Because of this, African, Bangladeshi, and Pakistani communities will grow substantially, both absolutely and relatively, over the next 20 years. African Caribbean and Indian communities will also grow, but not to the same extent. Analysis of place of birth by ethnic group shows that among all age groups, 34% of African Asians and 43% of Indians were born in the British Isles. In 1998, the employment rate among White people of working age was 75.1%. The average for all Black and Asian people was 57%. However, for people of Bangladeshi and Pakistani backgrounds, the respective figures were 35% and 41%. Rates for women in these communities were lower still. Asians and Blacks who left school have less success in gaining employment than White people. This is the case even when all relevant variables, such as educational attainment, are held constant.

The proportion of African Caribbean youth achieving five higher grade passes is considerably less than half the national average. Indian pupils achieve results above the national average, whereas Pakistani and Bangladeshi pupils achieve below the national average. Asian and Black youth are relatively more represented in higher education than their proportions in the general population. Students of Indian origin are 3 times as likely to be in higher education than their counterparts in the general population. However, about 70% of African Caribbean and 60% of Indian, Pakistani, and Bangladeshi students pursue degree studies at universities that were formerly polytechnics. Only 35% of White students do so. Comprehensive, free of charge education is available for all 5- to 18-year-olds. Education is compulsory up to age 16. Private, fee-paying schools also exist at all levels.

British governments have introduced policies to promote equality of opportunity and to combat overt racial discrimination. They have passed major antidiscrimination legislation but have taken steps to limit the number of ethnic minorities through immigration controls. The Immigration Act 1971 added further restrictions: To gain the right of abode in Britain people generally needed to be Commonwealth citizens and have some substantial connection with the United Kingdom (i.e., having a parent born in the United Kingdom). The 1981 British Nationality Act means that a person born in the United Kingdom is not automatically a U.K. citizen. To qualify for citizenship, the person must have a U.K.-born parent as well.

Free health and social services are available; however, studies have shown that access to health and social services is far from equal. Ethnocultural groups experience several barriers to accessing health care services, including poor quality or lack of accessible information and negative experiences of the health service. Ethnocultural groups are also overrepresented among the unemployed, low-income groups, and those in poor housing.

During the late 1960s and 1970s, the emphasis in immigration control shifted from workers to the family members of those who had already entered. The rules that governed the entry of family members were on the face of it, race neutral. In practice, however, relatives of Blacks and Asians experienced delays, indignities, and separation that would not have been tolerated had they been imposed on White families.

Asylum seekers have been in the eye of the immigration storm, stimulating three major Acts of Parliament over 6 years, with deterrent measures enacted to prevent or discourage arrivals. Visa requirements, detention, and reduced support for asylum seekers were put in place to reduce the number of asylum seekers.

The present government has declared that it is committed to creating One Nation, a country where racism is unacceptable. However, public attitudes vary and studies have shown that some people favor assimilation as opposed to multiculturalism and are intolerant of immigrants' religion and customs.

Recent Receiving Societies

Finland

Finland has a low level of immigration, with 2.6% of its total population of 5.2 million people born outside the country. Despite this low percentage of immigrants, Finland is only moderately low on the actual diversity index in Table 2.1, because of the presence of two ethnolinguistic groups (Finnish and Swedish). This degree of diversity is a historical residue and may not contribute to the way Finnish society receives and treats contemporary immigrants. On the diversity policy index, Finland is classified as low, probably more accurately representing its current approach to diversity.

The ethnic origins of the population are: Finnish, 93%; Swedish, 6%; Sami, 0.11%; Gypsy/Romany, 0.12%; and Tatar, 0.02%. About 1.6% are other foreign nationals, mainly from the former Soviet Union, Estonia, and Sweden (mainly ethnic Finn returnees). Most immigrants live in urban areas (4.2% of the Helsinki population is foreign born).

The overall average annual income is US$18,845. Immigrant groups, however, have a lower average income. The overall unemployment rate is 14.3%; noncitizens have an average rate of 46.7%, but this varies greatly across immigrant groups (up to 90%). Among immigrants, 56% have completed comprehensive school; 28%, upper secondary; and 15.5%, university.

National policies do not seek to encourage immigration. Traditionally, once immigrants have arrived, all the adaptation and changes are expected to be made by immigrants and their descendants rather than by the Finnish. Although the objective of official settlement policy is integration and multiculturalism, the national policies in practice can be considered to be seeking assimilation rather than integration. For example, a dispersion policy was adopted for immigrants, so that 3,000 Vietnamese were distributed over 100 municipalities.

Finnish attitudes toward refugees and other immigrants changed considerably between 1987 and 1993 in a negative direction. Increased immigration together with a large increase in unemployment may have affected these attitudes, as people feel socioeconomically threatened by immigration. Finns relate more negatively to those with the lowest labor market status than to those with a higher status. They have a negative attitude toward immigrants from Russia, Poland, Turkey, Vietnam, Chile, Somalia, and former Yugoslavia. They relate positively to Norwegians, British, North American, and Swedish immigrants.

Norway

Norway has a low level of immigration, with 6.7% of its total population of 4.5 million born outside the country. In the cities where the ICSEY data were collected, the percentage was higher, ranging from 6.4% in Trondheim to 21.2% in Oslo. In Table 2.1, Norway is rated as low on both diversity indices.

The origins of the main foreign born groups (as percentages of the total population) are: Pakistan, 0.47%; Sweden, 0.44%; Denmark, 0.42%; Vietnam, 0.33%; Bosnia, 0.27%; England, 0.24%; Turkey, 0.21; former Yugoslavia, 0.21%; Iran, 0.20%; and Sri Lanka, 0.19%. In addition there are 0.5% persons of Sami origin. Overall, one third of the foreign-born immigrants live in Oslo. Immigration is mainly by way of family reunification, refugees, and asylum seekers. The net migration rate is 1.62 migrants per 1,000 population. The overall population growth rate is 0.4%. The overall fertility rate is 1.77; the rate is largely the same for most immigrant groups. However, some ethnocultural groups have relatively higher rates (e.g., Pakistani, 3.7%). The average unemployment rate is 2.1%, but for the foreign born it is 9.2%. Overall, 29% of population has completed college or university. Western foreign-born immigrants have higher educational qualifications, whereas those of non-Western origin are lower. The educational system is comprehensive and free of charge for 6-to15-year-olds. This is followed by vocational training or academic streams leading to university study. Both mother tongue and Norwegian language training are available for immigrants. After having lived 3 years in Norway immigrants are allowed to participate in local elections. National elections are only open to naturalized immigrants.

Before 1960, with the exception of people with criminal records and Gypsies, anyone who sought refuge in Norway was welcome. In the 1960s, workers from Turkey and Pakistan were invited to come. An immigration stop was introduced in

1975. After this, only invited refugees, asylum seekers, and family reunifiers were allowed to come to Norway.

Dispersion is encouraged, accomplished by compensating municipalities for the extra efforts, facilities, and costs they incur for settling immigrants in their districts (such as housing, education, child care, primary health care, and social benefits). However, 73% of immigrants from Western countries and 83% from Third World countries live in the six largest metropolitan areas of the country.

Although giving up cultural heritage is not required, its maintenance is not encouraged, except by mother tongue instruction that is available for children. Formally, the government adopts an integration policy in which the principle of equal opportunities is central. However, Norwegians are in favor of assimilation. They generally have a positive attitude toward immigrants and accept that immigrants may maintain their own culture as long as it does not interfere with the public life of the society.

Portugal

Portugal is low on the immigration dimension, with 2.3% of its total population of 10 million born outside the country. Of these, 27% are from E.U. countries. Portugal, though being the lowest on the actual diversity index, is rated moderate on pluralism policy diversity.

The ethnic origin of those not from the European Union are Angola, Brazil, Mozambique, Cape Verde, Guinea Bissau, and Sao Tomé, all of whom are Portuguese speaking. About half of all immigrants live in the Lisbon area.

The net migration rate is –1.51 (negative!) migrants per 1,000 population. Thus, Portugal is still a country of net emigration rather than immigration. Returnees are an important element in Portuguese migration: In the 1980s to mid-1990s, 20,000 persons per year returned to live in Portugal. Earlier (in 1975–1976) there were 700,000 returnees from former African colonies. A substantial number of illegal immigrants live in Portugal, many of whom are able to be legalized. At present, immigration is increasing. The overall fertility rate in Portugal is 1.34.

Although the number of emigrants has decreased considerably in the 1980s and 1990s, it still is going on. In 1997 the number of Portuguese residing abroad was close to 4.6 million. Of these, 35% live in South America, 22% in North America, and 30% in Europe.

Preschool education is financed by a variety of organizations. Basic education is from ages 6 to 15 and is free. High school is 3 years and is followed by university.

In the case of family reunification, if the applicant is a Portuguese citizen, it leads to immediate citizenship for the reunifying persons. Immigrants who have lived at least 6 years in Portugal can apply for naturalization without being required to renounce their original nationality. When selecting persons for immigration, preference is given to immigrants from former colonial, Portuguese- speaking countries.

Traditionally, the Portuguese are tolerant of cultural diversity but intolerance has increased recently. Nevertheless, tolerance and positive attitudes prevail. This is possibly because Portugal has a long history of contact with other cultures. Marriage between Portuguese and native peoples was more frequent in Portuguese colonies than in colonies of other European countries.

Sweden

Sweden has a moderate level of immigration, but it borders on being relatively high. In their total population of 9 million, about 12% are first-generation immigrants, and another 7% are second generation. On the actual diversity index Sweden is also moderate, again bordering on being high. The ICSEY data were collected in the Stockholm metropolitan area with a population of 1.7 million, where there are about 18% first-generation immigrants and another 10% second generation. Historically Sweden has been ethnically diverse, with a large Finnish-speaking-population, and German influences from settlers in the older Hanseatic cities. There were four main periods of immigration: 1940–1947, refugee migration from neighboring countries; 1948–1972, labor migration from Finland and southern Europe; 1973–1989, refugee migration from non-European countries; and 1990–present, refugee migration from former Yugoslavia and the Middle East.

The main immigrant groups are Finns, Yugoslavs, Danes, Norwegians, Greek, Turks, and refugees from South America (mainly Chileans), Turkey, Lebanon (Assyrians), Iran, Iraq (mainly Kurds), Croatia, and Bosnia. There are three ethnolinguistic minorities: 25,000 Sami, 30,000 Finnish border people, and 10,000 Roma.

The net migration rate, 1.68 migrants per 1,000 population, is made up mainly by family reunification and refugees. The overall population growth rate is 0.29%, and the fertility rate is 1.83. However, birth rates are higher in particular groups (Ethiopia, Eritrea, and Somalia). The number of children born to these migrants to reach school age will grow considerably in the near future

The overall unemployment rate is 6.3% plus about 5% in training programs. There are 9 years of compulsory, comprehensive education starting at age 7 (or 6), followed by 2 to 3 years of vocational or academic training, followed by university. State schools are free. Recently, possibilities to start partly state-financed denominational or free schools were broadened. Language courses in Swedish as a second language are compulsory, with mother tongue lessons available on request.

Segregation in the housing market has increased rapidly (mainly between immigrants and the majority, with less between migrant groups). As a consequence, some schools are segregated.

General welfare policy applies to immigrants who are permanently residing in Sweden. Social, medical, and educational provisions meet high standards and are accessible.

Since 1973 immigration is only allowed for refugees and family members under the family reunification program. In 1989 criteria for admitting refugees were tightened, and in 1995 further restrictions were introduced.

On the diversity policy index, Sweden is rated as moderate. In Sweden there is a distinction made between an immigration policy and a policy for the integration of immigrants. Integration policy is summarized in three concepts: equality, freedom of choice, and partnership. Equality refers to the availability of the social welfare system to all permanent residents of Sweden, irrespective of citizenship. Freedom of choice refers to abandoning assimilation and accepting cultural diversity. Mother tongue instruction in schools and nursery schools is the most important instrument. Partnership refers to the need for reciprocity and working towards common objectives.

Several surveys show that public opinion does not support xenophobic offenses and felonies on xenophobic grounds. A large section of the public is seriously concerned about the impact on, and consequences of, refugee migration. Racism and xenophobia generally have not changed for the worse, but people's views about immigration have moved toward dissatisfaction with immigration policies. There has been a shift of public debate toward exclusion and intolerance. Most of the traditional democratic parties in the center of the political field are revising their views on migration policy and adopting elements of restriction and restraint.

IMMIGRANT GROUPS

We have adopted from cross-cultural psychology the view that we need to understand the cultural background of individuals to understand their behavior. For acculturation research, this requires that attention be paid to both cultural groups in contact. In the last section, we presented brief descriptions of the 13 societies of settlement as a way of establishing relevant features of the contexts into which immigrant youth settle. In this section, we describe core elements of the main immigrant groups in our study. We pay particular attention to the two immigrant groups that were sampled most often: Vietnamese (in seven countries) and Turks (in six countries). Three other groups were sampled in more than one country: South Asians (in four countries), Chinese (in two countries), Portuguese (in two countries), and Russians (in two countries). Thereafter, we present brief summaries of salient information for the other immigrant groups in the study.

Vietnamese

With few exceptions, such as the Vietnamese who came to Australia, Canada, and France as students, the first generation of Vietnamese in the seven countries surveyed were mainly refugees (the so-called boat people) who fled Vietnam after the fall of Saigon in 1975. Table 2.3 highlights features of the Vietnamese immigrants to the seven countries.

As refugees, Vietnamese have been protected by international laws and in most cases are entitled to the same social privileges and civil rights as members of the national group except perhaps the right to vote in parliamentary elections. The majority of Vietnamese refugees are ethnic Vietnamese, but some Vietnamese have a Chinese background. Unfortunately, we are unable to distinguish Sino-Vietnamese from ethnic Vietnamese in our study.

As can be deduced from the column labeled "Initial Arrival" in Table 2.3, France has a special relationship with the Vietnamese. Vietnamese immigration to France originated from the French colonization of Indo-China (Cambodia, Laos, and Vietnam, the most highly populated of the three) in the later part of the 19th century. During the many years under French rule, students found their way to France for study and work. After the French were defeated at Dien Bien Phu in 1954 by the Vietnamese Communists, civil servants, who had been loyal to the French regime, and families of mixed marriages sought refuge in France. Another wave of refugees fled Vietnam in 1975 when the Communists took over the southern parts of Vietnam. For historical reasons, France was a favored country of destination.

The Vietnamese immigrants generally have valued education, and children are encouraged by their elders to study. Moreover, the average educational background of Vietnamese immigrants is higher than of other immigrant groups who participated in the ICSEY project. Compared with other ethnic groups, Vietnamese children tend to have higher academic and school achievement.

In most countries the Vietnamese are not well organized institutionally. This may have a variety of reasons: dispersal and animosity between different ideological groups (e.g., Finland) or a suspicion of institutions caused by the prolonged war in Vietnam and the hardships of the refugee experience (United States). Family is the most important social unit for most refugees. Family has played an important role in the maintenance of personal identity and immigrants' sense of stability.

Vietnamese culture, based in Confucian and Buddhist roots, is strongly collectivist; the family structure is typically patriarchic, with children expected to obey their parents and fulfill their obligations within the family (Matsuoka, 1990;

TABLE 2.3
Vietnamese Immigration: Periods of Arrival, Ethnic Composition,
and Total Number

Country of Settlement	Initial Arrival	Subsequent Arrival	Ethnic Composition	Total
Australia	>1975 (students)	1976 (refugees) 1980s (migrants)	80% Vietnamese 20% Sino-Viet	154,830
Canada	>1975 (students)	1975 (refugees) 1980s (migrants)	Minority: Sino-Viet	113,000
Finland	1979 (refugees)		Minority: Sino-Viet	3,000
France	>1954 (students)	1975 (refugees)	Unknown	75,000
Norway	1975 (refugees)	1980s (migrants)	Minority: Sino-Viet	18,000
Sweden	1979 (refugees)	1980s–1990s (migrants)	Majority: Sino-Viet	12,000
United States	1975 (refugees)	1990s (migrants)	Majority: Vietnamese	1,122,528

Nguyen & Williams, 1989). Several studies show that Vietnamese parents have strongly encouraged the maintenance of cultural traditions at home, while encouraging their children to adapt to the larger society and become more independent in school (Nguyen, Messe, & Stollak, 1999; Zhou & Bankston, 1998). Children are expected to remain at home until marriage and to follow the advice of their elders in matters of dating, marriage, and career choice. Individual autonomy is subordinated to the needs of the family (Zhou & Bankston, 1994).

Turks

In 1998, about 5% of the Turkish population was living abroad. However, the distribution of the overseas population in terms of countries of residence has been highly skewed in favor of Europe, and in particular Germany. Of the close to 4 million Turks living abroad, about 3 million live in Europe, making them the largest foreign population in Europe (Economic Intelligence Unit, 2001). Furthermore, the overwhelming majority of them (about 2 million) resided in Germany. The ubiquity of Turks in Europe, and in particular Germany, is as a result of labor agreements reached between Turkey and various European counties. Turkey negotiated migration recruitment agreements, beginning with Germany in 1961, followed by the Netherlands, Belgium, Austria, and France, and ending with Sweden in 1967 (Crul & Vermeulen, 2003; Koray, 1997).

The Turkish immigrants filled vacant jobs that were less attractive to the nationals in many European countries. However, the majority of Turks were employed on a temporary basis as "guest workers." The one exception to the guest worker status accorded Turks in Europe was in Sweden, where labor unions managed to integrate them and accept them as workers with the same benefits as Swedes. In other words, Turks in Sweden were not regarded as guest workers who could be deported when their contracts came to an end. Turkish migrants to Finland are also unique in two ways: (a) the majority of them were refugees, and (b) there is a higher gender imbalance in favor of males, about one female to three males. This has resulted in high interethnic marriages between Finnish women and Turkish men. Thus the Finnish Turkish ICSEY sample mainly consists of children from mixed marriages.

An overview of the migration background of the Turks in the countries participating in the present study is presented in Table 2.4.

About 70% of emigrants from Turkey to Europe were ethnic Turks, and about 20% were Kurds. The rest consisted of various small ethnic groups such as Albanians, Georgians, and Armenians. In the ICSEY material, the term Turks refers to ethnic Turks only. About two thirds of the Turkish immigrants originated from rural areas and villages in central Turkey and from around the Black Sea, albeit a large number lived in large cities at the time of emigration. Generally, the Turks who emigrated to Europe had a low socioeconomic background and were poorly educated (Crul & Vermeulen, 2003).

TABLE 2.4
Turkish Immigration: Period of Arrival, Ethnic Composition,
and Total Number

Country of Settlement	Initial Arrival	Subsequent Arrival	Ethnic Composition	Total
Germany	>1955 >1961 (labor immigrants)	1980s (refugees)	80% ethnic Turks 20% Kurds	2,500,000
Finland	>1990 (refugees)		Unknown	2,287
France	>1966 early 1970s (labor immigrants)	1980s (refugees)	60% ethnic Turks 40% Kurds	380,000
Netherlands	>1964 (labor immigrants)	1970s (family reunification)	Mainly ethnic Turks Small percentage Kurds	331,000
Norway	>1968 (labor immigrants)	1980s (refugees) Family reunification	Majority ethnic Turks with some Kurds as refugees	14,671
Sweden	1960s	1970s (refugees)	33% ethnic Turks 33% Kurds 33% Assyrians	60,000

Research shows that Turkish immigrant youth are characterized by low educational attainment, although the second-generation youth perform better than the first generation (Crul & Doomernik, 2003; Phalet & Swyngedouw, 2003; Westin, 2003; Worbs, 2003). With their generally lower educational aspirations, it is perhaps not surprising that their unemployment rates are also high compared with their national peers. Moreover, they are overrepresented in unskilled work (Worbs, 2003). They tend to maintain a strong relationship with their Turkish culture, stick to traditional family values, have limited social contacts with nationals, prefer a marriage partner from Turkey, and have little Turkish language loss between generations (cf. Crul & Doomernik, 2003).

South Asians

People from South Asia are an important part of contemporary migrant flows. Included in this regional category are those from India, Pakistan, Sri Lanka, and Bangladesh who migrated as immigrants, or in some cases as refugees. In this study, immigrants from India and Pakistan were sampled in three countries (Canada, Norway, and the United Kingdom). In addition, in the same three countries there are secondary migrations from East Africa and from the West Indies to the Netherlands.

In Canada, immigrants from India initially settled on the west coast, working in the forestry and agricultural sectors, but are now mainly in urban areas. Indians are the second most numerous recent immigrant group (after Chinese), and close to 400,000 immigrants in Canada are of Indian origin. They are generally well educated and economically well established. Almost half of the Indians in the sample are Sikhs, and a quarter are Hindu.

In the United Kingdom, Indian immigrants also came directly from India and East Africa. They are mainly of Punjabi and Gujarati origin, divided about equally between Sikhs and Hindus, and number close to 1 million (1.6% of the population). They generally have high educational achievement and are upwardly mobile, many being employed as managers and professionals.

In Norway, the South Asian sample is of Pakistani origin. They came originally as guest workers in the 1970s and now number around 20,000 (0.46% of the population). In comparison with the immigrants to Canada and the United Kingdom, South Asians in Norway are less well educated and have among the lowest incomes. Many are employed in the service sector or own small businesses. However, their children are achieving well in school. Most are Muslims, with a majority being Sunni.

In the Netherlands, immigrants of Indian origin migrated from Surinam around 30 years ago when Surinam became independent. They came originally (around 1900) to Surinam from northern India, which then was under British rule, to work on the plantations. When they came to the Netherlands they spoke Dutch, had Dutch citizenship, and did not live together in concentrated areas. The majority are Hindu.

In Portugal, immigration from India increased substantially after 1974. There are currently 35,000 Indians, with around 80% of them living in the Lisbon area. There are four distinct communities (Hindus, Muslims, Ismaéliens, and Roman Catholics of Goa). They differ not only in religion, but also by education: Goans have high educational and occupational standing compared with the other groups.

Chinese

Chinese people from various parts of East and Southeast Asia constitute one of the major immigrant flows during the past century. In Australia, most early immigrants came as laborers and subsequently set up small businesses. More recently, Chinese have come as international students and as relatively well-qualified employees and professionals. They have come from China, Hong Kong, Malaysia, Singapore, and Taiwan. There are variations among these groups in educational and occupational attainment, with those from China more often in lower status occupations and those from Hong Kong and Singapore more often in professional jobs. Most Chinese in Australia are Christian.

In New Zealand, Chinese migration began in the 1860s when a small community established themselves as workers in the southern gold mines. They were the first non-European immigrants to New Zealand. In 1871, 4,364 Chinese resided in New Zealand; today, the Chinese population numbers more than 100,000 and represents almost 3% of the population The new migration to New Zealand has increased the Chinese population more than five-fold in the last 20 years, and at present almost three fourths of the Chinese population in New Zealand were born overseas. The vast majority of the newcomers originate from Mainland China, with Hong Kong, Malaysia, Singapore, Vietnam, and Cambodia each providing less than 1% of the Chinese migrants from North-Central Asia. Chinese from Taiwan form 3.4% of this group. On the whole, the Chinese are well educated.

Portuguese in France and Germany

Immigration from Portugal to France is a longstanding tradition, beginning well before Portugal's membership in the European Union. Now numbering 570,000, Portuguese immigrants live in the major cities and are predominantly working class, earning low salaries; however, their unemployment rate is low. Among the youth, educational attainment is low, with few graduating from secondary school. However, there are signs of upward social mobility among young people.

In Germany, Portuguese came as guest workers in the 1960s, and immigration increased after Portugal became part of the European Union in 1986. People with origins in Portugal now total 130,000, of whom 25,000 were born in Germany. As in France, they work mostly in blue collar jobs in industry but are increasingly moving into the service sector. They have relatively low educational achievement, which is continuing among the youth.

Russians in Finland and Israel

Two societies in our study received Russian immigrants, but under very different circumstances. In Finland, most Russian immigrants arrived as returnees or repatriates from a province adjacent to Finland, following the end of the Soviet Union. They currently number around 28,000, and the first generation are generally monolingual in Russian. Although they have Finnish ancestry, and see themselves as Finnish, they are commonly perceived as being Russian. Employment remains a problem for many in this community.

In Israel, Russians came in massive numbers after a policy change in the Soviet Union in the 1980s. By 1990, more than 700,000 Russian Jews had arrived, and they now number more than 1 million (15% of the population). They reside in most parts of the country, but they constitute 90% of the residents in some communities. They are typically well educated and have high occupational positions. In recent years, Russians have become a major force in Israeli political life.

Other Immigrant Groups

Angolans in Portugal

Angolans make up the third largest immigrant group in Portugal (after those from Brazil and Cape Verde), with 17,000 now residing there. Most live in the Lisbon area, where they work in blue collar jobs. Angolan youth are doing less well in school than their Portuguese peers.

Antilleans in the Netherlands

About 125,000 Antilleans live in the Netherlands. This is about one third of all Antilleans; the other two thirds mainly live in the Caribbean. Most immigrants are from Curaçao and Bonaire. They are descendants of slaves who originally were imported from West Africa. Almost all have Dutch citizenship. In terms of settlement they are an unstable group, with a continuing influx of first-generation Antilleans. Because of an economic recession, the number of Antilleans who came to the Netherlands has increased considerably in recent years. The Dutch government tends to deal with the recently arrived, relatively poorly educated young Antilleans as if they are non-Dutch. As a result, the Antilleans feel unfairly treated and are likely to retain a strong ethnic identity. About 50% of the families with children in this group are single-parent, female-headed families.

Armenians in the United States

Armenians came to the United States in small numbers early in the 1900s, settling mainly in New York and California. The largest numbers came in the 1970s and 1980s, mainly for political reasons, and in the 1990s, following the break-up of the Soviet Union. At present there are 385,000 persons of Armenian origin in the United States, more than 200,000 of whom are in the Los Angeles area. They have established cohesive community organizations. On average, they have achieved a high educational level and are generally successful economically. However, there are differences between the earlier, more established immigrants and the recent, generally more poorly educated immigrants. Armenian culture is characterized by a patriarchal family structure, with emphasis on close family ties, obligations to the family, and the expectation that young people will marry within the ethnic group.

Aussiedler in Germany

As in Finland and Israel, there is a right of return in Germany for ethnic Germans living in the former Soviet Union. Some had been there since the Middle Ages, but many settled later in the 18th century. Beginning in the early 20th century, these ethnic Germans were invited to return, and more than 4 million have done so. Before

1990, they were mainly German speaking and had settled well in Germany. However, later returnees, although seeing themselves as Germans, spoke little German and are perceived as Russians. The settlement of this latter group has been problematic, with high unemployment and low educational attainment.

Chileans (and Other Latin Americans) in Sweden and Norway

Following the military coup in 1973, many Chileans fled to Sweden and Norway. Soon afterward, immigrants from other Latin American countries arrived in Sweden, forming a heterogeneous Spanish-origin community. Although they generally have a high level of education, many could not find employment consistent with their academic achievement. At present there are around 20,000 persons with Latin American backgrounds in Sweden, and 8,000 in Norway, around half of them from Chile. There is a high level of naturalization and intermarriage with Swedes. Following the early wave of highly educated immigrants, there is now more diversity in economic status.

Ethiopians in Israel

The last two decades have witnessed a mass migration of almost the whole Jewish population of Ethiopia to Israel. They arrived in two major waves: Operation Moses (1984–1985) and Operation Solomon (May 1991). Relative to the total Israeli population, the Ethiopian newcomers and their offspring constitute a small immigrant group (less than 75,000 people, or 5% of the total number of immigrants settled in the country during the 1990s.) In addition to their distinctive language and culture, this group differs from other immigrants and the rest of Israeli population in their black African ancestry. Despite their strong commitment to the Jewish faith, the authenticity of Ethiopian Jews as "real" Jews was questioned by the Israeli authorities, and most of them had to undergo some sort of ritual conversion after their arrival. The dramatic nature of their immigration and their distinctive characteristics have set them apart as an immigrant group that has been granted increased assistance from the Israeli authorities.

Nevertheless, employment rates and percentage of students passing matriculation exams and attending universities are significantly lower than in the population at large.

Filippinos in Australia

Filippinos came to Australia originally to work in the marine and pearl-diving industries around the 1870s. More recently (starting in the 1960s), they came as students and professionals, and they continue to come under the family reunification scheme. Their economic status is lower than the average immigrant population despite relatively high educational attainment. Most Filippinos are Roman Catholic.

Koreans in Canada

The first Koreans arrived in Canada in the early 20th century, and immigration increased substantially starting in the 1960s. There are now close to 50,000 persons of Korean origin in Canada. Many are professionals, and they are often self-employed or operate small businesses. Their children achieve high educational standing and increasingly work as professionals. Most are Christians and are active in church-related Korean activities.

Maghrebians in France

This category includes a large number (more than 1.3 million) of immigrants from Algeria, Morocco, and Tunisia, all countries that were once ruled by France. Immigrants came mainly as laborers to the major industrial cities, where unemployment and discrimination are now serious problems. Most of those employed are blue collar workers. Among the youth, boys are achieving education on a par with French youth, but girls are not doing as well as their French peers. This population is mostly Muslim, although the second generation appears to be less involved in religion.

Mexicans in United States

Many people of Mexican origin in the United States are descended from inhabitants who lived in the area before the annexation of parts of Mexico by the United States in 1848. Thereafter, continuing streams of immigrants have arrived from Mexico, mainly for work, particularly in agriculture. There are now large communities of both recent arrivals and second and later generations of immigrants. Latinos currently make up approximately 32% of the population of California; three fourths of these are of Mexican origin. In Los Angeles public schools, children of Mexican background are the dominant group overall, and Mexican influence is pervasive throughout southern California in areas such as food, language, and music. Mexican culture stresses family interdependence and close ties to the extended family. The Roman Catholic church plays an important role in the daily lives of most Mexican Americans.

Mozambicans in Portugal

Almost 5,000 Mozambicans live in Portugal, most in the Lisbon area. They are mostly employed in blue collar jobs and as employees in small businesses. Youth are reported to be doing better than other immigrant groups from Africa.

Pacific Islanders in New Zealand

Pacific Islanders, mainly from Samoa, Fiji, and the Cook Islands constitute an important part of the cultural make-up of New Zealand. They arrived in large numbers in the 1960s and have continued to arrive since then. At present, there are more than 200,000 Pacific Islanders (5.6% of the population). Related to the indigenous Maori, they have been allowed special access to immigration; for example, there is a special annual quota of 1,100 for Samoans. They are concentrated in the major cities and have established churches and community centers there. Educational and occupational attainment are lower than the national average.

Timorese in Portugal

Before the Indonesian invasion of East Timor in 1975, there had been no Timorese migration to Portugal, even though Timor had been a colony of Portugal. Because of civil wars and political conflicts in East Timor, about 6,500 Timorese entered Portugal between 1976 and 1995, before approximately 4,500 of them moved on to Australia. In spite of a continuous flow of Timorese into Portugal, the total number settling in Portugal (between 1,500 and 2,000) has remained relatively stable because of this pattern of transmigration. Most Timorese in Portugal reside in Lisbon and Setúbal. It is a very young and active group. Timorese students have higher academic achievement than other ethnic groups (Viegas, 1997).

3 Methodological Aspects: Studying Adolescents in 13 Countries

Paul Vedder
Leiden University
Fons J. R. van de Vijver
Tilburg University

This chapter presents an overview of the methodological aspects of the study. It deals with a description of the sample, the sampling procedure, and the variables and instruments that were used for assessment. It also describes the procedures that were used for data collection and analyses. The chapter explains the way the results are presented, focusing less on comparisons of countries or groups and more on the interrelationships among variables and clusters of variables. Finally, it presents what we call the *standard treatment*, which is the statistical procedure we followed to ensure that the instruments used measure the same constructs across all the countries and ethnic groups in our sample.

PARTICIPANTS

Participants were 13- to 18-year-old adolescents and their mothers or fathers, sampled from 13 countries. In all countries, both immigrant and nonimmigrant (national) youth were sampled. Thirteen societies of settlement and 26 immigrant groups were sampled. Several immigrant groups were represented in more than one country. Given the relatively low numbers of members of particular ethnocultural groups in the population, sampling took place in cities or clusters of cities with relatively high concentrations of particular ethnocultural groups. Samples of the national groups were mostly from the same cities and neighborhoods as the immigrant adolescents. When immigrant youth were contacted through schools, national youth attending the same schools were also invited to participate. In no country did we have random samples.

Adolescents were approached individually or through schools and associations. In two countries, Canada and the Netherlands, families were first approached, mostly through associations and churches. This strategy was used only for groups to which schools gave no good access because of their low concentration in targeted schools. Material incentives were used to encourage participation in four countries: United States, Norway, Sweden, and Israel. Depending on the country and the respective rules, authorization from administrative bodies and parents, and consent from the adolescents were requested and obtained before the questionnaires were administered.

Adolescents

A total of 7,997 adolescents participated in the study. Demographic details are presented in Table 3.1. Vietnamese were examined in seven countries, Turks in six, South Asians (mainly Indians) in four, Chinese in two, and Russians in two. All other immigrant groups were examined in one country. These groups were Algerians, Angolans, Antilleans, Armenians, Aussiedler, Cape Verdians, Chileans, Ethiopians, Filipinos, Finns, Koreans, Kurds, Mexicans, Moroccans, Mozambicans, Pacific Islanders, Portuguese, Spaniards, and Timorese. These groups are described in more detail in chapter 2.

In the following presentation we use statistics such as t tests and Cohen's d, which is an effect size. Readers not familiar with statistics may simply follow the narrative that provides a description of the statistical outcomes.

The average age was 15.35 years ($SD = 1.56$) for the immigrant youth and 15.32 ($SD = 1.53$) for the national youth; this difference is not significant. Country-wise comparisons showed that for Canada, Germany, and Israel, average ages were significantly above the overall mean (all $ps < .05$), and for the United States, Portugal, and the Netherlands, average ages were significantly below the overall mean. The effect sizes were small with two exceptions.[1] We found two medium-size effects. Both Germany and Israel sampled adolescents above the average age ($ds = .73$ and .65, respectively). The United States and Portugal approached a medium negative effect size of $-.49$ and $-.46$, respectively, indicating a below-average mean age.

In some countries the age differences between immigrants and nationals were significant. In Canada, Finland, Portugal, and New Zealand, the immigrants were older than the nationals (all $ps < .05$); the effect sizes were .26, .22, .25, and .51, respectively. In Germany and Sweden, the immigrants were significantly younger (both $ps < .05$); the effect sizes were $-.19$ and $-.47$, respectively.

Samples differed in the proportion of males and females. Overall, slightly more girls (52.1%) than boys participated in the study. In Israel, relatively fewer girls

---

[1]The effect size for comparisons between the overall group and countries was computed as the difference of the country mean and the overall mean, divided by the overall standard deviation. When comparing nonoverlapping groups, the effect size was computed as the difference in the means of the two groups divided by their pooled standard deviation. We applied Cohen's (1988) cutoff values of .2, .5, and .8 for small, medium, and large effects, respectively.

TABLE 3.1
Sample Characteristics by Country for Immigrant and National Youth

	N	Age in Years	% Female	% 2nd Generation	Prop. Life in Country	Years of Schooling	Parents' Occupational Status
All							
Immigrants	5,366	15.35 (1.56)	53.4	65.3	.77 (.33)	9.43 (1.73)	1.87 (1.20)
Nationals	2,631	15.32 (1.53)	49.4	—	.99 (.07)	9.41 (1.61)	2.71 (1.10)
Australia							
Immigrants	456	15.22 (1.60)	60.7	69.3	.78 (.30)	10.02 (1.60)	2.45 (1.08)
Nationals	155	15.06 (1.45)	59.4	—	.99 (.06)	9.79 (1.48)	3.19 (1.74)
Canada							
Immigrants	257	15.87 (1.58)	55.6	49.7	.71 (.34)	10.61 (1.56)	2.89 (.99)
Nationals	139	15.49 (1.31)	55.4	—	1.00	10.03 (1.26)	2.99 (.98)
Finland							
Immigrants	442	15.30 (1.58)	50.1	23.5	.43 (.35)	8.41 (1.55)	1.78 (1.00)
Nationals	346	14.97 (1.36)	43.4	—	1.00	8.60 (1.34)	2.45 (.95)
France							
Immigrants	517	15.61 (1.45)	57.5	94.5	.95 (.16)	9.54 (1.43)	1.73 (1.17)
Nationals	151	15.52 (1.72)	58.0	—	1.00	9.33 (1.46)	2.56 (1.11)
Germany							
Immigrants	295	16.36 (1.36)	52.7	—	.76 (.29)	10.14 (1.97)	2.22 (1.09)
Nationals	249	16.61 (1.43)	56.5	—	1.00	10.76 (1.97)	3.27 (.79)
Israel							
Immigrants	461	16.31 (.90)	41.0	13.2	.40 (.28)	10.86 (.74)	2.31 (1.27)
Nationals	214	16.41 (.90)	39.7	93.4	.96 (.13)	10.0 (.00)	3.12 (1.04)

(continued)

TABLE 3.1 (continued)

	N	Age in Years	% Female	% 2nd Generation	Prop. Life in Country	Years of Schooling	Parents' Occupational Status
Netherlands							
Immigrants	354	14.87 (1.53)	49.7	88.9	.93 (.20)	10.58 (1.51)	2.34 (.98)
Nationals	101	14.74 (1.62)	60.4	—	1.00	10.63 (1.51)	3.48 (.73)
New Zealand							
Immigrants	256	15.70 (1.28)	54.2	67.6	1.00	—	—
Nationals	243	15.08 (1.17)	33.7	—	1.00	—	—
Norway							
Immigrants	484	15.24 (1.53)	50.1	68.7	.83 (.27)	8.87 (1.40)	1.79 (1.03)
Nationals	207	15.09 (1.52)	47.8	—	1.00	8.84 (1.41)	3.21 (.83)
Portugal							
Immigrants	426	14.79 (1.62)	62.6	—	.45 (.27)	8.05 (1.88)	1.13 (.65)
Nationals	355	14.44 (1.07)	46.3	—	1.00	8.47 (1.38)	1.39 (.69)
Sweden							
Immigrants	829	15.11 (1.60)	51.0	81.2	.88 (.25)	8.87 (1.49)	1.83 (1.01)
Nationals	214	15.86 (1.60)	51.9	—	1.00	9.55 (1.61)	2.79 (1.03)
U.K.							
Immigrants	120	15.18 (1.70)	45.0	95.8	.97 (.15)	9.18 (1.70)	2.23 (1.03)
Nationals	120	15.49 (1.57)	50.0	—	1.00	9.48 (1.57)	2.35 (.84)
U.S.A.							
Immigrants	472	14.60 (1.33)	60.7	69.6	.76 (.27)	9.29 (1.28)	2.25 (1.03)
Nationals	137	14.54 (1.40)	65.0	—	1.00	9.19 (1.32)	3.19 (.95)

Note. Figures refer to means and standard deviations, if not indicated otherwise. Parents' occupational status refers to the highest professional status of either parent (1 = unskilled; 2 = skilled; 3 = white collar; 4 = professional).

participated, whereas in the United States more than 60% of the participants were girls. In Portugal and New Zealand, relatively fewer girls participated in the national group than in the immigrant group. Neither in the national groups nor in the immigrant groups was gender related to adolescents' age, the number of years spent in school, or parents' level of education. At the national level, France was an exception to this rule. In the national group, French girls were almost half a year older than the boys (15.77 and 15.35, SDs 1.49 and 1.52, respectively), and they had been in school longer (9.66 and 9.26 years, SDs 1.44 and 1.40).

Table 3.1 shows that most immigrant adolescents were second generation. We defined second generation as either being born in the country of settlement or having immigrated before age 7. Finland and Israel had relatively low proportions of second-generation immigrants. These numbers are not a sampling artifact but rather reflect immigration policies of these countries. Finland recently became a country of immigration. Israel maintains an active immigrant policy toward Jews from Ethiopia and from the former Soviet Union (mostly from Russia); these were the two groups that participated in the Israeli study.

Among immigrants, irrespective of country and group, first-generation youth were older than second-generation youth. The mean age of first-generation youth was 15.78 years ($SD = 1.40$) and of second-generation youth was 15.08 years ($SD = 1.55$), $t(3,322) = 15.04$, $p < .001$, $d = .47$. The average number of years of schooling was 9.70 years ($SD = 1.58$) for first-generation youth and 9.32 years ($SD = 1.59$) for second-generation youth; this difference is significant, though small, $t(3,957) = 7.34$, $p < .001$, $d = .24$.

As expected, the average number of years of schooling was largely comparable across countries, suggesting that the school systems and enrollment patterns are largely comparable among the countries and groups. Still, some significant differences were found. The overall mean was 9.41 years ($SD = 1.70$). Australia showed an average above the overall mean with a small effect size ($d = .32$). Other countries with a significantly ($p < .05$) higher average were Canada ($d = .59$), Germany ($d = .59$), Israel ($d = .69$), and the Netherlands ($d = .70$). Four countries had scores that were significantly below the global mean: Norway ($d = -.32$), Sweden ($d = -.23$), Finland ($d = -.54$), and Portugal ($d = -.69$). The deviation of Norway, Sweden, and Finland from the general pattern can be explained by the fact that in these countries parents have the option to start their children in primary school 1 year later than in most other participating countries. Differences between immigrant samples and national samples with regard to years of schooling were significant in some countries, but the effect sizes were invariably small.

Adolescents also reported on their parents' occupational status. Occupational status was defined as the highest level obtained by either parent on the following scale: 1 (unskilled labor), 2 (skilled labor), 3 (white collar job), and 4 (professional job). Overall, the parents in the national samples had a significantly higher occupational status than did immigrant parents, $t(4,618) = 22.08$, $p < .001$; the effect showed a medium size (.59). The same was true in each country. The differences were significant in Norway, the Netherlands, Germany, Sweden, United States,

Australia, Finland, Israel, Portugal, and France. Effect sizes were large for the first five countries; medium for France, Australia, Finland, and Israel; and small for Portugal. Parental occupational status is slightly higher for first-generation immigrant youth than for second-generation immigrant youth. In the second generation, 17.1% of the parents worked at a professional level, whereas in the first generation 24.2% did, $\chi^2(3, N = 3,592) = 14.86$, $p < .01$.

Tables 3.1 and 3.2 contain information on parents' occupational status. The information in Table 3.1 is based on adolescents' reports and in Table 3.2 on self-reports by parents. The Pearson product moment correlation between the two scores was .82 ($p < .01$), and the means were about equal, paired $t(2,045) = -.57$, ns, supporting the validity of students' reports on parents' occupational status in terms of both correlation and level. Adolescent reports of parents' occupational status were used in the analyses, as these were available for many cases.

In summary, it can be concluded that with some exceptions, most relevant background variables did not differ substantially across ethnic groups and countries. There are two kinds of exceptions to this general observation. The first are sample particulars, such as the slightly higher ages in Germany and Israel, the slightly higher percentage of girls in the United States, and the differences between countries and groups in terms of generational status (first- or second-generation immigrants). These variables are potentially confounding variables in the main analyses of the project; whenever deemed appropriate we include these variables as covariates in the analyses. The second kind of exceptions are sample differences that reflect valid ethnic group or country differences. Examples are the higher occupational levels of national parents as compared with immigrant parents. These differences are also taken into account in the analyses where deemed appropriate.

Parents

A total of 3,165 parents participated. Demographic details are presented in Table 3.2. In most participating countries adolescents were asked to give a letter to their parents inviting them to participate. In Australia, Canada, and the Netherlands, some parents were contacted directly by research assistants. In Israel, Portugal, and New Zealand, no parental data were collected.

Countries showed noteworthy differences in the length of residence of parents; all countries differed significantly from the overall means of 15.20 ($SD = 8.22$) and 16.72 ($SD = 9.09$) years of stay for mothers and fathers, respectively. Finnish immigrant parents' average length of residence was considerably lower (about 10 years; $ds = -1.22$ and -1.04 for mothers and fathers, respectively). Australian and Canadian parents did not differ from the overall mean. American immigrants' length of residence was also relatively short in their new country ($ds = -.16$ and $-.26$ for mothers and fathers, respectively). Sweden and the Netherlands yielded scores slightly above average ($ds = .17$ to .49) whereas France and the United Kingdom yielded residence scores that were considerably higher than the overall averages ($ds = .75$ to .93). This pattern of differences may show a mixture of sam-

TABLE 3.2

Sample Characteristics of Participating Parents, by Country and by Groups With Sample Sizes of at Least 19 Participants

	N	Mother's Age	Father's Age	LOR Mother	LOR Father	Occupational Status
All						
Immigrants	2,302	41.61 (5.77)	45.37 (6.47)	15.20 (8.22)	16.69 (9.09)	2.32 (1.06)
Nationals	863	43.17 (4.97)	45.69 (5.49)	—	—	3.19 (.92)
Australia						
Immigrants	349	43.75 (5.23)	47.00 (6.47)	14.77 (6.97)	14.77 (6.96)	2.54 (1.06)
Nationals	124	43.22 (4.56)	45.71 (4.97)	—	—	3.16 (1.05)
Canada						
Immigrants	189	42.89 (4.68)	47.56 (5.61)	15.76 (8.51)	17.03 (9.35)	2.86 (1.03)
Nationals	105	—	45.25 (4.99)	—	—	2.53 (1.00)
Finland						
Immigrants	235	43.29 (7.59)	46.04 (8.09)	6.68 (5.65)	9.25 (6.66)	2.20 (.99)
Nationals	73	44.57 (4.25)	46.54 (5.31)	—	—	2.98 (1.06)
France						
Immigrants	212	42.81 (5.29)	47.41 (5.95)	22.16 (7.59)	24.59 (8.05)	—
Nationals	36	43.28 (3.79)	44.97 (4.88)	—	—	—
Germany						
Immigrants	29	40.31 (3.42)	43.69 (4.32)	—	—	2.37 (.93)
Nationals	90	41.30 (2.42)	44.48 (4.02)	—	—	3.35 (.70)
Norway						
Immigrants	124	42.82 (5.68)	46.08 (6.45)	—	—	1.73 (1.02)
Nationals	122	42.20 (4.86)	44.64 (5.25)	—	—	3.37 (.86)

(continued)

TABLE 3.2 (continued)

	N	Mother's Age	Father's Age	LOR Mother	LOR Father	Occupational Status
Sweden						
Immigrants	412	41.19 (5.64)	44.32 (6.26)	16.88 (7.52)	17.85 (7.80)	2.04 (1.07)
Nationals	133	46.50 (5.92)	48.84 (6.45)	—	—	2.95 (.90)
United Kingdom						
Immigrants	60	36.85 (1.89)	42.78 (2.45)	22.75 (3.85)	23.48 (3.70)	2.35 (1.03)
Nationals	59	38.42 (2.57)	42.32 (3.28)	—	—	2.46 (.83)
United States						
Immigrants	469	40.78 (5.31)	45.03 (6.34)	13.83 (7.33)	14.29 (7.43)	2.26 (1.00)
Nationals	131	43.65 (5.62)	46.32 (6.03)	—	—	3.32 (.84)
Netherlands						
Immigrants	337	39.82 (5.96)	43.40 (6.58)	17.09 (6.79)	21.23 (6.21)	2.30 (1.01)
Nationals	95	43.62 (4.16)	46.09 (4.64)	—	—	3.50 (.76)

Note. Values are means and standard deviations. LOR = Length of Residence in new country in years.

pling particulars and immigration rates (e.g., a short period of residence of Finnish migrant parents).

In the immigrant group, the analyses yielded a positive correlation between parents' age and their length of residence (fathers: $.16, p < .001, n = 1,595$; mothers: $.13, p < .001, n = 1,795$).

Parental occupational status, obtained for 27.3% of the sample, was defined using the same categories that were used for the adolescents. The highest level of either parent was used.

HOW THE DATA WERE COLLECTED

Data were collected in all countries by the researchers themselves or by research assistants who where either postgraduate students or teachers, who were selected and trained by the main researchers in each country. Research assistants were often members of the ethnocultural group with which they worked. Data collection involved completing a structured questionnaire. The questionnaires were self-explanatory, but when group administered, standard instructions were given at the start of the session. All participants were informed that participation was voluntary and that responses were anonymous. Most questionnaires were group administered in classrooms. In other cases, adolescents were approached individually, and the questionnaire was filled out individually. In supervised administration, the data collectors were instructed to see that the questionnaire was completed in a quiet room, sometimes at home, in schools, or at clubs. When whole classes participated, data were sometimes collected by the regular class teachers, who received special instructions. In Sweden, Finland, and New Zealand, mail surveys were used for groups with a low regional concentration. These were generally small groups. The adolescents were given some information about the project, in particular, the international aspect of the study. In most countries, ethnic language versions of the questionnaire were available, particularly for parents. However, adolescents and parents generally preferred using the national language version.

THE MEASURES WE USED

The questionnaire administered in each country was developed by the ICSEY collaborators to assess a wide range of variables that were shown in Fig. 1.1 of chapter 1. It was improved by extensive pilot testing in three cities (Los Angeles, Stockholm, and Bergen), followed by modifications to eliminate problems in wording. Measures were either developed for the project or taken directly or with some modification from existing scales. For most scales, response options ranged from 1 (strongly disagree) to 5 (strongly agree). We first developed an English version of the questionnaire. ICSEY countries in which English was a dominant language (Canada, the United States, the United Kingdom, New Zealand, and Australia) used this version, sometimes supplemented by translations in other languages for specific immigrant groups. In the other participating countries, the English version was translated into the national languages. We used back-translations to make sure that intended meanings represented in items would be similar or sufficiently comparable among different languages. When we expected that immigrant versions would be used by either adolescents or their parents, we followed the same translation protocol. However, in most countries the immigrants preferred using the national language version. In most cases we had ethnic-language-speaking research assistants who had an ethnic language version as a back-up in case an adolescent or parent was not sure about the meaning of a particular item.

Four versions of the questionnaire were used: one version each for immigrant youth, national youth, immigrant parents, and national parents. The immigrant youth version was the most extensive version. The variables that were measured can be divided in three clusters: demographic variables, intercultural relationships, and adaptation. This version is included in Appendix A.

In this section we give a short presentation of the variables and scales included in the youth and parent questionnaires. A further description is given in each of the next three chapters, which also includes a presentation of the conceptual background for each variable. The psychometric properties of most scales were established in the present study and are reported in Table 3.3.

Immigrant Youth Questionnaires

Demographic Variables

These variables included adolescents' age, gender, religious affiliation, country of birth, age of arrival if foreign born, and their parents' occupational status. The last variable was used to estimate parents' socioeconomic status (SES). When the parents of an adolescent differed as to their occupational status, the higher status was used for the categorization.

The samples included adolescents of both the first generation (born in the country of origin) and the second generation (born in the receiving country or arriving there before age 7). Adolescents from some groups were predominately from one or the other generation, so that generation and ethnic group could not be considered separately in analyses. For this reason we created a new variable: proportion of life spent in the new country, which equals 1 for those born in the country of settlement, the number of years they have spent in the host country divided by their age for foreign born. Proportion of life entails no variance for adolescents born in the country of settlement, as age is the denominator. We therefore created another related variable called length of residence, based on the number of years in the new country. Length of residence provides an indication of the duration of acculturation experiences; it equals age for those born in the new country.

Table 3.3 presents information about all the scales, including the number of items per scale, the scales' origins, and reliability for the immigrant and national samples. The complete questionnaire is in Appendix A.

The nature and quality of adolescents' intercultural relationships were measured with scales for acculturation attitudes (integration, assimilation, separation,

TABLE 3.3

Scales Used in the CSEY Study; Number of Items, Source, and Reliability Based on Adolescent Data From Present Study

Scale (Section in Questionnaire)	No. of Items	Source	Mean Cronbach's α Immigrants (SD)	Mean Cronbach's α Nationals (SD)
Acculturation attitudes		ICSEY; Berry, Kim, Power, Young, & Bujaki (1989)		
Integration (E)	5		.48 (.126)	—
Assimilation (E)	5		.58 (.109)	—
Separation (E)	5		.64 (.070)	—
Marginalization (E)	5		.55 (.107)	—
Cultural Identity				
Ethnic identity (D)	8	Phinney (1992), Roberts et al. (1999)	.82 (.095)	—
National identity (D)	4	Phinney & Devich-Navarro (1997)	.84 (.053)	.69 (.304)
Acculturation behaviors				
Ethnic language proficiency (B)	4	Kwak (1991)	.85 (.068)	—
National language Proficiency (B)	4	Kwak (1991)	.88 (.056)	—
Language use (B)	4	Kwak (1991)	.71 (.163)	—
Parents' use and proficiency of ethnic language (B)	4	ICSEY	.73 (.135)	—
Parents' use and proficiency of national language (B)	4	ICSEY	.74 (.090)	—
Ethnic peer contacts (F)	4	ICSEY	.79 (.056)	.82 (.054)
National peer contacts (F)	4	ICSEY	.78 (.070)	.70 (.102)
Family relationship values		Nguyen & Williams (1989), Georgas (1989), Georgas, Berry, Chrisakopoulou, & Mylonas (1996)		

(continued)

57

TABLE 3.3 *(continued)*

Scale (Section in Questionnaire)	No. of Items	Source	Mean Cronbach's α Immigrants (SD)	Mean Cronbach's α Nationals (SD)
Family obligations (students) (G)	10		.72 (.069)	.72 (.056)
Adolescents' rights (students) (G)	4		.78 (.112)	.75 (.111)
Family obligations (parents)	10		.73 (.085)	.74 (.067)
Children's rights (parents)	4		.73 (.090)	.78 (.066)
Perceived discrimination (H)	9	ICSEY	.83 (.039)	—
Psychological adaptation				
Life satisfaction (J)	5	Diener, Emmos, Larsen, & Griffin (1985)	.77 (.056)	.81 (.049)
Self-esteem (J)	10	Rosenberg (1965)	.75 (.105)	.83 (.051)
Psychological problems (K)	15	Beiser & Flemming (1986), Kinzie et al. (1982), Kovacs (1980/1981), Mollica, Wyshak, deMarneffe, Khuon, & Lavelle (1987), Reynolds & Richmond (1985), Robinson, Shaver, & Wrightsman (1991)	.88 (.037)	.89 (.030)
Sociocultural adaptation				
School adjustment (C)	7	Anderson (1982), Moos (1989), Sam (1994), Samdal (1998), Wold (1995)	.65 (.100)	.68 (.061)
Behavior problems (L)	10	Olweus (1989, 1994), Bendixen & Olweus (1999)	.80 (.077)	.82 (.058)

Note. ICSEY = International Comparative Study of Ethnocultural Youth.

and marginalization), cultural identity (ethnic and national identity), language proficiency (ethnic and national language), language use, contacts with peers from either their own ethnic group or youth from the national group, family relationship values, and perceived discrimination.

Acculturation Attitudes

This is a 20-item scale developed by the researchers. It assesses four acculturation attitudes: assimilation, integration, separation, and marginalization. The items concern five domains of life: cultural traditions, language, marriage, social activities, and friends. For example, the items in the social activities domain include four questions: "I prefer social activities which involve both [nationals] and [my ethnic group]" (integration); "I prefer social activities which involve [nationals] only" (assimilation); "I prefer social activities which involve [members of my own ethnic group] only" (separation); and "I don't want to attend either [national] or [ethnic] social activities" (marginalization).

Ethnic Identity

This was measured with eight items assessing ethnic affirmation (e.g., sense of belonging, positive feelings about being group member). This scale is based on the Multigroup Ethnic Identity Measure (MEIM; Phinney, 1992), but items were modified for the present study. An example is: "I feel that I am part of [ethnic] culture."

National Identity

Past research with immigrant adolescents used an eight-item scale to assess national affirmation and belonging in the United States (American identity; Phinney & Devich-Navarro, 1997). Three items from this scale, with an additional item assessing the importance of one's national identity, are used in the ICSEY questionnaire for the assessment of national identity. A sample item is: "I am happy that I am [national]."

Ethnic Language Proficiency

Proficiency in the ethnic language of an immigrant group is assessed by self-report. The scale inquires about a person's ability to understand, speak, read, and write their ethnic language. An example is: "How well do you speak [ethnic language]?" Answers are given on a 5-point scale ranging from 1 (*not at all*) to 5 (*very well*).

National Language Proficiency

Proficiency in the national language is assessed with the same self-report questions but with respect to the national language.

Language Use

Language use is measured with an adapted version of a scale developed by Kwak (1991). It refers to the extent to which youngsters use either their ethnic language or the national language when talking with their parents or their siblings. Their communication practices were measured on a 5-point scale ranging from 1 (*not at all*) to 5 (*all the time*). Higher scores reflect a relatively stronger preference for using the national language, whereas lower scores reflect a relatively stronger preference for using the ethnic language.

Ethnic Peer Contacts and National Peer Contacts

These two scales each have four items assessing the frequency of interaction with peers from their own ethnic group or from the national group. An example is: "How often do you spend free time with peers from your own ethnocultural group?" Participants responded on a scale ranging from 1 (*never*) to 5 (*very often*).

Family Relationship Values

This scale consists of two subscales. Ten items assess attitudes toward parental authority (henceforth family obligations), indicating adherence to hierarchical family structures based on age and gender. An example is: "Children should obey their parents." Four items assess the extent of acceptance of children's autonomy and freedom of choice, which we refer to as *adolescents' rights*. An example is: "When a girl reaches the age of 16, it is all right for her to decide whom to date." This scale was based on one developed by Georgas, Berry, Shaw, Chrisakopoulou, and Mylonas (1996).

Perceived Discrimination

This was assessed with immigrant youth only. The scale consisted of nine items: four items that assessed perceived frequency of being treated unfairly or negatively because of one's ethnic background by other students, other kids outside school, teachers, and other adults; and five items that assessed being teased, threatened, or feeling unaccepted because of one's ethnicity. An example is: "I have been teased or insulted because of my ethnic background." Participants responded on a scale ranging from 1 (*never*) to 5 (*very often*). Because the scale was constructed by ICSEY, the psychometric properties of the scale have not been established previously.

As explained in chapter 1, we distinguished two types of adaptation: psychological and sociocultural. Psychological adaptation was measured with scales for life satisfaction, self-esteem, and psychological problems. Sociocultural adaptation was assessed using scales for school adjustment and behavior problems.

Life Satisfaction

For measuring the overall degree of adolescents' satisfaction with their lives, we used a five-item scale. A sample item is: "I am satisfied with my life." The scale has been tested among diverse groups, such as adolescents and college students, and has shown good psychometric properties including good test–retest reliability, high internal consistency, and strong positive correlations with other subjective well-being scales (see Diener, Emmons, Larsen, & Griffin, 1985).

Self-Esteem

Global self-esteem was measured using Rosenberg's (1965) 10-item self-esteem inventory. A sample item is: "On the whole I am satisfied with myself." The original scale was designed as a unidimensional factor structure, which has been demonstrated in several studies (Hensley, 1977; Simpson & Boyal, 1975).

Psychological Problems

This scale contains 15 items designed to measure depression, anxiety, and psychosomatic symptoms. Items came from a variety of sources (e.g., Beiser & Flemming, 1986; Reynolds & Richmond, 1985). Sample items are: "I feel tired" and "My thoughts are confused."

School Adjustment

This was assessed by means of a seven-item scale based on Anderson (1982), Moos (1989), Sam (1994), Samdal (1998), and Wold (1995). A sample item is: "I feel uneasy about going to school in the morning."

Behavior Problems

This 10-item scale is an adaptation of Olweus' antisocial behavior scale (Bendixen & Olweus, 1999; Olweus, 1989, 1994). Two sample items are: "Cursed at a teacher" and "Purposely destroyed seats in a bus or a movie theatre." A 5-point response category ranging from 1 (*never*) to 5 (*many times during the past 12 months*) was used.

The version of the questionnaire for national adolescents was shorter. No questions were asked with respect to language proficiency and language use, ethnic identity, and perceived discrimination. An abbreviated version of the scales for acculturation attitudes was used, here referring to the national adolescents' acculturation expectations. A sample item is: "I feel that [immigrants] should adapt to [national] cultural traditions and not maintain those of their own."

As can be seen in Table 3.3, most scales had satisfactory to good reliability. The subscales for acculturation attitudes had slightly problematic reliabilities. The mean Cronbach's alphas are aggregated across countries and ethnocultural groups for the immigrants and across countries for nationals.

Parents' Questionnaires

Parents were asked to report their birthplace, citizenship, ethnicity, religion, age, occupation, employment status, educational qualification, and marital status. Parents also completed the scale for family relationship values. Immigrant parents gave additional information about year of arrival, immigration status, and prior occupation. They reported on both mother's and father's ethnic and national language proficiency and use (e.g., "How well does mother speak Dutch?" and "How frequently does father speak Turkish?") and responded to an abridged (12-item) version of the acculturation attitude scale that included items for only three domains.

For immigrant parents, the reliabilities (Cronbach's alpha) of the scales were satisfactory except for parental acculturation attitudes (see Table 3.3). We were not successful in defining scales for parental acculturation attitudes that had satisfactory psychometric qualities.

The questionnaire for national parents contained only demographic questions relevant to this group and the scale for family relationship values. The value of Cronbach's alpha for family obligations and for adolescents' rights were satisfactory (see Table 3.3).

ASSESSING COMPARABILITY OF CROSS-CULTURAL DATA: THE STANDARD TREATMENT

A first necessary step in cross-cultural data analyses involves the question: To what extent does an instrument measure the same construct (or set of constructs) in all cultural groups involved? Technically, this is known as structural equivalence (van de Vijver & Leung, 1997). The current study employed exploratory factor analysis to address structural equivalence.

How can structural equivalence be established in a data set that involved 13 countries and 41 immigrant groups (counting same groups in different countries as different groups)? In principle, two kinds of approaches can be envisaged. The first is the pair-wise comparison of factors obtained in the different groups. This results in 1,431 comparisons. Finding a pattern in such a large number of comparisons would be cumbersome. Therefore, the current project adopted a different procedure, which became known in the ICSEY group as the *standard treatment*. This procedure is based on a pooling of all the data from all the participants in a sample category (e.g., all immigrant youth). The procedure begins by computing the covariance matrix of the items of the scale to be analyzed per cultural group in the comparison (e.g., 13 covariance analyses for the comparison of the national groups). These covariance matrices are then averaged, with the sample size as weights. The overall covariance matrix provides us with a global average. It is our best estimate of the average covariance matrix.

TABLE 3.4

Results of the Standard Treatment

Scale	M	SD	Prop < .90*
Immigrant Adolescents			
Acculturation and cultural identity			
Assimilation	.96	.11	.07[c]
Integration	.91	.16	.18[d]
Marginalization	.96	.10	.07[e]
Separation	.99	.02	.00
Ethnic identity	.98	.06	.04[b]
National identity	1.00	.00	.00
Language			
Dominant national language usage	.99	.04	.02[a]
Proficiency in ethnic language (self-reported)	1.00	.00	.00
Proficiency national language (self-reported)	1.00	.00	.00
Peer contacts			
National peer contacts	1.00	.00	.00
Ethnic peer contacts	1.00	.00	.00
Values			
Adolescents' rights	.98	.09	.04[f]
Family obligations	.94	.25	.04[g]
Discrimination			
Perceived discrimination	.98	.11	.02[h]
Outcomes			
Life satisfaction	1.00	.00	.00
Self-esteem	.89	.27	.13[i]
Psychological problems	.99	.01	.00
School adjustment	.94	.06	.07[j]
Behavior problems	.96	.11	.04[k]
National adolescents			
Identity and acculturation			
National identity	.95	.17	.08[l]
Acculturation attitudes	.49	.20	1.00[m]
Peer contacts			
National peer contacts	.99	.02	.00
Ethnic peer contacts	.99	.00	.00

(continued)

TABLE 3.4 *(continued)*

Scale	M	SD	Prop < .90*
Adolescents' rights	.95	.14	.15[n]
Family obligations	.90	.26	.15[o]
Outcomes			
Life satisfaction	1.00	.00	.00
Self-esteem	.99	.00	.00
Psychological problems	.99	.00	.00
School adjustment	.95	.02	.08[p]
Behavior problems	.99	.00	.00

Note. Prop < .90 = Proportion of ethnic groups with values of Tucker's Phi lower than .90. The footnotes give a description of the ethnic groups (or countries) in which the factorial agreement was less than .90. The number in parentheses gives the value of Tucker's phi for that group (lower numbers point to less agreement with the global solution). [a]Turks in France (.76), Chileans in Norway (.89). [b]Vietnamese in the United States (.71), Armenians in the United States (.65). [c]Chileans in Norway (.80), Vietnamese in the United States (.88), Surinamese in the Netherlands (.29). [d]Turks in France (.20), Turks in Germany (.84), Aussiedler in Germany (.84), Vietnamese in the United States (.79), Russians in Israel (.32), Turks in the Netherlands (.83), Antilleans in the Netherlands (.80), Surinamese in the Netherlands (.76). [e]Turks in Germany (.82), Aussiedler in Germany (.73), Mexicans in the United States (.40). [f]Russians in Israel (.59), Ethiopians in Israel (.48). [g]Turks in France (.21), Aussiedler in Germany (.04). [h]Migrants from West African countries in France (.27). [i]Vietnamese in Australia (.14), immigrants from West Africa in France (.46), Vietnamese in the United States (.02), Armenians in the United States (.04), Cape Verdeans in Portugal (.03), Timorese in Portugal (.69). [j]Aussiedler in Germany (.85), Russians in Israel (.83), Cape Verdeans in Portugal (.87). [k]Vietnamese in Finland (.89), Surinamese in the Netherlands (.26). [l]Israel (.41). [m]Finland, France, Germany, Israel, New Zealand, Norway, Portugal, Sweden, the Netherlands, United States. [n]United Kingdom (.78), Israel (.54). [o]Portugal (.06), the Netherlands (.89). [p]The Netherlands (.89).

This procedure avoids two problems. First, by removing all differences in means obtained in the various ethnocultural groups from the data matrix, the procedure does not confound individual- and country-level differences (Van de Vijver & Poortinga, 2002). Carrying out a factor analysis on the raw data combining all participants from all countries confounds these two levels of differences. Second, by not working with standardized data, information about the measurement units in the various groups is retained in the computation of the overall covariance matrix.

The next step of the procedure is to determine the extent to which each sample shows a factor structure that is similar to the factor structure in the pooled, global data matrix. Thus, each sample is compared with the global mean.[2] If each group shows a sufficient level of agreement with the global solution, it is concluded that the structural equivalence is supported and that a scale measures the same construct(s) in each group. If structural equivalence would not be supported, additional analyses are required to explore the cause of the deviances of the factor structure (e.g., psychological constructs might not be identical, one or more items may not work in a particular cultural group). This procedure was conducted with adolescent data only. The number of parents in most groups was too small to warrant valid comparisons.

Factor Analyses

Tables B.1 to B.19 (see Appendix B) present the factor loadings of the pooled data for the immigrant adolescents.[3] The factors for each of the four acculturation scales were less strong in the sense that they explained less variance, yet all items pertaining to a particular acculturation attitude contributed in the expected way. Higher scores meant a stronger attitude (Tables B.1 to B.4).

Ethnic identity showed a pattern of relatively homogeneous loadings (Table B.5). The four items for national identity clearly defined a single factor, which explained 69.2% of the variance (Table B.6).

As can be seen in Tables B.7 to B.9, the three language scales (use, proficiency in national language, and proficiency in ethnic language) showed high eigenvalues of the first factor, explaining more than 60% of the variance in each case. Higher scores on the language use scale mean a relatively more frequent use of the national language, whereas high scores on the language proficiency scales indicate higher language proficiency. Moreover, (the absolute values of) the loadings were fairly homogenous, indicating that all items seemed to contribute in a similar way to the latent variable underlying the scales.

The two scales related to peer contacts (ethnic peer contacts and national peer contacts; Tables B.10 and B.11) showed high percentages of variance for the first factor (of over 60%) and a homogeneous set of factor loadings.

---

[2]The agreement between the factor loadings of items from two groups can be expressed using several congruence indexes (Van de Vijver & Leung 1997). The proportionality coefficient, also known as Tucker's phi (Tucker, 1951), is an often-applied congruence index. It is defined as $P_{xy} = \dfrac{\sum x_i y_i}{\sqrt{\sum x_i^2 \sum y_i^2}}$, in which x_i and y_i are factor loadings of item i in groups x and y. The index measures the identity of two factors up to a positive, multiplying constant. The latter allows for differences in factorial eigenvalues across cultural groups. Unfortunately, the index has an unknown sampling distribution, which makes it impossible to construct confidence intervals. Some rules of thumb have been proposed: Values higher than .95 are taken to indicate factorial invariance, whereas values lower than .90 (Van de Vijver & Leung, 1997) or .85 (Ten Berge, 1986) point to essential incongruities.

[3]For all scales in all groups, unifactorial solutions were chosen.

Two scales of family relationship values were used. For adolescents' rights, a similar pattern of homogenous loadings and a strong first factor was found (Table B.12). Family obligations showed more heterogeneity in factor loadings and a weaker first factor, yet all items supported to the measurement of the construct family obligations (Table B.13).

The items of the perceived discrimination scale were also fairly homogeneous with respect to the underlying construct (Table B.14). Most scales with outcome variables also showed this pattern of a strong first factor and fairly homogeneous loadings (Tables B.15 to B.19). Like in all other scales, the loadings of all items were in the expected direction.

Tables B.20 to B.30 show the results of the factor analyses of the pooled data of the national adolescents. The pattern of findings obtained for the immigrant adolescents is replicated here. All scales were unifactorial, often with substantial amounts of variance explained by the first factor and fairly homogeneous loadings of the rest of the items of the scale.

Table B.20 shows the results of the acculturation attitudes scale presented for the national adolescents. The distribution of the eigenvalues provided less support for the unifactorial nature of the scale than was found for the other scales. Inspections of solutions with more factors (not further documented here) did not show clearly interpretable results. Therefore, one factor was retained. This single factor was bipolar with the integration items loading positively and all other items loading negatively. A pattern in which integration items load on one pole and the other acculturation strategies on the other pole has been found before (e.g., Berry et al., 1977; Van de Vijver, Helms-Lorenz, & Feltzer, 1999).

In sum, in both adolescent groups all scales were unifactorial. Items of the scales loaded in the expected direction and in most cases the first factor explained a sizable proportion of the variance.

Measures That Make Sense to Youth in Different Groups and Countries: Structural Equivalence

This section describes the results of the standard treatment. The analyses were carried out for the adolescents of the immigrant and national groups separately. When the data of all parents of a single country were combined and the equivalence was examined across countries, evidence for structural equivalence of the scales was obtained. However, because of the cultural diversity within each country, this result should be interpreted with caution.

The analyses addressed the question of the extent to which the pattern of factor loadings that was found in the pooled sample could be replicated in each ethnocultural group (in the factors of Tables B.1 to B.19; Appendix B) or in each national group (as reported in Tables B.20 to B.30).

The results of the analyses for the immigrant and national adolescents are presented in Table 3.4. Support for the structural equivalence of the measures can be claimed if the comparison of the factor structure in an ethnic group with the global solution yields a Tucker's phi value of .90 or higher in each ethnic group.

High agreement indexes in all comparisons were found for assimilation, separation, marginalization, ethnic and national identity, proficiency in ethnic language, proficiency in national language, language use, peer contacts (national peer contacts and ethnic peer contacts), adolescents' rights, family obligations, perceived discrimination, life satisfaction, psychological problems, school adjustment, and behavior problems. These results strongly suggest that these scales measure the same psychological constructs in each ethnic group. Problematic was the intergroup comparability of scales for integration (18% of factorial agreement indexes lower than .90) and self-esteem (15%). Inspection of the loadings in the countries with deviant loadings did not suggest a clear pattern. Deviant loadings were found relatively often in particular ethnic groups, such as the Aussiedler in Germany and Vietnamese in the United States. However, even in these groups most factorial comparisons provided support for the structural equivalence of the scales. For example, in the group of Aussiedler, 4 of 21 scales showed values of Tucker's phi lower than .90. In general, such low values were infrequently found; of 967 comparisons (across all scales), 43 (4.4%) showed values of the agreement index lower than .90. The median value of Tucker's phi was .994. In all cases the low factorial agreement was caused by one or more items with a lower loading in the deviant group than in the global solution.

In the group of national adolescents, acculturation attitudes had an extreme pattern, with no country showing a value of Tucker's phi above .90. Clearly, acculturation attitudes do not show structural equivalence and cannot be used for cross-cultural comparisons of national samples. Both peer contact scales (national and ethnic peer contacts) and all outcome measures showed factorial agreements well above .90 and did not show a value of Tucker's phi lower than .90 in any comparison. For national identity and school adjustment, 8% of the coefficients yielded values lower than .90 in one country. Both value scales (adolescents' rights and family obligations) showed 15% values lower than .90. These findings point to slightly lower agreement than in the migrant group, although the overall agreement (except for acculturation attitudes) remains very fair.

It can be concluded that our analyses largely provide support for the structural equivalence of the scales, among both the migrants and the hosts, with the exception of acculturation attitudes among the national sample. We developed a research instrument that appears to be relevant for, and make sense to, youth in all the groups and societies we studied. It appears that the issues confronting immigrant youth, and our presentation of alternatives that are available to them, are sufficiently common to allow our comparative (or *etic*) approach to acculturation research.

ANALYSES AND PRESENTATION OF RESULTS

As described earlier, we found strong support for the structural equivalence of the scales used in this study. Structural equivalence is important for the interpretation of the data beyond countries and groups, but it does not preclude the influence of potentially confounding effects of country- and group-specific sample particulars (e.g., differences in age, gender composition, and immigrants' generational status). The Results section of each of the next two chapters starts with a report on the means of the various intercultural variables (chap. 4) and adaptation variables (chap. 5) for the immigrants, overall and for each of the 13 countries and for all national samples. These results are presented in the form of bar graphs. The figures presented take into account sample differences in gender, age, and proportion of life spent in the country. Including these control variables means that the graphs do not represent raw scores but rather estimated values (i.e., observed means that have been corrected for the confounding sample differences). These bar graphs give a general idea of how immigrant adolescents compare with national adolescents and how immigrant groups compare across countries. We have tested the statistical significance of all between-group and between-country comparisons but rarely report these. Instead, we report effect sizes as we have in the present chapter. We only report an effect size when the difference between groups was statistically significant. In this chapter we use Cohen's d as an indication of the difference between means as related to the variance of scores, and we continue to use this effect size where appropriate. Besides Cohen's d we use eta^2 (henceforth η^2) where we report the outcomes of variance analyses and R^2 when we report regression analyses. The latter two measures estimate the proportion of the total variance that is explained by the factor or variable tested (e.g., a value of .10 of η^2 in an analysis of variance of country differences in life satisfaction indicates that 10% of the variation in life satisfaction scores are due to country differences and 90% are due to individual differences and measurement unreliability).

As done in the previous part of this chapter, we give a narrative of the findings, allowing readers who are less familiar with statistics to grasp the meaning.

Earlier, we stated that apart from the possible confounding effects of variables such as age and gender, the samples could be expected to show valid ethnic group and country differences in background characteristics that are relevant for our psychological measures. Examples are the higher occupational levels of national parents as compared with immigrant parents. Many of these differences are expected, based on earlier studies or theoretical considerations that are presented in the introductory sections of the coming chapters. These expectations guide our further statistical analyses. Most concern relationships between specified sets of variables. When country or group is not involved in the comparison, we use standardized scores (scores standardized within country and group) as input to the analyses. Standardization eliminates confounding effects that influence between-country and between-group differences (sampling artifacts and response sets). When country or group are variables in the analyses, we conduct covariance analyses based on raw scores, controlling for gender, age, and part of life spent in the host country.

To condense the information based on individual variables, we conducted cluster analyses and exploratory factor analyses. Cluster analyses were used for categorizing adolescents in terms of intercultural characteristics irrespective of country and ethnic group. The analyses were conducted using scores standardized within country and ethnic groups. We used the k-means method. Because this method is sensitive to decisions as to the preferred number of clusters and the values for the initial cluster centers, we first conducted several exploratory analyses with 20% of the data selected at random. Based on the fit with the dominant theoretical framework guiding the study and on the interpretability of the resulting clusters, we decided to use four clusters. We then replicated this four-cluster solution using all the data. We refer to the resulting clusters as *acculturation profiles*. These profiles are presented in chapter 4. In chapter 5 we explore the relationship between these acculturation profiles and adaptation outcomes.

Exploratory factor analyses were used to combine variables. Choice of variables was determined by the exploratory factor analyses conducted in preparation for testing the overall model in chapter 6 (principal component analyses with varimax rotation). In addition to statistical criteria, such as eigenvalues, percentage of explained variance, and factor loadings, we also used theory-based arguments to choose the variables. The presentation of the resulting factor structures in chapters 4 and 5 gives an overview of the outcomes, focusing on the interrelationship between variables and preparing for the model testing in chapter 6.

In the chapters 6, 7, and 8 we mainly used the factor scores resulting from the factor analyses as input to the data analyses. Because these are factor scores, they are standardized scores, with the overall group as the basis for standardization.

Chapter 6 presents the outcomes of a structural equation model. This analysis brings together all relevant psychological constructs studied in the project. The model summarizes the interrelationships among intercultural variables and adaptation variables irrespective of country and group. The model was tested at the individual level in an attempt to map relationships, as these are found within individual immigrants. It is a parsimonious expression of the numerous relationships we observed. In chapter 6 we also analyze the impact on the interrelationships presented in the model of variables, such as age, generation, gender, parents' occupational status, and neighborhood, and two country-specific measures of diversity: cultural diversity and diversity policy. For this purpose we used multiple regression analysis and multivariate analyses of variance (MANOVA).

In chapter 7 we compare adolescents and their parents in terms of family relationship values. We explore the impact of intergenerational discrepancies in family relationship values on adolescents' adaptation. We also explore the relationship between acculturation profiles and intergenerational discrepancies. In addition to the type of analyses that were used for chapters 4 and 5, we conduct hierarchical multiple regression analyses. These allow us to determine the added value of particular variable clusters and intergenerational value discrepancies for explaining differences in adaptation among immigrant adolescents.

The analytical approach of chapter 8 is generally similar to that adopted in chapters 4 to 7. For instance, it tests the validity and implications of the structural equation model presented in chapter 6 for Vietnamese and Turkish youth.

4

The Acculturation Experience: Attitudes, Identities, and Behaviors of Immigrant Youth

Jean S. Phinney
California State University, Los Angeles
John W. Berry
Queen's University
Paul Vedder
Leiden University
Karmela Liebkind
University of Helsinki

This chapter examines the experiences, attitudes, and behaviors of adolescents from immigrant families in diverse societies as they move toward adulthood in the context of two (or more) cultural frameworks. To understand immigrant adolescents from diverse ethnocultural groups, we focus on two broad traditions of research. One tradition is the study of *acculturation,* a broad concept referring to the changes that take place following intercultural contact (Berry, 1997; Graves, 1967; Redfield, Linton, & Herskovits, 1936). A second tradition is the study of *cultural identity* among immigrants (e.g., DeVos & Romanucci-Ross, 1982; Liebkind, 1992a; Phinney, 1990; Rumbaut, 1994; Waters, 2000). Cultural identity can be thought of as an aspect of acculturation that focuses on immigrants' sense of self rather than on their behaviors and attitudes following immigration. Conceptually, it includes both ethnic identity and national identity. Research on acculturation and cultural identity approaches immigrant issues from different perspectives, yet each provides valuable background for studying immigrant adolescents. When we combine them, we can observe their independent and interactive roles in the experience of immigrant youth and the way these youth orient themselves to the cultures with which they are involved.

A central concern is with the process of acculturation in adolescents. The acculturation literature has focused on adults (e.g., Berry, 1997), although interest in immigrant adolescents is increasing (e.g., Fuligni, 2001; Portes & Rumbaut, 2001). The term *acculturation* originated in anthropology and was defined in terms of group processes:

> Acculturation comprehends those phenomena which result when groups of individuals having different cultures come into continuous first-hand contact, with subsequent changes in the original culture patterns of either or both groups. (Redfield et al., 1936, pp. 149–152)

In contrast to the emphasis in this definition on the changes that occur in groups, the concept of psychological acculturation was introduced by Graves (1967) to refer to changes in an individual who is in a culture contact situation. Individual changes are influenced both directly by the culture of the larger society and by the culture of which the individual is a member (the culture of origin for immigrants; Berry, 1997; Berry & Sam, 1997; Liebkind, 2001; Ward, 1996).

The acculturation process encompasses a broad range of phenomena. In this chapter we examine several aspects of psychological acculturation that are highly salient for adolescents in immigrant families. We consider the attitudes that adolescents have about dealing with their experiences in a new culture, specifically, the extent to which they wish to retain their ethnic culture and the extent to which they wish to become involved with the larger society. We explore their social contacts with peers, their language proficiency and use, and the values that they hold regarding family relationships. We also examine their perception of the discrimination that they experience.

Another major tradition in research on immigration concerns cultural identity, that is, the extent to which immigrants identify with their ethnic group and with the larger society. In early research in the United States, immigrants were seen as having to choose one identity or the other (e.g., Child, 1943) or risk becoming marginalized. Subsequent research has explored the range of alternative identities chosen by immigrant youth (Matute-Bianchi, 1986). The kinds of self-labels that immigrant youth adopt and the implications of self-identification for their adaptation are central issues for immigration research (Rumbaut, 1994). Underlying the self-labels used by immigrant adolescents is the developmental process of group-identity formation, which involves exploring and resolving the meaning for oneself of belonging to a particular group (one's ethnic identity) and to the larger society (one's national identity; Phinney, 1990; Phinney & Devich-Navarro, 1997).

In this chapter, we first present conceptual and empirical background on the acculturation experience, focusing on what we term *intercultural variables*, specifically, acculturation attitudes, cultural identities, language proficiency and usage, peer contacts, family relationship values, and perceived discrimination. We then present results from our study that address the general question: How do immigrant adolescents experience the acculturation process? The results are presented in two ways. First, we describe specific acculturation variables, their correlates, and their interrelationships. Second, using a person-oriented approach based on cluster analysis, we identify profiles of acculturation that reflect individual differences in the way adolescents acculturate. We conclude the chapter with a summary and discussion of the main findings.

ASPECTS OF THE ACCULTURATION EXPERIENCE: BACKGROUND AND MEASUREMENT

Acculturation Attitudes

The term *acculturation attitudes* refers to the ways people prefer to live in intercultural contact situations. Early research assumed that acculturating individuals would orient themselves either to one group or the other, in a sense choosing between them. This view was the basis for assessing the acculturation of an individual on a single dimension (e.g., Gordon, 1964 ; Suinn, Ahuna, & Khoo, 1992). However, an alternative view was proposed by Berry (1974, 1980), who argued that there are two dimensions along which individuals orient themselves. In this view, virtually everyone in an intercultural contact arena holds attitudes toward two fundamental aspects of acculturation: intercultural contact and cultural maintenance. This two-dimensional approach has been validated in several studies (e.g., Ryder, Alden, & Paulhus, 2000).

Among immigrants or other nondominant ethnocultural individuals, acculturation attitudes are based on two issues: To what extent do immigrants or other nondominant groups wish to have contact with (or avoid) people outside their group, and to what extent do they wish to maintain (or give up) their cultural attributes? When examined among the population at large (e.g., the dominant or national group), views about how immigrants and other nondominant ethnocultural groups should acculturate have been termed *acculturation expectations* (Berry, 2003) or, in earlier writings, *multicultural ideology* (Berry et al., 1977).

One way of illustrating the distinctions between intercultural contact and cultural maintenance, and between the views of dominant and nondominant groups is presented in Fig. 4.1 (Berry, 2003). The two basic dimensions are portrayed as independent of each other: for the nondominant ethnocultural groups on the left, and for the dominant group or national society on the right. For each issue, a dimension is shown, with a positive orientation at one end and a negative orientation at the other.

For members of the nondominant ethnocultural group, the main question is: "How shall *we* deal with these two issues?" whereas for the national society, the question is: "How should *they* (e.g., immigrants) deal with them?" These two issues define an intercultural contact space (the circles) within which individuals occupy a preferred attitudinal position. Each sector of the circles in Fig. 4.1 carries a name that has a long-standing usage in acculturation studies. From the point of view of nondominant ethnocultural groups (on the left of Fig. 4.1), when individuals do not wish to maintain their cultural heritage and seek involvement with other

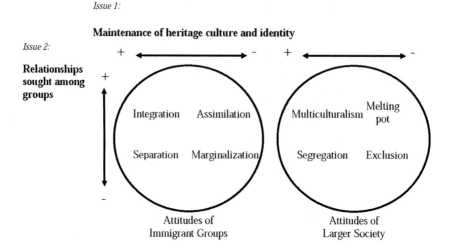

FIG. 4.1. Acculturation attitudes of immigrant groups and of the larger society.

cultures in the larger society, the *assimilation* attitude is defined. In contrast, when ethnocultural group members place a value on holding on to their original culture, and at the same time wish to avoid interaction with others, the *separation* alternative is defined. When there is an interest in both maintaining one's original culture and interacting with other groups, *integration* is the attitude. Here, individuals maintain a degree of cultural integrity, while seeking to participate as an integral part of the larger society. Finally, when there is little possibility or interest in cultural maintenance (often for reasons of enforced cultural loss), and little interest in having relations with other groups (often for reasons of exclusion or discrimination), *marginalization* is defined.

Immigrant and nondominant ethnocultural groups are not necessarily free to choose how to acculturate (Berry, 1974), as their experience depends to a large degree on the conditions in the larger society. The national society may enforce certain restrictions that constrain the choices immigrants can make. For example, integration can be chosen and successfully pursued by immigrants only when the national society is open and inclusive in its orientation toward cultural diversity (Berry, 1990). For integration to occur, a mutual accommodation is required, involving the acceptance by both dominant and nondominant groups of the right of all groups to live as culturally different people who interact within the same society. In this case, immigrants are able to adopt the basic values of the national society, and the national society is willing to adapt national institutions (e.g., education, health, justice, labor) to meet the needs of all groups living together in the larger plural society. These conditions are not met in all societies represented in this study, as noted in chapter 2.

Acculturation attitudes as presented from the point of view of the ethnocultural groups, shown on the left side of Fig. 4.1, do not take into account attitudes of the larger society. These attitudes are thought to play a powerful role in influencing the way acculturation takes place (Berry, 1974). The attitudes of the dominant group toward cultural maintenance and intercultural contact are shown on the right side of Fig. 4.1. The acceptance of cultural diversity and integration by the larger society defines the attitude of mutual accommodation now widely called *multiculturalism* (Berry, 1984a). When assimilation is preferred or sought by the dominant group, it can be termed the *melting pot* (and when strongly enforced, it becomes a pressure cooker). When separation is enforced by the dominant group, it is *segregation*. When marginalization is imposed by the dominant group, it is a form of *exclusion* (Bourhis et al., 1997). These orientations toward acculturation have been assessed frequently using various methods (reviewed by Berry, 1997; Berry, Kim, Power, Young, & Bujaki, 1989). The most common procedure is to select a number of domains relevant to intercultural relations (e.g., language use, food preference, parent–child relations) and then create four statements for the various domains, one for each of the four attitude sectors (e.g., van de Vijver et al., 1999). Another is to create two statements for a particular domain, one for each of the two underlying dimensions (e.g., Dona & Berry, 1994; Ryder et al., 2000).

These orientations toward acculturation have been conceptualized primarily with reference to adults. For adolescents in immigrant families, acculturation attitudes are shaped in large part by their families and communities. Attitudes about their own and other cultures are absorbed from the family, their peers, their school, and other adults with whom they interact. Adolescents can also differ in the kinds of friends they prefer, in their eagerness to learn a new language or retain their ethnic language, and the extent to which they adhere to the cultural values of their family. These preferences are the result of both contextual factors, such as the community they live in and their experience with discrimination, and personal characteristics, such as gender. Such preferences will, however, change over time, as adolescents expand their experience in society. In this chapter, we examine acculturation attitudes in relation to contextual and demographic factors, including length of residence in the society of settlement, and their association with other acculturation variables.

Acculturation attitudes were measured with a 20-item scale developed by the researchers, based on the model of Berry (Berry et al., 1989). The scale assessed four acculturation attitudes: assimilation, integration, separation, and marginalization across five domains about which young people in intercultural contact situations are likely to have preferences: cultural traditions, language, marriage, social activities, and friends. For each domain, one statement was created for each of the four attitudes. Responses to the following statements were given on a 5-point scale (1 = *strongly disagree*, 5 = *strongly agree*): "I prefer to have both (national group) friends and (ethnic group) friends" (integration); "I prefer to have only (ethnic group) friends" (separation); "I prefer to have only (national group) friends" (assimilation); and "I don't want to have either (ethnic group) or (national group) friends" (marginalization).

Cultural Identities: Ethnic and National

Cultural identity is a broad term used here to encompass both ethnic and national identities and their interplay. Identity for immigrants has been studied primarily in terms of ethnic identity. Much of the research has focused on the self-label chosen by immigrants (Rumbaut, 1994). Portes and Rumbaut (2001) show that the immigrant experience of adolescents differs substantially depending on whether young people use a label based on their country of origin (e.g., Mexican), a hyphenated label (e.g., Mexican-American), a pan-ethnic label (e.g., Latino or Hispanic), or a national label (e.g., American).

However, labels such as these do not necessarily indicate the strength of identification. Cultural identity refers to more than the group category or label that one chooses; rather, it involves a sense of belonging to one or more cultural groups and the feelings associated with group membership (Phinney, 1990). This sense of belonging to a cultural group is an aspect of one's social identity, as discussed by Tajfel and Turner (1986). For immigrants, social identity can include identification with one's ethnic group or culture of origin (ethnic identity) and the larger society (national identity). Both ethnic and national identities are assumed to change over time and context, and across generations of immigration (Phinney, 2003).

Ethnic identity and national identity can be thought of as two dimensions of group identity that may vary independently; that is, each identity can be either secure and strong or undeveloped and weak (e.g., Bourhis et al., 1997). Each of these dimensions can be considered separately in terms of their role in the acculturation process; however, they may interact and have differing implications depending on the strength of each identity. We first discuss these identities separately and then examine their relationship to each other. We also consider the relationship of cultural identity to other intercultural variables, including language, social relationships, and perceived discrimination.

The formation of an identity is a critical developmental task of adolescents, particularly in complex modern societies, and ethnic identity is an important aspect of this process, especially for immigrant youth. Ethnic identity is a dynamic construct that evolves and changes in response to developmental and contextual factors (Liebkind, 1992a, 2001; Phinney, 1990). With increasing age, more mature cognitive skills support the process of constructing a sense of self that integrates prior understandings and experiences. However, the process is highly dependent on the family, community, and national contexts to which the adolescent is exposed. For adolescents in immigrant families, the process of ethnic-identity formation involves examining the ethnic attitudes, values, and practices learned at home from their immigrant parents and considering them in relation to those of their peers and the larger society (Phinney, 1989). This process can lead to constructive actions aimed at affirming the value and legitimacy of their group membership (Brown, 2000; Tajfel & Turner, 1986), or to feelings of insecurity, confusion, or resentment over treatment of their group. Because of the variability among individuals and contexts, there can be considerable variation in the images that individuals construct of the behaviors, beliefs, values, and norms that characterize their group(s), together with their understandings of how these features are (or are not) reflected in themselves (Ferdman & Horenczyk, 2000).

Ethnic identity has been assessed in terms of the degree to which one has a sense of belonging and attachment to one's group (Phinney, 1992). It can vary from a low or weak ethnic identity, indicating lack of interest, involvement, and attachment, to a strong ethnic identity, accompanied by pride and positive feelings. In virtually all research with ethnic minority groups in the United States, ethnic identity scores are high, although there is wide individual variation. Members of immigrant ethnocultural groups consistently score higher on ethnic identity than do members of the dominant cultural group (i.e., European Americans in America). There is a large body of research establishing that a strong ethnic identity is positively associated with self-esteem and psychological well-being (e.g., Phinney, Cantu, & Kurtz, 1997; Roberts et al., 1999).

Compared to ethnic identity, there has been far less attention paid to conceptualizing and studying immigrants' identification with the larger society, that is, national identity. Some researchers have focused simply on the labels used. In the United States, where the label "American" is used to refer to national identity, immigrant groups typically change over time from using a label based on their country of origin (e.g., Chinese), to a hyphenated label (e.g., Chinese-American), to, in some cases, the single national label (e.g., American; Rumbaut, 1994). However, like ethnic identity, national identity is a more complex construct than is conveyed by a label; it involves feelings of belonging to, and attitudes toward, the larger society. Adolescents can vary from having a strong, positive sense of belonging to the larger society, to feeling that they are excluded or rejected by the larger society (Phinney & Devich-Navarro, 1997).

The relationship between ethnic and national identities is important because of the implications of this relationship for the acculturation process. The linear or one-dimensional model emphasized in much early research on acculturation suggested that the two identities are negatively correlated, so that when ethnic identity is strong national identity is necessarily weak, and vice versa. In that case, immigrants would have to identify either with their ethnic group or with the national society, but could not identify with both. In contrast, the more recent two-dimensional model suggests that the two identities may vary independently. It is then possible to identify strongly with both cultures and have a bicultural identity. This change from a one-dimensional to a two-dimensional model parallels the change noted earlier with respect to the conceptualization of acculturation attitudes. Just as for acculturation attitudes, research generally supports a two-dimensional model of ethnic and national identity among immigrants, in that linear measures of the two types of group identity are usually statistically independent. However, depending on the sample and the context, the correlation may be positive, negative, or near zero. These correlations, combined with information about the means for each identity, indicate the quality of the cultural identity in a particular context. A positive correlation, with high scores on both identities, suggests a bicultural or integrated identity; with low scores on both, a positive correlation suggests alienation. A negative correlation means that one can identify with only one culture; the means indicate which identity is stronger. The relationship may vary across immigrant groups (Hutnik, 1991; Phinney, Cantu, et al., 1997) and across national settings. A question of interest in the present study is the relationship between these identities across a range of groups and countries or regions (Phinney, Horenczyk, et al., 2001). In addition, we explore the demographic correlates of ethnic and national identities and their relation to other aspects of acculturation.

The two cultural identities were assessed independently by having adolescents evaluate the strength of each identity separately. These identities therefore refer to degree of identification, not just a category to which they do (or do not) belong.

Ethnic identity was measured with eight items assessing ethnic affirmation (e.g., sense of belonging, positive feelings about being group member). This scale is based on the MEIM (Phinney, 1992; Roberts et al., 1999). An example is: "I feel that I am part of [ethnic] culture." Items assessing the exploration aspect of ethnic identity were not included. The MEIM has been extensively used with adolescent and young adult participants in a wide variety of ethnic groups in several countries. It has consistently shown good to excellent reliability (a = .75 to .90).

National identity was assessed with three items based on an eight-item scale used to assess national affirmation and belonging in the United States (American identity; Phinney & Devich-Navarro, 1997). Three items from this scale, with an additional item assessing the importance of one's national identity, were used in the ICSEY questionnaire for the assessment of national identity. A sample item is: "I am happy that I am [Dutch]." In the study by Phinney and Devich-Navarro (1997), the scale showed no significant relationship to ethnic identity, indicating that in the U.S. setting it is an independent factor, in support of the two-dimensional model of cultural identity. It was not negatively correlated with ethnic identity, as would be suggested by a linear or one-dimensional model.

Language Proficiency and Use

Ethnic and national language proficiency and use are generally regarded as key indicators of acculturation (Birman & Tricket, 2001; van de Vijver et al., 1999) and are used in most measures of acculturation. Studies in which factor analysis has been used to identify components of acculturation find language to be one of the major contributors to the construct. For example, Suinn et al. (1992) found that language (together with music and movie preference) accounted for 41.5% of the variance. Cuellar, Arnold, and Maldonado (1995) found that language items accounted for 38.4% of the variance.

Learning the language of the country of settlement, or national language, is one of the major tasks of immigrants. The speed with which this is accomplished depends on many factors, including the needs and motivation of immigrants and the context in which they settle. The ethnic language is likely to be retained in the first generation but may decline if not used. For children of immigrants, the national language is learned in school, if not earlier. Learning the national language is a process that varies widely among immigrant groups. In some groups and some countries, learning the national language is accompanied by a loss of proficiency in the ethnic language, especially if the learners grow up in mixed communities where the national language is widely used.

Whereas immigrant adolescents face the task of learning the host language, second-generation adolescents often lose the ability to speak their ethnic language. If they choose to learn it, they face a very different task from that of immigrants learning the host language. A study (Kwak, 1991) comparing two groups of Korean adolescents in Canada (first-generation adolescents learning English and second-generation adolescents learning Korean) showed the influence of the larger society on the effectiveness of language learning. For the first generation, learning English was a necessity; their progress was superior to the learning of the Korean language by the second-generation adolescents and was not affected by personal characteristics. For the second generation, learning Korean was voluntary and was influenced mainly by the learner's positive attitudes toward Korean culture. The results showed that although language learning can be encouraged by individual factors such as the family setting, the effectiveness of language learning is limited without the consistent and systematic use of the target language in the larger society.

The relationship between language and ethnic identity is a much-debated topic. A clear but extreme position in this discussion is that ethnicity is largely defined by culture, which includes language, and even more specifically, the language in which it is transmitted between generations. This position corresponds to strong pleas for language maintenance or language revitalization (Chiang & Schmida, 1999; Fishman, 1996; Henze & Davis, 1999). Other scholars are more hesitant in giving language a prominent role in ethnic identity. They suggest that culture-specific knowledge, skills, and feelings can be transmitted through a newly acquired language as well (Genesee, 1987; Glenn & De Jong, 1996).

Indeed, many studies show that language loss is not synonymous to a loss of group membership, solidarity, and a sense of belonging. Ethnic language loss may occur without ethnic identity being reduced (Bentahila & Davies, 1992; Pandharipande, 1992). Nevertheless, several studies show that ethnic language is strongly associated with ethnic identity (Gudykunst & Ting-Toomey, 1990; Hurtado & Gurin, 1995). Other studies (cf. Cameron & Lalonde, 1994) suggest that ethnic language maintenance is important for second and later generation immigrants, but not for the first generation. Phinney, Romero, Nava, and Huang (2001) presented a review of studies and concluded that research has yielded conflicting findings about the relationship between language maintenance and ethnic identity. However, they found that adolescents from three American ethnic groups who have higher ethnic language proficiency and usage report stronger levels of ethnic identity (Phinney, Romero, et al., 2001).

Both competence in, and use of, the ethnic and national languages were examined in the current study. We examined the extent to which immigrant adolescents were proficient in each language, the frequency of use of both languages, and the way language differed in relation to the proportion of time in the new culture. Additional questions were the relationship of language to other intercultural variables, particularly acculturation attitudes and ethnic and national identity.

Competence in the ethnic language of immigrant adolescents was measured with a self-report based on a scale constructed by Kwak (1991). The scale assesses a person's abilities to understand, speak, read and write the ethnic language. Answers are given on a 5-point scale ranging from: 1 (*not at all*), 5 (*very well*). Competence in the majority language refers to the same self-report questions but with respect to the majority language.

Language use was measured with an adapted version of a scale developed by Kwak (1991). It refers to the extent to which adolescents use their ethnic language and the national language when talking with their parents and their siblings. Their communication practices were measured with a 5-point frequency scale for each language ranging from 1 (*not at all*) to 5 (*all the time*). Responses were transformed into a single linear scale, where low scores indicate use of ethnic language and high scores indicate use of the national language.

Peer Social Contacts

Social interactions with members of one's own ethnic group and with members of the larger society are another fundamental aspect of acculturation. An individual's involvement with people from one's own group and from the national society have often been employed as a way to validate a person's acculturation attitudes (Berry et al., 1989). Extent of social contact is widely used in assessing acculturation; in measures of acculturation, social networks have been found to account for 3% to 10% of the total variance (Cuellar et al., 1995; Suinn et al., 1992). Social networks are assumed to change as part of the acculturation process, as immigrants extend their contacts with the larger society. Nevertheless, ethnic ties typically remain strong, and across all groups there is evidence of in-group preferences, or *ethnic bias*, toward contacts with peers of one's own group (Hamm, 2000; Schofield & Whitley, 1983; Vedder & O'Dowd, 1999).

Adolescents are limited by the context in the kinds of choices they can make regarding their social networks. Immigrant parents may encourage or even insist that adolescents associate with in-group members, particularly in the case of romantic relationships. The extent of actual in-group and out-group interaction among peers is also constrained by school and community demographics. Studies in ethnically mixed schools suggest that students vary in the extent to which they stay with their own group (i.e., show ethnic bias) or mix with others (DuBois & Hirsch, 1990; Semons, 1991). Other studies (cf. Schnittker, 2002) show that the ethnic composition of particular activity settings or of the neighborhood in which immigrants live affects on acculturation experiences.

An initial question of interest in this study is the extent to which immigrant adolescents interact with peers from their own and other groups. Because we have information from participants on the ethnic composition of their neighborhoods, we can examine the role of neighborhood composition in social contact within and across ethnocultural groups. Social networks and friendships are also assumed to be associated with ethnic identity. Alba (1990) suggested that social interaction can provide a means by which ethnicity is experienced and expressed. Research with adolescents in the United States shows that interaction with peers from one's own ethnic group is strongly related to ethnic identity (Phinney, Romero, et al., 2001). The relationships of social interactions with ethnic and national identities and other acculturation variables are explored in this chapter.

Peer contacts were operationalized in terms of peer social interactions and cultural practices. The scale had four items each, assessing the frequency of interaction with peers from adolescents' own ethnic group and the national group: (a) number of friends, (b) free time spent with peers in school, (c) free time spent with peers out of school, and (d) frequency of playing sports with peers. A sample question is: "How often do you spend free time with peers from your own ethno-cultural group in school?" In addition, two items assessed participation in ethnic and national customs and activities. Participants responded on a 5-point scale ranging from 1 (*never*) to 5 (*very often*).

Family Relationship Values

The extent to which the original cultural values are retained following immigration is one indicator of acculturation, although it has been studied less than other aspects of acculturation. Values regarding family relationships are an important aspect of ethnic cultures that may change with acculturation (Georgas et al., 1996; Phinney et al., 2000; Sabogal, Marin, Otero-Sabogal, Marin, & Perez-Stable, 1987). Adolescents in immigrant families grow up in homes in which the values of their parents' culture of origin generally prevail. Immigrants to Western countries from non-Western cultural backgrounds can be characterized generally as valuing close family relationships, including obligations to the family, to a greater extent than do the members of their countries of settlement (Fuligni, 1998b; Phinney et al., 2000). For example, for Turkish immigrant adolescents in the Netherlands, family was an important part of their construction of identity and self-concept, but for their Dutch counterparts it was not (Verkuyten, 2001). Bowes, Flanagan, and Taylor (2001) demonstrated that adolescents' views on participation in household work were related to the sociopolitical characteristics of the nation; those from Bulgaria, the Czech Republic, and Hungary, as compared with those from Australia, the United States, and Sweden, did not expect payment for their work at home, indicating that a more communal relationship existed among family members.

In this chapter we explore variation in traditional cultural values regarding family relationships in terms of demographic variables, time spent in the society of settlement, and other acculturation variables. An additional question of interest regarding cultural values is the extent of disagreement in values between adolescents and parents in immigrant families. This question is explored in chapter 7, with data from both adolescents and parents.

The family relationship values scale was developed by the researchers based on scales of Nguyen and Williams (1989), Georgas (1989), and Georgas et al. (1996), with input based on the experiences of the researchers in diverse cultures. It consisted of 14 items that included two subscales. Ten items assessed attitudes toward family obligations, indicating adherence to hierarchical family structures based on age and gender. An example is: "Children should obey their parents." Four items assessed adolescents' rights, the extent of acceptance of adolescents' autonomy and freedom of choice. A sample item is: "When a girl reaches the age of 16, it is all right for her to decide whom to date." Responses were given on a 5-point scale ranging from 1 (*strongly disagree*) to 5 (*strongly agree*).

Perceived Discrimination

Immigrants have typically faced varying degrees of prejudice and discrimination in their countries of settlement. These experiences derive from their cultural and behavioral differences from the dominant culture, the past history of groups in contact, and negative attitudes toward immigration generally, based on the assumption that immigrants threaten jobs of citizens and are a burden on social services. Experiences of prejudice and discrimination are major factors among those making the acculturation process potentially stressful (Berry, 1997). However, stereotypes, prejudice, and discrimination are rarely accounted for in acculturation research (for exceptions, see Lalonde, Taylor, & Moghaddam, 1992; Liebkind & Jasinskaja-Lahti, 2000b). We do not yet know enough about how widely adolescents in immigrant families perceive discrimination and how such perceptions are related to the experience in their new country and to their overall adaptation. Earlier we examined the variation in perceived discrimination across countries of settlement (see chap. 2), where it was considered as a group-level variable. In this chapter we consider how it is related, at an individual level, to aspects of the acculturation experience. We examine differences in perceived discrimination in relation to acculturation attitudes, cultural identity, and time in the new society, as well as gender and parental occupation.

Research on discrimination among immigrants suggests that it has a reciprocal relationship to acculturation attitudes; that is, the attitudes of members of the larger society toward immigrants is likely to be reflected in the feelings of immigrants about the society (Berry & Kalin, 1979; Heider, 1958; Kalin & Berry, 1996). Thus we would expect that when immigrant adolescents feel that they are viewed negatively by others, they will be more likely to view society negatively and to reject being part of the larger society; that is, they would favor separation or marginalization over integration or assimilation.

Perceived discrimination may also be reciprocally related to cultural identity. A large study of adolescents from diverse American ethnic groups (Romero & Roberts, 1998) found that ethnic affirmation, that is, a positive sense of belonging to one's ethnic group, predicted more positive attitudes toward other groups, which in turn predicted lower perceived discrimination. These results support the multicultural hypothesis, namely, the proposition that only when people are secure in their own identity will they be in a position to accept those who differ from them. In national surveys in Canada (Berry & Kalin, 1995; Berry et al., 1977), results show that when people feel secure they are less prejudiced toward others, and when they feel threatened they are more prejudiced. Similar findings have been reported by Lebedeva and Tatarko (2004) studying various ethnic groups in the Russian Federation. Research with ethnic minority adolescents in the United States shows, similarly, that more positive attitudes toward one's own group contribute to positive out-group attitudes (Phinney, Ferguson, & Tate, 1997).

Conversely, the perception of discrimination may strengthen one's ethnic group identification and weaken ties to the national group. Branscombe and her colleagues (Branscombe, Schmitt, & Harvey, 1999; Schmitt & Branscombe, 2002) have emphasized that in disadvantaged groups, subjective perceptions of prejudice and discrimination can lead to increased identification with one's group. There is ample evidence for the direct association between perceived prejudice and minority group identification (e.g., Cozzarelli & Karafa, 1998; Schmitt & Branscombe, 2002; Ward & Leong, 2004). It is likely, however, that the effects on identity among immigrants experiencing prejudice and discrimination will ultimately depend on the contextual factors influencing the acculturation process (Phinney, Horenczyk, et al., 2001).

Perceived discrimination was assessed with a scale constructed by ICSEY members, consisting of seven items based partly on a scale developed by Hocoy (1993). Three items assessed perceived frequency of being treated unfairly or negatively because of one's ethnic background by peers, teachers, and other adults; and four items that assessed being teased, threatened, or feeling unaccepted because of one's ethnicity. Participants responded on a 5-point scale ranging from 1 (*never*) to 5 (*very often*).

Cultural, Religious, and Visibility Differences

In the literature on acculturation, there is evidence that a larger difference between two cultures in contact contributes to greater problems in intercultural relations (Ward, 1996). We would expect, therefore, that larger differences between immigrant groups and the societies in which they settle would be associated with more perceived discrimination and a weaker orientation to the larger national society. To investigate this proposition, we examined three dimensions on which the immigrant samples in this study could differ from the main population in the society in which they have settled: cultural values, religion, and visibility.

These dimensions of difference were assessed in various ways. For cultural values, differences were not derived from the questionnaires; rather, we extracted country scores for three values from Hofstede (2001): power distance, uncertainty avoidance, and individualism. Differences between scores for the 13 societies of settlement and scores for countries of origin of the immigrants were calculated and related to the intercultural variables.

For religion, we created four broad categories based on self-report in the questionnaire: no religion, Judeo-Christian, Muslim, and a combination of Eastern religions, primarily Buddhist and Hindu. All the societies of settlement were predominantly Judeo-Christian.

For an estimate of differences in visibility (between immigrants and the dominant populations of the 13 societies of settlement, which are mainly of European origin), we created three categories: high visibility (e.g., Angolans, Vietnamese), medium visibility (e.g., Moroccans, Turks), and low visibility (e.g., Finns, Russians). All the societies of settlement had predominantly European-origin populations.

We then examined variations on intercultural variables across these three categories. For all three dimensions, we expected that greater differences would be associated with higher levels of perceived discrimination and a weaker orientation to the larger society.

Summary

The acculturation experience of immigrant adolescents is a complex process involving many factors. Several important aspects of the acculturation process have been identified, including acculturation attitudes, cultural identities, language, peer contacts, family relationship values, and perceived discrimination. To understand acculturation, it is essential to consider these variables both individually and in combination. In the following sections, we use data from immigrant adolescents from the 13 countries to provide a detailed picture of the ways adolescents relate to their culture of origin and their society of settlement. Our goal is to present a broad picture of immigrant adolescents across different contexts rather than examine differences among specific groups and contexts. However, some salient country and ethnic group data are reported here. Complete details of means and standard deviation for countries and immigrant groups are presented in Appendix C.

We first present descriptive results for the intercultural variables of interest, the relationships of these variables to relevant demographic and contextual variables, and their relationships to each other. We address the following questions: What is the distribution of these variables across the immigrant and national youth in the societies of settlement? How do aspects of acculturation vary with demographic and contextual factors? How are these variables interrelated?

In addition, using a person-oriented approach based on cluster analysis, we address the questions: What individual patterns are evident in the ways in which adolescents acculturate? How are these patterns related to demographic and contextual variables?

INTERCULTURAL VARIABLES: DESCRIPTION AND PREDICTORS

In this section, we present descriptive results for each of the main intercultural variables (acculturation attitudes, ethnic and national identities, language, peer social contact, family relationship values, and perceived discrimination) and their relationship to demographic and contextual variables. The means are shown in separate graphs for all intercultural variables. Each graph shows the mean for all immigrant adolescents, for immigrant adolescents in each country, and for all national adolescents. These results are based on the sample described in chapter 3, where we provide information on the age, gender, parental occupation, and proportion of life spent in the new country of the adolescents. We used two additional variables, length of residence and neighborhood composition, to describe the acculturation experience.

Length of Residence

A categorical variable was created that allows for comparison among groups of adolescents who have lived for different lengths of time in their societies of settlement. We divided the immigrant youth into three approximately equal groups based on their length of residence: (a) 1,098 adolescents who were foreign born or arrived in the new country by or before the age of 6, (b) 1,177 adolescents who were foreign born and who had more than 6 but less than 12 years of residence, and (c) 1,122 adolescents who were native born or had more than 12 years of residence.

Neighborhood Composition

The variable neighborhood composition was based on adolescents' reports of the ethnic makeup of their own neighborhood. The proportion of adolescents in each of five categories was as follows: almost entirely a different ethnic group (22.8%); majority from a different group (25.4%); balanced, with an equal mix of people from own and other groups (30%); majority from own group (14%); and almost entirely from own group (7.8%). Notably, more than 78% lived in communities where the population was ethnically balanced or predominantly from another group.

Acculturation Attitudes of Immigrant and National Adolescents

Immigrant adolescents were scored on the extent to which they endorsed integration, separation, assimilation, and marginalization attitudes. For the national adolescents, acculturation attitudes refer to their view of how immigrants should fit into the new society. Mean levels for these attitudes, controlling for age, gender, and proportion of life spent in country of settlement are shown in Figs. 4.2 to 4.5.

Integration

Immigrant adolescents expressed the strongest preference for integration among the four acculturation attitudes, scoring 3.9 on a 5-point scale. Integration was the most favored attitude both overall and across all countries and ethnic groups (see Fig. 4.2). National adolescents, like the immigrant adolescents, endorsed integration most strongly, meaning that they believed immigrants should become integrated. However, they supported integration somewhat less than the immigrants themselves (3.7 vs. 3.9). This same pattern was found in all countries.

Separation

Separation was the second most strongly supported attitude among immigrants overall, but the general mean was only 2.6, below the theoretical midpoint of the scale, 3.0 (see Fig. 4.3). Thus, support for separation was considerably lower than support for integration. However, separation was not rated second by all groups; it scored third, below assimilation, for some groups, notably the Vietnamese in four countries (France, Norway, Sweden, and the United States), the Turks in Finland, and several groups in Portugal. Separation scores were generally higher among boys than among girls ($\eta^2 = .01$).

National adolescents were less supportive of separation (i.e., segregation) than immigrant adolescents (2.4 vs. 2.6). Among national adolescents, separation was less supported than assimilation.

Assimilation

Assimilation was rated third among immigrants overall, with a mean of 2.2, except for those cases noted earlier, where it was second (see Fig. 4.4). Boys generally had higher scores than girls ($\eta^2 = .01$). No significant relationship with age was found.

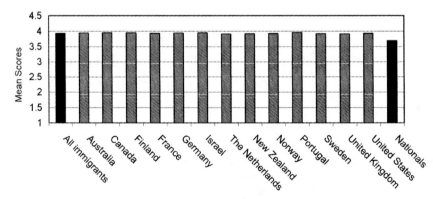

FIG. 4.2. Estimated mean scores for integration attitudes, controlling for age, gender, and proportion of life spent in country of settlement.

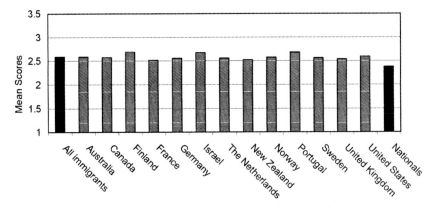

FIG. 4.3.   Estimated mean scores for separation attitudes, controlling for age, gender, and proportion of life spent in country of settlement.

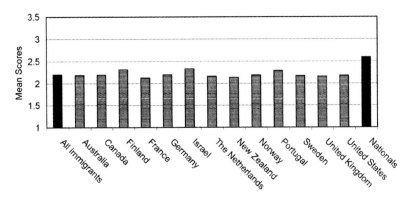

FIG. 4.4.   Estimated mean scores for assimilation attitudes, controlling for age, gender, and proportion of life spent in country of settlement.

In contrast to the immigrants, the national adolescents supported assimilation more than separation; their support for assimilation was considerably above that of the immigrant adolescents (2.6 vs. 2.2).

Marginalization

Marginalization was generally the least supported attitude among both immigrants and nationals, but there was some variation across groups. National adolescents had a stronger preference for marginalization (2.3) than did immigrant adolescents (1.8; see Fig. 4.5). Among immigrants, boys had higher scores than girls ($\eta^2 = .01$), and 17- to 18-year-olds had lower scores than the younger adolescents ($\eta^2 = .01$).

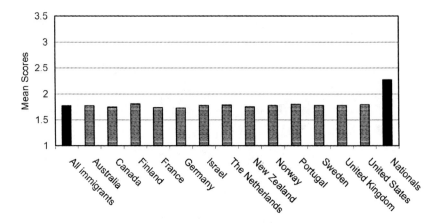

FIG. 4.5.   Estimated mean scores for marginalization attitudes, controlling for age, gender, and proportion of life spent in country of settlement.

Demographic Predictors of Acculturation Attitudes

Length of Residence. The three length-of-residence categories described earlier were used to examine differences in immigrant adolescents' acculturation attitudes with time in the new society. We used acculturation attitudes scores that were standardized within country and group. Only for separation attitudes was there a significant difference based on length of residence ($\eta^2 = .01$; see Fig. 4.6). The most recent arrivals endorsed separation attitudes significantly more than did longer term residents, with the difference most evident between those with less than 6 years and all others. Integration scores were generally higher with longer residence, but the difference was not significant. The other attitudes did not differ with length of residence.

Neighborhood Composition. The ethnic composition of immigrant adolescents' neighborhood was associated with acculturation attitudes. There was less support for integration among adolescents living in neighborhoods in which almost everyone belonged to their own ethnic groups than in neighborhoods in which at least half of the population was of a different ethnic background ($\eta^2 = .01$). Immigrant adolescents living in neighborhoods in which almost everyone belonged to their own ethnic group had higher separation scores than did those in more diverse neighborhoods ($\eta^2 = .01$).

Parental Occupation. There was relatively little variation in acculturation attitudes among immigrant adolescents in terms of parental occupation. Where there were differences, adolescents from higher SES backgrounds generally re-

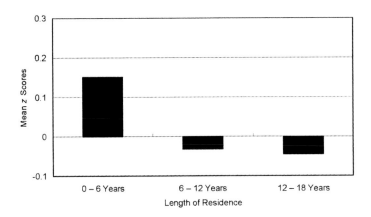

FIG. 4.6.   Mean levels of separation by length of residence.

ported lower separation scores than did those from lower SES backgrounds ($\eta^2 =$ .01). Other differences showed no interpretable pattern.

Ethnic and National Identities

The strength of ethnic and national identities provides evidence regarding the extent to which immigrant adolescents are retaining their sense of belonging to their ethnic group and becoming a member of the larger society. Because the two identities were measured independently on continuous scales, immigrant adolescents did not need to choose one cultural identity over another; rather, they expressed their sense of belonging to each group along a continuum. National adolescents only reported their national identity. The mean levels of ethnic and national identities are shown in Fig. 4.7.

Among immigrant adolescents overall, both ethnic and national identities were positive, above the midpoint. However, ethnic identity was very strong, with a mean of 4.3 on a 5-point scale, and was considerably stronger than national identity, which had a mean of 3.3. Ethnic identity was stronger than national identity in all countries and in most ethnocultural groups. As would be expected, national identity was substantially stronger among nationals (4.0) than among immigrants (3.2).

The Relationship Between Ethnic and National Identities

A conceptual question of interest is the extent to which ethnic and national identities are related to each other. A positive correlation with high scores on both identities suggests the likelihood of being bicultural; a negative correlation means that when one identity is strong, the other is weak. The mean scores of

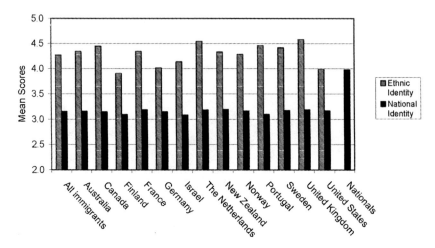

FIG. 4.7. Estimated mean scores for ethnic identity and national identities, controlling for age, gender, and proportion of life spent in country of settlement.

each identity and the correlation between them, by country, are shown in Table 4.1. A clear pattern emerged, in that the correlations were all positive in the settler societies, that is, those with a long tradition of immigration. Correlations of ethnic and national identities in these countries were .32 in New Zealand, .18 in Australia, .15 in the United States, and .09 in Canada. The only other country in which the correlations were positive was the United Kingdom (.10), where the sample was entirely South Asian (Indian). In all other countries, the correlations were negative, ranging from –.28 in Germany to –.04 in Israel. The correlations for ethnic groups within countries follow a similar pattern: They are positive for virtually all groups within the four settler societies and the United Kingdom. In the nonsettler countries the correlations are predominantly negative, but there are some interesting exceptions. For Vietnamese, the correlations are strong and positive in Finland, France, Sweden, and the United States, but negative in Norway. For Turks, the correlations are negative in all countries except for low positive correlations in Finland and Germany. Thus, in some countries, mainly settler societies, and for some groups, particularly Vietnamese, the two identities are compatible, suggesting that adolescents have a bicultural identity. In others, they are seen as incompatible, so that adolescents emphasize being either ethnically identified or nationally identified.

Demographic Predictors of Ethnic and National Identities

Length of residence in the new society was related to national identity but not to ethnic identity. Overall and in most countries, national identity differed signifi-

TABLE 4.1
Estimated Mean Scores for Ethnic and National Identities and Their Intercorrelation: The Pearson Correlations Are Based on Raw Scores

		N	Ethnic Identity M	Ethnic Identity SD	National Identity M	National Identity SD	Ethnic by National Identity r
Australia	All immigrants	304	4.34	0.08	3.16	0.06	.18***
	Vietnamese	112	4.35	0.08	3.16	0.05	.27***
	Chinese	83	4.33	0.09	3.15	0.06	.21
	Filippino	109	4.35	0.08	3.16	0.06	.07
Canada	All immigrants	256	4.45	0.10	3.15	0.07	.09
	Vietnamese	84	4.42	0.10	3.13	0.07	.17
	Koreans	81	4.43	0.10	3.13	0.07	−.01
	Indo-Canadian	91	4.49	0.07	3.18	0.05	.02
Finland	All immigrants	419	3.91	0.09	3.10	0.06	−.06
	Vietnamese	203	3.93	0.09	3.11	0.06	.18*
	Turks	57	3.97	0.09	3.15	0.07	.04
	Russians	159	3.85	0.05	3.05	0.02	−.37***
France	All immigrants	505	4.35	0.05	3.19	0.03	−.13***
	Vietnamese	82	4.31	0.07	3.17	0.05	.2
	Turks	61	4.36	0.04	3.20	0.01	−.14
	Algerians	110	4.35	0.05	3.19	0.03	−.03
	Moroccan	133	4.36	0.04	3.19	0.01	−.2
	Portuguese	119	4.34	0.06	3.19	0.03	−.19
Germany	All immigrants	250	4.01	0.07	3.15	0.05	−.28***
	Turks	95	4.04	0.06	3.17	0.04	.07
	Portuguese/ Spaniards	70	4.03	0.06	3.16	0.05	−.25*
	Aussiedler	85	3.96	0.07	3.11	0.05	−.39***
Israel	All immigrants	454	4.14	0.07	3.08	0.05	−.04
	Russians	296	4.11	0.05	3.06	0.03	−.28***
	Ethiopians	158	4.19	0.07	3.12	0.05	.00
Netherlands	All immigrants	348	4.54	0.06	3.19	0.04	−.27***
	Turks	165	4.56	0.04	3.20	0.01	−.22***
	Antilleans (Dutch)	87	4.50	0.08	3.15	0.06	−.43***
	Surinamese/ Hindu	96	4.55	0.04	3.20	0.02	−.08

(continued)

TABLE 4.1   (continued)

		N	Ethnic Identity M	Ethnic Identity SD	National Identity M	National Identity SD	Ethnic by National Identity r
New Zealand	All immigrants	159	4.33	0.03	3.20	0.01	.32***
	Chinese	37	4.32	0.04	3.19	0.01	.28***
	Pacific Islander	122	4.33	0.03	3.20	0.01	.31***
Norway	All immigrants	462	4.28	0.07	3.17	0.05	–.19***
	Vietnamese	137	4.28	0.08	3.16	0.05	–.14
	Turks	103	4.28	0.08	3.16	0.05	–.12
	Pakistanis	175	4.29	0.07	3.18	0.04	–.14
	Chilean	47	4.27	0.09	3.15	0.06	–.25
Portugal	All immigrants	190	4.46	0.07	3.10	0.05	–.19***
	Cape Verdeans	20	4.49	0.07	3.40	1.08	–.15
	Angolans	44	4.45	0.07	3.47	1.18	–.51***
	Indians in Portugal	30	4.51	0.07	3.40	1.11	.07
	Mozambicans	11	4.50	0.07	3.70	1.10	–.39***
	Timorese	85	4.43	0.06	3.72	1.06	.15
Sweden	All immigrants	815	4.42	0.07	3.18	0.05	–.19***
	Vietnamese	100	4.37	0.08	3.14	0.06	.20*
	Turks	277	4.43	0.07	3.18	0.04	–.24***
	Kurds	64	4.39	0.09	3.15		
	Finns	195	4.44	0.05	3.19	0.03	–.26***
UK	Indians	120	4.58	0.05	3.19	0.03	.10
USA	All immigrants	466	3.99	0.07	3.17	0.05	.15***
	Vietnamese	103	3.99	0.07	3.17	0.05	.21
	Armenians	193	3.97	0.08	3.15	0.06	.02
	Mexican	170	4.00	0.06	3.18	0.04	.51***

*$p < .05$. ***$p < .001$.

cantly with time ($\eta^2 = .01$); adolescents who had spent a more time in the new society had a stronger national identity (see Fig. 4.8). In contrast, ethnic identity did not differ with length of residence. Thus, generally there appears to be an increased sense of attachment to the national society with time, but no loss of attachment with one's own cultural group.

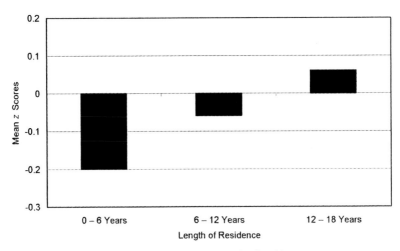

FIG. 4.8.   Mean levels of national identity by length of residence.

Seventeen- and 18-year-old adolescents had lower scores for ethnic identity than did younger adolescents ($\eta^2 = .02$). We found no clear relationship between age and national identity and no interactions of age and gender. Ethnic identity did not differ by parental occupational status, whereas national identity did differ by parental occupational status ($\eta^2 = .02$). Children of unskilled parents had the lowest national identity scores, followed by children of skilled parents. Children with parents in the two highest categories for occupational status had the highest scores. There were few significant differences in ethnic and national identities in relation to neighborhood composition, and the differences did not show an interpretable trend.

Language Proficiency and Use

Immigrant adolescents reported their proficiency in both the ethnic language and the national language, and reported the frequency of using each language. Mean levels of proficiency and usage by country are shown in Fig. 4.9. (Nationals did not report language proficiency.) Immigrant adolescents overall reported being highly proficient in the national language (4.5) and somewhat less proficient in the ethnic language (3.6). This was generally true across countries and ethnic groups. An exception was Russian immigrants in both Finland and Israel, who reported higher proficiency in their ethnic language. Overall, adolescents reported using the two languages almost equally.

Girls reported greater use of the national language than did boys ($\eta^2 = .01$), but there was no gender difference in proficiency. Parental occupational level was related to national language proficiency ($\eta^2 = .03$) and language use ($\eta^2 =$

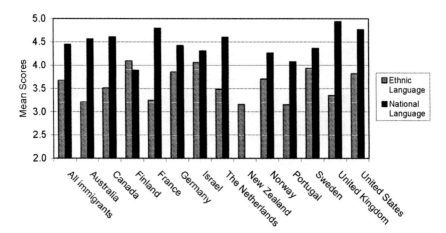

FIG. 4.9.   Estimated mean scores for ethnic language proficiency and national language proficiency, controlling for age, gender, and proportion of life spent in country of settlement. Scores are for immigrants only. (National language data were unavailable for New Zealand.)

.02); children whose parents worked at white collar or professional levels had greater national language proficiency and used the national language more than those in unskilled or skilled labor.

As expected, ethnic and national language proficiency and language use differed in relation to proportion of time in the new country. With longer residence, there was both greater national language proficiency ($\eta^2 = .07$) and greater usage ($\eta^2 = .05$), and lower ethnic language proficiency ($\eta^2 = .05$) and lower usage ($\eta^2 = .05$).

Neighborhood composition was an important factor in language use, as would be expected. In more diverse neighborhoods, national language use was higher than in neighborhoods that were predominantly of the adolescents' own group ($\eta^2 = .01$).

Peer Social Contacts

Adolescents in immigrant families had more frequent social contacts with peers from their own ethnic group (3.6) than with peers from the national group (3.3). National adolescents likewise had more contacts with peers from their own group than with immigrant peers, but for them, the difference was much greater (see Fig. 4.10).

Adolescents whose parents had lower occupational status had more frequent contacts with peers from their own ethnic group ($\eta^2 = .02$) and fewer contacts with peers from the larger society ($\eta^2 = .01$).

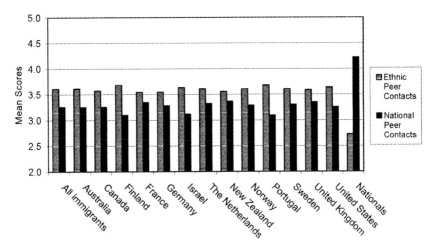

FIG. 4.10.   Estimated mean scores for social contacts with ethnic and national peers.

The frequency of national peer contact changed with length of residence (see Fig. 4.11; (η^2 = .01); adolescents with longer residence in the new country had more contact with peers from the national group. There were also fewer contacts with ethnic peers, but the effect was small. Neighborhood likewise was related to social networks in the expected direction. In more ethnically diverse neighborhoods, adolescents had more contact with national peers (η^2 = .01) and less contact with their own group peers (η^2 = .06) than in neighborhoods predominantly of their own group.

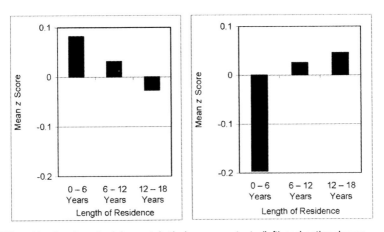

FIG. 4.11.   Immigrant adolescents' ethnic peer contacts (left) and national peer contacts (right), by length of residence.

Family Relationship Values

Family relationship values were assessed among both immigrant and national adolescents with two scales: family obligations and adolescents' rights. Higher scores indicate stronger endorsement of the values. Immigrant adolescents valued family obligations more (3.6) than did national adolescents (3.1) and valued adolescents' rights less (3.2) than did national adolescents (3.4; see Fig. 4.12). Among immigrant adolescents overall, the obligations score was higher than the rights score. For national adolescents, the mean rights scores were higher than the mean obligation scores.

There were no gender differences among immigrants in the endorsement of obligations overall or within countries. For rights, there were no gender differences overall; the few gender differences within countries varied as to which gender was higher. Endorsement of both obligations and rights showed few differences with age but did differ with parental occupation. Adolescents whose parents were in the lowest occupational status category valued family obligations the most, followed by adolescents whose parents were in the skilled and white collar category. Family obligations were least valued when parents were in the professional category ($\eta^2 =$ .02). Both family obligations scores and adolescents' right scores were unrelated to neighborhood composition.

Immigrant adolescents' endorsement of family obligations and of adolescents' rights were expected to differ with greater length of residence so as to approach the levels of the national adolescents. Differences with length of residence were generally in the expected direction, with lower obligations scores and higher rights scores with longer residence, but the effect sizes overall were small, and they are not reported. Because such differences have been found in other studies, we explored possible moderating effects. Gender, neighborhood composition, and country of settlement made a difference in the relationship between family obligations and length of residence. For girls, but not boys, obligations scores were lower among those with longer residence ($\eta^2 = .01$; <6 = .08, 6 − 12 = .00, and >12 = −.11). When adolescents lived in neighborhoods in which almost everyone was from another ethnic group than their own, obligations scores were lower with longer residence ($\eta^2 = .01$; <6 = .10, 6−12 = .03, and >12 = −.16); there were no such differences in other neighborhoods. Finally, obligations were lower with longer residence, with effect sizes large enough to report, in two countries, Sweden ($\eta^2 =$ .02; <6 = .06, 6−12 = .11, and >12 = −.26) and Israel ($\eta^2 = .02$; <6 = .12, 6 − 12 = −.12, and >12 = −.12). For adolescents' rights, there were no interpretable moderating effects.

Perceived Discrimination

Perceived discrimination was reported by immigrant youth only, not by national youth. The overall mean score for perceived discrimination was 2.1, indicating that most immigrant youth feel that they are not at all or only rarely discriminated

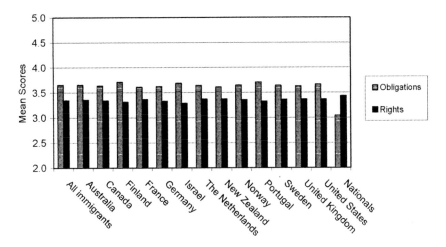

FIG. 4.12. Estimated mean scores for endorsement of family obligations and adolescents' rights, controlling for age, gender, and proportion of life spent in country of settlement.

against (see Fig. 4.13). Overall, males perceived more discrimination than did females ($\eta^2 = .01$); in all cases of gender differences within countries, males were higher on perceived discrimination. There were no consistent age differences overall and within countries. No meaningful relationships were found with parental occupational status, length of residence, or neighborhood composition.

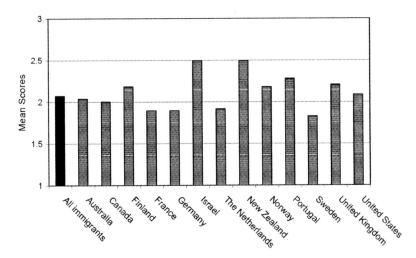

FIG. 4.13. Estimated mean scores for perceived discrimination, controlling for age, gender, and proportion of life spent in country of settlement, for immigrants only.

TABLE 4.2
Correlations Among Intercultural Variables and Contextual Variables

	1	2	3	4	5	6	7	8	9	10	11	12	13	14	15	16
1. Integration																
2. Separation	**-0.28**															
3. Assimilation	-0.09	0.06														
4. Marginalization	**-0.27**	**0.21**	**0.37**													
5. Ethnic identity	0.16	**0.22**	**-0.34**	**-0.20**												
6. National identity	**0.20**	**-0.29**	0.19	-0.03	-0.10											
7. Ethnic lang. prof.	0.09	**0.20**	-0.10	-0.03	**0.21**	**-0.22**										
8. National lang. prof.	0.07	-0.12	-0.15	-0.12	0.09	0.15	-0.09									
9. Language use	-0.01	**-0.20**	0.08	-0.02	-0.13	**0.35**	**-0.63**	**0.40**								
10. Ethnic peer conts.	0.05	**0.25**	-0.12	-0.06	**0.28**	-0.09	**0.27**	-0.02	**-0.22**							
11. Nat. peer contacts	0.16	**-0.22**	0.13	-0.05	-0.08	**0.26**	**-0.22**	**0.20**	**0.31**	-0.12						
12. Family obligations	0.09	0.18	-0.04	-0.08	**0.21**	0.03	0.08	-0.02	-0.07	0.17	-0.01					
13. Adolescent rights	0.11	-0.06	-0.05	-0.04	-0.02	-0.14	0.11	-0.06	**-0.22**	-0.05	0.01	-0.09				
14. Perceived discr.	-0.11	**0.21**	0.12	**0.20**	-0.06	-0.07	0.05	-0.10	-0.10	0.11	-0.15	-0.01	-0.10			
15. % of life in host country	-0.02	-0.10	-0.14	-0.03	0.15	0.05	-0.32	**0.44**	**0.32**	-0.05	0.14	-0.07	0.03	-0.16		
16. Occupational status	0.01	-0.04	0.00	-0.04	-0.09	0.19	-0.14	**0.20**	**0.27**	-0.09	0.07	-0.10	-0.06	-0.06	0.04	
17. Neighborhood	-0.06	0.08	-0.03	0.03	0.04	0.06	0.02	0.07	0.04	**0.24**	-0.09	0.09	-0.17	0.06	0.02	-0.13

Note. Correlations involving occupational status or neighborhood composition are Spearman Rho's (due to the ordinal nature of scale values); all other values are Pearson product–moment correlations. Lang. prof. = language proficiency; discr. = discrimination.

CORRELATIONS AMONG INTERCULTURAL VARIABLES

To gain understanding of the ways the various aspects of the acculturation process are related to each other, we used both correlations and factor analyses. Correlations among all the intercultural and contextual variables are shown in Table 4.2. Because of the large sample, almost all correlations are significant; correlations of .20 and above are shown in boldface. Only correlations of this magnitude or above are discussed.

Acculturation attitudes and cultural identities were interrelated in ways that were expected, providing a modest degree of support for their convergent validity. Specifically, ethnic and national identities were both positively related to a preference for integration and negatively related or unrelated to marginalization. In contrast, the two identities were related in opposite directions to assimilation and separation; ethnic identity was negatively related to assimilation but positively to separation, whereas national identity was positively related to assimilation but negatively to separation.

The associations of attitudes and identities with acculturation behaviors were generally in the expected direction but were modest. Among the acculturation attitudes, separation showed the strongest relationship with acculturation behaviors; separation attitudes were more strongly endorsed among those who used the national language less, had more peer contacts within their own group, endorsed family obligations more, and were more proficient in the ethnic language. Separation attitudes were also positively associated with perceived discrimination, as was marginalization, implying reciprocal attitudes. Those who do not wish to have relationships with members of the larger society believe that others are discriminating against them or experience actual discrimination.

With respect to the two cultural identities, national identity was positively related to national peer contacts and national language use, and negatively with ethnic language proficiency. Ethnic identity was positively associated with ethnic language proficiency and the cultural value of family obligations. The other intercultural variables were related as expected; for example, ethnic language proficiency was associated with ethnic peer contacts, and national language proficiency was associated with national peer contacts. However, ethnic and national identities were both unrelated to perceived discrimination.

Proportion of life in country, parental occupational status, and neighborhood ethnic context each bore some relation to intercultural variables, but the effects were varied. Proportion of life in the new country showed the strongest relationships, but these were only in the areas of language; those with a higher proportion of life in the new country reported greater national language proficiency and use and lower ethnic language proficiency. Parental occupational status was also related to language; higher status was associated with greater national language proficiency and usage. Neighborhood was related only to peer contacts, in the direction expected.

FACTOR ANALYSIS OF INTERCULTURAL VARIABLES

The second step in exploring the interrelationship among the intercultural variables was to carry out a factor analysis. Choice of variables was determined by the factor analyses conducted in preparation for testing the overall model in chapter 6 (principal component analyses with varimax rotation). In addition to statistical criteria such as eigenvalues, percentage of explained variance, and factor loadings, we also used theory-based arguments to choose variables and variable clusters.[1]

Eventually each variable was represented in a particular factor score. Four factors were distinguished: ethnic orientation, national orientation, integration orientation, and ethnic behaviors. Using the factor scores, we examined the influences of demographic variables of each on the four factors.

Ethnic Orientation

The ethnic orientation factor combines the scores of the variables ethnic identity, the acculturation attitude of separation, and family obligations (eigenvalue = 1.41; 46.82% explained variance). The ethnic factor was related to neighborhood composition, with higher scores associated with a higher proportion of the same ethnic group. The ethnic factor was lower with higher SES, assessed by parental occupation. The ethnic factor did not vary with length of residence in the society of settlement or with gender.

National Orientation

The national orientation factor refers to a combination of national identity and the acculturation attitude of assimilation (eigenvalue = 1.199; 59.97% explained variance). The national factor was stronger among those with higher SES, and among males. There were no differences with length of residence and no interpretable differences related to neighborhood ethnic density.

Integration Orientation

The integration factor includes the two acculturation attitudes of integration (loading positively) and marginalization (loading negatively) (eigenvalue = 1.263; 63.14% explained variance). The integration factor was higher among those with

---

[1]Using the outcomes presented in chapter 6 as the model for the variable clusters presented in this chapter means that we used an a priori approach and not an exploratory approach in this chapter. In each of the principal component analyses, we included only a preselected choice of variables. This had two important consequences for the outcomes. First, the number of participants included in the analyses in this chapter is greater than the number of participants included in the analyses in chapter 6 because missing cases are deleted list-wise. Including fewer variables in an analysis means fewer missing values and thus fewer excluded participants. Second, because the number of participants included in the analyses varies between the two chapters, the outcomes can be different.

higher SES and a lower ethnic neighborhood density. Males were lower on the integration factor. There were no differences based on length of residence.

Ethnic Behaviors

The ethnic *behaviors* factor combines ethnic language proficiency and contacts with ethnic peers (both positive loadings) and national language proficiency and contacts with national peers (both negative loadings; eigenvalue = 1.516; 37.89% explained variance). The etnic behaviors factor showed differences indicating that national language and contact with national peers were associated with higher SES, longer length of residence, and a neighborhood with lower density of one's ethnic group.

Three variables were not represented in any of the factors: language use, adolescents' rights, and perceived discrimination. The first two did not fit any of the factor structures used in chapter 6, and the third, perceived discrimination, appeared to be so important that is was kept as a separate variable.

THE ROLE OF CULTURAL, RELIGIOUS, AND VISIBILITY DIFFERENCES

For the three dimensions of difference (cultural, religious, and visibility), we expected that higher levels of difference in each case would be associated with greater perceived discrimination and a weaker orientation to the larger national society. Analyses with the three types of cultural values (power distance, uncertainty avoidance, and individualism) showed few significant relationships. We created a more comprehensive measure of cultural values by creating a factor score that combined differences on all three values, all of which loaded on one dimension (eigenvalue = 1.94; 64.5 % explained variance). Again, few significant relationships were found. It appears that cultural differences in values have little effect on intercultural relations, a conclusion that contrasts with much of the existing literature. However, in most other studies, the measure of cultural difference is perceived difference; in the current study, difference was assessed independently of the respondent's views. Perhaps the difference between these findings and those in the literature lies in the use in this study of a less subjective measure.

Regarding religion, the immigrant adolescents reported their religion and were grouped into the following four categories: no religion ($n = 581$), Christian or Jewish ($n = 2,319$), Muslim ($n = 1,238$), and Eastern religions (e.g., Hinduism and Buddhism; $n = 796$). All the societies of settlement were of predominantly Judeo-Christian religion. We first explored possible differences in perceived discrimination across the four religion categories. Means on perceived discrimination for all four religion groups were in the range of 2.0 to 2.1 and showed no meaningful differences.

To examine whether religious differences were related to adolescents' orientation to the larger society, we compared the religious groups on the four factor scores described earlier, controlling for gender, age, and length of residence. Integration orientation factor scores were highest in the Judeo-Christian group ($\eta^2 = .01$). For the national orientation, Muslim youth had the lowest scores, whereas the Hindu and Buddhist youth had the highest scores ($\eta^2 = .07$). For the ethnic orientation, Muslim youth had the highest scores and the nonreligious youth had the lowest scores ($\eta^2 = .10$). The ethnic behaviors factor scores were slightly higher in the Judeo-Christian and Muslim groups than in the groups reporting no religious affiliation or an eastern religion ($\eta^2 = .02$). These differences suggest that religion clearly is important for how immigrants engage in their intercultural relations.

The three visibility groups (high, medium, and low visibility relative to the predominantly European origin nationals) differed significantly on several variables, again with age, gender, and proportion of life in the country of settlement controlled. Perceived discrimination was significantly higher in the high-visibility group than in the medium- and low-visibility groups ($\eta^2 = .01$). However, the small effect size indicates that the effect of visibility was weak. Visibility was also related to the four factors. The high-visibility group had the highest scores on the national orientation factor ($\eta^2 = .07$) and the lowest scores on ethnic behaviors ($\eta^2 = .08$). Both these results were contrary to our expectation that high visibility would be associated with greater distance from the national culture and greater closeness to their own ethnic group. Actually, the least visible group had the highest scores for ethnic orientation ($\eta^2 = .05$). No relationship was found between visibility and the integration factor. These results provide no support for the view that those who are more visibly different feel less welcome and are less inclined toward being part of the larger society. On the contrary, particularly with respect to the national orientation factor and ethnic behaviors, the evidence seems to point to greater involvement among those who are most visibly different.

PROFILES OF ACCULTURATION

In addition to the analyses based on individual intercultural variables, a person-oriented approach was used to gain an understanding of differing profiles or patterns in the ways immigrant adolescents acculturate. Cluster analysis was carried out with the following variables: acculturation attitudes (integration, separation, assimilation, marginalization), ethnic and national identities, ethnic and national language, language use (low = ethnic language, high = national language), ethnic and national peer contacts, and family relationships (family obligations and adolescents' rights). Based on the fit with the dominant theoretical framework guiding the study and on the interpretability of the resulting clusters, we decided to use four clusters or four distinct profiles of acculturation: an integration profile, an ethnic profile, a national profile, and a diffuse profile. All adolescents for whom we had complete data fit one of the four profiles. We first describe the profiles and then examine their variation in relation to other variables.

Integration Profile

The most frequently occurring profile consisted of 1,576 adolescents (36.4% of the immigrant sample) who indicated relatively high involvement in both their ethnic and national cultures (see Fig. 4.14). These adolescents were high on both ethnic and national identities. They strongly endorsed integration and gave low endorsement to assimilation, separation, and marginalization. They reported high national language proficiency and average ethnic language proficiency; their language usage suggested balanced use of both languages. They had peer contacts with both their own group and the national group. They were near the mean on family relationships values. These adolescents appear to be comfortable in both the ethnic and national contexts in terms of identity, language, peer contacts, and values. Because they exemplify the concept of integration, their profile was termed the *integration profile*.

Ethnic Profile

A second profile, shown in Fig. 4.15, consisted of 975 adolescents (22.5%) who showed a clear orientation toward their own ethnic group, with high ethnic identity, ethnic language proficiency and usage, and ethnic peer contacts. They endorsed the separation attitude and scored low on assimilation, national identity, and contacts with the national group. Their support for family relationship values was well above the average. They therefore represent young people who are largely embedded within their own cultural milieu and show little involvement with the larger society. This profile was termed the *ethnic profile*.

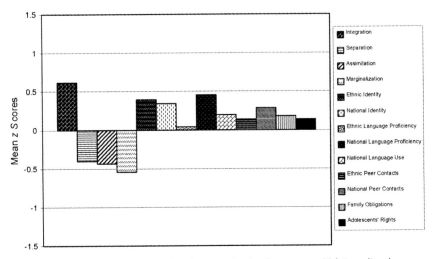

FIG. 4.14.   Integration profile, showing standardized scores on 13 intercultural variables.

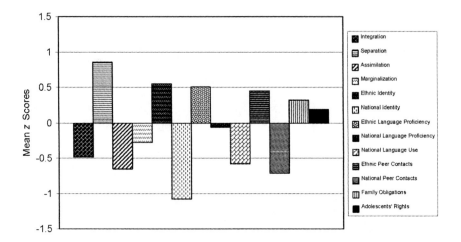

FIG. 4.15. Ethnic profile, showing standardized scores on 13 intercultural variables.

National Profile

A third profile, shown in Fig. 4.16, defined 810 adolescents (18.7%) who showed a strong orientation toward the society in which they were living. They were high on national identity and on assimilation and very low on ethnic identity. They were proficient in the national language and used it predominantly. Their peer contacts were largely with members of the national group, and they showed low support for family obligations. These adolescents appear to exemplify the idea of assimilation, indicating a lack of retention of their ethnic culture in terms of identity, language, peer contacts, or values. This profile was called the *national profile*.

Diffuse Profile

A final profile, shown in Fig. 4.17, is a pattern that is not easily interpretable. These 973 youth (22.4%) reported high proficiency in and usage of the ethnic language but also reported low ethnic identity. They had low proficiency in the national language, and they reported somewhat low national identity and national peer contacts. They endorsed three acculturation attitudes: assimilation, marginalization, and separation. This contradictory pattern suggests that these young people are uncertain about their place in society, perhaps wanting to be part of the larger society but lacking the skills and ability to make contacts. This profile appears similar to young people described in the identity formation literature as "diffuse," characterized by a lack of commitment to a direction or purpose in their lives and often socially isolated (Marcia, 1994). Therefore, this profile was termed a *diffuse profile*.

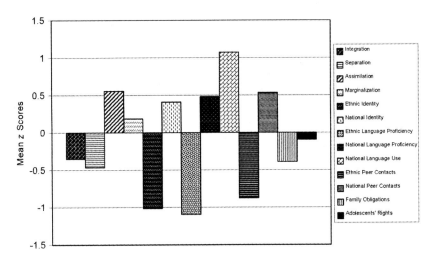

FIG. 4.16. National profile, showing standardized scores on 13 intercultural variables.

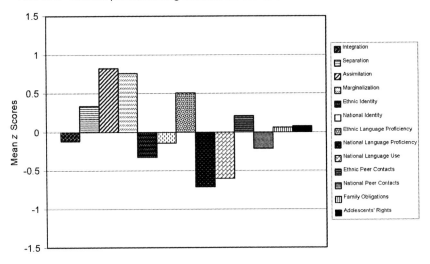

FIG. 4.17. Diffuse profile, showing standardized scores on 13 intercultural variables.

Acculturation Profiles and Perceived Discrimination

In carrying out the acculturation profile analyses, one intercultural variable, per-ceived discrimination, was not included; this was done so that its effect could be examined separately. We expected that perceived discrimination would be nega-tively related to adolescents' involvement in the larger society. Analysis of vari-ance showed a significant difference among the profiles in perceived discrimination (η^2 = .03). Significantly less discrimination was reported by adolescents with the integration profile (standardized m = –.165) and national profiles (standardized m = –.083) than the other two profiles. Those with the ethnic profile had a mean of .093. They were significantly higher in perceived discrimination than those with the integration and national profiles. Adolescents with the diffuse profile reported more perceived discrimination (m = .225) than those in the other three profiles. These results were essentially unchanged when length of residence was included as a covariate.

Variation in Acculturation Profiles

Length of Residence

An important conceptual issue is whether the different ways of acculturating shown by the profiles vary with longer residence in the new society. The profiles showed a clear pattern of differences across the three length-of-residence categories, $\chi^2(6, N = 2,855) = 383.56, p < .001$ (see Fig. 4.18). The integrated and national profiles were more frequent among those with longer residence; the proportion of integrated and national profiles among those born in the new society or with 12 or more years of residence was more than double that of those with the 6 or less years of residence. In contrast, the diffuse profile was dramatically less frequent in those with longer residence; more than 45% of those with 6 years or less residence showed a diffuse profile, whereas only about 12% of those with the longest residence showed this profile. On the other hand, the ethnic profile was almost equally frequent in all length-of-residence categories. Thus, as the figure shows, among the most recent arrivals, the diffuse profile dominated, and the national profile was very low. For those who lived in the society of settlement from birth or from their

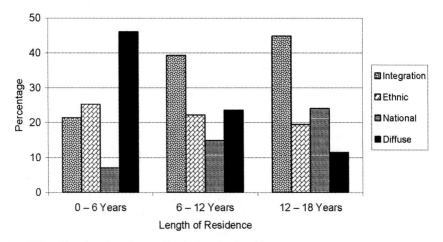

FIG. 4.18.   Acculturation profiles by length of residence.

early school years, the integrated profile dominated, and the national profile was second in frequency. In spite of these differences, a substantial group of adolescents, 20% to 25%, show strong and enduring involvement with their ethnic culture regardless of length of residence.

Neighborhood Composition

Neighborhood composition was significantly related to the acculturation profiles, $\chi^2(18, N = 4,190) = 65.79, p < .001$ (see Fig. 4.19). Results showed that the integration profile was most strongly represented in the balanced neighborhoods and dominated in all but one situation; in communities made up entirely of the adolescent's own ethnic group, the ethnic profile dominated. Furthermore, neighborhoods with a larger proportion of residents who were not from one's own group tended to have a higher proportion of national profiles than those with more same-group residents.

Gender, Age, and Parental Occupation

The proportion of males and females differed significantly across profiles $\chi^2(3, N = 4,321) = 45.62, < .001$, with girls more often showing the integrated profile and boys showing the diffuse profile. The integration profile was dominant in all three age categories (13–14, 15–16, 17–18 years). The ethnic profile was the second most dominant in the two youngest categories. The national profile was equally important in all age categories, whereas the diffuse profile was clearly more salient in the oldest group, 15- to 18-year-olds, than in the youngest group, $\chi^2(6, N = 4,334) = 24.41, p < .001$. Parental occupational status showed only a modest relationship to the profiles; the national profile was more common

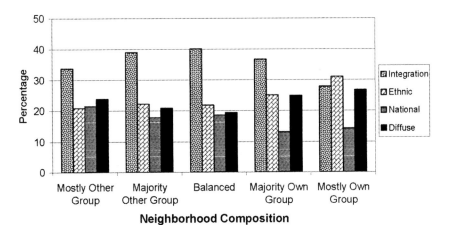

FIG. 4.19.   Acculturation profiles by neighborhood ethnic composition.

among those whose parents had higher status occupations, $\chi^2(12, N = 3,574) = 92.49, p < .001$.

Country of Settlement

The distribution of profiles differed widely across countries of settlement and ethnic groups (see Table 4.3). In the settler societies and in the United Kingdom, more than 50% of the adolescents showed an integrated profile: United States (53.5%), United Kingdom (53.0%), Australia (51.1%), and Canada (50.4%). The integration profile was somewhat less frequent but still the predominant profile in France (45.6%) and the Netherlands (39.1%); in the latter, the ethnic profile was also high (37.1%). The ethnic profile prevailed in Sweden (40.4%), where integration was also high (31.3%). Two countries were highest in the diffuse profile: Finland (44.1% diffuse, with the ethnic profile second, at 19.7%) and Israel (40.3% diffuse, with integration second, at 31.9%). Portugal was highest in the national profile (46.4%, with integration second, 29.4%). Finally, in two countries, Norway and Germany, all profiles were fairly evenly represented, with percentages of each profile between 14% and 30%.

The proportion of profiles by country is misleading, as profile distribution varied widely across ethnic groups within a given country. For example, within the United States, the integrated profile was predominant for the Mexican Americans and for the Armenians, but for the Vietnamese, the national profile was dominant (see Table 4.3 for profile distribution by country and ethnic group). Similar variation can be seen in other countries, such as the Netherlands.

SUMMARY AND CONCLUSIONS

Our results based on surveys from immigrant and national adolescents in 13 countries provide a broad picture of the acculturation experience of young people. These results involve analyses of intercultural variables central to the acculturation process, including acculturation attitudes, ethnic and national identities, language proficiency and usage, peer contacts, family relationship values, and perceived discrimination. These variables were examined individually and in combination, and were considered with reference to a number of demographic and background variables, including age, gender, parental occupation, length of residence in the new society, and ethnic composition of the neighborhood.

At the most general level, the results show clearly identifiable trends. Across most countries and ethnocultural groups, adolescents prefer integration and reject assimilation. They have strong ethnic identities and somewhat weaker but still substantial national identities. They report being more proficient in the national language than the ethnic language, but they use the two languages about equally. They have friends from both their own and other groups, and generally feel that they are rarely discriminated against. Thus, as a whole, immigrant adolescents show involvement with the new society while retaining their ethnic heritage, re-

TABLE 4.3
Distributions (percentages) of Four Acculturation Profiles,
by Countries and Groups

		N	Integration	Ethnic	National	Diffuse
Australia	**All immigrants**	**225**	**51.1**	**8.5**	**24.9**	**15.6**
	Vietnamese	56	60.7	7.1	17.9	14.3
	Chinese	68	41.2	4.4	29.4	25
	Filippino	101	52.5	11.9	25.7	9.9
Canada	**All immigrants**	**244**	**50.4**	**11.1**	**22.1**	**16.4**
	Vietnamese	77	44.2	5.2	19.5	31.2
	Koreans	80	42.5	22.5	18.8	16.3
	Indo-Canadian	87	63.2	5.7	27.6	3.4
Finland	**All immigrants**	**376**	**17.8**	**19.7**	**18.4**	**44.1**
	Vietnamese	202	18.3	10.4	18.8	52.5
	Turks	53	28.3	1.9	50.9	18.9
	Russians	121	12.4	43	3.3	41.3
France	**All immigrants**	**419**	**45.6**	**21**	**26.3**	**7.2**
	Vietnamese	71	46.5	8.5	39.4	5.6
	Turks	55	34.5	38.2	10.9	16.4
	Algerians	88	43.2	25	27.3	4.5
	Moroccan	117	51.3	27.4	16.2	5.1
	Portuguese	88	46.6	8	37.5	8
Germany	**All immigrants**	**242**	**29.8**	**21.1**	**19.8**	**29.3**
	Turks	96	22.9	28.1	9.4	39.6
	Portuguese/ Spaniards	67	52.2	28.4	9	10.4
	Aussiedler	79	19	6.3	41.8	32.9
Israel	**All immigrants**	**414**	**31.9**	**18.8**	**8.9**	**40.3**
	Russians	264	10.2	23.9	9.1	56.8
	Ethiopians	150	70	10	8.7	11.3
Netherlands	**All immigrants**	**294**	**39.1**	**37.1**	**13.6**	**10.2**
	Turks	152	30.9	53.9	2	13.2
	Antilleans (Dutch)	65	43.1	29.2	13.8	13.8
	Suranamese/ Hindu	77	51.9	10.4	36.4	1.3
Norway	**All immigrants**	**424**	**28.5**	**29.5**	**14.6**	**27.4**
	Vietnamese	129	26.4	13.2	24	36.4
	Turks	97	19.6	35.1	11.3	34

(continued)

TABLE 4.3 *(continued)*

		N	Integration	Ethnic	National	Diffuse
	Pakistanis	160	31.9	42.5	8.8	16.9
	Chilean	38	44.7	15.8	15.8	23.7
Portugal	**All immigrants**	**405**	29.4	**6.7**	**46.4**	**17.5**
	Cape Verdeans	106	47.2	13.2	32.1	7.5
	Angolans	102	22.5	1	70.6	5.9
	Indians in Portugal	71	32.4	7	54.9	5.6
	Mozambicans	45	11.1	2.2	86.7	0
	Timorese	81	22.2	7.4	4.9	65.4
Sweden	**All immigrants**	**763**	31.3	**40.4**	**7.3**	**21**
	Vietnamese	91	40.7	11	15.4	33
	Turks	261	25.3	47.1	5.7	21.8
	Kurds	60	25	61.7	3.3	10
	Latin Americans	163	40.5	41.7	6.7	11
	Finns	188	29.3	37.2	7.4	26.1
UK	**All Immigrants** (Indians)	**114**	52.6	**14**	**17.5**	**15.8**
USA	**All immigrants**	**413**	53.5	**12.8**	**16.9**	**16.7**
	Vietnamese	92	31.5	0	52.2	16.3
	Armenians	168	51.2	22	10.1	16.7
	Mexican	153	69.3	10.5	3.3	17

flecting a general preference for integration. These results are mirrored to a degree by adolescents from the larger society, who also see the integration of immigrants as the preferred form of acculturation.

Because the integration option is normative in the general discourse on immigrant adaptation in Western societies, both immigrants and national community members may tend to endorse it when asked to indicate their preferred acculturation orientation (Jasinskaja-Lahti, Liebkind, Horenczyk, & Schmitz, 2003). However, integration involves both the maintenance and the weakening of the culture of origin (Berry, 1997). Immigrant and national adolescents may differ on the preferred degree of weakening the immigrants' cultural identity (Jasinskaja-Lahti et al., 2003); the difference can be seen in the second most preferred acculturation attitude in this study. Among immigrants, separation was generally the second most preferred acculturation attitude, whereas among national adolescents, assimilation was the second choice.

However, the broad picture based on mean scores of the intercultural variables does not accurately reflect the variation among immigrant youth that is revealed using a person-oriented approach. Cluster analysis identified four distinct profiles that indicate different ways adolescents deal with the challenges of living in a culture different from their culture of origin. Only one of the four profiles, the integration profile, matches the pattern described in the preceding paragraph. The integration profile distinguishes adolescents who give clear evidence of being involved in, and comfortable with, both the ethnic and national cultures. This is the most common profile, including more than one third of the adolescents.

The other two thirds of adolescents are distributed approximately equally across three other profiles. More than one fifth of the adolescents show an ethnic profile, characterized by a strong orientation toward their own ethnic group. Their identity, language proficiency and use, peer contacts, and values are rooted primarily in their ethnic culture, and their attitudes reflect a preference for separation. Their attitudes, identity, and behaviors suggest relatively low involvement with the national culture.

A somewhat smaller group of adolescents reveal a national profile, which is almost a mirror image of the ethnic profile. Their acculturation attitudes, identity, language, peer contacts, and values are strongly oriented toward the national culture. For both of the ethnic and the national profiles, language is strongly related to cultural identity. The positive correlation of the ethnic language with ethnic identity is a key aspect of the ethnic profile; national language and national identity are linked in the national profile.

In general, language maintenance, shift, and loss do not occur independently of the sociostructural context, including demographic variables such as language users' absolute numbers and proportion of the total population and their geographic spread and distribution (Bourhis, 2001; Giles et al., 1977; Liebkind, 1999). The more demographic, political, economic, and cultural resources an ethnolinguistic group has, the more likely it is that it will maintain its group language and survive collectively as a distinct linguistic community (Barker & Giles, 2004; Bourhis, 2001). In the current study, proficiency in and use of the ethnic language were positively related to the proportion of an adolescent's own ethnic group in the neighborhood. This finding supports sociolinguistic theories of minority language maintenance, which hold that it is the individual's network of linguistic contacts that ultimately determines the proficiency in and use of a minority language (Allard & Landry, 1992; Landry & Bourhis, 1997).

It has been argued that language is a vital aspect of an ethnic group's identity, and there is some empirical support for this claim (Asante & Gudykunst, 1989). The language–identity link has, however, been subject to considerable debate (e.g., Edwards, 1992; Fishman, 1989; Liebkind, 1992a, 1996a, 1999). Most scholars agree that language can be an important component of ethnic identity but that this identity can, and does, survive the loss the original group language (Edwards, 1992; Giles & Robinson, 1990; Liebkind, 1999). In this study, however, the proficiency in and use of ethnic language among immigrant adolescents seemed to be closely related to their ethnic identity.

A fourth group of adolescents, characterized by a diffuse profile, constitutes 22% of the sample. They appear ambivalent and uncertain about their situation, endorsing three very different acculturation attitudes (separation, assimilation, and marginalization) and scoring relatively low on both ethnic and national identities. They are not proficient in the national language but express a desire to be part of the national society, and they report relatively high discrimination. In the classical literature on marginalization (Stonequist, 1937), such persons were described as being poised in psychological uncertainty between two worlds, neither one fully accepting them. This description has been proposed as particularly apt for adolescents by Mann (1965). For the marginal person, it has been found that the original goal was often one of assimilation, but this goal was thwarted by the experience of prejudice and discrimination (Mann, 1958). For youth with the diffuse profile in the present study, the pattern of high assimilation and high marginalization preferences, combined with high perceived discrimination, conforms closely to these classical descriptions of the marginal person.

The profiles differ in relation to contextual and demographic factors, highlighting the fact that no single pattern fits all immigrant adolescents. The amount of time adolescents have spent in a new society is a key demographic factor in understanding the acculturation experience. Our data are not longitudinal, but we derived a measure of length of residence based on place of birth and, for foreign-born adolescents, age of arrival in the new country. The results based on length of residence allow us to infer trends over time. Most notably, there is a trend toward adolescents' greater involvement in the country of settlement. This is accompanied by little difference in ethnic identity over time, although there is somewhat lower proficiency and usage of the ethnic language.

The increasing involvement in the new country over time can be seen in both the acculturation profiles and the individual variables. The national profile is found in only a small percentage (8%) of the most recent arrivals, that is, adolescents who were foreign born or had lived 6 years or less in the new country, but in almost one fourth (23%) of those with 12 years or more of residence. Individual variables show a similar trend. National identity, national language proficiency and usage, and contacts with peers from the national group are all higher with longer residence. The separation attitude, implying distancing from the national culture, is lower with longer residence. Support for family obligations is also somewhat lower with longer residence; that is, immigrant adolescents' attitudes are closer to the attitudes of national adolescents. The differences are small overall, but the lower support for family obligations is more evident among girls and in neighborhoods where most of the residents are from a different ethnic group other than that of the adolescent. Girls are likely to be more aware than boys of the extent to which traditional cultural values place heavier obligations on women.

Although national involvement is greater with longer residence, immigrant adolescents are not becoming assimilated. The assimilation attitude does not vary over time; that is, immigrant adolescents with longer residence do not show greater support for giving up their ethnic heritage to become part of the larger society. Furthermore, although ethnic language proficiency and usage are lower with longer residence, adolescents' identification with their ethnic group remains strong. Ethnic identity, in contrast to national identity, does not differ with length of residence. Ethnic identity appears to be more resistant to variation than other aspects of the acculturation process such as language. In fact, other research shows that ethnic identity remains strong into the third generation and beyond (Phinney, 2003). Furthermore, the ethnic profile showed only a limited decline, from 25% to 19.5%, from the most recent immigrants to those with the longest length of residence. These results clearly show that the acculturation process for these adolescents cannot be described as a linear progression from identification with one's culture of origin to assimilation into the national culture. Rather, the continued strong ethnic identity, together with the greater national involvement, suggests progression toward integration and biculturalism.

This trend over time toward integration is supported by both the profiles and the individual variables. Among the recent arrivals, the diffuse profile dominates. These adolescents, who do not identify with or have much involvement with either their ethnic group or the larger society, make up almost half of the most recent arrivals. In contrast, among adolescents with the longest residence, the integration profile dominates. Almost half the adolescents have this profile, and only 12% are categorized as diffuse. In terms of identity, the greater the time in the society of settlement, the greater is the likelihood of having both strong ethnic and national identities. These findings, although not longitudinal, suggest that over time, more adolescents will be integrated and bicultural.

Greater involvement in the country settlement can, however, imply different things. Snauwaert, Soenens, Vanbeselaere, and Boen (2003) assessed the acculturation attitudes of Moroccans and Turks in Belgium using three operationalizations of the integration alternative. When involvement in the society of settlement was defined primarily as having contact with members of the dominant group, they found that more than 80% of the immigrants preferred integration. However, when involvement was defined as endorsement of the dominant culture, only 37% were integrated. And when it was defined in terms of identity, only 10% were integrated; that is, they had an equally strong ethnic and national identity (Snauwaert et al., 2003). The findings of our study suggest that adolescents generally become increasingly integrated into their new society and may even develop a bicultural identity that combines their ethnic and national identities, but identity changes are slower than those of more behavioral aspects of acculturation.

Of particular interest is the role of perceived discrimination. Perceived discrimination is significantly lower among adolescents with the integrated and national profiles than among those with the ethnic and diffuse profiles. In addition, perceived discrimination is positively correlated with the separation and marginalization attitudes. These findings are consistent with research on the reciprocity of intercultural attitudes (Berry & Kalin, 1979; Heider, 1958; Kalin & Berry, 1996).

In our data, when adolescents feel that they are being discriminated against, they tend to be part of the ethnic and diffuse profiles; that is, the experience of discrimination is reciprocated, and the national society is rejected. On the other hand, when they do not feel discriminated against, adolescents are likely to be part of the integration and national profiles. Ideally, immigrant youth should have both ethnic and national support networks available in their new societies. However, immigrants who experience discrimination are increasingly likely to find support primarily in their ethnic networks. Although such networks have been shown to buffer the detrimental effects of discrimination (Jasinskaja-Lahti, Liebkind, Jaakkola, & Reuter, in press), in the long run, continuing discrimination and confinement only to ethnic networks may also contribute to the establishment of socially segregated immigrant communities.

Neighborhood ethnic composition and parental occupation are also implicated in the acculturation experience, although to a lesser degree. The most obvious effects are where the neighborhood is largely or exclusively made up of members of the adolescent's own group. Under these circumstances, ethnic language usage is high, and there are fewer contacts with national peers. The ethnic profile predominates in such neighborhoods. SES has a contrasting effect. Adolescents whose parents have higher status occupations are more oriented toward the national culture and report higher national language proficiency and usage.

Our results show that gender has a modest relationship to acculturation attitudes and experiences. Girls are more likely than boys to be found in the integration profile; they also report greater use of the national language. In contrast, boys are more likely to endorse the separation attitude and to be found in the diffuse profile. They also report higher levels of perceived discrimination. The age of the adolescents bears almost no relationship to any of the acculturation variables.

The larger context, beyond the variables assessed at the individual level, also play an important role in the relationship between acculturation orientations and identity (Phinney, Horenczyk, et al., 2001). For example, societies favoring assimilation expect immigrants to abandon their own cultural and linguistic distinctiveness for the sake of adopting the culture and values of the dominant group, whereas ethnic societies often define who can be full members of the society in ethnically exclusive terms (Bourhis et al., 1997). In societies favoring assimilation, immigrants who actively challenge the expectations of the national community by preferring separation are likely to be easy targets of prejudice and discrimination. In contrast, immigrants in segregationist countries are expected by the nationals to keep to themselves and minimize intergroup contact. In the latter case, immigrants who go against the current and want to assimilate are likely to experience the most prejudice and discrimination. If these immigrants also go against the current in their own community, which prefers separation, they are likely to lack support for their wish to assimilate into the host society (Jasinskaja-Lahti et al., 2003). It is possible that the diffuse profile found in this study reflects such predicaments.

Cultural and other differences between immigrant groups and the society where they settle have been assumed to play an important role in the acculturation experience. We examined perceived discrimination and orientation toward the larger society among individuals and groups who differed to varying degrees in cultural values, religion, and visibility from the larger society. Although perceived discrimination is higher in the most visibly different groups, the small effect size indicates a weak effect. Religious groups do not differ on perceived discrimination. However, Muslim youth report the weakest orientation toward the national society, and Eastern religion youth report the strongest orientation. Overall, the results do not provide strong support for the role of cultural or religious differences in acculturation. It may be that the effects of difference are more subtle, interacting with specific national settings, rather than being evident on a large scale.

In addition to the general findings, the results provide evidence of variation across the countries of settlement and across ethnic groups within countries. These were not explored in depth in this chapter. Variations among countries and ethnic groups are explored in chapter 8, where we focus on two ethnic groups in the same four countries of settlement and control many of the possible confounding variables. In the current analyses, differences among countries should be regarded as starting points for further study rather than as definitive conclusions. Because of the many differences we did not assess and cannot control, observed differences among countries may be the result of factors beyond the scope of the study. Members of different ethnic groups in multicultural societies actively (re)produce and negotiate intergroup relations and ethnic identity, taking into consideration local as well as national and global circumstances, resources, and boundaries. For example, although there may be asymmetrical power relationships between immigrant groups and the host population on a national level, in some local situations power relationships can be reversed. Young people, in particular, are actively negotiating forms of identity and belonging, and this process is marked by a plurality of differences, cultural syncretism, and the appropriation of social representations. In this process of negotiation, activities and affiliations are maintained that also increasingly cut across national boundaries (Verkuyten, 2005).

With these cautions in mind, one clear finding regarding the larger context emerges from the results. Countries described in chapter 2 as settler societies that have a long history of immigration and have been developed largely through immigration, such as Australia, Canada, and the United States, have the highest proportion of adolescents with an integration profile. Also, in these countries a bicultural identity is more evident. The strong positive correlation between ethnic and national identities suggests that in these countries adolescents are more likely to identify with both cultures, that is, to be bicultural. Overall, the results suggest that immigrants in these countries have more opportunity to become integrated into the new society.

In most other countries, there are fewer adolescents with an integration profile, and the correlation between ethnic and national identities is negative, indicating the difficulty of combining the two identities. For example, a separate identity, indicated by a negative correlation between the two identities and higher ethnic than national identities, is most common in countries with a shorter immigration history, such as the Netherlands and Germany. These results provide evidence that in the settler societies, which have more experience with immigration, integration and biculturalism are more available solutions to the challenge of living within two cultural frameworks. Exceptions to these general findings highlight the importance of considering the specific historical circumstances of the particular country and of the ethnic group sampled. For example, in the United Kingdom, the only group sampled was East Indians; for them, the positive correlation between the two identities may reflect that fact that they are English speaking and come from a former colony, and thus they find it easier to fit in.

In summary, the results presented in this chapter provide a picture of the complexity of the acculturation experience across a wide variety of countries and ethnic groups. Although one third of adolescents overall appear to be integrated into the society of settlement, in terms of attitudes, identity, language, and peer contacts, the remainder may be strongly embedded in their ethnic community, closely linked to the larger society, or unclear about their place in the new society and trying to make sense of it. The history of the country of settlement provides a broad background for these differences, with societies that have been formed largely through immigration providing more opportunities for new immigrants to become integrated. However, the process is not static. Clear patterns of change over time can be seen in differences related to the length of time adolescents have spent in the new society. Adolescents who have been in the new society longer are more likely to be integrated and less likely to be unclear about their situation. Nevertheless, there is also a strong tendency for those with a strong ethnic orientation to show relatively little change and to retain close ties to their ethnic group.

Several other factors influence the acculturation experience. Perceived discrimination is associated with adolescents' distancing themselves from the larger society and feeling that they do not belong. Neighborhood effects are apparent in most of the intercultural variables. Immigrant adolescents report more ethnic language use and have fewer contacts with national peers in more ethnically homogeneous neighborhoods. In more diverse neighborhoods, they report greater national language use and more contacts with national peers. Also in more heterogeneous neighborhoods, immigrant and national adolescents are more similar to each other in their values regarding family relationships. Higher SES, as indicated by parental occupational status, is associated with adolescents being more oriented toward the national society and being more proficient in the national language. Beyond these general conclusions, each ethnocultural group within a specific context faces particular acculturation issues. These differences can be understood only with further research on the history of the groups, their current attitudes and experiences, and the contexts in which they are undergoing acculturation.

5 Psychological and Sociocultural Adaptation of Immigrant Youth

David L. Sam
University of Bergen
Paul Vedder
Leiden University
Colleen Ward
University of Wellington
Gabriel Horenczyk
University of Jerusalem

The previous chapters focus on country-level and contextual variables (chap. 2), methodological considerations (chap. 3), and intercultural variables (chap. 4). This chapter examines the psychological and sociocultural adaptation of ethno-cultural youth with the following broad question in mind: "How well adapted are youth with an immigrant background in their society of settlement?" Specifically, we consider how well immigrant youth are doing with respect to psychological well-being (positive self-esteem and lower levels of mental health problems such as anxiety, depression, and psychosomatic symptoms), and how satisfied they are with their lives. The chapter also looks at the extent of their adjustment in school and their behavioral problems (i.e., antisocial behavior). With respect to adaptation, we also briefly explore the immigrant paradox phenomenon.

This chapter has three main parts. The first discusses the conceptual and empirical background to our broad questions, and the instruments used to measure the constructs. This part is not intended to be an exhaustive literature review on psychological and sociocultural adaptation; interested readers are directed to other sources, such as Ward (2001). The second part of the chapter presents a comparative overview of adaptation patterns across the different countries. Here, we compare the adaptation of immigrant youth in the different societies of settlement. In addition, we examine the relationship between the various adaptation outcomes and the factor structure of adaptation. We explore how the various adaptation outcomes are related to each other and how these relate to the four acculturation profiles previously identified in chapter 4. (Further exploration of the relationships between how youth engage in their intercultural relations and how well they adapt will be covered in chapter 6). The third part of the chapter discusses the findings in relation to the literature reviewed at the beginning of the chapter.

ADAPTATION: BACKGROUND AND MEASUREMENT

Psychological and Sociocultural Adaptation: The Distinction

Although adaptation is of significant concern to acculturation researchers, there has been considerable debate about its definition and measurement. Intercultural adaptation has been conceptualized in various ways, and its assessment has included diverse measurement of health status, communication competence, self-awareness, stress reduction, feelings of acceptance, and culturally skilled behaviors (Ward, 1996). Models of adaptation have been both data and theory driven. Hammer, Gudykunst, and Wiseman (1978), based on their factor analytic study of cultural competencies, identified a three-factor model of intercultural effectiveness: (a) the ability to communicate effectively, (b) the ability to manage psychological stress, and (c) the ability to establish interpersonal relationships. In contrast, Mendenhall and Oddou (1985), in their discussion of acculturation, drew conceptual distinctions among affective, behavioral, and cognitive components of adaptation including psychological well-being, functional intercultural interactions, and acceptance of appropriate attitudes and values.

In this research we rely on the distinction between psychological and sociocultural adaptation proposed by Ward and her colleagues (e.g., Searle & Ward, 1990; Ward, 1996, 2001). Broadly speaking, psychological adaptation refers to emotional well-being and satisfaction, and sociocultural adaptation is concerned with the acquisition of the culturally appropriate skills needed to operate effectively in a specific social or cultural milieu. The distinction between psychological and sociocultural adaptation is based on two of the major theoretical perspectives found in acculturation theory and research: stress and coping, and culture learning (Ward et al., 2001). Psychological adaptation, which highlights affective aspects of acculturation, is best interpreted within the stress and coping framework (Lazarus & Folkman, 1984). An example of research undertaken in this tradition is work on acculturative stress by Berry and colleagues (Berry, 1994, 1997; Berry & Kim, 1988; Berry, Kim, Minde, & Mok, 1987). Sociocultural adaptation, by contrast, is largely concerned with behavioral aspects of the acculturative experience and can be understood in terms of Argyle's (1969, 1982) analyses of social skills and interactions. Furnham and Bochner's work on social difficulty and the social psychology of intercultural encounters exemplify the culture learning tradition (Bochner, 1982; Furnham & Bochner, 1982).

The distinction between psychological and sociocultural adaptation has received empirical support. Kennedy's (1999) longitudinal study of acculturation among Singaporean sojourners demonstrated that the parallel measurements of psychological and sociocultural domains provided a better model of cross-cultural adaptation than a single global indicator. Research has further indicated that although psychological and sociocultural adaptation are related (Aycan & Berry, 1996; Ward & Kennedy, 1999), the magnitude of the relationship varies depending on acculturation conditions. The association is generally stronger under conditions of social and cultural integration. The magnitude of the relationship is greater among newcomers who are culturally similar rather than dissimilar to the society of settlement, it increases over time, and it is stronger among those adopting integrationist and assimilationist acculturation attitudes compared with the separated and the marginalized (Ward & Kennedy, 1996; Ward, Okura, Kennedy, & Kojima, 1998; Ward & Rana-Deuba, 1999). Ward (1996) also reported that the two types of adaptation tend to be predicted by different variables: Psychological adaptation is largely predicted by personality variables, life change events, and social support, and sociocultural adaptation is predicted by cultural knowledge, degree of contact, and positive intergroup attitudes (Ward, 2001).

The present study extends and refines work on psychological and sociocultural adaptation by including multiple measures of the two constructs and by incorporating both positive (life satisfaction, self-esteem) and negative (psychological symptoms, behavioral problems) indicators as outcome measures.

Life Satisfaction

Life satisfaction—or satisfaction with life—has been defined as the global evaluation of a person's quality of life based on his or her own chosen criteria (Shin & Johnson, 1987). In determining one's life satisfaction, judgments are based on a comparison with a standard that each individual sets for himself or herself. The preceding definition suggests that life satisfaction cannot be assessed by a universal set of criteria. Life satisfaction is based on the individual's own subjective evaluation. This is particularly important when the focus is on people of diverse ethnic backgrounds who may have different values or perceptions of what characterizes a good life.

In spite of the evidence that young immigrants exhibit no more symptoms of psychological disorders than their peers belonging to the society of settlement (Fuligni, 1998a), there is a dearth of studies that focus on the more positive aspects of adaptation among immigrant youth, and how immigrants compare with nonimmigrant peers. Life satisfaction studies should be of interest to acculturation researchers given the drastic and often rapid changes that occur during acculturation. Rapid changes in life have the potential to affect the stability of one's overall satisfaction (Inglehart & Rabier, 1986). In a study of young immigrants from the former Soviet Union to Israel, these adolescents reported lower life satisfaction than their nonimmigrant peers (Ullman & Tatar, 2001). Although studies of life satisfaction normally conceptualize it as an outcome variable, life satisfaction was found to be an important predictor of psychological well-being among Irish immigrants to the United States (Christopher, 2000).

To measure the overall degree of the adolescents' satisfaction with their lives, we modified the five-item scale developed by Diener et al. (1985). In our study, we used a 5-point response scale instead of the original 7-point response scale. The instrument has been tested among diverse groups, including college students. It has shown good psychometric properties including good test–retest reliability, high internal consistency, and strong positive correlations with other subjective well-being scales (see Diener et al., 1985). Following a review of different life satisfaction scales, Cummins (1995) proposed a "gold standard" for subjective well- being: For Diener et al.'s scale, this is $65.0 \pm 2.5\%$ of the maximum scale measure. In other words, for our 5-point scale, the gold standard is between 3.13 and 3.38, where scores below 3.13 should be interpreted as indicative of poor life satisfaction.

Self-Esteem

Self-esteem, or self-evaluation, is perhaps the most important aspect of the self-concept, and it has received the most theoretical and empirical attention over the last decades (Baumeister, 1995). This is primarily due to the high importance that has been attributed to it, particularly as a predictor of well-being as well as personal and social adjustment. Do immigrant adolescents differ from their national peers with respect to self-esteem? How does self-esteem relate to identity in particular and to other adaptation outcomes in general?

In this study, we regarded self-esteem as an adaptation outcome, even though the concept has been used both as a predictor and an outcome variable in ethnic identity and acculturation research (Deaux, 1996; Phinney, 1990). For example, Tran's (1987) causal modeling of the psychological well-being of Vietnamese refugees in the United States demonstrated direct and significant effects of self-esteem on life satisfaction.

The placement of self-esteem in models of acculturation and adaptation depends on both conceptual and empirical considerations. Our placement of self-esteem as an adaptation outcome reflects the view of this construct as malleable, subject to acculturation influences, and as an indicator of psychological well-being rather than as a relatively stable psychological disposition that functions as a resource in the adaptation process.

Conceptualizations of self-esteem vary considerably among theories and investigations, and these differences are reflected in the varied operationalizations and methods of measurement. The most common way of measuring self-esteem, however, is to ask a series of simple questions about global self-regard (e.g., Rosenberg, 1965). It should be noted that most distributions of self-esteem are skewed to the high end; therefore, individuals scoring lower than the mean or median, often characterized as having low self-esteem, are actually low only in a relative sense.

Following social identity theory (Tajfel, 1978; Tajfel & Turner, 1986), it has been postulated that being a member of a group and identifying with the group is an important determinant of a person's self-esteem. A lowered self-esteem is suggested to result if one's group is the subject of negative stereotypes, prejudice, and discrimination. Consequently it is common to measure self-esteem among immigrants as part of their psychological adaptation. Although a link between group identity in general and self-esteem in particular has been demonstrated (Crocker, Cornwell, & Major, 1993; Crocker, Voelkl, Testa, & Major, 1991), this link with respect to disparaged group members such as immigrants is variable (Verkuyten, 1994). A positive relationship between identity (both national and ethnic) and self-esteem, and a negative relationship between perceived discrimination and self- esteem (Phinney, Madden, & Santos, 1998) have been documented.

When it comes to comparing the self-esteem of immigrant and national adolescents, studies do not provide a clear picture, probably as a result of the different conceptualizations and measures used in the various studies together with group differences and contextual influences such as the extent of discrimination. Recent studies generally show that the levels of immigrants' self-esteem are not lower than those of their national counterparts (Leondari, 2001; Slonim-Nevo & Sharaga, 2000). Moreover, a recent study of immigrant girls in Norway found that their self-evaluations were more positive than those of nonimmigrant Norwegian girls (Stiles, Gibbons, Lie, Sand, & Krull, 1998). Along similar lines, Abouguendia and Noels (2001) reported that first-generation South Asian immigrants in Canada show higher self-esteem than second-generation immigrants. It may well be that the dual cultural frames of reference available to immigrants (because of their orientation to both national and ethnic cultures), which are generally weakened in subsequent generations, provide the newcomers with relatively powerful resources for developing and maintaining their self-esteem. Partial support for this interpretation can be derived from studies showing relatively high levels of self-esteem among immigrants who have an integration orientation (e.g., Eyou, Adair, & Dixon, 2000).

Self-esteem in our study was measured using Rosenberg's (1965) 10-item self-esteem inventory. The original scale was designed as a unidimensional scale, and this unidimensionality has been confirmed in several studies (Simpson & Boyal, 1975).

Psychological Problems

Do adolescents with immigrant backgrounds report more mental health problems than their national peers? Mental health problems, and in particular psychopathology, have been a topic of great concern since immigration to North America and Australia started. Working from a selection hypothesis that contended that potentially mentally ill people were more likely than others to emigrate, earlier studies generally concluded that immigrants suffered from serious psychological problems (Littlewood & Lipsedge, 1989; Ødegaard, 1932). There are two issues that need to be distinguished: Do immigrants actually have more problems, and if so, does the selection hypothesis account for it? There is currently hardly any evidence for the original selection view, although the controversy around what has become known as the "immigrant paradox" or the "healthy immigrant effect" have raised new discussions about health and selection (Jasso, Massey, Rosenzweig, & Smith, 2004). The immigrant paradox is briefly discussed at the end of the second part of this chapter.

Another working hypothesis, from a stress perspective, contends that immigration and acculturation are inherently stressful, and that these stresses may result in lowered mental health status (especially anxiety, depression), feelings of marginality and alienation, heightened psychosomatic symptom levels, and identity confusion. Aronowitz (1984) noted that among adult immigrants, early classic studies following the stress tradition reported strong associations between immigrant status and psychological disorders. However, more rigorous research and analysis have cast doubt on the inevitability of this association as several factors have been found to moderate the relationship (Berry, 1997). Similarly, immigrant children have not been found to demonstrate any greater tendency to have mental health problems than their host peers do (Bashir, 1993). However, studies have identified some commonalities with respect to the kinds of adaptation problems immigrant children and youth report. Specifically, younger children (i.e., younger than 15 years old) tend to manifest behavioral problems, and among adolescents, problems of identity associated with symptoms of anxiety and depression are more common (Aronowitz, 1984).

It is becoming increasingly common to examine the incidence of psychosomatic symptoms among immigrants, especially those from Third World countries. This is consistent with the view that culture shapes the way emotional problems are expressed, where people from developing countries such as China are more likely to express their emotional distress somatically (Tseng, 2001). However, there are no studies suggesting that immigrant children from developing countries report more psychosomatic symptoms than depression and anxiety, except for refugee youth (Bashir, 1993). Among refugee youth, in addition to psychosomatic complaints, other physical health problems such as parasitic infection have been reported (Nixon & Dugdale, 1984).

To assess psychological problems, we designed a 15-item scale for measuring depression, anxiety, and psychosomatic symptoms. Five items for each of the three areas were selected from the following sources: Beiser and Flemming (1986), Kinze et al. (1982), Kovacs (1980/1981), Mollica et al. (1987), Reynolds and Richmond (1985), and Robinson, Shaver, and Wrightsman (1991). As this instrument was specifically designed for this study, the psychometric properties of the instrument have not been established. However, the scale was found to have acceptable internal consistency (see Table 3.3).

School Adjustment

For most immigrant children and adolescents, school and other education settings are the major arenas for intergroup contact and acculturation. Thus, school adjustment can be seen as a primary task and as a highly important outcome of the cultural transition process. Within many immigrant communities, the importance attributed to school adjustment is particularly high: Newcomers tend to see schools as avenues to participation and mobility.

Much research has focused on the school performance of ethnic, national, and cultural minorities (e.g., Ogbu, 1995; Skutnabb-Kangas, 1999). However, relatively little empirical evidence is available on the school adaptation of immigrant students. In a review, Fuligni (1998a) concluded that children from immigrant families show a relatively high level of adaptation. He attributed this finding to immigrant families' emphasis on the value of education, family members' responsibilities and obligations to one another, and the dynamics of cultural identification. An Israeli study found no differences in the school functioning of high school students who immigrated from the former Soviet Union compared with Israeli-born children whose parents immigrated from the former Soviet Union during the 1960s and 1970s (Slonim-Nevo & Sharaga, 2000). Both groups exhibited good levels of social and educational adaptation.

The high levels of school adjustment, however, do not seem to characterize all immigrant groups in all receiving countries. Results from a large-scale study of second-generation American immigrants (Portes, 1999) show variations among groups constituting the immigrant student population with respect to both educational achievement and predictors of achievement. The groups that did best in school seem to have been integrated or assimilated into the national community, which may result in greater social and cognitive support to immigrant students.

Immigration-related and culturally dependent individual differences also seem to be associated with the school adjustment of newcomers. Based on her study of the adaptation of Chinese immigrant adolescents in Australia and Canada, Leung (2001) suggests that immigrants' academic achievement is influenced not only by societal-level variables, such as immigration and settlement policies, but also by individual variables, such as perceived amount of social support available, age, and the person's definition of success. Mastery of the new language is also highly important. Among immigrant children with poor school adaptation, the low level of proficiency in the national language seems to be a critical factor in their school failure (Bhattacharya, 2000).

The educational adaptation of immigrant children seems to be negatively affected by societal and school pressures toward rapid assimilation (Igoa, 1995; Sever, 1999). As suggested by Portes and Rumbaut (1990), "It is not the parents most willing to assimilate—in the sense of 'subtracting' from their cultural background—who seem to motivate their children effectively, but those most inclined to reaffirm their cultural heritage within ethnic neighborhoods" (p. 214). Olneck (1995) concluded that, "maintenance of ethnic loyalty, not assimilation, appears associated with stronger school performance among immigrant children" (p. 325).

The role of ethnic and national identity, and of acculturation orientations, in the educational adaptation of immigrants has been addressed in several studies. Results consistently show that a bicultural orientation is conducive to better school performance (Portes & Rumbaut, 2001). Furthermore, Horenczyk and Ben-Sha-lom (2001) measured three cultural identities among Russian immigrant students in Israel: Russian, Israeli, and Jewish. They found a linear relationship between the number of positive cultural identities and the level of school adjustment.

In this study, school adjustment was assessed using seven items. The scale was developed specifically for this study and was inspired by the work of Anderson (1982) and Moos (1979) on school and educational environments. Three of the items were adapted from the Health Behavior in School-aged Children—WHO Cross-National Survey research protocol for the 1993–2004 study (see Samdal, 1998; Wold, 1995), and four items were from a study by Sam (1994). As a collection of items from various sources, the psychometric properties of the scale have not been established previously.

Behavior Problems

With respect to behavior problems, our interest was in deviant overt behaviors among migrant youth, and here again we were interested in whether adolescents with immigrant background engage in more socially deviant behaviors than their national peers. In the research literature, these behaviors, including conduct disorders and delinquent behavior, have collectively been called antisocial behavior. For our purposes however, the term *behavior problem* is preferred for reasons such as uncertainties about the stability and persistence of the behavior among our study samples as well as wariness in applying a clinical and possibly stigmatizing label to a group (see Moffitt, 1993, for discussion about developmental taxonomy of antisocial behavior). Although we prefer to call these overt negative acts behavior problems, we use this term interchangeably with adolescent antisocial behavior and delinquency in this review, as these terms are more established in the literature.

Earlier studies suggested that immigrant children generally had lower school achievement (e.g., Leman, 1991; McLatchie, 1997) and that this lower school achievement might be expressed overtly in socially deviant behaviors (Rutter, 1995). Studies such as Fuligni (1997a, 1998) and Tomlinson (1989) indicate that immigrant children do well in school and in several cases outperform their national counterparts. Against this background, there is no reason to expect that immigrant youth are particularly prone to behavior problems compared with national youth. We nonetheless examined this relationship in our study.

Earlier theories also assumed that most delinquents came from socially disadvantaged backgrounds (Rutter & Giller, 1983) and that antisocial behavior arose from the strain caused by the gap between the cultural goals of the society and the means available for their achievement (Merton, 1938). Delinquency was seen as a normal way of living within a socially disadvantaged subculture (Mays, 1972). Many of these views have been toned down in recent years because the relationship has not been found to be consistent (Rutter, Giller, & Hagell, 1998). Studies using path analysis indicate that much of the risk from poverty for antisocial behavior is indirect. Adverse effects of prolonged economic stresses on family functioning are suggested to mediate the effect of social disadvantage on antisocial behavior. It is therefore important to control for the possible confounding role of SES when studying behavior problems among youth. In their epidemiological study of conduct disorders among West Indian immigrants in London, Rutter and his colleagues (Rutter, Yule, Norton, & Bageley, 1974, 1975) found that these were manifested almost entirely at school. Conduct disorders were almost completely absent at home, and their prevalence at home among the immigrants did not differ from that among their English peers. The researchers postulated that learning difficulties and racial discrimination might be influential factors. In a study of parental reports of problem behaviors and with reference to delinquent behavior, no significant difference was found between Dutch children in the Netherlands, Turkish children in Ankara, and Turkish immigrant children in the Netherlands (Bengli-Arslan, Verhulst, & van der Ende, 1997).

Our research team, in collaboration with Olweus, designed a 10-item scale to assess behavior problems. The items for the scale were developed on the basis of Olweus (1989, 1994) and Bendixen and Olweus (1999). The psychometric properties of the ICSEY 10-item scale have not been established in previous studies, but the original 35-item scale from which ours is developed has been shown to have satisfactory psychometric properties, with consistent gender differences; boys generally report more problems than girls.

The Immigrant Paradox

Our brief review points to the fact that children from immigrant families generally show satisfactory levels of both psychological and sociocultural adaptation. When children with immigrant backgrounds are compared with their national peers, they generally exhibit better health and less involvement in negative overt behaviors, and do as well as or better than their nonimmigrant peers with respect to academic achievement and psychological well-being (see Fulgini, 1998a). This pattern of adaptation has, in recent years received much attention in the U.S. literature on second-generation immigrants and has become known as the "immigrant paradox" (e.g., Garcia Coll, 2005; Hayes-Bautista, 2004). The immigrant paradox is the counterintuitive finding that immigrants have better adaptation outcomes than their national peers despite their poorer socioeconomic conditions. Another aspect of the paradox is that the first generation of immigrants has higher levels of adaptation than the second, so that over time adaptation of immigrant youth may decline toward the levels of the nationals or even below (Harris, 1999; Rumbaut, 1999; Suarez-Orozco & Suarez-Orozco, 2002, Waters, 1999).

However, the preceding findings regarding the immigrant paradox have limited generalizability in view of the fact that many of the studies are cross-ethnic group comparisons within one country. Furthermore, the notion of an immigrant paradox itself is relatively new and there is lack of clarity as to whether first- and second-generation immigrants should be compared with each other or, either together or separately, with nationals. It also is unclear whether we should expect second-generation immigrant youth to converge to the levels of adaptation of the nationals or that we should expect a deterioration effect irrespective of the nationals' level of adaptation. The notion of convergence suggests that the nationals are a model of adaptation to the immigrants, whereas such a notion of nationals as models is less likely to be valid when second-generation youth actually achieve lower levels of adaptation. We focus mainly on the comparison between first-generation adolescents and their national peers and we analyze whether (a) the adaptation of the second generation is less positive than that of the first generation, and (b) the adaptation scores of the second-generation immigrant youth either converge to the nationals (no statistically significant difference) or are lower than those of the nationals.

The present international study and data set enable us to go a step further to examine whether the unexpectedly good adaptation of immigrant youth can be confirmed across various immigrant ethnocultural groups and across different countries of settlement. It is important to add that although the ICSEY data set allows us to examine some aspects of the immigrant paradox, our examination of the phenomenon should be seen as exploratory because the ICSEY project was not designed with this goal in mind.

In our exploration we had two questions in mind: First, does the expected pattern (first-generation immigrant youth has better adaptation than national youth, and second generation converges to the nationals or has even lower scores) exist overall in the ICSEY data, or does it apply to some countries? The paradox has so far been reported only in the United States and we wondered whether context has played a part in its occurrence. This first question implies the issue of convergence of the second-generation immigrant scores to the scores of the nationals. If we do find convergence, we consider this support for the notion that the national youth represent a model for the second-generation immigrant adolescents. The pattern of convergence suggests that second-generation youth try to imitate national youth. Second, can the pattern referred to in the first question be found with both forms of adaptation (i.e., psychological and sociocultural) as we have assessed them in the ICSEY study?

ADAPTATION: AN OVERVIEW OF THE RESULTS

In this section we report first simple descriptive information about our measures of life satisfaction, self-esteem, and psychological problems (as aspects of psychological adaptation) and school adjustment and behavior problems (as aspects of sociocultural adaptation). We compare the levels of adaptation among immigrants from the various groups with the national youth samples. The figures consist of 15 bars, one bar showing the overall estimated mean for all immigrant youth, followed by 13 bars, one each for immigrants in the 13 ICSEY countries in alphabetical order, and then a bar for all national youth. Although the scales for the different measures ranged from 1 to 5, for the purpose of highlighting these scores, we do not use the full range of the scale. This chapter does not focus on immigrant group differences. Readers interested in the adaptation levels of the different groups in the various countries are referred to Appendix C.

In addition to the descriptive findings, we explored the relationship between the five adaptation measures and various background variables: age, gender, length of residence, ethnic composition of the neighborhood in which the adolescents live, and level of their parents' occupation. We also analyzed the impact of immigrant youth's religious background, their group's visibility, and the distance between their culture and the national culture. (These cultural difference variables are introduced in chapter 4 with respect to the relationships between adaptation outcomes and these background variables). This section also reports on the factor structure of the adaptation measures. Of special interest is how the different adaptation measures are related to cultural identity (both ethnic and national identities), and these relationships are reported. The chapter also examines the relationship between adaptation factors (i.e., psychological and sociocultural adaptations) and the acculturation profiles presented in chapter 4. The last part of the chapter focuses on the immigrant paradox.

PSYCHOLOGICAL ADAPTATION OF IMMIGRANT AND NATIONAL YOUTH

Life Satisfaction

As can be seen in Fig. 5.1 (as well as in Appendix C), the estimated mean scores for life satisfaction for both immigrant adolescents ($M = 3.52$) and their national peers ($M = 3.55$) were above 3.31, the mean score suggested by Cummins (1995) to be the gold standard for life satisfaction based on the scale of Diener et al. (1985). We can thus conclude that immigrant adolescents are satisfied with their lives. Although there were differences across groups, no group scored below the standard. There was no significant difference in life satisfaction between immigrants and their national peers. A significant but weak relationship was found between life satisfaction and age ($\eta^2 = .01$). Adolescents in the youngest age group (13–14 years) were more satisfied with their lives than their older peers.

Self-Esteem

Immigrant adolescents ($M = 3.75$) and their national peers ($M = 3.74$) did not differ with respect to their self-esteem. This is illustrated in Fig. 5.2. Across countries, differences in self-esteem scores between immigrant adolescents and national youth were very small, ranging from .01 to .04. Overall, the immigrant adolescent self-esteem was well above the theoretical midpoint of the scale (i.e., 3.0), suggesting a satisfactory level of self-esteem. Gender and age were unrelated to adolescents' self-esteem.

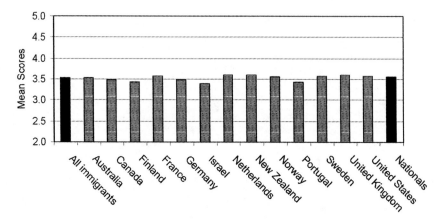

FIG. 5.1. Estimated mean life satisfaction scores for immigrant and national samples, controlling for age, gender, and proportion of life spend in country of settlement.

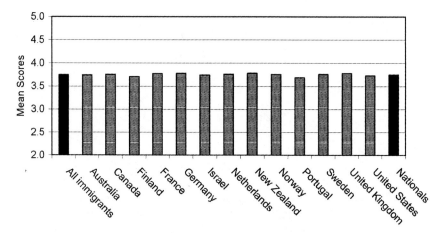

FIG. 5.2. Estimated mean self-esteem scores for immigrant and national samples, controlling for age, gender, and proportion of life spent in country of settlement.

Psychological Problems

Adolescents generally reported having few psychological problems (i.e., they scored well below the midpoint of the scale), and immigrant adolescents reported even fewer psychological problems ($M = 2.32$) than did their national peers ($M = 2.41$) ($\eta^2 = .01$; see Fig. 5.3). Comparing immigrants with the national youth within the 13 countries, there appears to be a systematic pattern of immigrants reporting fewer psychological problems than the nationals. Generally, the difference

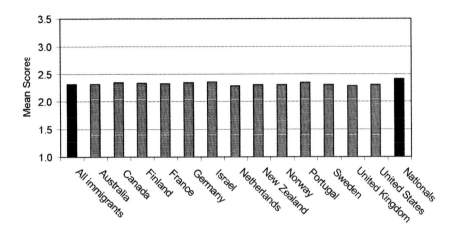

FIG. 5.3. Estimated mean psychological problem scores for immigrant and national samples, controlling for age, gender, and proportion of life spent in country of settlement.

between the mean scores ranged from .03 to .13, and the effect sizes relative to the grand mean also ranged from .04 to .84.

Apart from differences between immigrant youth and national youth, we found that immigrant boys generally had fewer psychological problems than immigrant girls ($\eta^2 = .01$). Furthermore, in the immigrant sample the psychological problems were slightly greater with increasing age ($\eta^2 = .01$).

SOCIOCULTURAL ADAPTATION OF IMMIGRANT AND NATIONAL YOUTH

School Adjustment

School adjustment (see Fig. 5.4) is high for both immigrants ($M = 3.89$) and national groups ($M = 3.74$). On the whole, school adjustment for immigrant youth was slightly better than for national youth ($\eta^2 = .01$). In the few cases where nationals reported better school adjustment (in Finland, Portugal, and Israel), the absolute mean difference was small (.02); the relative effect sizes based on the grand mean were all small as well (i.e., less than .02).

Further analyses show a slightly better school adjustment among girls compared with boys ($\eta^2 = .01$). Among immigrants, we found age to be negatively related to school adjustment ($\eta^2 = .01$). Contrary to our expectations, younger immigrants had better school adjustment scores than older youth. Furthermore, immigrant adolescents who had resided less than 7 years in the country of settlement had lower school adjustment scores than youth with longer residence ($\eta^2 = .01$). Parents' level of occupation was also related to immigrant adolescents'

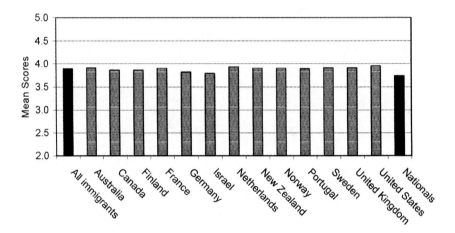

FIG. 5.4. Estimated mean school adjustment scores for immigrant and national samples, controlling for age, gender, and proportion of life spent in country of settlement.

school adjustment ($\eta^2 = .01$). Adolescents whose parents had jobs that typically required a university degree had better school adjustment than all other youth.

Behavior Problems

On the whole, all the adolescent groups reported relatively low levels of behavior problems ($M = 1.59$) (Fig. 5.5). National youth reported more behavior problems ($M = 1.70$) than immigrant youth ($M = 1.53$; $\eta^2 = .02$). In all 13 countries, immigrant adolescents reported fewer behavior problems than their national peers, and these were all significant. The largest difference was found in Portugal. In this country immigrant youth had a lower mean score for behavior problems than immigrant youth in any of the other countries ($M = 1.47$). The nationals had an intermediate mean score ($M = 1.69$). In the Netherlands we found the smallest difference score ($Ms = 1.55$ and 1.67 for immigrant and national youth, respectively). Girls had clearly fewer behavior problems than boys ($M = 1.50$ vs. 1.73; $\eta^2 = .03$).

ADAPTATION MEASURE: INTERRELATIONSHIPS AND FACTOR STRUCTURE

Table 5.1 shows the interrelationships among the adaptation measures for immigrant youth (above the diagonal) and for national youth (below the diagonal). There are two main points of interest with respect to the relationships: (a) they are all in the expected direction (e.g., high self-esteem is positively related to good school adjustment), and (b) the pattern of relationships is identical for the immi-

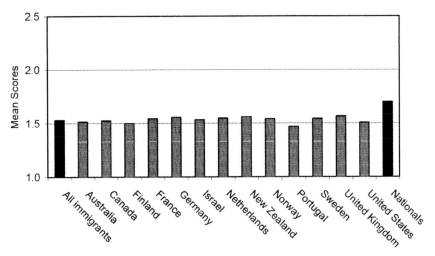

FIG. 5.5. Estimated mean behavior problem scores for immigrant and national samples, controlling for age, gender, and proportion of life spent in country of settlement.

TABLE 5.1

The Relationships (Pearson's *r*) Among Adaptation Measures for Immigrant and National Youth

	1	2	3	4	5
1. Life satisfaction		0.41	–0.33	0.28	–0.14
2. Self-esteem	0.59		–0.36	0.28	–0.11
3. Psychological problems	–0.37	–0.49		–0.36	0.22
4. School adjustment	0.34	0.32	–0.37		–0.33
5. Behavior problems	–0.13	–0.09	0.25	–0.39	

Note. (Minimum number of immigrants = 5,249; minimum number of nationals = 2,602). Correlations for immigrant youth are above the diagonal; for national youth, below the diagonal. All *p*s < .001.

grant and national youth. At the country level, there are some slight differences in these relationships in terms of the significance of the relationship, but the directions of the relationships are the same as expected.

Because the adaptation variables were significantly correlated with each other, it was reasonable to combine them into factors. This was achieved by carrying out a principal component analysis (PCA). We did this for the immigrant youth only, as the primary focus of the study is on immigrant youth. The other reason for carrying out the PCA was to verify whether the assumption we have followed so far in this chapter (i.e., that there are two forms of adaptation—psychological and sociocultural) is justified.

We conducted two PCAs. The first one included the adaptation outcomes for life satisfaction, self-esteem, and psychological problems, all measuring psychological adaptation. The factor loadings (self-esteem = 0.79, life satisfaction = 0.77, and psychological problems = –0.73) indicated a unifactorial solution. The second PCA was conducted with the scores for school adjustment and behavior problems, together labeled *sociocultural adaptation*. Again the loadings (school adjustment = 0.81, behavior problems = –0.81) indicated a unifactorial solution.

The psychological adaptation factor had an eigenvalue of 1.73 and explained 57.68% of the variance, and the sociocultural adaptation factor had an eigenvalue of 1.33 and explained 66.34%. There was a positive and significant correlation between psychological and sociocultural adaptation. For the entire sample, the overall Pearson correlation was .36. A similar trend in terms of the direction of the relationships was found in all the countries. The correlation coefficients ranged from .29 in Portugal to .44 in Australia.

ADAPTATION AND ACCULTURATION PROFILES

Four acculturation profiles—integration, ethnic, national, and diffuse—were identified in the previous chapter. The integration profile consisted of adolescents who highly endorsed the integration attitude and held both strong ethnic and national identities. They also had high national language proficiency and had high peer contacts with both the nationals and their own ethnic group members. The ethnic profile consisted of adolescents who showed a clear orientation toward their own ethnic group, were high on ethnic identity, had more contacts with their own ethnic group, and were high on ethnic language proficiency and use. The national profile was composed of adolescents who valued assimilation and were high on national identity and low on ethnic identity. They were proficient in the national language and used it more often. The diffuse profile was made up of individuals who were proficient in, and regularly used the ethnic language, although they were low on ethnic identity. They also reported low national identity and low interaction with their national peers, but high on both marginalization and assimilation.

On the basis of the scores on the variables reported earlier in this chapter, and of previous research (e.g., see Berry 1997; Berry & Sam, 1997), we expected the integration profile to have the best, and the diffuse profile the worst, psychological and sociocultural adaptations. As can be seen in Fig. 5.6 this is clearly the case. Immigrant youth with the integration profile have adaptation scores that are above the grand mean, whereas those with the diffuse profile are below the grand mean. The results for the national profile suggest that these individuals have relatively poor psychological adaptation, whereas they are not clearly distinct from other profiles with respect to sociocultural adaptation. In contrast, the ethnic profile shows good psychological adaptation but poor sociocultural adaptation.

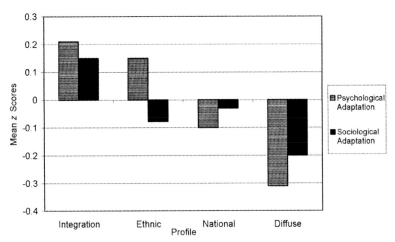

FIG. 5.6. Relationship between immigrant acculturation profiles and adaptation, controlling for age, gender, and proportion of life spent in country of settlement.

PREDICTORS AND CORRELATES OF ADAPTATION

Background Factors and Adaptation

Using the factor scores, we examined relationships between demographic variables and each of the factors. These analyses were carried out only for immigrants. Psychological adaptation was weakly but significantly related to gender ($\eta^2 = .01$); boys had a slightly higher score for psychological adaptation than girls. The psychological adaptation factor was unrelated to neighborhood composition, age, length of residence, and the level of parents' occupation, a proxy of SES.

As expected, immigrant boys scored lower on sociocultural adaptation compared with immigrant girls ($\eta^2 = .03$). However, age, length of residence, neighborhood ethnic density, and parents' level of education did not have any significant effect on sociocultural adaptation.

Adaptation and Cultural Identity

As clarified in earlier chapters, we conceive of cultural identity as a sense of belonging to one or more cultural groups. Strong ethnic or national identities provide a sense of emotional stability and personal security, and can be considered to be resources for well-being and adjustment. We found striking support for this notion (see Table 5.2).

Both ethnic and national identities (for immigrants) and national identity (for nationals) showed positive relationships with self-esteem, life satisfaction, and school adjustment, and negative relationships with psychological and behavior problems. Generally these same results were found at the country level.

TABLE 5.2
Relationship (Pearson's *r*) Between Adaptation Measures
and Cultural Identity

	Life Satisfaction	Self-Esteem	Psychological Problems	School Adjustment	Behavior Problems
Immigrant adolescents					
Ethnic identity	0.16***	0.18***	–0.08	0.13***	–0.06***
National identity	0.11***	0.08***	–0.03 *	0.14***	–0.09***
National adolescents					
National identity	0.22***	0.15***	–0.15***	0.19***	–0.07***

Note. Minimum number of immigrants = 5,241; minimum number of nationals = 2,598. *p < .05; ***p < .001.

Adaptation Across Generations: The Immigrant Paradox

As stated earlier, the immigrant paradox is the counterintuitive finding that immigrants have better adaptation outcomes than their national peers despite their poorer socioeconomic conditions. In our analyses of this phenomenon we included first- and second-generation immigrant youth as well as national youth. It was only when the ANOVA yielded a statistically significant finding and an effect size (η^2) of at least .01 did we go a step further to explore the following three contrasts to verify the existence of the paradox: (a) A pairwise comparison (Bonferroni) should reveal a statistically significant difference between first-generation immigrant youth and the national youth, indicating better adaptation for the immigrant youth; (b) either no statistically significant difference between second-generation immigrant youth and national youth or a statistically significant difference indicating that second generation immigrant youth had worse adaptation than their national peers; and (c) a statistically significant difference between first- and second-generation immigrant youth, indicating that first-generation immigrant youth have better adaptation than their second-generation peers. Together, the comparisons should reveal a pattern in which the first generation of immigrants has higher levels of adaptation than the second, and the adaptation of second-generation immigrant youth is the same as or below the levels of the nationals. It is only when a combination of comparison (a) with either comparison (b) or (c) yielded the expected findings do we refer to the overall pattern as *immigrant paradox*. We sought to answer two questions: Does the expected pattern exist overall in the ICSEY data or does it apply to some countries? Can this pattern be found with both forms of adaptation (i.e., psychological and sociocultural)?

Because age and gender have been found to be related to aspects of adaptation, we controlled for these factors when exploring the incidence of the phenomenon. Dividing the immigrants into first and second generations resulted in the exclusion of immigrants in certain countries such as France and Germany where we could not distinguish between the two generations because we lacked information on when they migrated and whether they were born in the country of residence or somewhere else. Furthermore, to have meaningful analyses, we excluded countries where the immigrant group of either generation was smaller than 24. By so doing, several immigrant groups (e.g., Chileans in Norway and Turks in Finland) were excluded from the analyses. In all, 17 immigrant groups in 10 countries met these criteria.

In a combined analysis with all the eligible groups, we found small nonrelevant differences between the first- and second-generation immigrants for both types of adaptation. We further explored differences among the groups for each type of adaptation separately for each of the 10 countries. We found statistically significant and relevant differences among the three groups (first- and second-generation immigrant youth, and national youth) for psychological adaptation in 4 countries (see Fig. 5.7) and for sociocultural adaptation in 6 countries (see Fig. 5.8).

In further analyses we first checked whether first-generation immigrant adolescents had better adaptation scores than their national peers. However, for psychological adaptation this pattern was not found in any of the countries. In three countries the nationals had better psychological adaptation scores than the first-generation immigrants, and in the fourth country, Sweden, the second-generation immigrant youth had more positive psychological adaptation scores than the national adolescents. Furthermore, in all countries where there

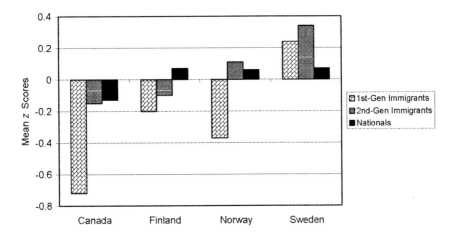

FIG. 5.7. Psychological adaptation factor scores for first- and second-generation immigrants and for nationals (controlled for age and gender).

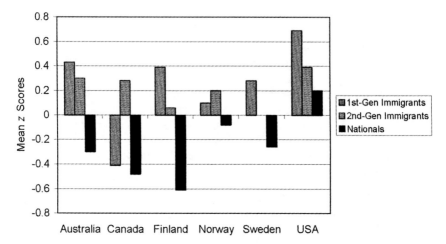

FIG. 5.8. Sociocultural adaptation factor scores for first- and second-generation immigrants and for nationals (controlled for age and gender).

are differences in psychological adaptation between generations (Canada, Finland, Norway, and Sweden), the second-generation immigrants show better adaptation than the first generation, but not better than the nationals, except in Sweden. These are contrary to the paradox: The findings neither confirm the expected pattern that first-generation immigrant youth had better adaptation scores than their national peers nor that the first generation has better adaptation than the second generation.

For sociocultural adaptation, we found statistically significant differences among the three groups of adolescents in Australia, Finland, Sweden, and the United States (η^2 sizes: Australia = .11, Finland = .17, Sweden = .03, and United States = .04). In these countries, the first-generation youth had better sociocultural adaptation than the nationals, and the adaptation of second-generation immigrant youth were close to the levels of the nationals. In contrast, in Canada and Norway second but not first generation immigrant youth had higher sociocultural adaptation scores than their national peers (see Fig. 5.8).

In Australia, Finland, Sweden, and the United States, Vietnamese immigrants were included in the sample. This allowed for a comparison of a common immigrant group across countries. With respect to psychological adaptation, we found that Vietnamese scored lower than their national peers (M for nationals = .07, η^2 = .02), and there was no significant difference between generations (first generation = –.26; second generation = –.19). These findings did not fit the expected pattern.

With respect to sociocultural adaptation, first-generation Vietnamese adolescents had higher scores (.19) than the nationals (–.01). Moreover, the second generation youth had scores well below the nationals (–.15, $\eta^2 = .01$). These two findings together fit the pattern defined earlier.

The first conclusion that may be drawn from these analyses is that the expected pattern of differences in adaptation scores between first-generation immigrant youth and their national peers, and between second-generation immigrant youth and their national peers is not characteristic of all immigrant youth in the Western countries of immigration that participated in the ICSEY study. The second conclusion is that the expected pattern showed up only with sociocultural adaptation.

Implied in the first result is the issue of whether immigrant youth's adaptation scores from first to second generation converge to the levels of adaptation characteristic of the nationals. With respect to sociocultural adaptation, we found this to be the case in four countries. This finding supports the notion that the national adolescents' adaptation serves as a kind of model for immigrants. However, when looking at the Vietnamese immigrants in four countries, we saw that with longer residence, immigrant youth's sociocultural scores may be worse than those of the nationals. This conflicts with the notion of the nationals as a model for second-generation immigrants.

Cultural, Religious, and Visibility Differences

Cultural Differences

We expected less positive adaptation in immigrant groups that were more culturally different from the society of settlement. However, using the same measure of cultural difference that we reported in chapter 4, we found no statistically significant relation between the degree of cultural difference and either psychological or sociocultural adaptation. As suggested previously, this lack of relationship may be because our measure of cultural difference is based on national value differences rather than on participants' perceptions of cultural differences.

Religious Differences

Our expectation, in line with previous findings, was that immigrants whose religions were different from the predominant Judeo-Christian beliefs of the societies of settlement would experience less positive adaptation. For psychological adaptation, we found the opposite to be the case: Muslims had the highest (standardized) score (+.20), whereas the other three groups had slightly negative scores. A similar tendency was found for sociocultural adaptation: Muslims had the highest score (.05) and nonreligious youth the lowest scores (–.10).

Visibility Differences

With regard to psychological adaptation of immigrants, the highest scores were obtained among the medium visibility group ($\eta^2 = .02$). This is difficult to interpret, as higher scores were expected in the low-visibility group, not in the medium group. For sociocultural adaptation, no statistically significant differences were found across the three visibility groups.

We may conclude that overall the relationship among these three forms of difference and adaptation scores did not confirm our expectations. This is clearly contrary to the existing literature (as reviewed by Masgoret & Ward, 2006; Ward, 2001).

SUMMARY AND CONCLUSIONS

The main questions that this chapter addressed were how well adapted immigrant youth were in relation to their national peers, and how this adaptation was related to background demographic factors, such as generation of immigration, and to acculturation profiles. In dealing with immigrant youth's adaptation, we examined five adaptation outcomes: life satisfaction, self-esteem, psychological problems, school adjustment, and behavior problems. These five adaptation outcomes were found to be closely related to each other in that they formed two clear factors: psychological and sociocultural adaptations, as previous studies have suggested (Ward, 2001). Consequently, later analyses in this chapter were limited to these two forms of adaptation outcomes.

Using the national youth as our comparison group, our results indicated that immigrant youth as a group are just as well adapted, and in some cases better adapted, than their national peers. On the whole, immigrant youth reported slightly fewer psychological problems, better school adjustment, and fewer behavior problems, although no significant differences were found between immigrants and their national peers in the areas of life satisfaction and self-esteem. In other words, although immigrant youth appeared to be better adapted socioculturally, they were not particularly different from their national peers in psychological adaptation.

Immigrant youth reported clearly fewer behavior problems than their national peers. Although several studies have suggested that immigrant and other ethnic youth are overrepresented in official crime statistics (Hofer & Tham, 1991; Junger & Polder, 1992), the use of self-reported delinquency suggests otherwise. Here, studies indicate that immigrant youth either do not differ from their national peers, or when they do differ, it is often in favor of immigrant youth: They report lower levels of delinquency (Junger-Tas, Terlouw, & Klein, 1994). Findings from our study provide additional support, suggesting that immigrant adolescents are characterized by fewer behavior problems when these are measured through self-report. Torgersen (2001) has pointed out that the main discrepancy between official crime statistics and self-reported antisocial behaviors is that self-reported anti-social behaviors fail to distinguish between the levels of seriousness in antisocial behaviors. According to Torgersen, when distinctions are made, immigrant youth do not differ from their national peers in serious delinquent behaviors (such as stealing), but they differ in the extent of minor and violent delinquent behaviors. Specifically, immigrant youth report lower minor delinquent behaviors (e.g., painting graffiti) but more violent delinquent behavior (e.g., fighting with the use of weapons) than their national peers (Torgersen, 2001). In our study, we focused on petty delinquent behaviors, and this may explain the clear differences between immigrant youth and their national peers.

Immigrant youth also had better school adjustment scores than national adolescents. Immigrant youth's high scores in this respect parallel immigrant parents' high expectations for their children's school adjustment and academic achievements. Through these expectations they are indirectly promoting good school adjustment from their children (Rumbaut, 2000; Suarez-Orozco, 1989).

Based on our broad findings, we believe the phenomenon of the so-called immigrant paradox may be an overgeneralization. Of the 13 ICSEY countries, we could explore this phenomenon in only 10 countries, and of these 10, we found only one aspect of the phenomenon (first-generation immigrants outperforming their national peers) in 4 countries, and only in sociocultural adaptation. The paradox does not exist in psychological adaptation; rather, we found the opposite of the paradox. With respect to the convergence of immigrants' adaptation toward that of the national, we found evidence in all 4 countries. However, when looking only at Vietnamese immigrant adolescents in these 4 countries, we found no convergence. Vietnamese second-generation immigrant youth had sociocultural adaptation scores that were considerably lower than those of their national peers.

One explanation for first-generation immigrants doing better socioculturally than second-generation immigrants may be that the culture of immigrant families has a protective effect on their children's acculturation (Harris, 2000). In this case it may be that immigrant parents more closely monitor the social activities of their first-generation children than their later-generation children, as parents may not want to leave their children unsupervised in a society with which they are not familiar. This in turn may protect the children from antisocial behavior.

Making comparisons between immigrant and national youth is difficult because of the many ways they may differ. In the absence of psychometrically established cutoff points, it is not uncommon to use national samples as the reference group or norm. Thus, deviations from the national mean are seen as either better or poorer adaptation. In this study where the nationals were sampled from the same area and schools as the immigrants, and more important from a nonclinical population, we think that using the nationals as a reference groups is justified and that we can stand by our conclusion that immigrant youth are generally well adapted. It is also important to add that poorer or better adaptations of immigrants compared with the nationals are relative rather than absolute evaluations.

Further support for our conclusion that immigrant youth are well adapted comes from the response categories of the scales used. The midpoint of all the adaptation outcome scales was 3, and these were more or less defined as neutral. In all cases, the immigrant scores were either well below this midpoint of negative scales, as they were for psychological problems and behavior problems, or well above it for positive scales, as they were for life satisfaction, self-esteem, and school adjustment. This means that in all the cases, immigrant youth reported that they fell on the positive side of the adaptation scales. One of the scales we used in this study—life satisfaction—has an established cutoff point of "good life satisfaction" (see Cummins 1995, 1998), and using this cutoff point as a standard, immigrant children in all the countries clearly had good life satisfaction.

With immigrant youth generally showing good adaptation, our study lends further support to several studies in the late 1990s from the United States, suggesting that immigrant children generally adapt well and in some cases better than their national peers (Fulgini, 1998; Harris, 2000; Kao, 2000; Rumbaut, 2000; Zhou, 1997).

Of the various background sociodemographic factors we examined in relation to immigrant youth adaptation, only gender and age appeared to have a consistent relationship, although the direction of the relationships varied with respect to the outcome in question. Although boys were generally better psychologically adapted, girls were socioculturally better adapted. Previous studies have suggested that women may be more at risk for acculturation problems than men (Beiser et al., 1988; Carballo, 1994). Furthermore, several studies have shown that women exhibit more symptoms of psychological distress in terms of depression and anxiety, whereas men are more frequently diagnosed with behavioral and personality disorders, and these gender differences have been observed across cultures (Tanaka-Matsumi & Draguns, 1997)

Our results also point to the fact that younger immigrants (13- and 14-year-olds) were generally better adapted than older immigrants. Although several studies have suggested that adaptation is generally easier for younger immigrants (Aronowitz, 1984, 1992; Beiser et al., 1988), it is not easy to explain why this is the case, partly because of the lack of longitudinal studies. One explanation often given is that the younger the acculturating individual, the more "flexible" the person is in terms of cultural conflicts between one's original cultural heritage and that of the new society. Additionally, older adolescents are faced with more and different challenges from those of their younger peers as they go through the transition from adolescence to adulthood (Erikson, 1968).

Although the inverse relationship between the extent of ethnic homogeneity of one's neighborhood and the incidence of psychiatric problems has been known for years (Murphy, 1965), systematic studies in this area are difficult to come by. The positive effect of large ethnic community on adaptation has often been seen as being due to the buffering effect of social support. Contrary to our expectation, good adaptation was not related to the ethnic composition of the neighborhood.

In the Introduction we refer to the cultural learning perspective, which suggests that the cultural distance between nationals and immigrants should have an inverse relationship with immigrants' adaptation. Specifically, we had expected, among other things, that Muslims, who represent cultures that are very different from the prevailing Anglo-Christian cultures of the ICSEY countries, would show negative adaptation. The finding of this study contradicts what we expected. Perhaps the experience of in-group support linked to a strong sense of religiosity protects youth from the otherwise negative effect that cultural distance may have. The positive relationship between feelings of belonging and adaptation is well documented (Baumeister & Leary, 1995). Perhaps this sense of belonging or bonding is even positively affected by more or less adverse living conditions.

It is perhaps important to add that religiosity has been found to positively influence one's subjective well-being (Diener, 2000; Diener, Scollon, Oishi, Dzokoto, & Suh, 2000), raising the possibility that being a Muslim may have contributed positively to their psychological adaptation. Furthermore, Muslim societies have been found to be relatively tight in terms of regulation of behaviors (Gelfand, 2005); thus, socially inappropriate behaviors such as those used in our sociocultural adaptation measure will not be expressed. In other words, in spite of large cultural distance, there may not be any reason to expect poor adaptation among immigrant youth from Muslim cultures.

In summary, the results presented in this chapter point to the fact that immigrant youth are well adapted when compared with their national peers, and that their adaptation patterns in terms of the relationships among different outcomes are similar to the national youth. To a lesser degree, the adaptation outcomes are dependent on some sociodemographic factors and, in particular, on gender and age. Finally, the integration profile seems to be the most adaptive profile for acculturating individuals. In general terms, there seem to be support to the view that how immigrant youth acculturate is related to how well they adapt.

6 Predicting Immigrant Youths' Adaptation Across Countries and Ethnocultural Groups

Paul Vedder
Leiden University

Fons J. R. van de Vijver
Tilburg University

Karmela Liebkind
University of Helsinki

In chapters 4 and 5, we present background information and findings about the acculturation, intercultural relationships, and adaptation of the adolescents in our sample. Those two chapters provide the building blocks of an overall model of the relationships among acculturation, intercultural relationships, and adaptation that is tested in this chapter. At the end of chapter 4 we identify four intercultural factors: ethnic orientation, national orientation, integration, and ethnic behaviors. These four factors, which combine different variables, should not be confused with the four acculturation profiles (integration, ethnic, national, and diffuse) that are also described in chapter 4 and that combine different individuals.

At the end of chapter 5 we present a factor analysis of the five adaptation variables. The two resulting factors were labeled *psychological adaptation* and *sociocultural adaptation*. These two factors are also used in this chapter. The model presented in this chapter specifies the hypotheses regarding the relationships among the four intercultural factors and the two adaptation factors. The central question is whether there are systematic relationships at the individual level between the intercultural experiences of immigrant youth and how well they adapt. That is, using the terms employed in chapter 1, we are seeking an answer to the question "Does *how* adolescents acculturate relate to *how well* they adapt?"

In the preceding chapters little attention is paid to countries of settlement or to immigrant groups. In this chapter we explore whether and to what extent the relationship between acculturation experiences and adaptation outcomes is affected by two country characteristics: their cultural diversity (including level of immigration) and their policies with respect to diversity. In addition, we analyze to what extent the strength of this relationship depends on demographic factors such as age, generation (first- or second-generation immigrants), gender, and SES.

In the model presented in this chapter, the four intercultural factors are examined in relation to the two adaptation outcomes. A recurring issue in the acculturation literature is whether immigrants can combine involvement and identification with the national culture and involvement and identification with their ethnic culture. Some acculturation researchers have proposed, and found evidence, that the combination of the two cultures, rather than involvement with just one, is the most adaptive mode of acculturation and the most conducive to the immigrants' well-being (cf. Berry, 1997; Howard, 1998; LaFromboise et al., 1993; Phinney & Devich-Navarro, 1997). Our first hypothesis stems from this research tradition.

Hypothesis 1a: Involvement and identification with both the national and the ethnic cultures are associated with more positive adaptation outcomes for immigrant youth than involvement with either the national or the ethnic culture alone.

Other researchers are more hesitant about the relationship between cultural orientation and adaptation. For instance, Birman, Trickett, and Vinokurov (2002) suggest that the roles of ethnic and national identities in the adaptation of immigrants are linked to the acculturative demands of both the overall community context and the demands of agents in various life spheres within this context. Immigrant youth tend to perceive stronger assimilative expectations in their school settings and to have stronger assimilative tendencies with regard to school adjustment than with respect to other domains of adaptation. These researchers employed the differentiation between two kinds of adaptation proposed by Ward (2001). As stated in earlier chapters, Ward distinguished between psychological and sociocultural adaptation. Psychological adaptation refers to feelings of psychological well-being or satisfaction, whereas sociocultural adaptation refers to the abilities and skills needed to adjust to new social settings, such as knowledge of the national language and culture. Psychological adaptation is primarily based on affective responses, whereas sociocultural adaptation is based on behaviors and the effectiveness of interactions in a new cultural milieu, including the skills that facilitate these interactions. According to Ward, these two types of adaptation are interrelated but are predicted by different variables. Psychological adaptation is more personality oriented and depends on the availability of social support. For immigrant youth, personality development and the availability of social support may be related more to their orientation toward their own community than to their orientation toward the national community and culture (Oppedal, Røysamb, & Sam, 2004; Ward, 2001). Sociocultural adaptation, on the other hand, is more affected by the intensity and quality of relationships with members of the national society (Ward, 2001). We use this information as the basis for two further hypotheses dealing with the relationship between cultural orientation and adaptation.

Hypothesis 1b: Orientation toward the national group has a stronger impact than orientation toward one's ethnic group on sociocultural adaptation of immigrant youth.

Hypothesis 1c: Orientation toward one's ethnic group has a stronger impact than orientation toward the national group on psychological adaptation of immigrant youth.

We assume that a vital aspect of immigrants' acculturation experience is the level of discrimination they perceive, which reflects the attitude in the larger society toward the immigrants and likely has a decisive impact on the immigrants' acculturation and adaptation. Therefore, like other researchers (e.g., Sellers & Shelton, 2003), we treat perceived discrimination as an independent variable that contributes to the explanation of immigrants' adaptation outcomes. In recent studies, considerable empirical evidence has been provided that perceiving oneself as a target or victim of discrimination by members of a dominant group is one of the major acculturative stressors that is clearly associated with psychological symptoms among immigrants (Jasinskaja-Lahti, Liebkind, & Vesala, 2002; Liebkind & Jasinskaja-Lahti, 2000b; Sellers & Shelton, 2003; Ying, 1996).

Hypothesis 2: Perceived discrimination is negatively related to both psychological and sociocultural adaptation of immigrant youth.

Apart from intercultural variables and perceived discrimination, numerous other factors are assumed to influence adaptation. These include demographic factors not affected by migration such as gender and age, and contextual factors such as current immigration levels and immigration policy of the country of settlement (Berry, 1990). In the preceding chapters we deal with the separate impact of most of these contextual factors on acculturation and adaptation by using them as control variables in the analyses. In this chapter we focus instead on the role of these factors as possible moderators of the relationship between acculturation and adaptation. To what extent does the strength of this relationship depend on demographic factors such as age, generation (first- or second-generation immigrants), gender, and SES? Including possible moderator variables in our models helps in determining which relationships between acculturation processes and adaptation apply broadly and which are limited to particular groups or particular contexts.

THE ROLE OF BACKGROUND VARIABLES

Age

With increasing age, adolescents have more mature cognitive skills to support the process of constructing a sense of self that integrates prior understandings and experiences. However, the process is highly dependent on the family, community, and national contexts to which the adolescent is exposed. With regard to ethnic identity (Liebkind, 1992a, 2001; Phinney, 1990), this process can lead to constructive actions aimed at affirming the value and legitimacy of one's group membership (Brown, 2000; Tajfel & Turner, 1986) or to feelings of insecurity, confusion, or resentment over treatment of one's group.

Age-related trajectories, however, are not consistent across a variety of aspects of acculturation, and age does not have a straightforward relationship to acculturation and adaptation. In this chapter we explore whether age moderates the relationship between acculturation and adaptation. The few studies addressing this matter are not conclusive. Kaplan and Marks (1990), using a measure that combined language usage and ethnic identity items, with high scores indicating higher levels of assimilation, showed that higher levels on this measure in Mexican-American young adults correspond to higher levels of distress, whereas higher levels on this measure in older Mexican-Americans corresponded to lower levels of distress. The researchers suggest that this moderating effect of age may be caused by age-related differences in coping with discrimination and alienation; young adults cope less well than older Mexican-Americans. For this same ethnic group, Krause, Bennett, and Tran (1989) concluded that a low level of knowledge of the national language, combined with financial problems, had a negative impact on feelings of control, self-esteem, and psychological well-being irrespective of participants' age. Liebkind (1996a) suggests a moderating effect of age for female immigrants. Adult females have typically been seen as carriers of the culture; in a new society, they are more likely to remain at home and maintain traditional practices. Younger females, particularly those from traditional cultures that are restrictive toward women, may identify with Western values that allow women greater freedom. These differences may cause stress within the family and have a negative effect on the women's adaptation.

In chapters 4 we report no effects of age on acculturation and in chapter 5 we present minor effects on adaptation. In this chapter we explore whether age affects the relationship between acculturation and adaptation. Because of inconclusive previous results, we formulated no hypothesis.

Gender

Evidence on gender differences in acculturation, particularly with respect to identity development, is largely inconclusive. Whereas some studies have reported differences between immigrant men and women in the strength of cultural identities (Abu-Rabia, 1997; Eisikovits, 2000; Liebkind 1993, 1996a), many investigations have failed to find gender differences (e.g., Nesdale, Rooney, & Smith, 1997). As noted earlier, Liebkind (1996a) contended that female adults from traditional cultures are the main carriers of these cultures. Other studies (e.g., Tang & Dion, 1999), however, suggest that this position of female immigrants is combined with more traditionalist acculturation attitudes and expectations in male immigrants, suggesting that the gender issue has not been resolved, either with respect to cultural identity or with respect to a broader field of acculturation topics. We therefore did not formulate a hypothesis with respect to gender.

In chapter 4 we report that gender had a modest relationship to acculturation attitudes and experiences. Girls were more likely than boys to endorse integration strategies and to be characterized by the integrated profile; they also reported greater use of the national language. In contrast, boys were more likely to be characterized by the diffuse profile. They also reported higher levels of perceived discrimination. In chapter 5 we report a slightly better psychological adaptation for boys than for girls and a better sociocultural adaptation for girls.

Generation and Length of Residence

Whether persons are first- or second-generation immigrants is also related to acculturation and adaptation. Immigrants generally arrive in a new country with a strong sense of their national or cultural origin and with varying degrees of willingness to adopt the identity of their new society (Berry & Sam, 1997; Liebkind, 2001; Phinney, 2003). Subsequent generations face identity issues associated with their sense of belonging to their ancestral culture and to their country of settlement. The longer immigrants stay in a new society, and the younger they started their acculturation, the more positively and smoothly it will proceed (Beiser et al., 1988; Liebkind, 1996a).

In chapter 4 we report that with longer residence, national identity, national language proficiency and usage, and social contacts with peers from the national group were all higher and the separation strategy, implying distancing from the national culture, was lower. In chapter 5 we report there was no relationship between length of residence and both forms of adaptation. In chapter 5 we also explore the immigrant paradox and show that overall first-generation immigrant adolescents did not have higher adaptation scores than second-generation immigrant youth. In some countries, however, first-generation youth had better sociocultural adaptation than second-generation youth.

In this chapter we focus on whether the relationship between acculturation and adaptation differs between first- and second-generation youth. We found only one earlier study exploring a possible differential effect of generation. Wall, Power, and Arbona (1993) showed that first-generation Mexican-American immigrant adolescents who had a stronger orientation toward the national society were more susceptible to antisocial peer pressure than first-generation Mexican-American youth who were more involved with their Mexican cultural background. The same result was not found for second-generation Mexican-American youth. This evidence is too scant to warrant the formulation of a hypothesis with respect to a possible moderating effect of generational status on the relationship between acculturation and adaptation.

SES

Some studies show that SES affects the acculturation processes. Higher levels of SES are usually accompanied by a stronger orientation toward the national society and a stronger tendency to exhibit behaviors and values that facilitate contact with members of the national society (Ward, 2001). In chapter 4 we report that adolescents whose parents had higher status occupations were more oriented toward the national culture and reported higher national language proficiency and usage. No relationship between SES and either form of adaptation was found (see chap. 5).

Research exploring the moderating effect of SES for the relationship between acculturation and adaptation is scarce. An exception is the study by Shen and Takeuchi (2001), which showed that SES moderates the relationship between acculturation and depressive symptoms. Chinese-Americans with higher scores on an acculturation factor (a combination mainly of language usage, generation, and proportion of life spent in the United States, with higher scores reflecting higher levels of "Americanization") experienced more stress but only if they had lower SES. Shen and Takeuchi found that higher SES serves as a buffer against stress. In the ICSEY study, SES was assessed by parental occupational status. Because research evidence is inconclusive, we did not formulate a research hypothesis about the moderating effect of SES on the relationship between acculturation and adaptation.

Ethnic Composition of the Neighborhood

The possible influence of the neighborhood ethnic composition has received attention in empirical studies and theoretical analyses, which all point to the relevance of context (cf. Birman et al., 2002; Mollenkopf, 2000; Nguyen et al., 1999). For instance, Birman et al. (2002) suggested that the roles of ethnic and national identities in the adaptation of immigrants are linked to the acculturative demands of both the overall community context and the various life spheres within that context.

In chapter 4 we report that where the neighborhood was largely or exclusively made up of members of the adolescent's own group, ethnic language usage was high and social contacts were largely within one's own group. Moreover, the ethnic profile predominated in such neighborhoods. We found no relationship between the neighborhood ethnic composition and youths' psychological well-being and their social adjustment.

Schnittker (2002) showed that for Chinese immigrants in the United States the relationship between acculturation and adaptation outcomes, particularly self-esteem, varies with the ethnic composition of particular activity settings or of the neighborhood in which they live. English language use was related more positively to self-esteem in predominantly non-Chinese neighborhoods, whereas Chinese cultural participation was more positively related to self-esteem in predominantly Chinese neighborhoods. Birman et al. (2002) treated contexts from the perspective of immigrants as settings of demands. Using this interpretation in the Schnittker study, we can infer that complying with the demand to use English in the non-Chinese setting makes one feel good, whereas in the predominantly Chinese neighborhood complying with the demand to participate in neighborhood cultural activities makes one feel good. Based on this model of compliance we formed the following hypothesis.

Hypothesis 3: The (positive) relationship between ethnic orientation and psychological adaptation is stronger for adolescents living in a neighborhood predominantly of one's own group than for youth living in ethnically more diverse neighborhoods.

Cultural Diversity

As proposed in chapter 1, the ICSEY project was partly inspired by the notion that a country's level of immigration and cultural diversity and its policy with respect to cultural diversity would interact with identity choices and adaptation. National policies supporting multiculturalism would be expected to allow immigrants the option of being bicultural, and the choice of this option should have an impact on well-being (Grosfoguel, 1997; Icduygu, 1996). Direct evidence for links between policies and ethnic identity, however, is weak. Some studies show that the decisive factors for identity formation and psychological adaptation are not national policies but actual living circumstances (e.g., dispersal vs. high local concentration of a particular group), personal relationships (with family, peers), and activity settings (school, the neighborhood) (Crul, 2000; Gold, 1992; Keaton, 1999). These circumstances may be independent of the national policies (Oriol, 1989). However, national immigration policies may also have an impact on immigrants' well-being. Bourhis et al. (1997) suggest that a country's immigration level and immigration policy reflect the majority's attitudes toward immigrants. Both policy and attitudes may influence immigrants' attitudes and interethnic contacts and thus have an impact on individual immigrants' well-being.

We propose that there are some relationships between characteristics of the society of settlement and the adaptation of immigrant youth that transcend specific ethnocultural groups and countries. We focused on two variables: cultural diversity and diversity policy. Cultural diversity combines four country scores for diversity that were introduced in chapter 2: the percentage of immigrants in the population, the index of ethnolinguistic fractionalization (Inglehart, 1997), Sterling's (1974) ethnic diversity index, and the index of cultural homogeneity (Kurian, 2001). Diversity policy is a three-way classification used by Banting and Kymlicka (2004) and was introduced in chapter 2.

In this chapter we analyze the impact of diversity on the various measures of intercultural experiences and adaptation developed in the previous chapters guided by the following hypothesis.

Hypothesis 4a: Youth living in societies with higher levels of cultural diversity experience better psychological adaptation than youth living in societies with lower levels of cultural diversity.

Hypotheses 4b: Youth living in societies with national policies supporting cultural diversity experience better psychological adaptation than youth living in societies that are less supportive of cultural diversity.

MODEL TESTING: VARIABLES AND GENERAL PRINCIPLES

Most variables included in the data analyses stem from self-report measures. However, some of the context variables, particularly levels of cultural diversity and diversity policy, stem from additional sources of information about the migrants and their countries of settlement that could have a bearing on acculturation processes. In our analyses we consider these sets of variables separately. In this chapter we report analyses at the individual level. Apart from analyses using cultural diversity scores, the scores included in the analyses were standardized within country and ethnic group to avoid confounding country and group differences. The analyses involving cultural diversity scores were conducted with factor scores based on adolescents' raw scores.

Variables Included in Model Testing

Only complete cases were included in the structural equation modeling (SEM) presented later in the chapter. As a consequence, statistics such as sample sizes and factor loadings are not identical to those presented in previous chapters.

Demographics

The demographic variables used in the analyses in this chapter were age, gender, generation (first-and second-generation immigrants; the latter include youth who were born in the new society or arrived before the age of seven), and SES (measured in terms of parents' highest level of occupational status).

Acculturation Experiences

Perceived discrimination at the individual level was the only measure of direct acculturation experiences employed. Whereas perceived discrimination can be seen as both a cause and a result of the acculturation process, there is sufficient empirical ground for treating perceived discrimination as a predictor variable that affects many immigrants along similar lines. In this chapter we deal with perceived discrimination as a predictor variable.

Acculturation Process

Several variables were used for measuring the acculturation process. These variables are introduced in chapters 3 and 4. The constructs of ethnic and national identity and acculturation attitudes are often used interchangeably (e.g., Nguyen et al., 1999). However, in this study, the term *ethnic identity* is used to refer to the aspect of acculturation that focuses on the subjective sense of belonging to one's own ethnic group or culture (Phinney, 1990). In an earlier publication (Phinney, Horenczyk et al., 2001), we showed that Berry's (1990, 1997) model of acculturation is a useful starting point for understanding variation in ethnic and national identities and their interrelationships.

We conducted exploratory factor analyses to find a small set of factors underlying the variety of acculturation variables. Comparable analyses are presented in chapter 4. In contrast to the analyses in chapter 4, here we included only immigrant adolescents who had scores for all variables in the theoretical model tested in this chapter. There are fewer adolescents than those included in the earlier analyses, and the outcomes were different. The factor analyses allowed us to identify unifactorial subsets of scales. The selection of variables was based on theoretical considerations such as the one about acculturation and cultural identity presented in the preceding paragraph; an exploration of the correlations between variables presented in chapter 4; and statistical criteria such as eigenvalues, percentage of explained variance, and factor loadings.

The first factor analysis involved an ethnic orientation. This factor was based on ethnic identity, the obligations subscale of the family relationships scale, and the acculturation attitude of separation (eigenvalue = 1.390; 46.3% explained variance). This factor refers to various aspects of relationships or identification with an immigrant adolescents' own ethnic culture. Higher scores mean a stronger orientation toward one's own group.

The second factor analysis involved national orientation. At the individual level, the factor was made up of national identity and assimilation attitude (eigenvalue = 1.171; 58.6% explained variance). This factor refers to various aspects of relationships or identification with the national culture. Higher scores mean a stronger orientation toward the national society.

The third factor represents an integration orientation; the factor was made up of the acculturation attitudes of integration and marginalization (eigenvalue = 1.290; 64.5% explained variance). This factor combined attitudes toward both the ethnic and the national cultures. Higher scores indicate positive attitudes to both cultures (i.e., more integration and less marginalization).

The fourth factor analysis involved ethnic behaviors. The following scales constituted a single factor: frequency of social contact with peers (either from adolescents' own ethnic group or the national group), ethnic language proficiency, and national language proficiency (eigenvalue = 1.378; 34.5% explained variance). Higher scores indicate more contacts with ethnic peers and a higher proficiency in the ethnic language, whereas lower scores indicate a stronger orientation toward friends of the national group and a higher proficiency in the national language.

Adaptation Outcomes

Self-esteem, psychological problems, and life satisfaction represented psychological adaptation; school adjustment and behavior problems represented sociocultural adaptation. The analyses presented in chapter 5 confirm this distinction. The scale scores for psychological problems contributed to both components, but more strongly to the psychological adaptation component than to the sociocultural adaptation component. Therefore, psychological problems were included in psychological adaptation. New analyses were conducted for both kinds of adaptation separately. The psychological adaptation factor was based on three scales: self-esteem, life satisfaction, and psychological problems (eigenvalue = 2.730; 57.7% explained variance). Higher scores indicate greater well-being.

The sociocultural adaptation factor was based on two scale scores (behavior problems and school adjustment; eigenvalue = 1.297; 64.8% explained variance). Higher scores indicate better sociocultural adaptation.

The factor analyses allowed us to combine most of the measures presented in earlier chapters into factor scores. Exceptions were the scale dealing with language usage and the family relationships subscale referring to adolescents' rights. The small correlations with the other scales suggest that these scales may be related to other concepts not studied here. In accordance with our intention to keep our basic model as simple as possible, we did not include these variables.

Cultural Diversity

As stated earlier, the cultural diversity score is based on four variables: percentage of immigrants in the population, index of ethnolinguistic fractionalization (Inglehart, 1997), Sterling's (1974) ethnic diversity index, and index of cultural homogeneity (Kurian, 2001). An exploratory factor analysis (PCA) showed that the four variables all loaded on a single factor labeled *cultural diversity* (eigenvalue = 3.326; 83.16% variance explained). Bivariate correlations among the variables ranged from .46 to .89. However, because not all indexes were available for all participating countries, we did not use factor scores but rather computed for each country a mean of at least three of the four indexes (standardized across countries). At the individual level, all adolescents received their own country's cultural diversity score.

To explore the relationships among cultural diversity, perceived discrimination, the acculturation process, and adaptation outcomes, we repeated the factor analyses of chapter 4 and 5, now with the raw scores, yielding scores standardized across countries. The outcomes of these analyses are presented in Appendix D. Percentages of explained variance varied between 38.4 (ethnic behaviors) and

67.9 (sociocultural adaptation). The interpretations of the factors are similar to those presented earlier.

THE THEORETICAL MODEL: THE RELATIONSHIPS AMONG INTERCULTURAL VARIABLES AND ADAPTATION

The theoretical model representing the expected relationships among intercultural variables and adaptation variables is presented in Fig. 6.1. The project focuses on the total process of acculturation. The overarching construct of acculturation can be divided into constituent constructs, some of which are input variables and others are output variables. More specifically, the four factors described earlier (national orientation, ethnic orientation, integration, and ethnic behaviors) are assumed to precede the outcome variables (sociocultural adaptation and psychological adaptation). Perceived discrimination is at the top right corner; it is considered a basic starting point of the acculturation experiences of the immigrants.

It should be clear that the relationships proposed among the variables are a deliberate simplification of the complex reality of cultural adaptation in the acculturation process. For example, it is assumed here that perceived discrimination is an

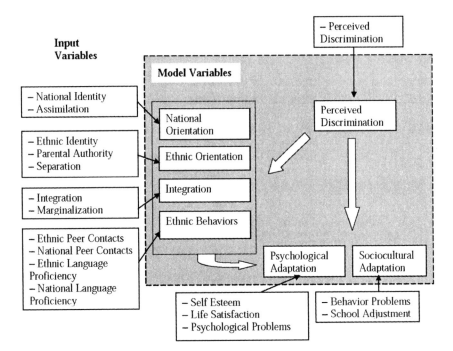

FIG. 6.1. The basic model: The expected relationships among perceived discrimination (antecedent), acculturation (intermediate) and adaptation (outcome) variables are given in the rectangle labeled "Model variables," and the scales used to measure the model variables are presented in the box called "Input variables."

antecedent variable. In practice, this variable may also be the result of acculturation experiences over time. In this sense, the whole acculturation process as outlined in Fig. 6.1 can be seen as a recurring loop. Similarly, although the integration factor may have an impact on outcome variables, the relationship may also be in the opposite direction. Thus, Fig. 6.1 may not be exhaustive and may leave out important feedback loops. However, our research design does not allow for an accurate estimation of feedback loops and mutual causation.

TESTING THE MODEL: OUTCOMES

As a first step in the analyses, we compared the relative importance of the three levels of data (individual, ethnic group, and country) to determine which data level is most important in explaining the data. Are differences in, say, psychological adaptation mainly due to individual, group, or county differences? To answer such questions, we estimated the percentage of variance attributable to each level, using country of residence and group as random factors and the psychological variables as dependent variables. The results are presented in Table 6.1.

From the percentages in the table it is clear that the major source of variation is individual differences. However, orientation toward one's own group and ethnic behaviors showed sizable differences across cultural groups. Country is a slightly more important source of variance than ethnic group for integration, orientation toward the national group, and both adaptation variables.

Intercultural Aspects of Acculturation and Adaptation Outcomes

We initially tested the model presented in the preceding section, using the Amos SEM program (Arbuckle, 2003) but did not obtain an acceptable fit. One reason may be that the four variables (national orientation, ethnic orientation, integration, and ethnic behaviors, as presented in Fig. 6.1) shared a substantial amount of variance, as suggested earlier (p. 151). To overcome this problem, we defined a latent variable

TABLE 6.1
The Percentage of Variation in Scores Due to Country, Ethnocultural Group, and Individuals, for Immigrant Youth ($N = 4,767$)

Dependent Variable	Country	Group	Individual
Perceived discrimination	0	6	94
Ethnic orientation	1	20	79
National orientation	7	5	89
Integration	3	1	95
Ethnic behaviors	0	32	68
Psychological adaptation	4	0	95
Sociocultural adaptation	3	1	95

called *ethnic contact* based on the four intercultural variable factors. The four original intercultural factors showed the following loadings for this latent variable (see the final outcome model in Fig. 6.2[1]): orientation toward own group, .40; orientation toward the national group, –.33; integration did not contribute; ethnic behaviors had a fixed loading of 1 in the nonstandardized model of Fig. 6.1 and a loading of .85 in the standardized model. The standardized loadings are represented in Fig. 6.2 with dotted lines. Higher values indicate that immigrant adolescents are more oriented toward their own group and less toward the national group.

The proportion of variance explained by the various variables was 72.9% for ethnic behaviors, 3% for integration, 16.1% for orientation toward own group, 10.9% for orientation toward national group, 1.19% for ethnic contact, 11.2% for sociocultural adaptation, and 22% for psychological adaptation.

The final empirical model presented in Fig. 6.2 follows the logic and structure of the original theoretical model (Fig. 6.1). However, a few modifications were needed to obtain an acceptable fit. A new latent variable labeled *ethnic contact* was added. Although three of the intercultural factors (national orientation, ethnic orientation, and ethnic behaviors) seem to affect psychological adaptation indirectly through this new latent variable, two of these factors also have direct effects on

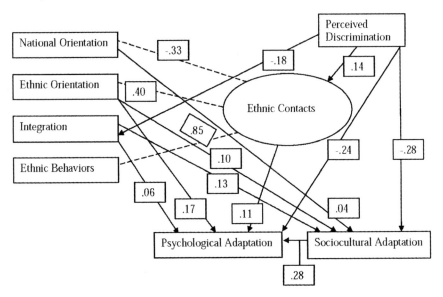

FIG. 6.2. Test of the theoretical model specifying relations between intercultural variables and adaptation outcomes at the individual level; values shown are standardized regression weights.

---

[1]All of the coefficients of Fig.6.2 were statistically significant ($p < .05$). The overall fit of the model presented in Fig. 6.2 was very good, $\chi^2(N = 4,767; df = 4) = 7.123; p = 0.13$; adjusted goodness of fit index (AGFI) = .997; non-normed fit index (NNFI) = .995; root mean squared error of approximation (RMSEA) = .013). The loss of participants is due to missing data, as the analysis involves only full cases.

both of the adaptation outcomes measured. This means that in addition to the common effect through the latent super variable *ethnic contact*, they also have some unique effects on adaptation.

The model generally provides support for our hypotheses. Hypothesis 1a states that a combined involvement and identification with both the national and the ethnic cultures will be associated with more positive adaptation outcomes than a preference for either the national or the ethnic culture alone. In support of this hypothesis, we found that integration had a positive impact on both adaptation scores. This effect was slightly stronger on sociocultural adaptation than on psychological adaptation.

Hypothesis 1b states that a national orientation will have a stronger impact than ethnic orientation on sociocultural adaptation. We found that orientation toward the national group had a positive effect on sociocultural adaptation only. But its effect on sociocultural adaptation was weaker than that of ethnic orientation. Hence, we found no support for this hypothesis.

Hypothesis 1c states that ethnic orientation will have a stronger impact than national orientation on psychological adaptation of immigrant youth. We found that ethnic orientation has an effect on both types of adaptation, but as expected, the effect on psychological adaptation is stronger than the one on sociocultural adaptation. The ethnic behaviors factor did not have a direct impact on adaptation outcomes but did have an indirect effect, via ethnic contacts. As can be seen from Fig. 6.2, ethnic contact had a significant impact on psychological adaptation but did not have a significant relationship with sociocultural adaptation. The results suggest that adolescents' orientation toward their own group is more important for their psychological well-being than for their sociocultural adaptation.

As shown in Fig. 6.2, perceived discrimination negatively affected psychological adaptation and contributed to poorer sociocultural adaptation. This supports our second hypothesis. It is interesting that perceived discrimination seemed to increase immigrants' general orientation toward their own group, as is expressed in the arrow running from perceived discrimination to the latent variable ethnic contacts. At the same time, perceived discrimination had a negative influence on integration, that is, on the simultaneous orientation toward both the national society and one's own group. Perceived discrimination was an important variable vis-à-vis the acculturation outcomes of our study. In our results, perceived discrimination showed a stronger relationship with outcome variables than any other variable.

The final path to be discussed in Fig. 6.2 went from sociocultural to psychological adaptation.[2] This finding suggests that the indicators of psychological adaptation such as self-esteem and life satisfaction are influenced by adaptation outcomes that contribute to the factor score for sociocultural adaptation (e.g.,

---

[2]It was revealing during the analyses that drawing an arrow from psychological to sociocultural adaptation had a strong negative influence on the model fit. It was only when the arrow went from sociocultural to psychological adaptation that the fit was good.

behavior problems) and that psychological adaptation can be seen as the final outcome in the model, containing or reflecting the psychological consequences of the acculturation experiences that were measured, as well as of sociocultural adaptation.

The Impact of Background Variables

To explore and test whether the relationship between intercultural variables and adaptation variables is moderated by demographic and contextual variables, we conducted MANOVAs with the scores for psychological and sociocultural adaptation as dependent variables. Perceived discrimination (standardized within country and ethnic group), integration, ethnic orientation, national orientation, and ethnic behaviors were independent variables. In each analysis we included one of five background variables: age in years, generation (first- or second-generation immigrant), gender, parents' occupational status (unskilled, skilled, white collar, and professional), and neighborhood composition (level of ethnic homogeneity). The analyses yielded three statistically significant interactions[3] ($p < .01$), all with respect to gender. These were: Gender × Perceived Discrimination, Gender × Ethnic Behavior, and Gender × National Orientation. We did not find a significant interaction effect for any other background variables, meaning that we did not find support for Hypothesis 3 about the moderating effect of neighborhood.

To interpret the findings for gender, we repeated the MANOVAS for males and females separately and with perceived discrimination, ethnic behavior, and orientation toward the national group as covariates to find the extent to which these acculturation variables would explain variance in psychological and sociocultural adaptation. The outcomes are presented in Table 6.2.

Generally, the impact of acculturation variables or factors on adaptation outcomes was stronger for boys than for girls. The differential effect of gender is most apparent from the differences with respect to the relationship between perceived discrimination and sociocultural adaptation; the relationship is stronger for boys than for girls (η^2s = .10 vs. .06). A similar gender effect is apparent from the impact of ethnic behaviors on psychological adaptation (η^2 = .02 for boys and .00 for girls) and from the impact of national orientation on psychological adaptation (η^2 = .03 for boys and .01 for girls).

Cultural Diversity

The country scores for cultural diversity (standardized across all countries and based on the four indexes presented in chapter 2 and earlier in this chapter) and country ratings for diversity policy (based on the three-way classification presented in chapter 2, and earlier in this chapter) are presented in Table 2.1.

---

[3]We were only interested in the first-order interaction terms between independent variables and factors, to find out whether the regression lines describing the relationship between an independent variable and an outcome variable would run parallel across the levels of a variable.

TABLE 6.2

MANOVA Examining the Effect of Acculturation Variables on Psychological and Sociocultural Adaptation, for Boys and Girls Separately

	Male	Female		Male		Female	
	Wilks' Lambda $F_{(2, 2227)}$	Wilks' Lambda $F_{(2, 2520)}$		$F_{(1, 2228)}$	η^2	$F_{(1, 2521)}$	η^2
Perceived discrimination	220.00***	165.60***	Psych. ad.	313.86***	.123	285.42***	.102
			Socioc. ad.	254.13***	.102	157.71***	.059
Ethnic behaviors	32.86***	.54	Psych. ad.	44.35***	.02	.51	
			Socioc. ad.	6.10*	.003	.93	
Orientation toward national group	54.16***	11.06***	Psych. ad.	77.52***	.034	22.11***	.009
			Socioc. ad.	7.44*	.003	2.55	.001

Note. MANOVA = multivariate analysis of variance. $*p < .05$. $***p < .001$.

Multiple regression analyses were conducted to explore the impact of cultural diversity on acculturation variables and adaptation outcomes. To control for country- and group-related sample differences with respect to adolescents' demographic characteristics we used a stepwise procedure.[4] Table 6.3 presents the outcomes of the analyses.[5]

Generally, the impact of cultural diversity is absent or weak. The (four) weak effects are nevertheless interesting. First, in countries with higher levels of cultural diversity, immigrant youth report slightly higher levels of discrimination than in countries with lower levels of cultural diversity. This finding suggests that greater diversity in a society offers the opportunity for greater discrimination against members of the various cultural groups; conversely, when there is little diversity, there can be fewer such opportunities. Second, higher levels of cultural diversity also correspond to a slightly stronger involvement with peers from one's own ethnic group and language.

TABLE 6.3
Multiple Regression Analysis Examining the Impact of Cultural Diversity on Acculturation Variables and Adaptation Outcomes

Dependent Variable	β	R^2	F
Residual perceived discrimination	.08**	.01	19.50**
Residual ethnic orientation	−.01	.00	.07
Residual national orientation	.23**	.05	192.51**
Residual integration	.01	.00	.11
Residual ethnic behaviors	.08**	.01	21.58**
Residual psychological adaptation	−.08**	.01	19.56**
Residual sociocultural adaptation	.01	.00	.16

$**p < .01$.

[4]First, we conducted regression analyses in which perceived discrimination and each of the factor scores (ethnic orientation, national orientation, integration, and ethnic behaviors) was used as dependent variables (standardized across countries) and five demographic variables as predictors (adolescents' age, gender, proportion of life spent in the country of residence, neighborhood ethnic composition, and adolescent-reported parents' occupational status). For each of the dependent variables we saved the unstandardized residual scores. These were used as dependent variables in consecutive regression analyses in which the cultural diversity score was used as the only predictor. The outcome of this two-step procedure represents the unique contribution of cultural diversity to the prediction of perceived discrimination, the acculturation process variables, and the adaptation variables after taking into account the influence of the specified demographic variables.

[5]The relationship between demographic variables and the intercultural and adaptation variables has already been dealt with in chapters 4 and 5 and was summarized in the Introduction to this chapter. Although for this chapter we recalculated the scores (the actual sample size was 3,399 because of data loss due to incomplete cases), the differences are small and do not warrant a new presentation.

Third, at the same time, in the countries with higher levels of cultural diversity immigrant youth are more strongly oriented toward the national group than in countries with lower levels of cultural diversity. This is clearly the strongest effect found. The combination of a stronger orientation in more diverse societies toward both their ethnic group and the national society (which we have termed the *integration orientation*) might indicate that greater diversity provides a salient context in which youth feel more able to orient themselves toward both groups rather than having to choose between them.

Finally, higher levels of cultural diversity corresponded to slightly lower levels of psychological adaptation. This latter finding begs for an explanation, as generally higher levels of cultural diversity were expected to have a positive impact on acculturation experiences and adaptation outcomes. To examine whether the findings with respect to perceived discrimination might explain the negative impact of cultural diversity on psychological adaptation, we repeated the regression analyses with perceived discrimination as a covariate. Perceived discrimination explained 11.3% of variance and cultural diversity 0.2% ($\beta = -.04$). After taking perceived discrimination into account, the impact of cultural diversity on psychological adaptation weakens (from 0.6% to 0.2%). This lends some support to our explanation of the negative relationship between cultural diversity and psychological adaptation. The finding suggests that it is not so much cultural diversity but the elevated levels of perceived discrimination accompanying the higher levels of cultural diversity that negatively impact psychological adaptation. Nevertheless, the overall findings on adaptation do not support the hypothesis that higher levels of cultural diversity correspond to more positive adaptation.

We explored two other possible explanations for the unexpected negative impact of cultural diversity on psychological adaptation, but we found no additional explanations for the finding. First, although we have already considered perceived discrimination as a covariate, we can also explore its role as a moderator variable. If there is a lot of prejudice and discrimination in addition to a high level of cultural diversity, the result for adaptation would likely to be negative, whereas absence of discrimination in combination with high cultural diversity could be beneficial for adaptation. Hence, perceived discrimination might function as a moderator of the relationship between cultural diversity and psychological adaptation.

The second possibility concerns the role of individuals' orientations toward the national culture as a moderator of the relationship between cultural diversity and psychological adaptation: When the orientation toward the national society is strong, high cultural diversity may be related to less positive psychological adaptation if this also implies that cultural diversity is seen as a threat to one's own social position (e.g., the view that "other immigrant groups spoil my own group's and my personal opportunities in my new society"), whereas a weak orientation toward the national group, combined with strong cultural diversity, may be related to a more positive psychological adaptation. We did not find support for either of these alternatives.

We may conclude that a country's cultural diversity is positively related to acculturation processes, particularly to national orientation in combination with an involvement with one's own ethnic group and ethnic language (ethnic behaviors), but negatively related to psychological adaptation, although the relationships are generally weak.

We also explored the moderating effect of cultural diversity on the relationship between acculturation factors and adaptation. We followed the same procedure as depicted earlier for the background variables. Statistically significant interactions were found between cultural diversity on the one hand, and ethnic orientation, national orientation, ethnic behaviors, and perceived discrimination on the other hand. These interactions indicate that these latter variables have a different impact on psychological and sociocultural adaptation depending on the level of cultural diversity of the countries of residence of the immigrant adolescents. However, the contribution to explained variance in adaptation scores was generally low, with a maximum of 0.9%. In comparing the participating countries, we did not find an interpretable pattern.

The possible impact of diversity policy on acculturation and adaptation also was analyzed with multiple regression analyses using the same unstandardized residual scores (see note 4) for perceived discrimination, the acculturation process factors, and the adaptation variables as dependent variables, and the rating for diversity policy as the only predictor. The outcome of this procedure represents the unique contribution of cultural diversity policy ratings to the prediction of perceived discrimination, the acculturation process variables, and the adaptation variables after taking into account the influence of the specified demographic variables. Table 6.4 presents the outcomes.

As with the impact of cultural diversity, the impact of the diversity policy is generally weak or absent. Pluralism policy does not have an impact on perceived discrimination and ethnic behavior. Neither does it affect psychological adaptation, whereas we had expected a positive impact. However, countries in which pol-

TABLE 6.4
Multiple Regression Analysis Examining the Impact of Cultural Diversity Policy on Acculturation Variables and Adaptation Outcomes

Dependent variable	β	R^2	F
Residual perceived discrimination	−.03	.00	2.10
Residual ethnic orientation	.04*	.00	6.16*
Residual national orientation	.11**	.01	39.60**
Residual integration	.07**	.01	16.72**
Residual ethnic behaviors	.03	.00	2.52
Residual psychological adaptation	−.02	.00	1.99
Residual sociocultural adaptation	.07**	.01	15.78

$*p < .05.$ $**p < .01.$

icy is more supportive of cultural diversity tend to have immigrant youth who have an integration orientation—that is, they combine a stronger orientation toward their own group with a stronger orientation toward the national group—and who have higher integration scores. Moreover, immigrant youth in these countries tend to have higher scores for sociocultural adaptation than immigrant youth living in countries characterized by policies that are less supportive of cultural diversity. Overall, it appears that diversity policy supports a preference for both an integration orientation and better sociocultural adaptation.

The exploration of possible moderator effects of diversity policy did not yield any relevant findings (a maximum of .2% explained variance and no interpretable patterns).

SUMMARY AND CONCLUSIONS

In this chapter we test the assumption that the combined involvement and identification with the national and the ethnic cultures would be associated with more positive adaptation outcomes for immigrant youth than involvement and identification with either the national or the ethnic culture alone (Berry, 1997; Howard, 1998; LaFromboise et al., 1993; Phinney & Devich-Navarro, 1997). Using the distinction between psychological and sociocultural adaptation of immigrants (Ward, 2001), we assumed in accordance with previous research that orientation toward the national group would have a stronger impact than orientation toward one's own ethnic group on sociocultural adaptation, whereas the opposite would be true of psychological adaptation.

Among the four factors examined in relation to adaptation, an ethnic orientation made the strongest contribution to adaptation. It had direct positive effects on both types of adaptation, with a stronger effect for psychological than for sociological adaptation. Second in importance was the integration factor, which also contributed positively to both types of adaptation. However, the effect of the integration factor was stronger for sociocultural adaptation than for psychological adaptation.

A national orientation made a modest positive contribution to sociocultural adaptation, in accordance with previous research (Ward, 2001). Its role in psychological adaptation was less clear. It was negatively associated with ethnic contact, which in turn was positively linked to psychological adaptation, so that overall a stronger national orientation was associated with poorer psychological adaptation.

The results of the model testing, as described earlier, show that the ethnic orientation factor is positively related to sociocultural adaptation. This result may appear to conflict with findings reported in chapter 5, which show that youth with an ethnic profile have relatively low scores for sociocultural adaptation. Similarly, the current chapter shows a positive relationship between the national orientation factor and sociocultural adaptation, whereas in chapter 5 we report that youth with a national profile had relatively low scores for sociocultural adaptation.

This apparent contradiction is the result of different analytical methods, samples, and variable used in the two analyses The four profiles in chapter 5 are compared in terms of mean scores, that is, the level of adaptation, whereas the model tested in the current chapter is a correlational analysis, that is, the relative positioning of each individual with respect to several variables. Furthermore, the profiles refer to subgroups of individuals with a particular combination of scores for all intercultural variables, whereas the factor scores used in this chapter deal with all immigrant youth, and each factor score refers to a small subset of variables combined in a factor score.

The results of our study also indicate that the psychological adaptation of immigrant youth is dependent on their sociocultural adaptation; behavioral problems and poor school adjustment of immigrant adolescents clearly contributed to lower self-esteem and life satisfaction among the immigrant youth studied. This result supports previous studies that indicate that, among immigrant youth, psychological and sociocultural adaptation may be intertwined. By far the most commonly reported pattern of mental health problems among immigrant adolescents in Western European societies is behavioral deviance in the form of antisocial behavior and conduct disorders (Aronowitz, 1992; Liebkind, Jasinskaja-Lahti, & Solheim, 2004).

We explored possible moderator effects of various background variables such as age, generation, gender, and SES on the relationship between intercultural factors and the adaptation factors. We found that only gender had a moderating effect; the relationship between acculturation experiences and processes on adaptation was stronger for boys than for girls. Although a stronger orientation toward their own group in terms of ethnic behaviors seemed to be beneficial for the adaptation of the boys, this was not the case for the girls. Perhaps an explanation may not be found in the gender differences as such but in the dominant attitudes toward gender equality in Western societies. Immigrant girls whose ethnic behavior is more oriented toward their own group, also with respect to gender inequality, may deviate more visibly than boys from the dominant attitude toward gender equality. They are likely to be seen as either supporting gender inequality or as oppressed. As a result, they might experience more stress, which negatively affects their adaptation. This difference in attitudes between the broader society and the immigrant girls toward gender equality may counter the otherwise beneficial effect that a community of co-ethnics tends to have on the adaptation of immigrant girls (Liebkind, 1996a).

Some contexts support the adaptation of immigrants better than others. This applies at the local as well as the national levels (Schnittker, 2002). With respect to an impact of context at the local level, we assumed that adaptation would be fostered by a match between the acculturation orientations of the immigrant youth and the ethnic composition of the neighborhood in which they live. Our data did not confirm our assumption regarding the impact of the local context, specifically with respect to the ethnic composition of the neighborhood.

At the national level we assumed that the psychological adaptation of immigrant youth would be positively affected by the cultural diversity and diversity policy in the country of settlement. This assumption was partially supported. The overall cultural diversity of the country of settlement did have some specific direct effects on acculturation and adaptation variables. In keeping with our assumptions, we found that both cultural diversity and diversity policy were directly related to both an increased orientation toward the national group and stronger involvement with one's own ethnic group and ethnic language. This combined effect indicates an integrated orientation.

Not in keeping with our assumptions is the finding that higher levels of cultural diversity coincide with lowered psychological adaptation, as well as with increased experiences of discrimination. We found some indications that the lowered psychological adaptation in culturally more diverse societies may be due to the increased experiences of discrimination in those societies, but we could not completely explain the negative impact of cultural diversity on psychological adaptation. We explored other alternative explanations as well but found no satisfactory solution. Although we found no relationship between diversity policy and psychological adaptation, we did find that immigrant youth in societies supporting a policy of cultural diversity reported slightly better sociocultural adaptation than youth in societies less supportive of such policy.

One aspect of the context is the discrimination that immigrants experience. In this study, as well as in other studies (Liebkind et al., 2004; Shrake & Rhee, 2004), perceived discrimination has turned out to be strongly negatively related to various aspects of young immigrants' well-being. As we have acknowledged, our explanatory model is a simplified one, and the whole acculturation process can be seen as a recurring loop or a circle, where causes and consequences and even mere coincidences are difficult to disentangle. This is particularly clear with respect to perceived discrimination. Clearly, the subjective interpretation of events as discriminatory (i.e., perceiving oneself as a target or victim of discrimination by members of a dominant group) is one of the major acculturative stressors associated with decreased well-being among immigrants (Berry, 1997; Noh & Kaspar, 2003). According to our results, not only does perceived discrimination go along with reduced psychological and sociocultural adaptation, but it also is associated with a reduced orientation toward integration. In addition, we found a positive relationship between perceived discrimination and ethnic contact (a variable combining variance from the three factors of national orientation, ethnic orientation, and ethnic behaviors), implying that those experiencing much discrimination orient themselves primarily to their own group.

This latter relationship can be explained in at least two ways. Ethnic behaviors and discrimination experiences usually reinforce each other. Whereas immigrants perceiving discrimination may stick only with each other to receive social support, members of the larger society may, as a consequence, increasingly consider them to be outsiders who are unwilling to fit in (Birman & Trickett, 2001; Birman et al., 2002; Jasinskaja-Lahti et al., in press).

The relationship can be explained also with the rejection-identification model of attributions to prejudice presented by Branscombe and her colleagues

(Branscombe et al., 1999; Schmitt, Branscombe, Kobrynowicz, & Owen, 2002). According to this model, perceived discrimination in disadvantaged groups leads to increased identification with one's group. In addition, perceived prejudice tends to encourage minority members' hostility toward the majority group (Branscombe et al., 1999), which in turn may increase experiences of discrimination.

Taken together, our results point to the fact that the acculturation process is a complex web of mutual relationships among contextual, intercultural, and adaptation variables. Among immigrant youth, a truly bicultural orientation is beneficial for their sociocultural adaptation, and sociocultural adaptation in turn enhances their psychological well-being. Psychological well-being is also enhanced by a strong orientation toward one's ethnic group. The adolescents' own ethnic group evidently provides the social support needed to buffer the negative effects of perceived discrimination, as more discrimination is associated with a stronger ethnic orientation. However, in the long run, this could entail a vicious circle, increasing discrimination further and resulting in an increase in the separation or marginalization orientation of the immigrant groups. The extent to which increasing cultural diversity will lead to these unwanted outcomes, instead of supporting the beneficial effects of the bicultural orientations of the immigrants themselves, is likely to depend on the political and attitudinal climate of the societies of settlement. This climate is characterized by attitudes that vary between seeing cultural diversity as an asset and seeing it as a liability. The degree to which members of the larger society accept a multicultural ideology may ultimately prove to be the key to the successful management of a culturally diverse society (Arends-Tóth & Van de Vijver, 2003; Berry, 2001; Berry et al., 1977; Breugelmans & Van de Vijver, 2004; Schalk-Soekar, Van de Vijver, & Hoogsteder, in press).

7

Family Relationship Values of Adolescents and Parents: Intergenerational Discrepancies and Adaptation

Jean S. Phinney
California State University, Los Angeles
Paul Vedder
Leiden University

The family is a critical context for the acculturation of immigrant adolescents. Earlier chapters report on the role of contextual variables reported by adolescents, such as parental SES and neighborhood ethnic diversity, and group- or country-level factors, such as immigration history or diversity of the society of settlement. However, until now we have not considered the immediate family. The focus of the present chapter is on the values held by both adolescents and parents concerning family relationships. In particular, we examine disagreements, or discrepancies, between adolescents and parents on these values. We investigate demographic factors related to intergenerational value discrepancies between immigrant and national families and explore the relationship of value discrepancies to adolescent adaptation.

FAMILY RELATIONSHIP VALUES: CONCEPTUAL BACKGROUND

Family Relationship Values in Immigrant and National Families

In all cultures, parents socialize their children into the values and practices of their society (Whiting & Whiting, 1975). Immigrant parents bring with them the values of their culture of origin and strive to preserve them in their new environment and teach them to their children. In most cases the values they hold differ from those of the society of settlement. There is evidence that members of non-European cultures hold stronger values related to family interdependence and respect toward parents than do people of north and west European origin (Georgas, Berry,

167

Kagitcibasi, Poortinga, & van de Vijver, in press; Kagitcibasi, 1996). Immigrants from such backgrounds continue to emphasize these values (Aycan & Kanungo, 1998; Fuligni et al., 1999; Georgas, Berry, Shaw, Christakopoulos, & Mylonas, 1996; Nguyen & Williams, 1989; Phalet & Schönpflug, 2001). Adolescents in the United States from Asian and Latin American backgrounds hold stronger values regarding their obligations to assist, respect, and support their families than do adolescents from European backgrounds (Fuligni et al., 1999; Phinney, Kim-Jo, Osorio, & Vilhjalmsdottir, 2005; Phinney et al., 2000). Adolescents from cultures that emphasize family interdependence consider their household chores to be communal activities, whereas those from Western societies are more likely to believe that individual chores should be compensated (Bowes et al., 2001).

In contrast, Western childrearing practices focus less on family interdependence and more on autonomy in children and adolescents. Family structures are typically less hierarchical and more egalitarian (Greenfield, 1994; Rothbaum, Pott, Azuma, Miyake, & Weisz, 2000). Adolescents feel that they have the right to make decisions about their personal life in areas such as dating and marriage (Crocket & Silbereisen, 2000; Dekovic, 1999; Smetana & Asquith, 1994).

As a result of differences between the cultures of immigrants and the cultures of settlement, immigrant parents face the task of teaching their children the values of their culture of origin while living in a new society that holds different values. Their children are exposed to the values of their parents but also to the values of the larger society in which they live. As a result, the children may adhere less strongly to their parents' values. For example, Vietnamese adolescents in Australia endorsed traditional cultural values less than did their parents (Rosenthal et al., 1996). Vietnamese-Australian adolescents reported high levels of parental control as a source of intergenerational disagreement (Herz & Gullone, 1999). Because immigrant adolescents are socialized both in the family context and in contexts more representative of the national culture, such as schools, immigrant families may experience greater value differences between adolescents and parents than do national families, in which adolescents' and parents' values are more similar. Such value differences may be a cause of conflict in immigrant families.

However, when value discrepancies between parents and children are viewed from an acculturation perspective, one can easily make the error of attributing discrepancies solely to acculturation. In fact, value discrepancies between parents and adolescents are a developmental phenomenon reported in most cultures. In research with samples in Western countries, disagreements between adolescents and parents are common (Dekovic, 1999; Smetana, 1995; Steingberg, 1990). Fuligni (1998b) found that American adolescents from immigrant groups did not differ from nonimmigrant groups in levels of conflict and cohesion with their parents. Similar levels of conflict have been reported in samples from families in Hong Kong (Yau & Smetana, 1996). Thus, discrepancies may be part of normal developmental processes rather than an aspect of acculturation. To explore this issue, it is important to have comparable data from both immigrant and national families.

Much of the research on intergenerational differences has not surveyed parents directly but rather has relied on adolescents' reports of both their own and their parents' values (see Sam, 1995). It is therefore not clear whether reported differences between immigrant adolescents and parents are actual differences or simply adolescents' perceptions of such differences. In our data, surveys with parents allow us to compare adolescents' reported values with the parents' own reports. We explore the extent of differences between adolescents and parents within families and compare immigrant and national families. Greater intergeneration differences in values in immigrant than in national families would suggest that acculturation processes make a contribution to the development of such differences.

The data also allow us to explore whether and to what extent family values are related to the acculturation attitudes and behaviors of immigrant adolescents and parents. Prior research with immigrant families in Canada (Aycan & Kanungo, 1998) shows that parents' acculturation attitudes have an impact on socialization in the family. From chapter 4 we know that acculturation strategies vary considerably among immigrant adolescents. In this chapter we report that parents' acculturation attitudes also vary. We can therefore examine whether immigrant adolescents' and parents' acculturation attitudes are related to value discrepancies. We expected value discrepancies to be greater when parents and adolescents differ in their attitudes or preferences toward the ethnic and national cultures.

A related question is whether intergenerational discrepancies increase over time for immigrant families. Changes in values are part of the acculturation process, and both parents and children in immigrant families are likely to face pressure to shift toward the attitudes of their new culture. However, children are likely to experience broader exposure to the culture of the larger society through social interactions at school. Parents have more difficulty in learning a new language than do their children (Portes & Schauffler, 1994). As a result, children and adolescents have been found to adopt new attitudes and values more rapidly than do their parents (Buriel & De Ment, 1997; Liebkind, 1992b; Portes, 1997; Szapocznik & Kurtines, 1993). Nguyen and Williams (1989) show that parents' values did not vary with length of residence in the United States, but adolescents' values did. As a result, the intergenerational discrepancy increased with years in the United States. Similarly in the ICSEY data, we examine whether the value discrepancy between adolescents and parents was greater with longer residence.

Family Obligations and Adolescents' Rights

Two types of family relationship values were studied. *Family obligations* refer to values found in cultures stressing interdependence, which are typical of many immigrant groups. Parents are expected to be the authorities, and children should be respectful and obedient to their parents. Children should share in household chores and should live at home until they marry. In contrast, *adolescents' rights* refer to values held by most Western countries, involving increasing autonomy as children get older. For example, adolescents are seen as having the right to decide whom they may date and marry.

Intergenerational Value Discrepancies and Adaptation

Intergenerational value discrepancies are important because differences in values between parents and children can cause conflicts that lead to disruption in family cohesion and result in adjustment problems for adolescents (Smetana, 1995; Steinberg, 1990). Research with immigrant families has shown that harmonious adolescent–parent relations led to students' higher educational achievement and psychological well-being (Rumbaut, 1997). The more Vietnamese adolescents and their parents in Australia perceived themselves as having disagreements at home, the more frequently they reported having conflicts over family, school, and social activity (Rosenthal et al., 1996). Regardless of ethnocultural group, high school students in Hong Kong committed more disciplinary violations when they had greater conflicts with their mother at home (Stewart et al., 1998). These research results suggest that conflicts with parents adversely affect the adaptation of adolescents.

Intergenerational discrepancies may have different implications for families from differing backgrounds. In Western societies, disagreements between parents and adolescents may be considered part of normal developmental processes (Steinberg, 1990) and therefore not be as disruptive as in non-Western cultures that place greater value on family harmony (Markus & Lin, 1999). In cultures where norms of respect for parents prevail, differences within the family may be associated with greater problems. We explore this issue by comparing the relationship of intergenerational values discrepancies with adaptation in both immigrant and national families.

Research Questions and Hypotheses

On the basis of prior developmental research, we expected to find intergenerational value discrepancies in both immigrant and national families. We expected that values regarding family obligations would be endorsed more strongly by both immigrant and national parents than by their adolescent children, but that values related to adolescents' rights would be endorsed more strongly by adolescents than by their parents. These differences between adolescents and parents are what we refer to as *intergenerational value discrepancies.*

We also expected differences between immigrant and national families. We showed in chapter 4 that immigrant adolescents differ from national adolescents on both family obligations and adolescents' rights. We expected to find these differences also between their parents, with immigrant parents endorsing family obligations more strongly and adolescents' rights less strongly than national parents. Overall, we expected intergenerational value discrepancies to be greater in immigrant than in national families. In addition, in immigrant families, we expected the discrepancy to be greater with longer residence in the new society. We examined other factors that may influence discrepancies, including gender, age, neighborhood, and parental education.

Finally, we expected that larger value discrepancies would be associated with poorer psychological and sociocultural adaptation (controlling for relevant variables); we explored whether this relationship was stronger among immigrant than national youth. For immigrant families, we examined whether these relationships vary across acculturation profiles and whether they vary depending on original levels of values scores.

IMMIGRANT AND NATIONAL ADOLESCENTS AND THEIR PARENTS: SAMPLE AND PROCEDURES

The participants were 2,374 immigrant adolescent–parent dyads and 968 national adolescent–parent dyads (see Table 7.1). The numbers are considerably smaller than for the study as a whole because not all parents of adolescents participated.

Family relationship values were measured by 14 items that assess the two types of values, family obligations (10 items) and adolescents' rights (4 items), as described in chapter 3. Adolescents and parents answered identical questionnaire items. To explore the psychometric properties of the family obligations and the adolescent rights subscales, we compared the factor structures and the reliabilities (Cronbach's alpha) for four groups: immigrant adolescents and parents, and national adolescents and parents. Factor structures were comparable across the four groups, and reliabilities ranged between .73 and .90.

TABLE 7.1
Number of the Participating Parent–Adolescent Dyads in 10 ICSEY Nations, With Percent Females (in parentheses)

	Immigrants	Nationals
Australia	350 (68)	124 (59)
Canada	189 (59)	105 (54)
Finland	184 (54)	72 (42)
France	212 (55)	35 (63)
Germany	29 (52)	90 (62)
Netherlands	338 (49)	95 (59)
Norway	125 (54)	123 (54)
Sweden	416 (50)	132 (54)
UK	60 (43)	59 (51)
USA	471 (61)	137 (65)
Total	2,374 (55)	968 (57)

Note. ICSEY = International Comparative Study of Ethnocultural Youth.

The immigrant parents had a choice of language versions, either their ethnic language or the national language. In most countries, parents were given only one questionnaire, and these were completed either by the mother (48%), the father (20.5%), both parents (29%), or others on behalf of the parents, for example, a grandparent or aunt (2.5%). We found a small effect for the person who completed the questionnaire. With respect to family obligations and adolescents' rights, fathers would grant their children fewer rights while insisting upon more obligations from their children; mothers were less restrictive with respect to rights and less demanding with respect to obligations than were fathers. Whenever appropriate, we controlled for this effect in further analyses. In Sweden and Finland, mothers and fathers received separate questionnaires; their mean scores were computed for the present analyses.

In three countries (Israel, New Zealand, and Portugal) parents did not participate at all; hence adolescents from these countries were not included in our analyses. Parental participation rates in some countries were very low for both immigrants (e.g., 29 parents in Germany) and nationals (e.g., 35 parents in France). Given these sampling limitations, our focus was not on country or ethnic group comparisons but rather on intergenerational value discrepancies, differences in discrepancies between immigrant and national families, the factors that predict such discrepancies, and the relationship of discrepancies to adaptation. Ethnic and country comparisons are reported in chapter 8 for Vietnamese and Turks.

The proportion of adolescents with a participating parent was slightly higher for immigrant adolescents (49.4%) than for national adolescents (44.7%), and slightly higher for girls (50.8%) than for boys (44.5%). The overall mean of the parental occupation was 2.14 ($SD = 1.247$), slightly above the level of skilled workers (2.0).

There were few differences between adolescents whose parents participated and those whose parents did not participate. The average age of the adolescents with a participating parent was very similar to that of the other adolescents (15.36 and 15.35 years, respectively). The parental occupational level of immigrant adolescents with a participating parent was close to the overall sample mean, whereas the parental occupation level of the other immigrant adolescents was below the mean ($d = -.41$). The national adolescents with participating parents had the highest parental occupational level ($d = .75$), and the other national adolescents also had a mean score above the overall mean ($d = .19$). No differences were found either in generational status or in length of residence between immigrant adolescents with and without a participating parent.

Countries showed noteworthy differences in length of residence of parents; all countries differed significantly from the overall means of 15.14 ($SD = 8.19$) and 16.69 ($SD = 9.07$) years of residence for mothers and fathers, respectively. For example, the immigrant parents' length of residence in Finland and the United States was shorter than the average, whereas in France and the United Kingdom it was longer than the overall mean. These differences result from both the selection of the immigrant groups and the immigration histories in each country.

Parental reports of their occupational status were comparable to parental occupation as reported by adolescents. Parents also reported on their highest achieved level of education. The correlation between parents' occupational status and their level of education was .64, indicating considerable overlap of the two measures. Furthermore, educational level was available for more dyads than was occupational status. Hence, we used parents' education as a proxy for SES. SES was used as a control variable in this chapter and in the next chapter when dealing with intergenerational value discrepancies in Vietnamese and Turkish families. The overall mean for parents' self-reported level of education was 5.30 (SD = 1.83), just above high school completion. The immigrant parents on average had finished secondary school or high school (M = 5.00, SD = 1.83), whereas the national parents on average had some years of college education (M = 5.98, SD = 1.83).

Immigrant parents reported that their use of, and proficiency in, the ethnic language was higher than in the national language (Ms = 4.46 and 2.76, SDs = .69 and .87, respectively).

IMMIGRANT AND NATIONAL FAMILIES: SIMILARITIES AND DIFFERENCES

In chapter 4, with data from adolescents, we reported that, as expected, immigrant adolescents valued family obligations more than did national adolescents, and immigrant adolescents valued adolescents' rights less than did their national counterparts. Analyses of the parents' scores gave similar results. Immigrant parents scored higher on family obligations (M = 4.02) than did national parents (M = 3.21; η^2 = .24), and immigrant parents scored lower on adolescents' rights (M = 2.82) than did the national parents (M = 3.70; η^2 = .13).

We next examined whether and to what extent adolescents and parents differed in the endorsement of family relationship values. Analyses of mean scores for family obligations as reported by adolescents and parents showed that in both the immigrant and national families, parents believed more strongly than did their adolescents that children should fulfill certain family obligations (immigrant adolescents: M = 3.67, SD = .68; immigrant parents: M = 4.02, SD = .64, n = 2,341, Cohen's d = .53; national adolescents: M = 2.97, SD = .60; national parents: M = 3.19, SD = .62, n = 966, Cohen's d = .36).

Analyses of the mean scores for adolescents' rights as reported by adolescents and parents showed that both the immigrant and the national adolescents believed they had more rights than their parents felt they should have (immigrant adolescents: M = 3.52, SD = 1.14; immigrant parents: M = 2.84, SD = 1.06, n = 2,358, Cohen's d = .62; national adolescents: M = 4.17, SD = .99; national parents: M = 3.64, SD = .89, n = 963, Cohen's d = .56).

A central question of interest was whether immigrant families experience greater intergenerational discrepancies than do national families. For family obligations, we calculated an intergenerational discrepancy score by subtracting adolescent scores on obligations from those of parent. For adolescents' rights, we calculated intergenerational discrepancy by subtracting parent scores on rights from adolescent scores. Thus, in both cases, overall group-level discrepancy scores were positive. In these analyses we used adolescents' gender, age, and proportion of life spent in the country of residence, together with parents' level of occupation, as control variables.

For family obligations, the discrepancy score was significantly higher for immigrant families ($M = .35$) than for national families ($M = .20$; $\eta^2 = .01$; see Fig. 7.1). No meaningful differences between immigrant and national families were found with respect to the adolescents' rights discrepancy scores.

CORRELATES AND PREDICTORS OF FAMILY RELATIONSHIP VALUES AND INTERGENERATIONAL DISCREPANCIES

Length of Residence and Family Relationship Values

Among immigrant adolescents, as we reported in chapter 4, family obligation scores were slightly lower with longer residence in the society of settlement, but the effect size was very small. Similar results but with larger effect sizes were found for girls and in neighborhoods with mostly other ethnic groups. Because fewer adolescents participated in the data for the current chapter, we repeated the analyses. We used value and discrepancy scores standardized within country and group, as this procedure controls for confounding effects that influence between-country and between-group differences (e.g., sampling artifacts and response sets; see chap. 3).

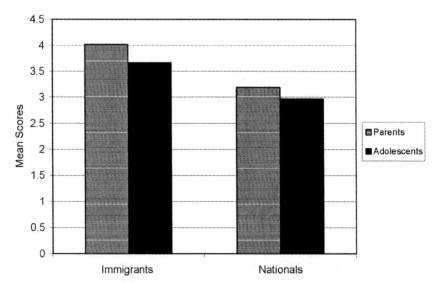

FIG. 7.1.   Mean family obligation scores for immigrant and national parent–adolescent dyads, showing intergenerational discrepancies.

In accordance with our expectations, adolescents' scores for family obligations were lower with longer residence ($\eta^2 = .01$); adolescents with less than 6 years of residence endorsed family obligations more strongly than did adolescents with longer residence (see Fig. 7.2). As in chapter 4, gender made a difference; girls showed lower obligations score with longer residence ($\eta^2 = .01$; less than 6 years = .13, 6–12 years = –.00, and more than 12 years = –.12), but boys did not. However, for immigrant parents, the obligations scores were not related to adolescents' length of residence. Scores regarding adolescents' rights were not associated with length of residence for either adolescents or parents.

We expected that intergenerational discrepancies would be greater in immigrant families with longer residence in the new society, based on the assumption that adolescents' attitudes change more rapidly than adults', resulting in a larger discrepancy over time. This expectation was not confirmed overall for either family obligations or adolescents' rights. However, among adolescents with a diffuse profile, that is, who appeared uncertain or confused about their place in the new society, the discrepancy for family obligations was greater with longer residence ($\eta^2 = .05$; less than 6 years = –.08, 6–12 years = –.01, and more than 12 years = .48).

Values in Relation to Gender, Age, Neighborhood, and Parental Education

In immigrant families, gender was unrelated to either the value scores or the discrepancy scores. In the national families, family obligation scores for boys (.11) were slightly higher than scores for girls (–.12; $\eta^2 = .01$). Overall, the discrepancy

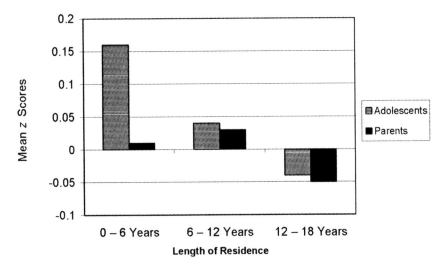

FIG. 7.2. Family obligation scores of immigrant adolescents and their parents, by length of residence. (Standardization scores do not show actual parent–adolescent differences, which are shown in Fig. 7.1.)

scores for family obligations were slightly larger for girls than for boys, but the difference was meaningful only for national families (.13 for girls and –.17 for boys; $\eta^2 = .02$). There were no gender differences for discrepancies in adolescents' rights. Adolescents' age was not related to the values and the discrepancies scores in either immigrant or national families.

In immigrant families living in neighborhoods in which almost all people come from a different ethnic group, rights discrepancy scores were higher than in more ethnically homogeneous neighborhoods ($\eta^2 = .01$). There were no other differences for values or for obligations discrepancies. In national families living in communities where many immigrants lived, adolescents' family obligations scores were higher than in families living in neighborhoods with fewer immigrants ($\eta^2 = .02$).

In immigrant families, parents' level of education was related only to parents' reported family obligations; parents with at least a high school education believed that adolescents had fewer obligations to the family than did less educated parents ($\eta^2 = .02$). In national families, both adolescents and parents in families with more educated parents believed less strongly in adolescents' obligations ($\eta^2 = .02$ and $\eta^2 = .04$, respectively). However, for discrepancies, there were no differences related to parental level of education. For adolescents' rights, there were no differences in adolescents' or parents' scores or the discrepancy with parental level of education.

Actual cultural diversity and diversity policy (the two country-level diversity variables introduced in chapter 2) were examined in relation to family relationship values and discrepancy scores. No important or easily interpretable relationships were found between discrepancies and diversity variables for either immigrant or national families.

The Role of Acculturation Profiles in Values and Value Discrepancies

In the Introduction we raised the question of whether intergenerational discrepancy scores for family obligations and adolescents' rights reflect a common developmental phenomenon or result from the acculturation experiences of immigrant parents and their children. The impact of acculturation is evident in the results showing that discrepancies are greater in immigrant than in national families. Family relationship values and intergenerational discrepancies may also be related to the different ways adolescents acculturate.

The acculturation profiles identified in chapter 4 describe four ways immigrant adolescents manage the challenge of living in two cultures: an integrated profile, an ethnic profile, a national profile, and a diffuse profile. These profiles were related to adolescents' and parents' scores on family relationship values, but there was considerable variability in the effects. Adolescents' obligations scores showed the strongest relationship to the profiles ($\eta^2 = .09$). The lowest obligations scores were in the national profile (–.56) and the highest were in the ethnic profile

(.31). Parents' obligations scores showed a similar pattern, but the effect was considerably weaker ($\eta^2 = .01$). The discrepancy for family obligations also differed significantly among the four profiles ($\eta^2 = .03$). Adolescents with the national profile had larger discrepancy scores (.32) than all other adolescents, and those with an ethnic profile had smaller discrepancy scores (–.20), than the other two profiles (integration, .29; diffuse, .39).

Adolescents' rights scores were also related to the profiles ($\eta^2 = .01$); diffuse adolescents reported lower rights than either ethnic or integrated youth. Parents' rights scores were unrelated to profiles, and there were no differences among the profiles in the discrepancy in rights.

Intergenerational Discrepancies and Parental Acculturation Attitudes

Intergenerational value discrepancies may also be related to the acculturation attitudes of immigrant parents. In this section we examine whether parents' separation or assimilation preferences have an impact on discrepancies beyond the impact of adolescents' acculturation profile.

Because the items measuring parental acculturation attitudes could not be combined into a psychometrically satisfying scale (as shown in chapter 3), we used just two items that are indicative of acculturation attitudes. We focused on items dealing with cultural traditions, specifically, the item measuring a separation preference in cultural traditions ("I feel that [my ethnic group] should maintain their own cultural traditions and not adapt to those of [national group]"), and the item measuring an assimilation preference ("I feel that [ethnic group] should adapt to [national] cultural traditions and not maintain those of their own"). These items were used in separate hierarchical regression analyses for each of the profile groups with each discrepancy score as the dependent variable; proportion of life spent in the country and parents' highest level of education were included as controls.

With respect to family obligations, a stronger parental preference for separation was associated with a larger discrepancy in all profile groups except the diffuse group. As expected, the effect was strongest for adolescents with a national profile ($R^2 = .03$, $\beta = .16$). For these adolescents, who favor involvement with the national culture, a stronger parental preference for separation predicted a larger intergenerational discrepancy in family obligations. We found similar, although weaker, effects of parents' separation preference among adolescents with an the ethnic profile ($R^2 = .02$, $\beta = .12$) and with an integration profile ($R^2 = .01$, $\beta = .11$). Thus, even for adolescents who remain oriented to their own ethnic group or toward both their own culture and the larger society, parents' higher separation preference is associated with larger discrepancies.

Similar analyses with intergenerational rights discrepancy scores as the dependent variable did not yield relevant or statistically significant outcomes.

INTERGENERATIONAL DISCREPANCIES
AND ADOLESCENT ADAPTATION

As just shown, differences with parents over cultural values are a reality for many adolescents, and differences with regard to family obligations are larger in immigrant than national families. An important question, therefore, is whether these differences have an impact on adaptation. In chapter 5 we introduced the concepts of psychological adaptation (adolescents' self-esteem, life satisfaction, and absence of psychological problems) and sociocultural adaptation (school adjustment and absence of behavior problems). The relationship of these adaptation variables to intergenerational discrepancies for obligations and rights was analyzed with a series of hierarchical regression analyses that controlled for adolescents' age, their proportion of life spent in the country of residence, parents' level of education, and adolescents' gender.

The results are shown in Table 7.2. As expected, higher intergenerational discrepancies in family obligations were associated with poorer psychological and sociocultural adaptation for both immigrant and national adolescents. There were no important differences between the immigrants and nationals with respect to the strength of the relationship between intergenerational discrepancies and adaptation. Discrepancies in adolescents' rights did not contribute to the prediction.

An additional question is whether the relationship between intergenerational family relations value discrepancies and adolescents' adaptation differs among adolescents with differing acculturation profiles. To answer this question, hierarchical regression analyses were carried out, similar to those described earlier, but separately for the four acculturation profiles.

Across all four profiles, the obligations discrepancy had a negative impact on adaptation, but the effect varied depending on the profile and the type of adaptation. The strongest effect was for adolescents with an integration profile (a balanced orientation toward both the own and the national culture). For these adolescents, a discrepancy in obligations had a negative effect on sociocultural

TABLE 7.2
The Relationships Among Intergenerational Value Discrepancies and Adaptation

Group	Type of Adaptation	R^2 Discrepancies	β Rights Discrepancy	β Obligations Discrepancy
Immigrants	Psychological	.02***	ns	−.14***
	Sociocultural	.02***	ns	−.14***
Nationals	Psychological	.02***	ns	−.13***
	Sociocultural	.04***	ns	−.19***

Note. R^2 is a measure of the predictive power of the discrepancy, and β indicates whether higher scores on each type of discrepancy correspond to higher scores (a positive value) or to lower scores (a negative value) on each type of adaptation.
***$p < .001$.

adaptation ($R^2 = .06$ and $\beta = -.24$) but not on psychological adaptation. For adolescents with a national profile, characterized by closer ties to the larger society, a discrepancy in obligation scores had a significant negative impact on psychological adaptation ($R^2 = .04$ and $\beta = -.20$) and a significant but lesser effect on sociocultural adaptation ($R^2 = .03$ and $\beta = -.17$); that is, the psychological adaptation, and to a lesser extent the sociocultural adaptation, of adolescents who are oriented toward the larger society were influenced by differences with their parents over obligations. For those with a diffuse orientation, who lack a clear sense of their position in society, differences with their parents over obligations affected both psychological adaptation ($R^2 = .02$ and $\beta = -.12$) and their sociocultural adaptation ($R^2 = .02$ and $\beta = -.11$). Generally, those with an ethnic profile were the least influenced by discrepancies; only sociocultural adaptation was affected ($R^2 = .02$ and $\beta = -.12$).

A final question was whether the relationship between intergenerational value discrepancies and adaptation depends on the original level of adolescents' or parents' obligations or rights scores. Intergenerational discrepancies may have different implications in families that strongly endorse collectivist values of family interdependence compared with families who place more emphasis on independence. For example, when strong norms of respect for parents prevail, as in many immigrant cultures, differences within the family may be associated with greater problems for immigrant adolescents. To explore this issue, we examine the relationship of intergenerational value discrepancies to adaptation, considering initial levels of adolescents' and parents' scores on family relationship values. Immigrant and national adolescents and parents were divided into three groups based on their obligations and rights scores (low: scores < 3; medium: scores 3–4; high: > 4). The resulting groups varied in size. Especially in the national group, the high-obligations group based on either adolescents' or parents' scores were too small to allow for a valid comparison with other groups. The only interpretable patterns were found in the immigrant families; these results are summarized in Table 7.3.

The results suggest three patterns, which provide insight into the role different levels of values play in psychological adaptation. First, as shown in the first two panels of Table 7.3, when adolescents' scores on obligations are low—that is, the adolescents do not strongly endorse the cultural value of family obligations—the discrepancy between them and their parents on this value has a negative impact on both their psychological and sociocultural adaptation. Adolescents' rejection of obligations that are expected by the parents may lead to increased stress, which contributes to poorer adaptation.

Second, as shown in the third panel of Table 7.3, when parents score high on adolescents' rights—that is, parents grant adolescents greater autonomy in decision making—a larger discrepancy regarding rights has a stronger positive impact on adolescents' psychological adaptation, and the discrepancy regarding obligations has a stronger negative impact on adolescents' psychological adaptation. When adolescents experience strong parental approval of autonomous decision making

TABLE 7.3
The Impact of the Level of Immigrant Adolescents' and Parents' Scores
for Obligations and Rights on the Relationship Between Intergenerational
Value Discrepancy Scores and Adolescents' Psychological and Sociocultural
Adaptation

	β Discrepancy Rights	β Discrepancy Obligations	R^2
Dependent variable: Psychological adaptation			
Obligations (Adolescent scores)			
Low	ns	−.15 **	.03***
Medium	ns	−.13 ***	.02***
High	ns	ns	ns
Dependent variable: Sociocultural adaptation			
Obligations (Adolescent scores)			
Low	ns	−.14**	.03**
Medium	ns	−.08*	.01*
High	ns	ns	ns
Dependent variable: Psychological adaptation			
Rights (Parent scores)			
Low	ns	−.11	.02***
Medium	.10*	−.12**	.02**
High	.17**	−.21**	.07***
Dependent variable: Sociocultural adaptation			
Obligations (Parent scores)			
Low	ns	ns	ns
Medium	ns	−.09*	.01*
High	−.07*	−.18***	.04***

$*p < .05; **p < .01; ***p < .001.$

in their personal relationships, this contributes to their psychological well-being. However, this same desire for autonomy may be frustrated by the parents' expectations regarding family obligations, so that adolescents do not get to enjoy their rights, resulting in the negative impact of intergenerational discrepancies.

A third pattern is shown in the fourth panel of Table 7.3. When parents report high scores regarding family obligations, both types of discrepancies are associated with poorer sociocultural adaptation. As parents report higher expectations for the fulfillment of obligations, the discrepancies appear to create greater tension that detracts from positive adaptation.

SUMMARY AND CONCLUSIONS

The family is a critical context for the development of adolescents, and the values that parents hold regarding the family provide the background against which adolescents make their way toward adulthood. For immigrant adolescents, the cultural values of their parents often differ from the values that predominate in the families of their peers from the larger society. As a result, immigrant adolescents are exposed to different value systems regarding their obligations to the family and their right to make autonomous choices in their personal lives. In this chapter, we explored the values regarding family relationships held by adolescents and parents in both immigrant families and families from the national societies of settlement. We examined differences in values between adolescents and parents and between immigrant and national families, to gain an understanding of the relationship between acculturation processes and these differences. Our results support many of the findings of prior research on family relationships among immigrants in various cultural contexts (e.g., Chun & Akutsu, 2003; Georgas, Berry, Kagitcibasi, Poortinga, & van de Vijver, 2005; Phalet & Schönpflug, 2001; Rosenthal et al., 1996). We extend these findings on the basis of samples of adolescents and parents from immigrant and national families in 10 countries.

As expected, family relationship values in immigrant families differ from those of national families in their societies of settlement. Specifically, immigrant adolescents and their parents believe that adolescent children have more obligations to the family and fewer individual rights than do their counterparts in national families. These results are in accord with much other research on cultural values (e.g., Fuligni et al., 1999; Kagitcibasi, 1996; Nguyen & Williams, 1989), showing that immigrant families from non-European backgrounds support the values of interdependence more strongly than do families from European backgrounds. The underlying differences between the cultural values of immigrants and those of their society of settlement may create intergenerational discrepancies that are a potential source of stress during the acculturation process (Berry & Sam, 1997). These differences provide the basis for expecting that immigrant adolescents may have greater difficulty in overall adjustment. Nevertheless, as we report in chapter 5, immigrant adolescents do not show greater adjustment problems than their national peers. Two issues need to be considered: (a) whether there are in fact greater differences over values between parents and children in immigrant families and (b) whether these differences contribute negatively to adjustment.

Developmental research has shown that differences between adolescents and parents exist in most cultures as part of normal adolescent development (Steinberg, 1990). In keeping with this evidence, we found that across both types of families, adolescents feel less strongly than their parents that they have obligations to the family, such as obeying and helping out their parents and living at home until married. Similarly, in both types of families, adolescents believe more strongly than their parents that they have the right to make their own decisions about dating and marriage. Furthermore, there are no differences in discrepancies in relation to gender, age, or neighborhood ethnic composition. Parents' level of education played a small role in both immigrant and national families in that obligations scores were slightly lower with higher parental education. Overall, intergenerational discrepancies in family relationship values appear to be a normal developmental phenomenon, common to immigrant and national families alike.

Nevertheless, acculturation processes may contribute to this phenomenon, leading to greater discrepancies in immigrant families. We found this to be partially true. Adolescents and parents in immigrant families differ significantly more than do adolescents and parents in national families on family obligations, although they do not differ more on adolescents' rights. These results suggest that acculturative pressures, beyond the effect of normal developmental processes, contribute to differences between immigrant adolescents and their parents.

Furthermore, intergenerational discrepancies were related to acculturation processes in complex ways. The ways adolescents handle their lives in the country of settlement, as well as their parents' attitudes regarding acculturation, have an impact on intergenerational discrepancies in family obligations. When adolescents show a national profile—that is, they are strongly oriented to the national culture in terms of attitudes, identity, and behaviors—the discrepancy in family obligations is greater than it is among adolescents with other acculturation profiles. This effect is even stronger when the parents more strongly favor retention of their own culture. Thus, the intergenerational discrepancy is larger in the presence of what might be called an *acculturation gap*, that is, when adolescents lean toward assimilation and parents wish to maintain their own cultural traditions without assimilating.

Conversely, when adolescents are oriented toward their ethnic culture, the discrepancy is less. However, even among ethnically oriented adolescents, the discrepancy is larger when parents strongly support retention of cultural traditions. Thus, intergenerational discrepancies are influenced by both adolescents' and parents' attitudes and behaviors related to acculturation.

We expected the discrepancy to be larger with longer residence in the new society. There is substantial research showing that immigrant adolescents adopt new attitudes and values more rapidly than do their parents (Buriel & De Ment, 1997; Liebkind, 1992b; Nguyen & Williams, 1989; Portes, 1997; Szapocznik & Kurtines, 1993). Therefore, with longer residence, the values of immigrant adolescents may become closer to those of the larger society, whereas their parents' values remain little changed, creating a larger value discrepancy within the family. Our overall results in this chapter support this view with regard to family obligations; adolescents with 6 years of residence or less in the new society show higher levels of support for family obligations. This effect is stronger among girls than among boys. However, in conjunction with the results reported in chapter 4, we see that differences in length of residence are found under some conditions but not others. Furthermore, the expectation that intergenerational value discrepancies would be greater with longer residence was supported only among adolescents who appeared uncertain about their place in society. We cannot therefore assume that our findings apply in all settings or samples.

Much previous research stresses the negative impact of intergenerational differences on the adaptation of immigrant youth (e.g., Birman & Trickett, 2001; Chun & Akutsu, 2003; Gil, Vega, & Dimas, 1994; Szapocznik & Kurtines, 1993). A central concern in this study was whether intergenerational discrepancies have a negative impact on adaptation across a range of adolescents from both immigrant groups and the national societies, and if so, whether the impact is greater in immigrant families. In answer to the first question, we found that larger intergenerational discrepancies with regard to family obligations are associated with poorer psychological and sociological adaptation in both immigrant and national families. This result was expected in immigrant families, where parents strive to maintain their cultural values. However, even in the national families, in which family obligations were endorsed less than in immigrant families, discrepancies between adolescents and parents are associated with poorer adaptation. Clearly, the phenomenon is not simply one of acculturation.

Discrepancies might be expected to be more disruptive in immigrant cultures that place greater value on close family relationships than in national cultures that place more emphasis on independence. However, our results did not support this view; the impact of discrepancies regarding obligations is no greater in immigrant than in national families. The fact that discrepancies have a similar negative effect on adaptation across both types of families also suggests a common developmental phenomenon.

Nevertheless, our results show that acculturation processes do make a difference in the role of intergenerational discrepancies. In immigrant families, but not in national families, the initial levels of obligations or rights reported by adolescents and parents are important to the relationship between discrepancies and adaptation. Most notably, the negative impact of discrepancies on adaptation in family obligations is greater when adolescents' scores regarding family obligations are low or when parents' scores are high. Together with the finding on the role of acculturation profiles, length of residence, and the acculturation gap, this finding suggests that developmental and acculturative processes are intertwined in the impact of value discrepancies on immigrant families.

In summary, the complex set of results regarding family relationship values confirms many previous findings and provides new information on acculturation and family relationship values. As expected on the basis of prior research, immigrant youth and their parents differ from national youth and their parents. Immigrant adolescents and parents value obligations to the family more highly, and adolescents' right less highly, than do national families. In spite of the absolute differences in levels of endorsement between immigrant and national families, adolescents in both types of families value obligations less than do their parents, suggesting that intergenerational discrepancies are at least in part a common developmental phenomenon. Nevertheless, the difference between adolescents and parents is greater in immigrant families, providing support for the idea that immigrant adolescents may experience greater difficulty in their family relationships. Furthermore, with greater time spent in the national cultural setting, immigrant adolescents feel less obligated to their families, and the intergenerational difference in family obligations is greater.

Finally, larger intergenerational discrepancies are associated with poorer adaptation, consistent with earlier research. However, this relationship is no greater in immigrant families than in national families. This result extends findings from a small subset of the data from the current study (Phinney & Ong, 2002) to a large and diverse sample. The assumption that immigrant adolescents are more prone to poor adjustment because of acculturation differences within the family needs to be reconsidered in light of evidence that nonimmigrant families show a similar impact of intergenerational differences. The fact that immigrant adolescents show overall levels of adaptation equal to, or better than, those of their nonimmigrant peers, in spite of larger intergenerational discrepancies, provides evidence of the strengths of immigrant families in meeting and dealing with the challenges of the acculturation experience.

8

Vietnamese and Turkish Immigrant Youth: Acculturation and Adaptation in Two Ethnocultural Groups

Paul Vedder
Leiden University

David L. Sam
University of Bergen

Fons J. R. van de Vijver
Tilburg University

Jean S. Phinney
California State University, Los Angeles

The study of acculturation among diverse ethnic groups in a wide range of countries of settlement poses substantial challenges. One approach to this diversity is to combine data from very different groups and settings and focus on the large picture. We do this in much of this book to provide a broad and general description of the acculturation and adaptation of immigrant youth in 13 countries. However, this approach leaves unanswered the questions of whether our findings and our model can be generalized to all the groups and countries studied, and how acculturation experiences and outcomes differ among specific ethnic groups and countries. Because of the small numbers in many of the ethnic groups that we sampled and the diversity of groups selected in each country, we could not examine this question in all groups and settings. Nevertheless, for two immigrant groups, Turks and Vietnamese, we obtained large enough samples across different countries to permit further analyses. Vietnamese were sampled in seven countries and Turks in six. The large sample sizes obtained for these two immigrant groups allowed us to explore the generality of our findings in two specific groups. Furthermore, because both groups were sampled in the same four countries, we could make comparisons both between two ethnic groups in the same country and among the four countries based on immigrants from the same ethnic groups.

In this chapter, following some background information on Turkish and Vietnamese immigrants, we address two main goals. First, we examine ethnic- and country-level differences by making controlled comparisons between the two groups and among the four countries. We pose the following questions: To what extent and in what ways do acculturation experiences and outcomes vary between the two ethnocultural groups (Turks and Vietnamese)? How do these experiences and outcomes vary among four countries of settlement (Finland, France, Norway, and Sweden)? To answer these questions, we used only data from Vietnamese and Turks in the four countries of settlement that they have in common.

Second, we explore the generality of the findings reported for all youth earlier in the book. We pose the following question: To what extent does our theoretical model of the relationship between immigrant youth's intercultural relations and adaptation outcomes (presented in chap. 6) apply to the two largest groups, Vietnamese and Turks? To answer this question, we use data from all the Vietnamese youth (in seven countries) and all the Turkish youth (in six countries).

VIETNAMESE AND TURKISH IMMIGRANTS

Globally, Vietnamese and Turks constitute two very large and distinct immigrant groups. They have attracted several research investigations in their countries of settlement (for studies of Vietnamese immigrants see Berry & Blondel, 1982; Liebkind et al., 2004; Nguyen et al., 1999; Sam, 1994; Thai, 2003; for studies of Turkish immigrants, see Ataca & Berry, 2002; Bas, Asci, Karabudak, & Kiziltan, 2004; Demir & Tarhan, 2001; Eskin, 2003; Janssen et al., 2004).

In chapter 2, ethnographic descriptions of Turks and Vietnamese are presented as cultural and social contexts within which we can understand each group's acculturation and adaptation. Of particular importance for this chapter are the background features that distinguish the two groups. The bulk of the Turkish immigrants came as guest workers, where the goals were a short-term sojourn followed by return home at the end of the job contract. Most Turkish immigration has been to European countries. Because this migration took place largely in the mid 1960s and early 1970s, the majority of the Turkish adolescents in our study are second-generation immigrants. Turkish second-generation immigrants have been characterized as having strong orientation toward the Turkish culture (Crul & Doomernik, 2003), probably because, as guest workers, they expected to return home and therefore wished to maintain their ethnic culture.

In contrast, the majority of Vietnamese are refugees; they have settled widely around the world and are found on most continents. The bulk of their emigration took place in the late 1970s and 1980s; therefore, Vietnamese families generally have been in their countries of settlement for shorter periods. Nevertheless, as refugees with little realistic possibility of returning home, most expect to remain in the country of settlement. They tend to have a strong drive to build a new future in their new country of residence (Nguyen et al., 1999; Zhou & Bankston, 1998).

These differences between the two groups are fundamental to interpreting differences found in their acculturation experiences and outcomes.

GROUP AND COUNTRY VARIATION IN ACCULTURATION EXPERIENCES AND OUTCOMES: VIETNAMESE AND TURKISH YOUTH IN FOUR COUNTRIES

In this section we ask: How do acculturation experiences and outcomes differ between ethnocultural groups (Vietnamese and Turks) and among countries of settlement (Finland, France, Norway, and Sweden)? We address this question by returning to issues addressed earlier in the book for all immigrants, but now using only Vietnamese and Turkish youth residing in four common countries, that is, with subsamples that allow for more controlled comparisons. However, we do not simply assume comparability but rather strive for comparability by including relevant control variables in the analyses.

We first examine variation in the four acculturation profiles identified in chapter 4 that describe different patterns exhibited by immigrant youth in dealing with their experience in two cultures. We then consider differences in perceived discrimination and in the four factors, or orientations, that were presented in chapter 4. We also explore the extent to which family relationship values and intergenerational discrepancies, reported in chapter 7, differ by ethnicity and country. Throughout this section, we examine the relationship of the major variables to the two types of adaptation described in chapter 5: psychological and sociocultural.

The Turkish and Vietnamese Samples in Four Countries

A description of the Vietnamese and Turkish adolescents and parents in the four-country subsamples used in these analyses is provided in Table 8.1. The two groups differed in several ways. The Turkish youth were more likely than the Vietnamese youth to be second generation and to have resided longer in the country of settlement. More Vietnamese than Turks lived in ethnically mixed neighborhoods, whereas more Turks than Vietnamese lived in neighborhoods that were predominantly of their own group. The Turks showed more religious homogeneity, with 88.3% indicating that they were Muslim. Slightly more than half of Vietnamese adolescents indicated that they were Buddhist, and about one fifth were Roman Catholic.

The parents show generally similar patterns. Parents' reported level of education was used as a proxy for SES. The overall mean for Vietnamese and Turkish parents' self-reported level of education was 4.05 ($SD = 1.87$), which represents a value slightly above some secondary or high school (which was coded as 4). The Vietnamese parents on average were slightly more educated ($d = .04$) and the Turkish parents were less educated ($d = -.05$). Parental occupational status was slightly lower in the Turkish group than in the Vietnamese group. The relatively low occu-

TABLE 8.1
Sample Characteristics: Vietnamese and Turkish Immigrant Groups in the Four Common Countries

	Vietnamese Youth	Turkish Youth
Number (percent female)		
Finland	219 (52)	58 (62)
France	85 (57)	61 (50)
Norway	142 (54)	106 (47)
Sweden	101 (47)	284 (52)
Mean age	15.64 (SD = 1.55)	15.12 (SD = 1.58)
Length of residence		
0–6 years	37%	38%
>6 to <12 years	46%	39%
> 12–18 years	18%	23%
Generation		
First	48%	18%
Second	52%	82%
Proportion of life in new country	.70 (SD = .33)	.88 (SD = .27)
Religion		
Muslim	7.0%	89%
Buddhist	56%	4%
Roman Catholic	21%	2%
Nonreligious	17%	6%
Percent of parents in study	54%	46%
	Vietnamese Parents	Turkish Parents
Number		
Finland	133	39
France	38	31
Norway	37	23
Sweden	71	130
Parental occupation		
Unemployed	9%	7%
Unskilled	48%	60%
Skilled	18%	17%
White collar	10%	11%
Professional	15%	6%
Education		
4 = some high school	4.13 (SD = 1.99)	3.96 (SD = 1.73)
Length of residence	10.04 years (SD = 7.46)	19.54 years (SD = 7.09)

pational status of the Turks as observed here appears to be a true reflection of their general SES in the society of residence rather than a sampling artifact.

Acculturation Profiles: Ethnic Group Differences

In chapter 4, using a person-oriented approach, we identify four distinct profiles of acculturation that characterized groups of adolescents: an ethnic profile, indicating identification and involvement with one's ethnic group; a national profile, indicating identification and involvement with the society of settlement; an integration profile, indicating involvement in both the ethnic and national cultures; and a diffuse profile, indicating no clear sense of place in the new society. We examined the distribution of these profiles among Vietnamese and Turkish youth. We expected to find the ethnic profile more common among the Turks and the national profile more common among the Vietnamese (see chap. 2; Crul & Doomernik, 2003; Nguyen et al., 1999; Zhou & Bankston, 1998). We also explored whether the findings reported earlier, that adolescents with the integration profile had better adaptation scores than adolescents characterized by the other acculturation profiles, apply specifically to Vietnamese and Turks. Factor analysis reported in chapter 5 with the adaptation variables identified two adaptation factors that were used in the current analyses: psychological adaptation (life satisfaction, self-esteem, and psychological problems, the latter with negative loadings) and sociocultural adaptation (school adjustment, positively loaded; behavior problems, negatively loaded).

A comparison of the profile distributions for the Vietnamese and Turkish adolescents is shown in Fig. 8.1, together with the distribution for all immigrant youth in all countries of residence. The distributions differed between the Vietnamese and Turkish group, $\chi^2 (3, N = 959) = 104.70, p < .001$. For the Turks, the ethnic profile was clearly dominant, and the national profile was the least represented. In contrast, for the Vietnamese, the ethnic profile was the least common and the national profile was more common than for the Turks. The integration profile, most common in the total sample, was not the dominant profile for either group. It is surprising that the Vietnamese youth were strongly represented in the diffuse group. However, further analyses showed that the high proportion of Vietnamese with a diffuse profile is due largely to the higher numbers of first-generation youth in this ethnic group. Our prior results with the entire sample showed that the diffuse profile is more common in more recent arrivals (see chap. 4). For the Vietnamese, similarly, the diffuse profile was strongly overrepresented among youth with 12 years or less of residence (0 to 6, 21% of all Vietnamese adolescents; > 6 to < 12, 18%), but much lower among those with more than 12 years of residence (5%). In the latter group, there were more adolescents with an integrated or national profile than with a diffuse profile. Therefore, the large numbers of diffuse Vietnamese youth appear to be due to the recency of their immigration rather than to difficulties in the acculturation process.

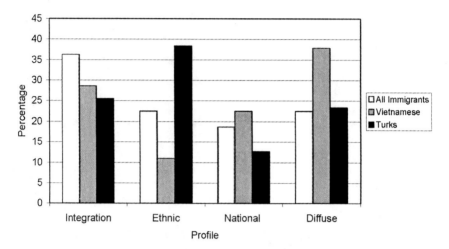

FIG. 8.1. Acculturation profile distribution for all immigrants irrespective of country of residence and for the Vietnamese and Turkish immigrant adolescents in four common countries.

We explored the relationship between acculturation profiles and adaptation outcomes in the Vietnamese and Turks. Prior results (see chap. 5) show that immigrant youth with the integration profile had better adaptation scores than youth with any other profile. Those with the diffuse profile had the lowest scores. Individuals with the national profile had relatively poor psychological adaptation, but they were not clearly distinct from other profiles with respect to sociocultural adaptation. In contrast, the ethnic profile showed good psychological adaptation but poor sociocultural adaptation.

The scores for psychological adaptation by profile and ethnocultural group (including all immigrants for comparison) are shown in Fig. 8.2. There were no differences in psychological adaptation by ethnocultural group; the scores for Vietnamese and Turks were largely similar. Scores significantly varied by profile, irrespective of ethnocultural group ($\eta^2 = .05$). Comparisons of the scores per profile (Bonferroni) showed that psychological adaptation scores for the integration profile were higher than those in the national and diffuse profiles; the ethnic profile yielded higher scores than did the diffuse profile. These results are generally similar to those reported in chapter 5 for the entire sample. The national profile appears to be related to poor adaptation for the Turks, but this effect was not sufficiently strong to result in a statistically significant interaction effect.

Analysis of sociocultural adaptation by profile and ethnic group showed no difference by ethnocultural group, but an effect of profile ($\eta^2 = .02$) (see Fig. 8.3). Scores for the integration and ethnic profiles were higher than scores for the national profile. In contrast to our results for the entire sample, the national profile, rather than the diffuse profile, yielded the lowest scores for sociocultural adaptation. Figure 8.3 also shows that among the Turkish youth, the ethnic profile, not the integration profile, was associated with higher levels of sociocultural adaptation.

The sample sizes did not allow for testing country-level differences in profiles for Turks and Vietnamese.

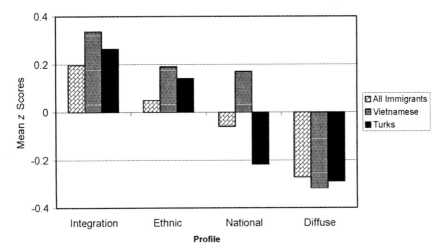

FIG. 8.2. The estimated scores for psychological adaptation of Vietnamese and Turkish adolescents by acculturation profile in four common countries, controlling for age, gender and proportion of life spent in country of residence.

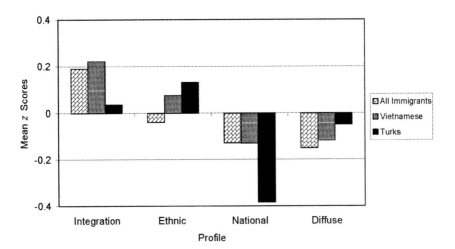

FIG. 8.3. The estimated scores for sociocultural adaptation of Vietnamese and Turkish adolescents by acculturation profile in four common countries, controlling for age, gender and proportion of life spent in country of residence.

ion and Adaptation: Differences by Ethnocultural Group
⌐⌐⌐ ⌐⌐⌐⌐try of Settlement

The acculturation profiles discussed previously provide a person-oriented approach to understanding variation in the ways adolescents acculturate, by identifying categories of individuals with particular characteristics. A second way to understand acculturation is a variable-oriented approach, such as factor analysis, which groups together variables that are correlated with each other. In chapter 4, using factor analysis with the intercultural variables, we identify four factors that underlie the acculturation experience: the integration orientation, which includes the two acculturation attitudes of integration (loading positively) and marginalization (loading negatively); the ethnic orientation, which includes ethnic identity, the acculturation attitude of separation, and family obligations; the national orientation, which includes a combination of national identity and the acculturation attitude of assimilation; and ethnic behaviors, which combines ethnic language proficiency and contacts with ethnic peers (both positive loadings), and national language proficiency and contacts with national peers (both negative loadings). Perceived discrimination was included as a separate variable. Adaptation was examined in terms of the two types used earlier: psychological and sociocultural.

To examine ethnic differences in the intercultural and adaptation variables in this section, the factor scores were recalculated for Vietnamese and Turkish adolescents using raw scores. The outcomes of these analyses in terms of the factor structure, eigenvalues, and percentages of explained variance were largely similar for the two groups and the interpretation of the factors was similar to that presented in chapters 4, 5, and 6.

When dealing with country differences, we used estimated mean scores, as in chapters 4 and 5. In the estimates the possible effects of adolescents' age, gender, and percentage of life spent in country of residence were taken into account; that is, samples were made comparable with respect to these background variables. We particularly looked at the dependence of the scores on country of residence, immigrant group, and their interaction. Statistically significant interactions indicate that the relationship between either acculturation or adaptation and the immigrant group depends on the country of residence of that group. All relationships were tested with univariate analyses of covariance.

Differences in Perceived Discrimination

Because of the importance of perceived discrimination in the adaptation of immigrant youth (see chap. 6), we examined this variable first, exploring differences based on ethnocultural group and country of settlement. The results show that country of residence makes a difference in the extent to which one perceives discrimination ($\eta^2 = .04$). Both the Vietnamese and Turkish adolescents in Norway reported higher levels of perceived discrimination than the Vietnamese and Turks in the other three countries. Overall there were no differences between the Vietnamese and Turks, but there was an interaction ($\eta^2 = .01$), reflecting different group levels in the four countries (see Fig. 8.4). The Turkish youth in Finland perceived less discrimination than the Vietnamese, whereas the Turkish youth in Norway perceived more discrimination. A possible explanation regarding the Turkish immigrants in Finland is that, as reported in chapter 2, a relatively high proportion of the adolescents had a dual or mixed ethnic background (i.e., Turkish father and Finnish mother).

Differences in Orientation Factors

The integration orientation factor differed by both ethnicity and country of settlement. Vietnamese adolescents had slightly higher integration scores than their Turkish peers ($\eta^2 = .01$) in all countries. Both groups of adolescents in Norway had lower scores than their peers in Finland and Sweden ($\eta^2 = .02$).

For the ethnic orientation factor, Turkish youth had higher scores than Vietnamese ($\eta^2 = .03$), irrespective of country, and the scores in Finland were lower than in the other countries ($\eta^2 = .03$); however, there was an interaction of ethnic group and country ($\eta^2 = .09$), as shown in Fig. 8.5. The higher ethnic orientation scores of the Turks were found in three countries, but not in Finland. As noted before, many of the Turkish youth had one Finnish parent, a fact that may attenuate their ethnic orientation.

Higher scores on the ethnic orientation factor were shown earlier to be positively related to more perceived discrimination in the entire sample (see chap. 6). However, that finding does not help explain the high levels of perceived discrimi-

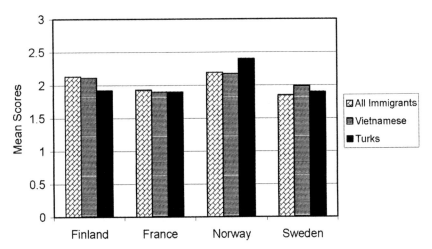

FIG. 8.4. Estimated perceived discrimination scores of Vietnamese and Turkish immigrant youth in four countries, controlling for age, gender, and proportion of life spent in country of settlement.

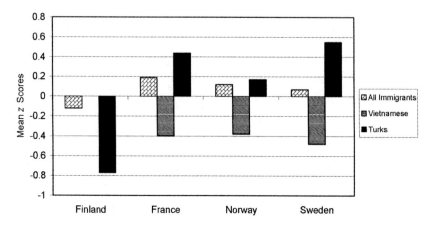

FIG. 8.5.   Estimated scores on the ethnic orientation for Vietnamese and Turkish immigrant youth in four countries, controlling for age, gender, and proportion of life spent in country of settlement.

nation reported by Vietnamese and Turks in Norway, as in this case the ethnic orientation scores were relatively low.

For the national orientation factor, the Vietnamese generally had higher scores than the Turks ($\eta^2 = .02$). The national orientation scores were higher in Finland and lower in Sweden than in the other countries ($\eta^2 = .06$). There was also an interaction ($\eta^2 = .01$): National orientation was higher for the Vietnamese than for the Turks in three of the countries, but in Finland the scores of the two groups were at about the same level.

The patterns for the ethnic behaviors were largely comparable with those found for the ethnic factor. Scores were lower in Finland than in France, and in France they were lower than in Norway and Sweden ($\eta^2 = .12$). Generally, the Vietnamese had lower scores than the Turks ($\eta^2 = .02$), but again the exception was Finland. Here, Turkish adolescents had a very low mean score (–1.31), whereas the Vietnamese had a modest score (–.25; interaction effect: $\eta^2 = .13$). The Turks in Finland reported low ethnic behaviors, ethnic orientation, and perceived discrimination, supporting the links among these variables. However, a similar relationship was not found for the Turks in Norway.

In summary, these results reveal considerable differences among the two groups and the four countries with respect to acculturation experiences. Turks generally scored higher on the ethnic orientation and the ethnic behaviors, whereas the Vietnamese had higher scores for the integration and national orientations. No difference was found between Turks and Vietnamese for perceived discrimination. Country comparisons showed that Norway had both the lowest scores on the integration factor and the highest levels of discrimination. These results have implications for adaptation, which is explored in the next section.

Orientation Factors, Perceived Discrimination, and Adaptation

Results reported in earlier chapters suggest that an integration orientation is associated with better psychological and sociocultural adaptation of immigrant adolescents. In addition, a stronger ethnic orientation is generally related to better psychological as well as sociocultural adaptation, whereas a stronger national orientation only contributes to better sociocultural adaptation. Discrimination is detrimental to both types of adaptation. Because the Turkish youth showed a stronger ethnic orientation and the Vietnamese showed stronger integration and national orientations, and because of the relationship of these orientations of adaptation reported in chapter 5, Turkish youth were expected to have slightly better scores for psychological adaptation and the Vietnamese adolescents were expected to have better scores for sociocultural adaptation. In addition, based on the results on perceived discrimination among the two groups in Norway (in the preceding section), we expected adolescents in that country to have lower adaptation scores than their counterparts in the other three countries.

The results partially support our expectations. Turkish adolescents had higher scores on psychological adaptation than the Vietnamese ($\eta^2 = .01$), whereas Vietnamese adolescents generally had better sociocultural adaptation than Turkish youth ($\eta^2 = .04$).

The immigrant youth in Norway, with both the lowest integration and the highest perceived discrimination scores, had lower psychological adaptation than their peers in Finland and Sweden ($\eta^2 = .03$). Furthermore, the immigrant youth in Norway scored lower on sociocultural adaptation than their peers in France and Sweden ($\eta^2 = .03$).

The Role of Cultural Diversity

As we have shown, the acculturation experiences and adaptation outcomes of Vietnamese and Turkish immigrant youth vary by country of settlement. We explored whether the links among country, acculturation experiences, and adaptation outcomes could be accounted for by the countries' scores for cultural diversity. Cultural diversity is an index developed from existing country-level data related to cultural, ethnic, and linguistic homogeneity (vs. heterogeneity) and the percentage of immigrants in a country (see chaps. 2 and 6).

In chapter 6 we report that in countries with higher levels of cultural diversity, immigrant youth report slightly higher levels of discrimination than in countries with lower levels of diversity. Higher levels of cultural diversity also corresponded to a slightly stronger involvement with peers from one's own ethnic group and with one's ethnic language. At the same time, in the countries with higher levels of cultural diversity, immigrant youth were more strongly oriented toward the national group than in countries with lower levels of cultural diversity. Finally, higher levels of cultural diversity corresponded to slightly lower levels of psychological adaptation.

For these analyses, we calculated new values for the relevant variables that control for age, gender, proportion of life in country of residence, and ethnocultural group. We compared these with newly calculated values for each variable in which, in addition to demographic variables, we also controlled for cultural diversity.[1] These comparisons allowed us to determine whether actual diversity accounts for country-level differences in acculturation and adaptation scores of Vietnamese and Turkish adolescents. The results for perceived discrimination showed that differences in perceived discrimination between countries are explained to a large extent by differences in cultural diversity of the countries. The direction, however, was unexpected: Lower levels of diversity correspond to higher levels of perceived discrimination. Similar analyses for psychological adaptation showed that taking the countries' cultural diversity into account results in a more positive picture of adolescents' psychological adaptation in Norway and a more negative picture of youth's adaptation in France than the original scores indicated. These findings suggest that the diversity in Norway reduces the psychological adaptation of Turkish and Vietnamese youth, whereas in France diversity supports immigrant youth's adaptation We also found that actual diversity positively affects the likelihood that immigrants value an orientation toward their own group and their integration orientation, whereas it does not affect their orientation toward the national group. The latter varies between countries irrespective of the countries' diversity.

Family Relationship Values and Intergenerational Discrepancies: Ethnic Group and Country Differences

Our focus in this section is on group and country influences in family relationship values and intergenerational value discrepancies. As in chapters 4 and 7, we consider two types of values: family obligations, which are the responsibilities that adolescents have to their parents and family; and adolescents' rights, which are adolescents' autonomy and freedom of choice in social relationships. These were reported by both adolescents and their parents. We calculated the intergenerational discrepancy for both obligations and rights as the differences between adolescents and parents. We used estimated scores that are corrected for particular background variables. The adolescent scores were corrected for adolescents' gender, age, and proportion of life spent in the country of residence. Parents' scores were corrected for parents' level of education. In the analyses of the intergenerational discrepancies, we included parents' level of education and proportion of life spent in the country of residence.

---

[1] In a second round of analyses we used each of these two new variables and explored the extent to which country of residence would explain the variance in scores. If cultural diversity scores cover the role of countries of residence in acculturation and adaptation, we should find that country of residence explains more variance in the first new variable—the one in which we did not account for actual diversity scores—than in the second one. Further information on the analyses and the outcomes is available from Paul Vedder (vedder@fsw.leidenuniv.nl).

Family Obligations and Intergenerational Discrepancies

Country of settlement made a difference in adolescents' family obligation (η^2 = .03); Turkish and Vietnamese adolescents in Sweden generally had higher obligations scores than did adolescents in Finland and Norway. Ethnic group as such did not make a difference in the obligations scores, but there was an interaction of country and ethnic group (see Fig. 8.6); Turkish and Vietnamese adolescents' scores differed depending on the country (η^2 = .06). In three countries, Turkish adolescents reported supporting family obligations more than did the Vietnamese adolescents; in Finland, the reverse was true. Turks in Finland had particularly low scores.

As with the adolescents, parents' scores on family obligations varied by country (η^2 = .05). Turkish parents in Finland and Vietnamese parents in Sweden reported that adolescents had less family obligations than did parents in France and Norway. In addition, the scores for Turkish and Vietnamese adolescents varied by country (η^2 = .10; see Fig. 8.7). In Sweden, Turkish parents reported more obligations than did Vietnamese parents, whereas in Finland and Norway the order is reversed; in France the group difference is negligible.

Intergenerational discrepancies did not vary between Vietnamese and Turkish families, but they varied considerably by country (η^2 = .07). In three countries parents clearly reported more obligations than did adolescents, but in Sweden adolescents and parents differed little (Finland: M = .33; France: M = .54; Norway: M = .56; Sweden: M = .05).

With the entire sample, adolescents' family obligations were lower with longer residence in the country of settlement but only among girls (see chap. 7). For the current sample of Vietnamese and Turks, there was a small effect of length of resi-

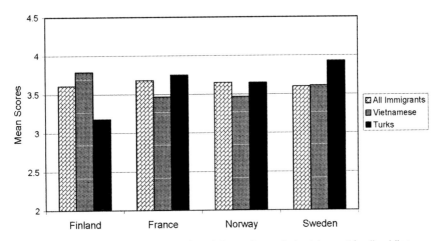

FIG. 8.6.   Estimated mean scores for adolescent-reported adolescent family obligations by group and country, controlling for age, gender, and proportion of life in country of residence.

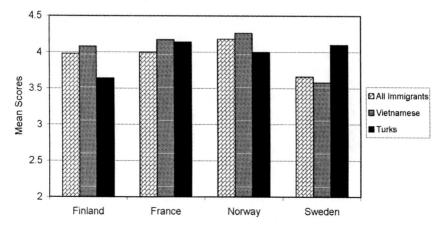

FIG. 8.7. Estimated mean scores for parent-reported adolescent family obligations by group and country (controlling for parents' level of education).

dence that varied by country ($\eta^2 = .01$). In Sweden and Finland, irrespective of ethnic group, adolescents' family obligation scores were lower with longer residence. Length of residence was unrelated to parents' reported obligations scores and obligations discrepancy scores.

Adolescents' Rights and Intergenerational Discrepancies

As was the case for many of the results regarding obligations, country of settlement made more of a difference in adolescents' reported scores for adolescents' rights ($\eta^2 = .20$) than did ethnicity. In France, scores were considerably lower ($M = 2.42$) than in Finland ($M = 4.07$), Norway ($M = 3.67$), or Sweden ($M = 3.89$). However, Turkish and Vietnamese adolescents' scores differed depending on the country ($\eta^2 = .03$); in Finland, Turkish adolescents had higher scores than Vietnamese, whereas in Sweden the Vietnamese had higher scores.

The parents' reported scores for adolescents' rights, like those of the adolescents, varied by country ($\eta^2 = .08$), irrespective of ethnic group. Parents in Finland and Sweden reported that adolescents had more rights than did parents in France and Norway. Furthermore, Turkish parents generally granted their children more rights than did Vietnamese parents ($\eta^2 = .02$). Vietnamese and Turkish parents' scores for adolescents' rights varied somewhat by country ($\eta^2 = .04$); generally, Turkish parents reported granting more rights than Vietnamese parents, but in France, Turkish parents reported exceptionally low rights scores for their children. Vietnamese parents' scores varied little by country.

Intergenerational discrepancies with regard to adolescents' rights varied by country ($\eta^2 = .07$; Finland: $M = .67$; France: $M = -.31$; Norway: $M = .77$; Sweden:

$M = .61$). In three countries adolescents had stronger desires for rights than their parents wanted to grant them. In France, however, parents, particularly Vietnamese parents, grant their children more rights than their children actually claimed. This could perhaps be because the Vietnamese in France have been there much longer than the Vietnamese in the other three countries (see chap. 2). We found no differences in discrepancies between Vietnamese and Turkish families.

Intergenerational Discrepancies and Adolescent Adaptation

In the entire sample, as reported in chapter 7, intergenerational discrepancies were associated with poorer psychological and sociocultural adaptation. We expected similar results for the Turkish and Vietnamese samples. The results were only partly as expected. Higher intergenerational discrepancies for the family obligations were associated with poorer sociocultural adaptation ($\beta = -.18$) but only among the Turkish adolescents ($R^2 = .03$).

In earlier results with the entire sample (see chap. 7), adolescents' acculturation profile had an impact on the relationship between intergenerational value discrepancies and adolescents' adaptation. With the Turks and Vietnamese subsample, we found significant effects for sociocultural adaptation only. First, for Vietnamese adolescents with a diffuse acculturation profile, larger intergenerational obligation discrepancies corresponded to lower levels of sociocultural adaptation ($\beta = -.21$). Second, for Turkish youth with an integrated profile, larger discrepancies with respect to family obligations were associated with lower sociocultural adaptation scores ($\beta = -.47$). It is possible that for these Turkish adolescents who want to integrate—that is, to combine values and behaviors of the broader society and the home—intergenerational discrepancies weigh more heavily and thus have a more negative impact than for those with other profiles.

THE GENERALITY AND SPECIFICITY OF THE ADAPTATION MODEL

The second major goal of this chapter was to examine the generality of the model tested with the entire ICSEY sample. The findings from chapters 4 and 5 culminated in the testing of the model of the relationships among the intercultural variables and the adaptation outcomes in chapter 6 (see Fig. 6.1). The model generally supported our hypotheses regarding these relationships. We found, as expected, that a combined involvement and identification with the national and the ethnic cultures (i.e., an integration, or bicultural, orientation) was associated with more positive adaptation outcomes for immigrant youth than involvement and identification with either the national or the ethnic culture alone. We also found, as expected, that immigrant youths' ethnic orientation had a stronger (positive) impact on their psychological adaptation than on their sociocultural adaptation. In contrast, an orientation toward the national society had a stronger impact on sociocultural adaptation. Perceived discrimination negatively affected adaptation, but a stronger ethnic orientation was beneficial to adolescents' psychological well-being, even though a stronger ethnic orientation was related to higher levels of perceived discrimination.

In this section, we test the generality and specificity of the model with Vietnamese and Turkish samples to determine the extent to which these findings apply independently to two specific ethnic groups. In addition to expecting general agreement with the previous findings, we expected the strengths of the relationships to differ between the two groups because of the differences in their immigration histories. For testing the model we used the same factor scores that were used for testing the overall model in chapter 6.

The Turkish and Vietnamese Samples in All Their Countries of Settlement

The sample used to test the model consisted of all the Vietnamese and Turkish immigrant youth who had completed all of the questionnaire: 938 Vietnamese (in seven countries) and 732 Turkish adolescents (in six countries). Table 8.2 provides a demographic description of these participants. The table shows that this sample, although larger than the one used for comparisons in the previous section, is demographically similar. For example, the Turkish youth had longer residence in their countries of settlement than the Vietnamese youth, and the Vietnamese parents generally had somewhat higher status occupations.

Testing the Model With Vietnamese Youth

The outcomes of the model testing (using SEM) with the Vietnamese are presented in Fig. 8.8.[2] The model encompasses the idea that the four acculturation attitudes, the two cultural identities, and the two acculturation behaviors (language and social contacts) have much in common. Exploratory factor analyses were employed in chapter 6 to identify patterns among these variables, leading to the identification of four factors (integration orientation, ethnic orientation, national orientation, and ethnic behaviors). As in the general model in chapter 6, these factors constituted a single underlying super factor, labeled *ethnic contacts.*

The values represented in Fig. 8.8 are the mean standardized regression weights for all Vietnamese in the seven countries in the analyses. The fit of the model was satisfactory.[3] The variables accounted for 9.8% of the variance in

---

[2]The regression coefficients and path coefficients were constrained to be equal across the seven participating countries (although not further reported here, the change in fit statistics of models with less or with more constraints suggested that equality of the coefficients mentioned was the solution with best fit). In line with the model presented in chapter 6, the error terms of integration, ethnic identity, and majority identity were allowed to correlate.

[3]The Chi-Square was significant, $\chi^2(N = 941, df = 106) = 175.24, p < .01$, which is not so good, but the Chi-Square/df ratio of 1.65 stayed well below 2, which was very good. The value of the AGFI was .91, which is satisfactory; the NNFI was .86, which is below the suggested threshold level of .90. Finally, the value of the RMSEA was .026, which is very good.

TABLE 8.2
Sample Characteristics: Vietnamese and Turkish Immigrant Groups in Nine ICSEY Nations

	Vietnamese Youth	Turkish Youth
Number (percent female)		
Australia	241(66)	
Canada	77 (49)	
Finland	205 (52)	55 (62)
France	81 (57)	50 (50)
Germany		103 (49)
Netherlands		153 (47)
Norway	139 (54)	97 (47)
Sweden	98 (47)	274 (52)
United States	97 (59)	284 (52)
Mean age	15.54 $(SD = 1.59)$	15.21 $(SD = 1.64)$
Length of residence		
0–6 years	32%	15%
> 6 to <12 years	40%	20%
> 12–18 years	27%	65%
Generation		
First	56%	14%
Second	44%	86%
Proportion of life in new country	.73 $(SD = .32)$	.91 $(SD = .23)$
Religion		
Muslim	6%	91%
Buddhist	47%	2%
Roman Catholic	29%	1%
Nonreligious	15%	5%
Percent of parents in study	67 %	51%
	Vietnamese Parents	Turkish Parents
Number		
Australia	199 (66)	
Canada	47 (57)	
Finland	133 (53)	39 (59)
France	38 (68)	31 (45)
Germany		9 (11)
Netherlands		144 (46)

(continued)

TABLE 8.2 *(continued)*

	Vietnamese Parents	Turkish Parents
Number		
Norway	37 (62)	23 (52)
Sweden	71 (45)	130 (48)
United States	94 (60)	
Parental occupation		
Unemployed	7%	12 %
Unskilled	38%	47%
Skilled	24%	25%
White	17%	10%
Professional	14%	7%
Education		
4 = some high school	4.66 (*SD* = 1.78)	3.92 (*SD* = 1.56)
Length of residence	12.6 years (*SD* = 6.67)	19.2 years (*SD* = 6.33)

Note. ICSEY = International Comparative Study of Ethnocultural Youth.

sociocultural adaptation and 22% in psychological adaptation. These percentages are comparable to those found for the general model in chapter 6, which included all immigrant youth.

An inspection of Fig. 8.8 shows considerable similarity with the analysis of all immigrant youth (Fig. 6.1). However, a closer inspection of the direction and size of the coefficients also suggests some differences. As in the general model, the factor ethnic contacts was based on the positive contributions from ethnic behaviors and ethnic orientation, and the negative contribution of national orientations. However, ethnic orientation did not contribute to the prediction of sociocultural adaptation, and integration had a negligible contribution to the prediction of psychological adaptation. Furthermore, unlike the general model, ethnic contacts did not play a role in predicting sociocultural adaptation but only in predicting psychological adaptation. In addition to the indirect effects of the three factors (ethnic orientation, national orientation, and ethnic behaviors), adolescents' ethnic orientation also had a direct effect on psychological adaptation. This means that in addition to the common effect, the ethnic orientation factor had a unique contribution.

In the Vietnamese sample, in contrast to the general model, no clear support was found for the hypothesis that a combined involvement and identification with the national and ethnic cultures would correspond to more positive adaptation outcomes than an orientation toward either the national or the ethnic culture alone. Similarly, no support was found for the hypothesis that the national orientation would be more strongly related to sociocultural adaptation than would the ethnic orientation. However, in accord with the general model, we found that the ethnic

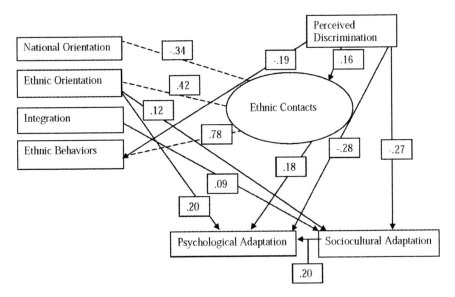

FIG. 8.8.   The outcome of the test (structural equation modeling) of the basic model specifying relations between intercultural variables and adaptation outcomes for Vietnamese immigrant adolescents; the values represented are standardized regression weights (averaged across countries).

orientation had a stronger impact on psychological adaptation than did the national orientation. These findings suggest that for the Vietnamese, identification and involvement with their own culture were more important for maintaining a good psychological adaptation than was a national orientation. The model captured more variation in psychological adaptation than in sociocultural adaptation. Finally, as in the general model, perceived discrimination had a dominating and negative impact on both types of adaptation.

Testing the Model With Turkish Youth

The outcomes of the model testing (using SEM) with the Vietnamese are presented in Fig. 8.9. The same coefficients were constrained to be equal across countries, as in the Vietnamese model. The values represented in the figure are the mean standardized regression weights for the six participating countries. For all Turkish adolescents together, the fit of the model was weak but still satisfactory.[4]

---

[4]Although the Chi-Square was significant, $\chi^2 (N = 738, df = 89) = 178.25, p < .01$), the Chi-Square/$df$ ratio of 2.00 pointed to a good fit. Both the AGFI (.88) and the NNFI (.83) yielded poor values, whereas the RMSEA (.04) was very good.

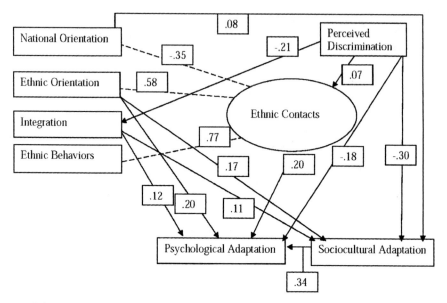

FIG. 8.9. The outcome of the test (structural equation modeling) of the basic model specifying relations between intercultural variables and adaptation outcomes for Turkish immigrant adolescents; values represented are mean standardized regression weights.

In the Turkish group the model explained 14% of the variance in sociocultural adaptation scores and 27.6% of the variance in psychological adaptation scores. The predictive power of the model was clearly better in the Turkish than in the Vietnamese group. As with the model presented in chapter 6 and the model for the Vietnamese, the latent variable ethnic contacts combines a strong ethnic orientation at the behavioral level with a preference for the ethnic group in terms of cultural identity.

In the Turkish model the ethnic contacts factor mainly contributed to psychological adaptation. Even with respect to this variable, the model showed that besides the indirect impact of the acculturation factors through ethnic contacts on adaptation, both ethnic orientation and integration had unique contributions to both psychological and sociocultural adaptation. In the Turkish sample the impact of adolescents' ethnic orientation was about equal for both adaptation types. Thus, we did not find support for the expectation that ethnic orientation would have a stronger impact on psychological adaptation than on sociocultural adaptation. Neither did we find support for the idea that orientation toward the national group would have a stronger impact than an ethnic orientation on sociocultural adaptation.

With respect to Turks, the model testing lent support to the hypothesis that a combined orientation toward the national and the ethnic cultures corresponds to more positive adaptation outcomes than an orientation toward either the national or the ethnic culture alone. This appeared to be more so for psychological adaptation than for sociocultural adaptation. Finally, as in the prior models, perceived discrimination negatively affected adaptation outcomes.

Overall, the model testing for the Turkish youth shows that adaptation scores in this group can best be explained in terms of an orientation toward integration. However, this is different from saying that the Turks are characterized by high levels of integration. As was shown in the first section of this chapter, Turks are predominantly represented in the ethnic profile rather than in the integration profile.

SUMMARY AND CONCLUSIONS

A problem that plagues psychological acculturation research with immigrants is its limitation in generalizing beyond the group and the country where the study was carried out (Berry et al., 1987; Cohon, 1981; Virta, Sam, & Westin, 2004). This is partly because immigrants do not constitute a homogenous group and contextual features in their societies of settlements vary greatly. The present study is no exception. The findings reported in chapters 4, 5, 6, and 7 have been based largely on 30 different immigrant groups in 13 countries of settlement. Although in most of our analyses we controlled for age, gender and other sociodemographic factors, we cannot be certain that our findings can be generalized across societies of settlement and across immigrant groups. Hence, in the present chapter we focused on Turkish and Vietnamese youth to verify the generality of our findings to ethnicity and country of residence. The chapter addresses the questions whether acculturation experiences and adaptation outcomes are similar or vary between ethnic groups and across countries, and whether our theoretical model of immigrant youth adaptation is general or ethnic specific.

Before interpreting our findings, one methodological caveat needs to be mentioned. The two immigrant groups, Vietnamese and Turks, have widely different backgrounds: The Vietnamese youth have a refugee background and are equally divided between first- and second-generation immigrants. The Turkish youth have a background of labor migration and are primarily second-generation immigrants. Thus, in these samples, immigration history and immigrant group are confounded. Ideally, additional immigrant groups should have been included in our analyses, as any comparison between two naturally occurring groups is inherently ambiguous (Campbell, 1961; Segall, Dasen, Berry, & Poortinga, 1999). Unfortunately, we did not have other immigrant groups large enough to be included in these analyses.

Comparisons Between Vietnamese and Turkish Immigrants

We explored similarities and differences for the two groups in several ways. First, we used a person-oriented approach based on the acculturation profiles reported earlier. The results showed that the majority of the Turks belong to the ethnic profile. This finding seems to be consistent with the nature of Turkish immigration and resettlement in Europe. The Turkish immigration from the onset was regarded as temporary, hence the name guest workers. Consequently, the countries receiving Turkish immigrants did not put into place structures that would facilitate the integration of the Turks in the new society, and neither did the Turks themselves work toward becoming integrated into the new society. For instance, until recently Turks in Germany could not readily secure German citizenship (Østergaard-Nielsen, 2001). As guest workers, many Turks believed they would eventually return home, even though this return migration is nowhere in sight, constituting what has become known as the "myth of return" (Rack, 1982; Zetter, 1999). For many Turks, it was deemed advantageous to keep a strong ethnic identity, maintain a separation attitude, and stay proficient in their original language. Turkish parents have undoubtedly passed on to their children their wish to remigrate back to Turkey, and they seem to have succeeded in promoting ethnic retention. This is clearly reflected in the predominance of the ethnic profile among Turks and the relatively higher family obligation scores among the Turkish sample compared with the Vietnamese.

Because refugee status often entails an indefinite life in exile, it is reasonable for Vietnamese parents and their offspring to make the best of their life in the new society, perhaps becoming as much a part of the new society as possible. Furthermore, the United Nations Convention for Refugees guarantees refugees a number of social welfare benefits and civil rights such as education in their society of settlement. It is likely that an expected indefinite life in a new society, together with the social and civil rights, contribute to the predominance in the national profile among the Vietnamese. In addition, a large number of Vietnamese youth were in the diffuse profile. However, this finding is largely explained by the large numbers of Vietnamese youth who are relatively recent immigrants. Among all immigrant youth, the diffuse profile was disproportionately represented among adolescents with the shortest length of residence in the new society. Thus, the large proportion of Vietnamese with a diffuse profile reflects their shorter length of residence.

Our results regarding the adaptation of Vietnamese and Turks in four countries generally support the results we obtained with the entire immigrant sample. The integration profile is the most adaptive profile for both groups. However, the majority of Turks and Vietnamese were not found in the integration profile, suggesting that many Vietnamese and Turkish adolescents have suboptimal adaptation outcomes. Furthermore, both in our earlier results and in related research (Ward, 2001), the ethnic profile tends to be associated with better psychological adaptation and the national profile tends to be associated with better sociocultural adaptation. The differences between the two groups with respect to the ethnic and the national profiles may explain why the Turkish youth have slightly better scores for psychological adaptation, whereas the Vietnamese adolescents should have better scores for sociocultural adaptation. The relatively better psychological adaptation found among Vietnamese youth within the national profile gives some credence to their desire to identify as much as possible with the national society, in view of the possibility that they may remain permanently in their country of settlement.

It is surprising that for the Turks, the ethnic profile is more adaptive than the integration profile. Perhaps this is because the ethnic profile was the most common, adding to a sense of consensus and providing some degree of extra social support. In addition, the national profile is highly maladaptive for the Turks in terms of their sociocultural adaptation. The latter finding is exceptional in that it conflicts with the general picture that the diffuse profile, rather than the national profile, is the most maladaptive. It is important to clarify that this finding does not contradict another result, namely, that a national orientation is conducive to better sociocultural adaptation. The latter result was found for all participating immigrant youth as well as for the Turkish participants in particular. When dealing with profiles, we are considering a particular subsample of immigrant adolescents who are characterized more than other adolescents by a preference for using the national language, interacting with national peers and wanting to assimilate. In this case we are dealing with a relatively small group of Turkish adolescents whose attitudes, aspirations, and behaviors are geared to the national group, so that they stand in marked contrast to the dominant acculturation strategy in their own group, which is characterized by a strong bonding with and orientation toward their own group. Most likely the youth with the national profile lack support from their own ethnocultural community. From other studies (e.g., Nesdale et al., 1997), we know that this may lead to distress and adaptation problems when this loss of support is not sufficiently compensated by support from the national group. Although we have no information about the support that Turkish youth with a national profile receive from the national group, generally we know that in Western countries the attitudes toward Muslims are predominantly nonsupportive (Pew Research Center, 2005).

For Turkish adolescents with an integration profile, larger intergenerational discrepancies with respect to family obligations were associated with lower sociocultural adaptation scores. It is possible that these integrative Turkish adolescents want to integrate, both in the broader society and at home, and thus intergenerational discrepancies are particularly stressful.

Differences between Turks and Vietnamese are also seen in the testing of the overall adaptation model. The results suggest that the relationship between acculturation processes and adaptation outcomes in the Vietnamese sample is best explained by an ethnic orientation, whereas for the Turks, the relationship is best explained by an integration orientation. In both groups perceived discrimination negatively affects adaptation outcomes, but the strength of this effect is clearly weaker among the Turks than among the Vietnamese. Furthermore, the relatively weak relationship between perceived discrimination and the ethnic contacts factor among the Turks suggests that, for them, discrimination does not promote a tendency to seek support within their own group.

Overall, there are fewer ethnic group differences than differences based on country of settlement. However, the observed group differences provide important insights into the acculturation of adolescents from Vietnamese and Turkish backgrounds.

Comparisons Across Countries of Settlement

In most of our comparisons, there is a stronger effect of country than of ethnic group. Norway emerged as a particularly interesting example. In Norway we found both the lowest scores on the integration factor and the highest levels of discrimination. Integration tends to correspond to better adaptation, whereas discrimination is detrimental to it. The combined effect should lead to low adaptation scores in Norway. The Vietnamese and Turkish youth in Norway, having both the lowest integration and highest perceived discrimination scores, indeed had lower adaptation scores than youth in other countries. It is difficult to explain why Turks and Vietnamese in Norway should have relatively higher perceived discrimination scores. Overall, Norway did not have higher reports of perceived discrimination (see chap. 4). This makes Norway an intriguing exception with respect to the Vietnamese and Turks.

Another, perhaps related, finding is that cultural diversity in Norway reduces Vietnamese and Turkish youth's psychological adaptation. In chapter 6 we suggest that this might be due to the positive relationship between cultural diversity and perceived discrimination, but as stated before, levels of perceived discrimination are not exceptional in Norway, and more important, when comparing the four common countries, we found that lower cultural diversity scores coincide with higher levels of perceived discrimination. The low level of cultural diversity may mean for the Vietnamese but particularly for the Turks in Norway (see Fig. 8.4) that they lack a sense of support from their own ethnocultural group because of the relatively low numbers of their own group in Norway. In addition, for the Turks in Norway cultural diversity may have an exceptional meaning. Perhaps they, more than their peers in other countries, perceive it as an indicator of xenophobia on the part of the national society. Cultural diversity is not seen as an opportunity to find support in their own ethnocultural group but as something that might make the national society resentful of immigrants. This suggestion is of course a speculation that awaits validation in further research.

When there was a difference by ethnic group, in most cases there was also an interaction, indicating that the relationship varied by country. For example, Turkish youth in Finland perceive less discrimination, whereas Turkish youth in Norway perceive more discrimination. The interaction effects are most evident in comparisons involving Turkish adolescents in Finland. Most of them have a Turkish father and a Finnish mother. Whereas Turkish adolescents generally have a stronger ethnic orientation and are more characterized by ethnic behaviors than Vietnamese adolescents, Turkish adolescents in Finland have a weaker ethnic orientation and are less involved with peers from their own group and use their own language less than their Vietnamese peers. A similar interaction effect occurs with respect to Turkish adolescents' national orientation. Generally, the national orientation of Vietnamese adolescents was stronger than that of the Turkish adolescents, but in Finland the Turkish and Vietnamese adolescents' scores are on average at about the same level. The important point is that particular situations yield results contrary to the overall picture.

The actual ethnic, cultural, and linguistic diversity of the countries of settlement is an additional factor influencing acculturation. When diversity is taken into account, country differences in perceived discrimination, adolescents' orientations toward their own ethnic group or toward integration, and both psychological and sociocultural adaptation are reduced. The findings show that an increase in cultural diversity increases the likelihood that immigrants will be oriented toward their own group but that such diversity has no impact on the likelihood of orienting toward the national group. Cultural diversity, which is a country-level score, may not be indicative of contact with the national group at the personal level.

The importance of country differences in cultural diversity is particularly clear for perceived discriminations. In countries with lower cultural diversity scores we found higher levels of perceived discrimination. Accounting for cultural diversity completely diminished the differences in perceived discrimination between countries.

The impact of country can also be seen with respect to family relationship values. Among Vietnamese and Turkish immigrants in the four countries studied, family relationship values depended more on the country of residence than on ethnocultural group. Except in Finland, Turkish adolescents in France, Norway and Sweden generally reported higher obligations scores than their Vietnamese peers in the same countries, and this may be a reflection of the strong ethnic orientation Turks have compared with Vietnamese. On the other hand, Vietnamese parents in general reported higher obligations scores than their Turkish counterparts except in Sweden. The high obligations scores among Vietnamese parents may be part of the Vietnamese culture—children are expected to show respect and obey their parents (Matsuoka, 1990; Nguyen et al., 1999; Nguyen & Williams, 1989; Zhou & Bankston, 1998). It is, however, difficult to explain why Vietnamese parents in Sweden have comparatively lower obligation scores.

Generalizability of Findings

The findings presented earlier regarding the impact of ethnic group and country of residence on acculturation and adaptation suggest that we need group and country-specific explanations for acculturation processes, adaptation outcomes, and their interrelations. The role of group and country in acculturation and adaptation is a critical issue to pursue in acculturation research. Nevertheless, the findings of the present chapter primarily support the view that acculturation and adaptation and their interrelationship can be understood in broadly applicable regularities and characteristics irrespective of ethnic groups and countries.

The findings of this chapter suggest that with few exceptions, conclusions drawn from chapters 4, 5, 6, and 7 can be generalized across countries and across ethnocultural groups, at least within the parameters of this study, but there are some aspects of the intercultural relations and the adaptation outcomes that may be specific to particular immigrant groups and countries of residence. These conclusions are in line with many cross-cultural psychological research findings: Some findings are general to all human beings and some are specific to a particular cultural group (Berry et al., 2002).

9 Understanding Immigrant Youth: Conclusions and Implications

Jean S. Phinney
California State University, Los Angeles
John W. Berry
Queen's University
David L. Sam
University of Bergen
Paul Vedder
Leiden University

OVERVIEW AND RESEARCH QUESTIONS

Immigration is becoming an increasingly important issue worldwide, and research is accumulating from many countries around the globe. However, there have been few studies that examine immigrant youth from an international perspective. The project reported in this book sought to gain understanding of the process of acculturation and the outcomes of this process in a sample of more than 5,000 adolescents from a wide range of immigrant groups residing in 13 countries of settlement. We were interested in three basic questions:

1. *How* do immigrant youth live within and between two cultures— their ethnic or heritage culture and the culture of their new country? We were guided in this inquiry by notions about acculturation drawn from the literature, particularly the concepts of acculturation attitudes and cultural identity.

2. *How well* do immigrant youth adapt to their intercultural situation in the personal, social, and academic areas of their lives? To explore this issue, we drew on the concepts of psychological and sociocultural adaptation.

3. What is the relationship between *how* adolescents engage in their intercultural relations and *how well* they adapt? We hoped to be able to draw conclusions about the best way for youth to orient themselves to their heritage culture and their new society to achieve positive outcomes and avoid negative consequences.

In designing the study, we selected countries of settlement that varied systematically in terms of their diversity to provide a theoretical basis for interpreting our results. The countries of settlement varied on two dimensions of diversity. The first, a society's cultural diversity, included the society's history of immigration, the current percentage of immigrants, and its linguistic and cultural diversity. The second, diversity policy, refers to the extent to which the society of settlement espouses cultural diversity as a resource to be supported or, alternatively, seeks to reduce diversity and maintain cultural homogeneity. As background for the study, chapter 2 presents information on the 13 societies of settlement and portrayals of the 26 immigrant groups included in the study.

Participants in the study were 13- to 18-year-old adolescents and, for some adolescents, their mothers or fathers. In all countries, we drew nonrandom samples, usually from the main cities in which immigrants have settled. Samples included youth and some of their parents from major immigrant communities, as well as nonimmigrant (national) youth, usually from the same areas. Participants were surveyed using a common questionnaire developed by the ICSEY researchers. We assessed a range of intercultural variables that describe the acculturation experience (acculturation attitudes, cultural identities, language proficiency and use, peer social relations, family relationship values, and perceived discrimination) and two types of adaptation variables: psychological adaptation (including life satisfaction, self-esteem, anxiety, depression, and psychosomatic symptoms) and sociocultural adaptation (involving school adjustment and behavior problems). Statistical procedures used to explore the psychometric properties of the measures provided support for the structural equivalence of the measures in both the immigrant and the national samples; that is, the instruments appeared to measure the same constructs across all groups and countries, and hence were deemed suitable for use in a comparative study.

HOW DO IMMIGRANT ADOLESCENTS ACCULTURATE?

The concept of acculturation was developed in anthropology to help describe and understand how cultural groups change following their contact with other groups. The focus of anthropologists was on collectivities (such as societies, communities, and institutions) rather than on individuals. In contrast, psychologists are interested in individuals and individual differences. This project incorporated both the group and individual perspectives, and we provide both cultural-level and individual-level information and analyses. As psychologists, we have sought to study patterns of similarities and differences in cultural and individual acculturation phenomena. In particular, we investigated the issue of the extent to which there are variations in the ways individuals engage the acculturation process.

At the individual level, we found that there are clearly different ways immigrant adolescents live in their new society. These are best exemplified by acculturation profiles described in chapter 4. Cluster analysis, a procedure that identifies groups of individuals who share particular characteristics, was carried out with all the immigrant youth using the intercultural variables (acculturation attitudes, cultural identities, language, peer social relations, and family relationship values). The analysis yielded four acculturation profiles that describe groups of adolescents with distinct ways of handling the acculturation process.

One group of adolescents exhibits an integration profile. Their acculturation attitudes reflect a preference for integration and a rejection of assimilation and separation. They have strong ethnic identities but also substantial, if somewhat weaker, national identities. They report being more proficient in the national language and using it more than the ethnic language, but they also maintain their ethnic language. They have friends from both their own group and other ethnocultural groups, including the national society. Overall, they give clear evidence of being involved in the new society while retaining their ethnic heritage.

A second group consists of adolescents with an ethnic profile. They have strong ethnic identity, high ethnic language proficiency and usage, and social contacts primarily with their ethnic peers. They endorse the separation attitude and score low on assimilation, national identity, and contacts with the national group. They represent young people who are largely embedded within their own cultural milieu and show little involvement with the larger society.

A third group exhibits a national profile. They are high on national identity and on the assimilation attitude, and very low on ethnic identity. They are proficient in the national language and use it predominantly. Their peer contacts are largely with members of the national group. These adolescents show a strong orientation toward the larger society in which they are living and little retention of their ethnic culture.

A final group shows a diffuse profile. These adolescents endorse three contradictory acculturation attitudes—assimilation, marginalization, and separation— and are low on both cultural identities. They report low proficiency in and use of the national language. Their profile reflects uncertainty and ambiguity about their place in society.

Acculturation Strategies

The four acculturation profiles not only show variety in the ways immigrant adolescents acculturate, they also highlight the fact that the attitudes, identities, and behaviors we studied do not function in isolation but are intimately interrelated. This interrelationship can be seen first in the correspondence between acculturation attitudes and the cultural identities. For example, attitudes toward integration are positively correlated with both ethnic and national identities, and marginalization attitudes are negatively correlated with both identities. Assimilation and separation attitudes are correlated with the two identities in the expected way, positively with one identity and negatively with the other. The cultural values of family obligations and adolescents' rights are also related in expected ways to acculturation attitudes and identity.

Furthermore, acculturation attitudes are linked to the two behavioral variables of language usage and social contacts with peers. For example, integration attitudes are associated with use of both the ethnic and national languages, and with social relationships with peers from both groups.

More broadly, the acculturation profiles suggest that attitudes, identities, and behaviors cluster together in different ways to form distinct groups of youth. These groupings are easily interpretable on the basis of earlier research findings on individual variables. The clustering of variables into consistent patterns suggest a broader concept of *acculturation strategies* that provide a comprehensive picture of how individuals live in contact settings (Berry, 1997). The view that individuals are not simply pawns or victims of their circumstances but rather actively seek out and create their own ways of living (e.g., Bandura, 1997) lends support to the use of the term strategies to refer to differing ways of handling the complexity of living in two different cultural contexts.

Alternative Views of Ways of Acculturating

The empirical procedure used in the cluster analysis could, in principle, yield any number of profiles, including only one. The fact that we found four profiles supports our expectation that there are variable ways youth can live in their intercultural world. Moreover, the four profiles closely resemble the four sectors of the acculturation framework presented in chapter 4.

Other researchers have arrived at somewhat different conclusions regarding the ways immigrants acculturate. In the sociological literature, Portes and Rumbaut (2001) use the overall concept of *segmented assimilation* to distinguish among various possible outcomes of the acculturation experience among immigrant minorities. They present a number of alternatives that are based in part on the extent to which adolescents and parents follow similar or different approaches. *Consonant acculturation* refers to the situation where both children and parents become incorporated into the mainstream society, similar to our concept of assimilation, seen in the national profile. *Consonant resistance to acculturation* refers to isolation of both parents and adolescents within the ethnic community, similar to our concept of separation or an ethnic profile. *Selective acculturation* implies retention of the ethnic culture, particularly among parents, while the children become bilingual, a pattern suggesting integration, but with possible conflict within families. Finally, *dissonant acculturation* involves different patterns of change among parents and children that may lead to families' losing the ethnic culture while not becoming part of the mainstream, similar to our concept of marginalization. However, there are differences between their conceptualization and ours. Their core concept is that of assimilation, rather than the more generic acculturation, suggesting that the expected eventual outcome for immigrants in the settings they studied in the United States is assimilation; alternative outcomes are dissonance in the family or resistance to acculturation. Other American scholars (e.g., Ogbu, 1997; Zentella, 1997) point to the importance of culture maintenance, suggesting that there are other possible ways of acculturation besides assimilation. Ogbu (1997) described a type of separation called cultural inversion, and Zentella (1997) discussed a kind of contextual separation focusing mainly on immigrant children's educations situation.

Preferred Ways of Acculturating

Our results show differences in the extent to which particular ways of dealing with acculturation are preferred or adopted among immigrant youth. The most strongly endorsed acculturation attitude among immigrant adolescents both overall and across all countries and ethnocultural groups is integration. Not only do immigrant youth endorse this attitude most, the national adolescents also believe that immigrants should become integrated. The preference for integration is also reflected in the acculturation profiles. Among the four profiles, the integration profile is the most common profile, characterizing about one third of the adolescents; only one fourth or fewer of the adolescents showed any other single profile.

Adolescents' second most endorsed attitude, is separation, that is, retaining their ethnic culture and not necessarily adopting aspects of the national culture. This preference for separation over assimilation was a surprise, given the common assumption that contemporary immigrant youth are less involved in their heritage culture and more involved with national or international peer cultures. However, the same preference is reflected in the profiles. The ethnic profile, which includes stronger separation attitudes, is somewhat more common than the national profile. In the sample as whole, well over half of the adolescents are in either the integration or the ethnic profile, both of which show strong support for the maintenance on one's ethnic culture, with or without involvement in the national culture. These results clearly attest to the importance for most immigrant youth of holding onto their heritage culture.

Nevertheless, the patterns of preferred ways of acculturating cannot be considered universal. The distribution of profiles varies considerably over time and across contexts. We cannot assume that the same frequencies will be found in all conditions; rather, the specific situation must be taken into account.

Acculturation and Length of Time in a New Society

Our project did not include longitudinal data that would allow for the study of changes among immigrants over time in a new society. However, we used several proxy variables, including generation, proportion of life in the new society, and length of residence, that allow us to examine differences among adolescents who vary in the length of their exposure to the new society. Although any conclusions are tentative in the absence of longitudinal data, the results are sufficiently consistent to indicate patterns of change that are likely to occur over time.

A basic issue in acculturation research is whether immigrants undergo a linear change, from a strong identification and involvement in their culture of origin to a more or less complete identification and involvement in the culture of settlement, that is, assimilation, or whether there are alternative pathways of change over time (Berry, 1980, 1984b). Our results provide evidence that the process of change is not a linear progression. On the one hand, with longer residence in the new society, there is greater involvement with the national culture: National identity is stronger; national language proficiency and use are higher; contact is greater with peers from the larger society; and more immigrant adolescents exhibit a national profile, characterized by an orientation toward the larger society. On the other hand, there is not a parallel decrease in identification with the ethnic group. Over time, the proportion of adolescents with an ethnic profile does not change; ethnic identity continues to be strong and adolescents have no fewer contacts with their ethnic peers. Only their ethnic language and proficiency are lower. The result is involvement and identification with both cultural groups. The clear implication is that with longer residence, adolescents are more likely to be bicultural and integrated, rather than assimilated.

Nevertheless, some differences in ethnic involvement can be seen over time. Immigrant adolescents with longer residence endorse family obligations less than more recent arrivals, and this difference is greater for girls than for boys and in neighborhoods where most residents are not from their own ethnocultural group. In contrast, parents' support for family obligations is unrelated to length of residence. These results are in accord with other research showing that immigrant adolescents' cultural values change more rapidly than do their parents' (Nguyen & Williams, 1989). This difference is reflected in a discrepancy between adolescents and parents. Contrary to prior research, we found no difference overall in the intergenerational discrepancy in family obligations with longer residence. However, among adolescents with a diffuse profile (i.e., those who appear uncertain or confused about their place in the new society), the discrepancy is greater over time. The results provide little evidence for the assumption that there is an inevitable increase in differences between immigrant adolescents and their parents over time in a new society. Rather, the likelihood of such an increase differs across adolescents and across settings.

HOW WELL DO IMMIGRANT YOUTH ADAPT?

A question that has engaged the attention of cross-cultural psychologists for decades is how people born and raised in one society manage to live in another society that is culturally different from their original society (Sam & Berry, in press). A related question is what happens to adolescents of parents who have migrated from one cultural context to another. Early scholarship on how well people fare during cross-cultural transitions painted a rather pessimistic view of the outcome, contending that it was harmful (Malzberg & Lee, 1956; Ødegaard, 1932; Plato, 348 B.C./1892). However, recent studies suggest otherwise, pointing to the precarious nature of cross-cultural transitions but at the same time indicating that a negative outcome is not inevitable (Beiser et al., 1989; Berry & Sam, 1997; Rogler, Cortes, & Malgady, 1991). In short, many people are able to weather the cultural changes and come out of it unscathed.

Research based on young immigrants has concluded that adolescents with immigrant backgrounds adapt equally well as their national peers and in some cases are better adapted (Aronowitz, 1984; Fulgini, 1998b). Some current research presents a more complex picture, suggesting that the adaptation of immigrants is initially as good as, and sometimes even better than, that of their national peers, but that this initial advantage deteriorates over time (Garcia Coll, 2005; Hayes-Bautista, 2004).

In this project, we examined two types of adaptation: psychological adaptation (including life satisfaction, self-esteem, and psychological problems measured in terms of anxiety, depression, and psychosomatic symptoms) and sociocultural adaptation (including school adjustment and behavior problems, that is, antisocial behavior in school and in the community). Although the measures by which adaptation was assessed did not include all possible aspects of adaptation, the two adaptation variables showed good psychometric properties and appear to provide adequate assessments of attitudes and behaviors that are salient for youth.

On the whole, immigrant youth show slightly fewer psychological problems, fewer behavior problems, and better school adjustment compared with their national peers but do not differ in life satisfaction and self-esteem. Although immigrant youth appear to be better adapted socioculturally, they are similar to their national peers in psychological adaptation. These conclusions are based on our samples of immigrant and national youth, and our samples may not be representative of all such youth. However, our findings are generally consistent with several previous research findings (Fuligni, 1998a; Rumbaut, 2000). Most previous research has been based on immigrants in a single country and, at best, two countries. Our results go further than previous studies in that they are based on a large number of immigrant youth and their national peers living in 13 countries, and hence provide a basis for generalizing such findings.

The positive outcomes for immigrant youth that have been reported in recent research have provoked interest among researchers because of the expectation that immigrants will inevitably have problems resulting from the stress of living between two cultures. Failure to find poorer adaptation among immigrant youth compared with their national peers has resulted in the notion of the *immigrant paradox*, the counterintuitive finding that immigrants show better adaptation outcomes than their national peers. The paradox also refers to the finding that first-generation immigrants often have higher levels of adaptation than the second generation and that over time the adaptation of immigrant youth may decline toward the level of the nationals or even below. To ascertain the existence of the phenomenon, several analyses would need to be carried out, including comparisons of all immigrants with residents of the society of settlement, comparisons of first-generation with second-generation immigrants, and comparisons of second-generation immigrants with national residents.

In this study, there is no overall evidence of differences that would support the assumptions of the immigrant paradox. However, the patterns varied widely depending on the country and the type of adaptation, with some cases showing the expected differences and other cases showing the opposite. In four countries—Australia, Finland, Sweden, and the United States—the first-generation immigrant youth have better sociocultural adaptation than the national samples, and the adaptation of second-generation immigrant youth were close to the levels of the nationals, in support of the paradox. Nevertheless, for psychological adaptation, there is some evidence of the opposite effect. In all countries where there are differences in psychological adaptation between generations (Canada, Finland, Norway, and Sweden), the second-generation immigrants show better adaptation than the first generation, but not better than the nationals, except in Sweden. These findings are contrary to the paradox.

The Role of Acculturation

Given the findings of generally small differences in adaptation between immigrant and national youth, how can we say that the experience of acculturation plays a role in adaptation? This issue has been addressed by Lazarus (1997), who suggested that there is much more going on in an immigrant's life than his or her experience of acculturation, such as emotional reactions to developmental and other life transitions. The issue has been studied empirically by Chataway and Berry (1989), who used a three-group design (English-speaking and French-speaking Canadian university students, and Chinese international students at the same university) to distinguish cultural differences from language differences and from common difficulties experienced in the transition to university life, such as loneliness and uncertainty about the future. It has been further studied by others (e.g., Abouguendia & Noels, 2001; Lay & Nguyen, 1998 ; Safdar, Lay, & Struthers, 2003) who have proposed assessing daily hassles that are common to all young people. They found that such daily hassles were indeed related to psychophysical distress, which then negatively affected psychosocial adjustment.

Our view on the role of acculturation is that, although on average there are few differences between the immigrant and national samples, there are large differences *within* the immigrant youth samples, and these differences depend on how the youth are going about their acculturation. All youth are challenged by new experiences, regardless of their immigrant status, but immigrant youth are exposed to more and different challenges, which reside in their intercultural status. When these experiences, such as language use, identity choice, and the experience of discrimination, are examined, they show that acculturation plays an important role in how well immigrant youth adapt, both psychologically and socioculturally.

WHAT IS THE RELATIONSHIP BETWEEN *HOW* ADOLESCENTS ACCULTURATE AND *HOW WELL* THEY ADAPT?

Our findings clearly support the view that the ways adolescents manage their intercultural situation is related to how well they adapt in their society of settlement. Results from two types of analyses of our data show this to be true. First, as reported in chapter 5, levels of adaptation vary in relation to the adolescents' acculturation profiles, that is, their pattern of involvement with their ethnic and national cultures. Adolescents with the integration profile show the most positive psychological and sociocultural adaptation, and those with the diffuse profile exhibit the poorest adaptation, both psychologically and socioculturally. This pattern is in keeping with the conclusion drawn by Berry and Sam (1997) in their review of numerous studies of acculturation and adaptation.

Adolescents with the ethnic profile show good psychological adaptation but not as good sociocultural adaptation. If integration is not an option or is not feasible for immigrant youth, an orientation toward the ethnic culture appears to be the next best choice. In contrast, those characterized by the national profile are poorly adapted both psychologically and socioculturally, but not as poorly as those in the diffuse profile. The results from the sample of all immigrant youth are largely confirmed in the subsamples of Vietnamese and Turkish youth with regard to psychological adaptation (see chap. 8). However, in the Turkish group there are some discrepancies with respect to sociocultural adaptation. The ethnic profile, rather than the integration profile, is associated with better sociocultural adaptation, and the national profile, rather than the diffuse profile, with worse.

The model tested in chapter 6 provides additional support for the benefits of integration as a way of acculturating in general. The model includes four factors (integration orientation, ethnic orientation, national orientation, and ethnic behaviors) based on the intercultural variables, with perceived discrimination as a separate variable. We also employed the two factor scores based on the adaptation variables: psychological adaptation and sociocultural adaptation. We found that an integration orientation is beneficial for both the psychological and the sociocultural adaptation of immigrant adolescents. Among immigrant youth, a truly bicultural orientation is beneficial for their sociocultural adaptation, and sociocultural adaptation in turn enhances their psychological well-being. Psychological well-being is also enhanced by a strong orientation toward one's ethnic group.

Overall, the results show that a joint positive orientation toward the ethnic culture and the national society is conducive to a better adaptation of both types than an orientation to either the ethnic culture or the national society alone. In contrast, a limited or negative orientation toward either the ethnic culture or the national society independently underlies adaptation problems. These findings are broadly applicable in the sample as a whole and in the subsample of Turkish immigrant youth, and they are in accord with other research (reviewed by Berry, 1997; Berry & Sam, 1997), suggesting that integration provides the most positive basis for adaptation in a new society. Remarkable in the Vietnamese sample is that adolescents' orientation toward the national culture plays no independent and direct role in predicting adaptation outcomes, whereas in the overall model test and in Turkish sample a stronger national orientation contributes to better sociocultural adaptation.

Evidence of the benefits of integration has led to criticisms in recent years that this finding may be a measurement artifact, arising from social desirability (Rudmin, 2003). Furthermore, Snauwaert et al. (2003) have demonstrated that the endorsement of the different acculturation strategies depends on the way these strategies have been conceptualized and operationalized (i.e., whether the strategies have been defined in terms of identity, behaviors, or attitudes). However, in this study we have multiple conceptions and measures of integration as a way of acculturating carried out in numerous samples. This complexity undermines the criticism that any one factor can explain away the consistency of the finding that integration is associated with better adaptation.

Furthermore, our results provide considerable evidence that adaptation outcomes are moderated by additional demographic and contextual factors that limit or enhance the options that immigrant adolescents have. Whenever the social context facilitates an integration approach, it is likely to be the best approach. However, integration always entails a common task that needs to be carried out by both the society of settlement and the immigrants; there needs to be agreement between both groups that integration is an acceptable way to engage in intercultural relations (Berry, 2003). The degree of acceptance or rejection by the larger society of integration as the way for immigrants to acculturate is reflected in their individual attitudes and national policies toward multiculturalism (Berry & Kalin, 1995; Berry et al., 1977). Striving for integration may lead to frustration among immigrants in some contexts, for example, when members of the larger society object to the immigrants' wishes to retain their ethnic culture. This resistance to integration may be based on the perception in the larger society that the retention of ethnic customs and language usage are an indication of a preference for separatism and unwillingness to join the society. When immigrants are seen this way, their presumed negative attitude toward the society tends to be reciprocated, leading to negative attitudes and discrimination toward immigrants (Berry & Kalin, 1979; Kalin & Berry, 1996). When immigrants experience discrimination, the most adaptive approach may be for them to seek support in their own culture. Thus, the adaptation of immigrant youth is likely to reflect how well their goals and preferences match the opportunities afforded to them in their society of settlement. As we have noted, national youth express a preference for integration for immigrants as the way they should be acculturating. The fact that most immigrant youth indicate a desire to be part of their new society suggests that integration will be most adaptive as long as it is available to them.

DEMOGRAPHIC FACTORS IN ACCULTURATION: GENDER, AGE, SES, AND ETHNICITY

Given the diversity we find in the ways of acculturating, an important question is whether the factors that are associated with different profiles, orientations, and adaptation outcomes play any role in the relationship among them. Among the demographic variables we studied, gender is the most strongly related to acculturation experiences and outcomes. However, SES (socioeconomic status) and ethnicity also made a difference.

Gender

Our results show that, in general, girls have more psychological problems than boys, but they have better school adjustment and fewer behavior problems. These results are in keeping with previous research with both immigrant youth (Portes & Rumbaut, 2001) and nonimmigrants (Tanaka-Matsumi & Draguns, 1997) showing that adolescent girls are more likely than boys to internalize problems and have higher levels of depression, whereas boys are more likely to externalize problems and act out. Thus, some gender differences in immigrant adolescents reflect common developmental phenomena and are not necessarily an outcome of acculturation.

Other gender differences are closely linked to the immigrant experience. Our results suggest that girls fit in more smoothly to their new society than do boys. Immigrant girls, compared with boys, report more positive attitudes toward integration and are more frequently represented in the integration profile. They also use the national language more than do boys. Conversely, boys report greater endorsement of separation attitudes and feel more discriminated against. This result is at variance with the view that among immigrants, females are more likely to be the carriers of culture, concerned with maintaining cultural traditions, and males become more involved with the larger society (Liebkind, 1996b). However, this latter view may pertain to parents rather than to children. In immigrant families, women are often expected to stay home and care for children, and men have jobs that bring them into contact with the larger society.

For adolescents, the role of gender may be quite different. In school, girls have the same opportunity as boys for exposure to the new society. Girls are likely to find school a congenial atmosphere, both because they typically do better in school than boys (Henderson & Dweck, 1990; McCord, 1990) and because a school atmosphere that promotes gender equality may allow them greater freedom than they experience at home. Positive attitudes toward school may contribute to the better school adjustment of girls. On the other hand, an orientation toward integration might create more stress at home, especially when parents want their daughters to remain close to the cultural traditions of the family (Liebkind, 1996b). Stress at home may be a factor in the poorer psychological well-being of girls.

For immigrant boys, poorer school adjustment may contribute to behavior problems and feelings of being discriminated against. In keeping with their poorer sociocultural adaptation, boys are more highly represented in the diffuse profile, characterized by apparent difficulty of finding a way to manage the challenges of dealing with two cultures. They may then turn toward their own group for support and favor separation, as is suggested by the rejection-identification model (Schmitt et al., 2002). In summary, immigrant boys appear to experience fewer psychological problems than girls but at the cost of having more difficulty in fitting in to the larger society. These gender differences are of course broad generalizations that must be interpreted with caution because of the wide variation at the individual level.

Age and Development

In a sample of young people ranging from 13 to 18 years, we would expect considerable difference by age in their patterns of acculturation and adaptation. However, there are relatively few effects of age. Some results suggest that older adolescents are not doing as well as younger adolescents. Younger immigrants have better school adjustment scores and are more satisfied with their lives than their older peers. The diffuse profile, indicative of uncertainty about their current situation, is more frequent in the older groups, 15- to 18-year-olds, than in the youngest group (13- to 14-year-olds). These results may be an aspect of normal adolescent development as young people experience confusion when they seek to establish a sense of identity (Erikson, 1968). However, age is confounded with age of arrival. We did not study the impact of age of arrival, but it is likely that adolescents who arrive at an older age have more difficulty in adjusting. When groups with equal length of residence are compared, older adolescents would necessarily have arrived in the country of settlement at an older age, a fact that may explain the evidence that they are not doing as well as younger immigrants.

There are few other differences with age; no age differences were found for most acculturation variables. For example, although older adolescents were expected to value family obligations less and to differ more with their parents, no age effects were found for these values, or for the discrepancies between adolescent and parent. An obvious factor is that acculturation is inevitably confounded with developmental processes that are occurring simultaneously (Schönpflug, 1997). In many cases, immigrant adolescents did not differ from their national peers; for example, the two groups did not differ in the impact of intergenerational discrepancies on adaptation. The similarities in adaptation between immigrant and national youth suggest common developmental processes that are occurring in both groups. When acculturation does make a difference in acculturation and outcomes, a large number of factors other than age, both individual and contextual, are involved. It is therefore perhaps not surprising that age alone provided little explanatory power.

SES

SES is an important demographic factor in the adaptation of immigrant youth and one that has been found to have a consistent relationship to acculturation experiences and outcomes reported in the literature (Berry & Sam, 1997). This is the case in our study, with higher SES, based on parental education, associated with a stronger orientation toward the national culture and a greater national language proficiency and use. Similarly, the national profile is more common among adolescents whose parents have higher status occupations. Furthermore, immigrant adolescents from higher SES families show lower support for separation attitudes, that is, an exclusive focus on one's ethnic group. These results are consistent with other evidence that higher SES is associated with greater contact with the national society (e.g., Ward, 2001). These results may reflect the fact that it is difficult to be financially and professionally successful in a new society without becoming involved in the language and culture of the society.

Ethnicity and Ethnocultural Group

The ethnocultural group to which adolescents belong provides particular goals, values, attitudes, and behaviors that make a difference in their acculturation experience. Ethnocultural group membership makes a substantial difference specifically in ethnic orientation and ethnic behaviors, as is shown in Table 6.1, and these in turn are important predictors of adaptation outcomes. We could not examine the role of ethnicity with reference to all the ethnocultural groups in the sample. However, for the two groups that were widely represented in different countries, we can see clearly the impact of ethnicity. Specifically, the Turkish and Vietnamese youth who are living in the same four countries show differences that can be reasonably attributed to differences between the groups. For the whole sample, the integration profile is the most adaptive profile, but the majority of Turks and Vietnamese are not found in the integration profile for reasons that are linked to their differential immigration history and goals. This finding suggests that many Vietnamese and Turkish adolescents may have suboptimal adaptation outcomes. However, another finding, particularly in the Turkish group, seems to contradict this suggestion. The ethnic profile is most characteristic of the Turkish adolescents, and in this group this profile is more adaptive than the integration profile. Also for the Turks, the national profile is the least adaptive.

In the Vietnamese sample, the relationship between profile and adaptation outcomes is similar to the relationship found for the immigrant youth in all countries: The integration profile is most adaptive, the ethnic profile is second most adaptive, and the diffuse profile is least adaptive.

Yet for the Vietnamese, the diffuse profile is the most frequent, and the integration profile is second. These findings together suggest that adaptation of the Vietnamese adolescents is less optimal than for the Turkish youth. For the Vietnamese this difference is related to the fact that more Vietnamese youth are first generation. As is typical of substantial numbers of recent immigrants in the sample as a whole, many of them have not yet made up their minds about their cultural bonds and their position in the new society, and thus show a diffuse profile.

Among both Vietnamese and Turks, perceived discrimination negatively affects adaptation outcomes. The strength of this effect is clearly weaker among the Turks than among the Vietnamese. There are two possible explanations for this difference. For the Turks, a preference for separation and the ethnic profile may indicate a form of group cohesion that serves as a buffer against the negative effects of discrimination. For the Vietnamese, the impact of discrimination may be the consequence of their higher frequency in the diffuse profile: A culturally confused person may be more susceptible to discrimination than a person with strong bonds in his or her own ethnocultural group (Branscombe et al., 1999).

CONTEXTUAL FACTORS IN ACCULTURATION: COUNTRY OF SETTLEMENT, NEIGHBORHOOD, AND FAMILY

Another approach to the question of the relationship between how immigrant youth acculturate and how well they adapt is to look at the way the various contexts influence this relationship. We examine three contexts that vary in proximity to the adolescent: country of settlement, neighborhood, and family.

Country of Settlement

The study was carried out in 13 countries, all of which are of predominantly Western European origin. The analyses in chapter 6 show that country of settlement made only a small contribution to variation in acculturation outcomes. The contribution to variance explained was largest for national orientation, but this was only 7%. Nevertheless, in spite of their overall common European origin, these countries differ widely in terms of their experience with, and attitudes toward, immigration and diversity.

A nation's immigration policy and the cultural diversity of the country are examples of distal context variables that are likely to affect acculturation. Bourhis et al. (1997) suggest that a country's immigration level and immigration policy reflect the larger society's attitudes toward immigrants. Both policy and attitudes may influence immigrants' attitudes and interethnic contacts, and thus have an impact on individual immigrants' well-being. In the present study we found that both greater cultural diversity (e.g., language diversity and proportion of immigrants) and diversity policy (administrative intentions) are directly positively related to both an increased orientation toward the national group and a stronger involvement with one's own ethnic group, together with a more extensive use of the ethnic language. To the extent that societies support an integration orientation among immigrants, these immigrants are likely to manifest this orientation at the behavioral level. However, higher levels of cultural diversity also coincide with increased experiences of discrimination and lower psychological well-being. It is likely that greater diversity provides more opportunity for individuals to discriminate against each other, and as noted, discrimination negatively affects psychological adaptation.

The distribution of profiles also varied in relation to immigration history. The proportion of immigrant youth in the integration profile was more than 50% in historically immigrant receiving or settler societies such as Australia, Canada, and the United States, and 31% or less in European countries where immigration is more recent, such as Norway and Finland. This variation can also be seen in the four common countries in which Turkish and Vietnamese immigrants resided: Finland, France, Norway, and Sweden. Norway emerged as a particularly interesting example. Norway has both the lowest scores on the integration factor and the highest levels of discrimination. Integration tends to correspond to better adaptation, whereas discrimination is detrimental to it. The combined effect resulted in lower adaptation scores for immigrants in Norway than in other countries.

Some of the differences among the four countries can be explained by differences in cultural diversity among the countries. The findings suggest that an increase in cultural diversity increases the likelihood that immigrants will be oriented toward their own group, but it has no impact on the likelihood of orienting toward the national group. Cultural diversity also is important to perceived discrimination. Although higher levels of cultural diversity generally correspond to higher levels of perceived discrimination (see chap. 6), the comparison involving only Norway, Sweden, Finland, and France (see chap. 8) show that Norway, a country with low cultural diversity, is characterized by higher levels of perceived discrimination. For immigrants in Norway, particularly the Turkish immigrants, low diversity may be linked to low support from their own group. Earlier we suggested that such support can buffer against the negative experience of discrimination (Branscombe et al., 1999). The lack of support may make immigrant youth more susceptible to discrimination experiences. However, it is important to keep in mind that generally the reported levels of perceived discrimination were low in all groups and all countries.

Other countries besides Norway have unique situations. Whenever we found differences by ethnic group, in most cases we also found interaction effects, indicating that the group differences in acculturation or adaptation varied by country. For example, Turkish youth in Finland perceive less discrimination, whereas the Turkish youth in Norway perceive more discrimination. The Turkish adolescents in Finland are an exceptional sample in that most of the adolescents have a Turkish father and a Finnish mother. Whereas generally the Turkish adolescents have a stronger ethnic orientation and are more characterized by ethnic behaviors than the Vietnamese adolescents, the Turkish adolescents in Finland have a weaker ethnic orientation, are less involved with peers from their own group, and use their own language less than their Vietnamese peers. This result may stem in part from having a Finnish parent.

Neighborhood Composition

At a more proximal level, the possible influence of the neighborhood ethnic composition has received attention in empirical studies and theoretical analyses (cf. Birman et al., 2002; Kalin & Berry, 1982; Mollenkopf, 2000; Nguyen et al., 1999; Schnittker, 2002). When adult samples are used in examining the impact of neighborhoods on acculturation, outcomes may be confounded with the choices people make regarding the kind of neighborhood in which to live. Those who prefer separation are more likely to live in communities made up predominantly of their own group. Because adolescents typically have no choice as to their place of residence, they provide a valuable population for examining neighborhood effects.

There is a clear correspondence between the neighborhood ethnic composition and the four acculturation profiles. The integration profile is most strongly represented in neighborhoods that are mostly other groups or are ethnically balanced. In communities made up almost entirely of adolescents' own ethnocultural group, the ethnic profile dominates. Furthermore, neighborhoods with a larger proportion of residents who are not from one's own group tend to have a higher proportion of youth with a national profile than those with more same-group residents. However, there is no direct relationship between neighborhood ethnic composition and adaptation outcomes.

These overall results are reflected in the behaviors and attitudes of immigrant youth. Neighborhood composition is an important factor in language proficiency and use. In neighborhoods that are more diverse, national language proficiency and use are higher than in neighborhoods that are predominantly of the adolescents' own group, possibly because the need for a *lingua franca* is satisfied by learning and using the national language. Furthermore, immigrant adolescents' family obligations scores are higher in own-group communities and lower in more diverse communities, where they are likely to be exposed to the values of the larger society.

When adolescents live in neighborhoods with residents primarily from their own group, they have less chance to interact with peers from other groups. We found that youth living in neighborhoods with primarily their own group had proportionally more contacts with peers of their own group than with peers of the national group. People from other groups are unfamiliar and may be perceived negatively, leading to reciprocal negative attitudes. On the other hand, adolescents whose neighborhoods include large numbers of national group members may benefit from the positive effect of contact between ethnic groups, as suggested by the contact hypothesis (Pettigrew & Tropp, 2000).

The Family Context

The most proximal context of acculturation explored in the present study is the family context. We focused on family relationship values that generally have been shown to differ between the immigrants' cultures of origin and the cultures of the countries of settlement (Georgas, Berry, van de Vijver, Kagitcibasi, & Poortinga, in press). These values were adolescents' and parents' attitudes about adolescents' obligations toward the family and adolescents' rights to make autonomous decisions in matters of intimate relationships. Our study confirmed earlier studies (Fuligni et al., 1999, Kagitcibasi, 1996; Nguyen & Williams, 1989) in showing that immigrant adolescents and their parents believe that adolescent children have more obligations to the family and fewer individual rights than do their counterparts in national families. It qualified the findings from earlier studies (Buriel &

De Ment, 1997; Liebkind, 1992b; Nguyen & Williams, 1989; Portes, 1997; Szapocznik & Kurtines, 1993) in showing that the discrepancy between adolescents and parents over family obligations is greater with longer residence. Over time, adolescents feel less obligated to the family, whereas parents do not vary in their sense of adolescents' obligations. We found confirmation for this last result in the group of adolescents with a diffuse profile only, that is, the adolescents who appeared uncertain about their place in the new society.

The intergenerational discrepancy is larger in families where adolescents lean toward assimilation and parents wish to maintain their own cultural traditions without assimilating, that is, where there is an acculturation gap. Conversely, when adolescents are oriented toward their ethnic culture, the discrepancy is less, although even for these adolescents the discrepancy is larger when parents strongly support retention of their cultural traditions. Thus, intergenerational discrepancies are influenced by both adolescents' and parents' attitudes and behaviors related to acculturation.

The intergenerational discrepancy in family relationship values is important for immigrant families because of the finding that a greater intergenerational discrepancy is associated with poorer psychological and sociocultural adaptation. Scholars assume that intergenerational discrepancies are indicative of conflicts between parents and their adolescent children (see Kwak, 2003, for an overview). These conflicts are deemed to lead to increased levels of stress that negatively affect adaptation. Research has rarely examined the relationship between intergenerational value discrepancies and family conflicts. However, even if studies show a link between value discrepancies and conflicts, we would still have to show that conflicts lead to poorer adaptation. Theories of stress and coping (e.g., Billings & Moos, 1981; Heller & Swindle, 1983) suggest that whether conflicts lead to stress levels that negatively affect adaptation depends both on the support that adolescents receive for coping with conflicts and on the severity of the conflicts. In the Netherlands, the ICSEY survey contained a measure of family conflicts and family support. Preliminary analyses of these data suggest that the availability or lack of support is more important to the adaptation of immigrant adolescents than are conflicts.

In summary, country of settlement, neighborhood ethnic composition, and family value orientations are three contexts affecting the relationship between acculturation and adaptation. The contexts vary in the closeness to the individual: Cultural diversity is defined at a national level and may be very distant from individual immigrants. The neighborhood is part of the daily life sphere, for which an adolescent may seek shelter at home, in school, or at clubs. Family relationship values represent the closest context, present in everyday contacts between parents and children and among children.

PERCEIVED DISCRIMINATION

Perceived discrimination is usually assumed to be an important factor in the adaptation of immigrant youth. In our study there is a strong association between more perceived discrimination and poorer psychological and sociocultural adaptation. In our overall model, perceived discrimination contributes most to the prediction of adaptation outcomes, either directly or through its impact on other acculturation variables. Because this is a correlational study, the direction of effect is unclear (Phinney et al., 1998), and we cannot say definitively that discrimination contributes to poorer adaptation; perhaps those who do not adapt well are seen less favorably in the larger society and thus elicit discrimination. Furthermore, self-reports of discrimination are subject to personal bias and may differ from actual incidents of discrimination. Nevertheless, the relationship between the perception of discrimination and adaptation is evident. For example, Vietnamese and Turkish youth in Norway report the highest level of perceived discrimination. These youth also report the poorest adaptation, underscoring the negative impact of perceived discrimination.

Perceived discrimination also has a role in the negative relationship between the cultural diversity of a country and the levels of psychological adaptation. Greater diversity in the society is associated with higher levels of discrimination, which in turn negatively affects psychological adaptation. Furthermore, more discrimination is reported by adolescents with ethnic and diffuse profiles than by those with integration or national profiles. Again, the direction of effect is not clear. An ethnic orientation may be seen as a preference for separatism, and it may therefore provoke negative reactions from a society that wants immigrants to become integrated or even assimilated. Alternatively, it may be that the adolescents' own ethnic group provides the social support needed to buffer the negative effects of perceived discrimination; thus, discrimination may strengthen their ethnic identity. There is evidence that perceived discrimination that is attributed to prejudice toward one's group strengthens the orientation toward the ethnic group as a source of comfort or as a basis for defense against further discrimination (Branscombe et al., 1999; Schmitt et al., 2002). It is likely that the relationship is interactive, with both separation and discrimination reinforcing each other.

Individual characteristics are also related to discrimination in our study. Adolescents who are the most highly visible in appearance report more discrimination, as do boys. However, parental occupational status and length of residence are unrelated to the perception of discrimination. Overall, the findings with respect to the role of perceived discrimination support the view that some individual characteristics and some contexts are associated with higher levels of discrimination. The absolute levels of discrimination across settings and groups are generally low, indicating that most adolescents experience little discrimination. Nevertheless, to the extent that discrimination is experienced, immigrant adolescents do not do as well. This relationship appears to be robust, with evidence from adult immigrant samples providing support (e.g., Noh, Beiser, Kaspar, Hou, & Rummens, 1999).

GENERALIZABILITY OF FINDINGS

In chapter 6, we report the percentage of variance that could be attributed to societies of settlement, to immigrant groups, and to individuals. The pattern was clear:

Most of the variance was due to individual differences, with a modest amount due to immigrant group for two variables related to their ethnicity. We have already noted the success we had in achieving equivalence of measures across societies and groups. When the finding regarding equivalence and the limited degree of variance due to culture (both country and ethnocultural group) are combined, we can ask whether our main findings with respect to orientations to acculturation, to adaptation, and to the relationships among them are applicable to understanding the acculturation of immigrant youth in general.

Several factors may limit the generality of our findings. As psychologists, we place an emphasis on individuals and on individual differences. Researchers using other approaches might reach different conclusions: Anthropologists might have found a larger role for culture; sociologists, a larger role for institutions; or political scientists, greater importance for national policies. The common developmental issues which are faced by youth within the age range that we sampled may also influence our findings. Had we sampled younger immigrants, or those experiencing acculturation in later life, we might well have found a smaller role for individual differences and a greater role for the various cultural backgrounds of immigrants. However, within the range of societies and the age group with which we worked and the methods that we used, we believe that our results are broadly applicable and constitute a basis for generalizing to immigration phenomena in other societies of Western origin (or rooted in Western culture), such as Turks settling in Italy or Russians in Canada.

DIRECTIONS FOR FUTURE RESEARCH

This study provides a broad picture of acculturation and adaptation among immigrant adolescents but leaves many questions unanswered. Our findings are based primarily on measures completed by adolescents in 13 countries of settlement, all of which have populations that are of predominantly European origin. Furthermore, in each country, only selected regions were studied. These countries and regions provide a limited sample of countries worldwide where migration and acculturation are taking place. Clearly, there is need for studies of migrant youth in other regions of the world, including Asia, South America, and Africa, where the conditions of migration and settlement are very different from those in countries we studied. Such studies would allow us to determine the extent to which the patterns of acculturation and adaptation that we found are similar in settings that differ in their social, political, and economic structure, and their prevailing cultural norms.

Our data are primarily self-report. Future research would benefit from studies in which other sources of information are used, including parent and teacher ratings of adolescents, academic records, and direct measures of community structure and ethnic composition. Ethnographic descriptions of the communities sampled that go beyond the descriptive material presented in chapter 2 would be valuable in providing a better understanding on the contexts of acculturation and allowing for more informed interpretations of findings.

Our focus was on adolescents. Although limited information was obtained from some of the parents, our conclusions predominantly concern young people who are making the transition to adulthood, with all the attendant adolescent issues of finding a place in their world. We do not know the extent to which our results may apply to adults who have settled into their lives in a new society. Aronowitz (1984) noted that findings with adult immigrants cannot necessarily be applied to adolescents. Adults deal with other issues, such as finding employment and housing, learning a new language as an adult, and coping with strains on parental and spousal roles due to different cultural norms in their new society. Research with adults, using methods and research design similar to ours, could explore whether our view of how adolescents handle acculturation and how they adapt applies to adults as well.

The variables studied and the measures used to assess them are a limited selection from a wide variety of constructs and measures that could be used. The specific variables chosen and the way they were measured likely affected the outcomes we obtained. For example, in studying cultural identity, we assessed the two dimensions independently (an ethnic identity and a national identity) rather than only one, or more than two. Our results revealed their independence; that is, they were not correlated. A negative correlation would have suggested the presence of a single, bipolar dimension. However, there may be other dimensions of cultural identity, such as identity as a member of worldwide youth culture, that could be explored in future research. For acculturation attitudes, we assessed four preferences, rather than the two underlying dimensions, that is, cultural maintenance and participation in the larger society. This choice of four attitudes may have influenced our finding of four acculturation profiles, although the presence of other variables in the cluster analyses suggests that the four acculturation attitudes were not the determining factors in finding four profiles. Nevertheless, research using other measures might reveal additional profiles. Within the four acculturation attitudes, we assessed preferences across five quite different domains of daily life, such as language and dating, a fact that probably contributed to the relatively low internal consistency of these attitude measures. An important task is the further development and testing of measures of acculturation that can capture the construct of acculturation reliably in all its complexity.

Our study dealt largely with proximal factors in the acculturation context, primarily family and neighborhood. The fact that the main source of our information is self-reports put a limitation on the possibilities for examining distal influences (cf. Vedder, 2004). The issue of proximal and distal acculturation influences is important when considering what acculturation research can add to planning interventions that could support the adaptation of immigrants. Future studies might consider including acculturation contexts that vary systematically in terms of their proximity to immigrant adolescents and collect information about these varying acculturation contexts from persons who are the main actors in such contexts.

Finally, the study was based on specific conceptual frameworks to the exclusion of others. The choice of concepts such as acculturation attitudes, cultural identities, and psychological and sociocultural adaptation was guided partly by the involvement of researchers who have been central in the development of these concepts in acculturation research and partly by the known relevance of these concepts to the processes of acculturation and adaptation. Our findings are consistent with work from other perspectives. For example, personal stories (in both fiction and non-fiction) portray many of the same processes and outcomes that we found (e.g., Padolsky, 1994). In anthropology and education (e.g., Gibson, 1988), the processes of acculturation and adaptation are described as "accommodation without assimilation," which resembles our findings regarding the integrative way of living interculturally. We are reassured when our findings correspond in important ways to those stemming from other research and scholarly traditions. Nevertheless, other researchers have adopted different concepts and frameworks, including coping (as a mediator between stress and adaptation), ethnic attitudes (of both the immigrant and national samples), and daily hassles (which are experienced by all youth, independent of acculturation experiences). The extent to which our findings are congruent across differing conceptual frameworks is a question that will require additional studies by researchers with a range of backgrounds and perspectives.

IMPLICATIONS

What do our results suggest for governments and their agencies (such as immigration and settlement services) and institutions (such as schools and health care services), and for individuals who are navigating their way through the complex process of immigration, acculturation, and adaptation? Our answer depends on the information and policy needs of each of these domains.

Implications for Governments

Many national governments now have, or are considering the development of, policies and programs to regulate the immigration process and the settlement of people who come to reside in their societies. We believe that our findings have some implications for these areas of public life.

There are many kinds of migration in the contemporary world. Many of these variations have been included in our study. We have studied immigrants who are selected by governments (1) to promote national development (e.g., in Australia, Canada, and the United States), (2) to accommodate the return of nationals from their diaspora (e.g., in Finland, Germany, and Israel), or former colonial people (e.g., in the Netherlands, Portugal), (3) to address humanitarian needs (e.g., refugees and asylum seekers in many countries), and (4) to obtain temporary workers (e.g., guest workers in Germany and the Netherlands), as well as those who are arriving illegally (e.g., in the United States). We have not examined these variations explicitly, except for the contrast in chapter 8 between Vietnamese (who are mostly refugees) and Turks (who are mostly guest workers). However, the consistency in findings with respect to how individuals and groups acculturate and how well they adapt suggests that we have found patterns that could well apply to people from all cultural backgrounds who are migrating to all societies in the Western world for a variety of reasons. If this is the case, the message for settlement policies and programs is fairly clear.

Our findings suggest that there should be support and encouragement for immigrants to pursue the integration path, as both psychological and sociocultural adaptation are more positive among those who orient themselves in this way. As we proposed in chapter 4 (see Fig. 4.1), the integration way of acculturating involves acceptance of two kinds of orientation in both the immigrant groups and the larger society. First, cultural maintenance should be desired by the immigrant community and permitted (even encouraged) by the society as a whole. Second, participation and inclusion in the life of the larger society should be sought by the immigrants, and permitted and supported by the larger society. Given these features, integration requires several initiatives:

1. Provide support for immigrant and ethnocultural community organizations so that cultural loss is limited or prevented, their ethnic identity is sustained, and their way of life is allowed to be maintained and to thrive.

2. Develop policies and programs to encourage the participation of immigrants in the daily life of the national society so that they do not remain isolated in their own communities or alienated from the larger society.

3. Develop policies and programs for the general population to encourage their acceptance of the cultural diversity that will follow from Point 1, and the participation of diverse peoples in the life of the larger society that will follow from Point 2. Public education about the value of diversity, and antidiscrimination and equity laws are appropriate vehicles for these initiatives.

The integration path appears to be generally the most beneficial. However, other ways of acculturating, particularly the ethnic or separation orientation, can be beneficial in some cases. The ethnic orientation contributes to both types of adaptation, but to a lesser extent than integration. This implies that a policy allowing immigrants to maintain separation if they wish, for example, by allowing immigrants to settle within their own ethnic communities, is preferable to a policy that pushes immigrants to assimilate, for example, by denying ethnic cultural and language rights or by promoting scattered settlement over wide areas of a country. Clearly, a policy of exclusion, leading to the marginalization of youth, has nothing to recommend it as a public policy.

The legislation and policies installed and formulated by the governments eventually are implemented by a variety of institutions. Many institutions have daily interaction with immigrants and ethnocultural groups. Public institutions, such as schools and health care, generally reflect the national policies that are promoted by the dominant group. For example, when the assimilation path is pursued, schools tend to reflect only the values and knowledge of the dominant society, and health care accepts and uses only the medical and pharmaceutical knowledge of the mainstream health system. If the integration path is adopted as public policy, institutional change is required to reflect the joint goals of cultural diversity and inclusion. In schooling, the multicultural education movement under way in many societies has brought about curriculum change so that all people now living in the society can find themselves represented in the classroom, without stereotyping or derogation and with adequate portrayal of their way of life. So, too, in health care: although Western biotechnology has dominated, other forms of medical practice (such as traditional Chinese medicine or Auyervedic medicine from India) have begun to find acceptance in multicultural health.

Implications for Individuals and Families

For individuals and their families, our results have clear implications for the promotion of successful adaptation following migration. In keeping with the recommendations for governments and institutions, the core message for individuals is to seek ways to follow the integrative path as much as possible, in preference to the other ways of acculturating. However, this general conclusion may need to be qualified in differing contexts. For example, in more public areas of life (such as in school and in the general community), a form of integration that verges on assimilation may allow a better fit with the larger society and its institutions, especially when attitudes in the larger society are intolerant of the maintenance of heritage cultural practices in public. Alternatively, in more private contexts (such as family and ethnocultural group life), a form of integration that verges on the separation orientation may allow for a better fit with co-ethnics in daily interactions. These variations in the way of acculturating require some degree of flexibility and the ability to mix and match strategies. In our conceptualization of integration, such blending and merging are possible ways of obtaining the best of both worlds, especially when there are two or more worlds to be enjoyed and mastered.

The results also provide information about discrimination and its negative effects on personal well-being. If public policy and institutional change work toward the acceptance of diversity and equality, as we propose, then discrimination might decrease in the long term. Discrimination is unlikely to disappear, and individuals need to be aware of its negative effects. However, a strong ethnic identity, which can be promoted by cultural diversity programs, may have a buffering effect against the experience of discrimination (as suggested in the case of Turks). Adolescent who are confident in their own ethnicity and proud of their ethnic group may be better able to deal constructively with discrimination, for example, by regarding it as the problem of the perpetrator or by taking proactive steps to combat it. In fact, forbearance in the face of discrimination may be beneficial for one's adaptation (Noh et al., 1999). Similarly, knowing that the uncertainty and confusion that characterizes the diffuse acculturation profile diminishes over time may help young people to carry on despite the difficulties they experience.

For those who are counseling immigrant youth undergoing acculturation, our findings may help them understand better the processes and problems these youth are experiencing. Teachers, therapists, and parents may all profit from knowing that the integrative way of acculturating is likely to lead these young people to more satisfactory and successful transitions to adulthood in their culturally diverse societies.

References

Abouguendia, M., & Noels, K. A. (2001). General and acculturation-related daily hassles and psychological adjustment in first- and second-generation South-Asian immigrants to Canada. *International Journal of Psychology, 36,* 163–173.

Abu-Rabia, S. (1997). Gender differences in Arab students' attitudes toward Canadian society and second language learning. *Journal of Social Psychology, 137,* 125–128.

Alba, R. (1990). *Ethnic identity: The transformation of White America.* New Haven, CT: Yale University Press.

Allard, R., & Landry, R. (1992). Ethnolinguistic vitality beliefs and language maintenance and loss. In W. Fase, K. Jaspaert, & S. Kroon (Eds.), *Maintenance and loss of minority languages* (pp. 171–195). Amsterdam: John Benjamins.

Anderson, C. (1982). The search for school climate: A review of the research. *Review of Educational Research, 53,* 368–420.

Appleyard, R. (2001). International migration policies: 1950–2000. *International Migration, 39,* 7–19.

Arbuckle, J. L. (2003). *Amos 5.0 update to the Amos user's guide.* Chicago: SPSS.

Arends-Tóth, J. V., & van de Vijver, F. J. R. (2003). Multiculturalism and acculturation: Views of Dutch and Turkish-Dutch. *European Journal of Social Psychology, 33,* 249–266.

Argyle, M. (1969). *Social interaction.* London: Methuen.

Argyle, M. (1982). Intercultural communication. In S. Bochner (Ed.), *Cultures in contact: Studies in cross-cultural interaction* (pp. 61–80). Oxford: Pergamon.

Aronowitz, M. (1984). The social and emotional adjustment of immigrant children: A review of literature. *International Migration Review, 18,* 237–257.

Aronowitz, M. (1992). Adjustment of immigrant children as a function parental attitudes to change. *International Migration Review, 26,* 86–110.

Asante, M. K., & Gudykunst, W. B. (Eds.). (1989). *Handbook of international and intercultural communication.* Newbury Park, CA: Sage.

Ataca, B., & Berry, J. W. (2002). Psychological, sociocultural and marital adaptation of Turkish immigrant couples in Canada. *International Journal of Psychology, 37,* 13–26.

Aycan, Z., & Berry, J. W. (1996). Impact of employment-related experiences on immigrants' psychological well-being and adaptation to Canada. *Canadian Journal of Behavioural Science, 28,* 240–251.

235

Aycan, Z., & Kanungo, R. (1998). Impact of acculturation on socialization beliefs and behavioral occurrences among Indo-Canadian immigrants. *Journal of Comparative Family Studies, 29,* 451–467.

Bandura, A. (1997). *Self efficacy: The exercise of control.* New York: Freeman.

Banting, K., & Kymlicka, W. (2004). Do multiculturalism policies erode the welfare state? In P. Van Parijs (Ed.), *Cultural diversity versus economic solidarity* (pp. 227–284). Brussels: Editions De Boeck Université.

Barker, V., & Giles, H. (2004). English-only policies: Perceived support and social limitation. *Language and Communication, 24,* 77–95.

Bas, M., Asci, F., Karabudak, E., & Kiziltan, G. (2004). Eating attitudes and their psychological correlates among Turkish adolescents. *Adolescence, 39,* 133–140.

Bashir, M. R. (1993). Issues of immigration for the health and adjustment of young people. *Journal of Paediatrics and Child Health, 9,* 42–45.

Baubock, R., Heller, A., & Zolberg, A. (Eds.). (1996). *The challenge of diversity: Integration and pluralism in societies of immigration.* Aldershot, England: Avebury.

Baumeister, R. F. (1995). Self and identity: An introduction. In A. Tesser (Ed.), *Advanced social psychology* (pp. 51–97). New York: McGraw-Hill.

Baumeister, R. F., & Leary, M. R. (1995). The need to belong: Desire for interpersonal attachments as a fundamental human motivation. *Psychological Bulletin, 117,* 497–529.

Beiser, M. (1999). *Strangers at the gate.* Toronto, Canada: University of Toronto Press.

Beiser, M., & Flemming, J. A. E. (1986). Measuring psychiatric disorder among Southeast Asian refugees. *Psychological Medicine, 16,* 627–639.

Beiser, M., Wood, M., Barwick, C., Berry, J. W., deCosta, G., Milne, W., Fantino, A. M., Ganesan, S., Lee, C., Tousignant, M., Naidoo, J., Prince, R., & Vela, E. (1988). *After the door has been opened: Mental health issues affecting immigrants and refugees in Canada.* Ottawa: Ministries of Multiculturalism and Citizenship, and Health and Welfare.

Bendixen, M., & Olweus, D. (1999). Measurement of antisocial behaviour in early adolescence and adolescence: Psychometric properties and substantive findings. *Criminal Behaviour and Mental Health, 9,* 323–354.

Bengli-Arslan, L., Verhulst, F. C., & van der Ende, J. (1997). Understanding children's (problem) behaviours from cultural perspective: Comparison of problem behaviours and competences in Turkish immigrant, Turks and Dutch children. *Social Psychiatry and Psychiatric Epidemiology, 32,* 477–484.

Bentahila, A., & Davies, E. (1992). Convergence and divergence: Two cases of language shift in Morocco. In W. Fase, K. Jaspaert, & S. Kroon (Eds.), *Maintenance and loss of minority languages* (pp. 197–210). Amsterdam: John Benjamins.

Bergman, L., Magnusson, D., & El-Khouri, B. (2003). *Studying individual development in an interindividual context.* Mahwah, NJ: Lawrence Erlbaum Associates.

Berry, J. W. (1974). Psychological aspects of cultural pluralism. *Culture Learning, 2,* 17–22.

Berry, J. W. (1980). Acculturation as varieties of adaptation. In A. Padilla (Ed.), *Acculturation: Theory, models and some new findings* (pp. 9–25). Boulder, CO: Westview.

Berry, J. W. (1984a). Cultural relations in plural societies: Alternatives to segregation and their socio-psychological implications. In M. Brewer & N. Miller (Eds.), *Groups in contact* (pp. 11–27). New York: Academic Press.

Berry, J. W. (1984b). Multicultural policy in Canada: A social psychological analysis. *Canadian Journal of Behavioural Science, 16,* 353–370.

Berry, J. W. (1990). Psychology of acculturation. In J. Berman (Ed.), *Cross-cultural perspectives. Nebraska Symposium on Motivation* (Vol. 37, pp. 201–234). Lincoln: University of Nebraska Press.

Berry, J. W. (1994). Acculturative stress. In W. J. Lonner & R. Malpass (Eds.), *Psychology and culture* (pp. 211–215). Needham Heights, MA: Allyn & Bacon.

Berry, J. W. (1997). Immigration, acculturation and adaptation. *Applied Psychology, 46*, 5–68.

Berry, J. W. (2001). A psychology of immigration. *Journal of Social Issues, 57*, 611–627.

Berry, J. W. (2003). Conceptual approaches to acculturation. In K. Chun, P. Balls-Organista, & G. Marin (Eds.), *Acculturation: Advances in theory, measurement and applied research* (pp. 17–37). Washington: American Psychological Association Press.

Berry, J. W., & Blondel, T. (1982). Psychological adaptation of Vietnamese refugees in Canada. *Canadian Journal of Community Mental Health, 1*, 81–88.

Berry, J. W., & Kalin, R. (1979). Reciprocity of interethnic attitudes in a multicultural society. *International Journal of Intercultural Relations, 3*, 99–112.

Berry, J. W., & Kalin, R. (1995). Multicultural and ethnic attitudes in Canada. *Canadian Journal of Behavioural Science, 27*, 301–320.

Berry, J. W., Kalin, R., & Taylor, D. (1977). *Multiculturalism and ethnic attitudes in Canada*. Ottawa, Canada: Supply and Services.

Berry, J. W., & Kim, U. (1988). Acculturation and mental health. In P. R. Dasen, J. W. Berry, & N. Sartorius (Eds.), *Health and cross-cultural psychology* (pp. 207–236). Thousand Oaks: Sage.

Berry, J. W., Kim, U., Minde, T., & Mok, D. (1987). Comparative studies of acculturative stress. *International Migration Review, 21*, 491–511.

Berry, J. W., Kim, U., Power, S., Young, M., & Bujaki, M. (1989). Acculturation attitudes in plural societies. *Applied Psychology: An International Review, 38*, 185–206.

Berry, J. W., Poortinga, Y. H., Segall, M. H., & Dasen, P. R. (2002). *Cross-cultural psychology: Research and applications* (2nd ed.). Cambridge, England: Cambridge University Press.

Berry, J. W., & Sam, D. L. (1997). Acculturation and adaptation. In J. W. Berry, M. H. Segall, & C. Kagitcibasi (Eds.), *Handbook of cross-cultural psychology: Vol. 3. Social behaviour and applications* (2nd ed., pp. 291–326). Boston: Allyn & Bacon.

Bhattacharya, G. (2000). The school adjustment of South-Asian immigrant children in the United States. *Adolescence, 35*(137), 77–85.

Billings, A. G., & Moos, R. H. (1981). The role of coping responses and social resources in attenuating the stress of life events. *Journal of Behavioral Medicine, 4*, 139–157.

Birman, D., & Trickett, E. J. (2001). Cultural transitions in first-generation immigrants: Acculturation of Soviet Jewish refugee adolescents and parents. *Journal of Cross-Cultural Psychology, 32*, 456–477.

Birman, D., Trickett, E. J., & Vinokurov, A. (2002). Acculturation and adaptation of Soviet Jewish refugee adolescents: Predictors of adjustment across life domains. *American Journal of Community Psychology, 30*, 585–607.

Bochner, S. (1982). The social psychology of cross-cultural relations. In S. Bochner (Ed.), *Cultures in contact: Studies in cross-cultural interaction* (pp. 5–44). Oxford, England: Pergamon.

Body-Gendrot, S. (2003, June). *The second generation in the banlieues: The temptation of violence?* Paper presented at the Bellagio Conference on the Second Generation in Europe and in the U.S. Bellagio, Italy.

Bonifazi , C., & Strozza, S. (2003). Integration of migrants in Europe: Data sources and measurement in old and new receiving countries. *Studi Emigrazione, Vol. XL*(152).

Bourhis, R. (2001). Acculturation, language maintenance, and language shift. In J. Klatter-Folmer & P. Van Avermaet (Eds.), *Theories on maintenance and loss of minor-*

ity languages. Towards a more integrated explanatory framework (pp. 6–37). Munster, Germany: Waxmann.

Bourhis, R. Y., Moïse, L. C., Perreault, S., & Senécal, S. (1997). Towards an interactive acculturation model: A social-psychological approach. *International Journal of Psychology, 32,* 369–386.

Bowes, J. M., Flanagan, C., & Taylor, A. J. (2001). Adolescents' ideas about individual and social responsibility in relation to children's household work: Some international comparisons. *International Journal of Behavioral Development, 25,* 60–68.

Branscombe, N. R., Schmitt, M. T., & Harvey, R. D. (1999). Perceiving pervasive discrimination among African Americans: Implications for group identification and well-being. *Journal of Personality and Social Psychology, 77,* 135–149.

Broeders, D. (2001). *Immigratie en integratieregimes in vier Europese landen* [Immigration and integration policies in four European countries]. Hague, the Netherlands: Netherlands Scientific Council of Governmental Policy.

Brown, R. (2000). Social identity theory: Past achievements, current problems and future challenges. *European Journal of Social Psychology, 30,* 745–778.

Brubaker, R. (2001). The return of assimilation? Changing perspectives on immigration and its sequels in France, Germany, and the United States. *Ethnic and Racial Studies, 24,* 531–548.

Buriel, R., & De Ment, T. (1997). Immigration and sociocultural changes in Mexican, Chinese, and Vietnamese families. In A. Booth, A. Crouter, & N. Landale (Eds.), *Immigration and the family: Research and policy on U.S. immigrants* (pp. 165–200). Mahwah, NJ: Lawrence Erlbaum Associates.

Cameron, J., & Lalonde, P. (1994). Self, ethnicity, and social membership in two generations of Italian Canadians. *Personality & Social Psychology Bulletin, 20,* 514–520.

Campbell, D. T. (1961). The mutual methodological relevance of anthropology and psychology. In F. L. K. Hsu (Ed.), *Psychological anthropology* (pp. 333–352). Homewood, IL: Dorsey.

Canetti-Nisim, D., & Pedahzur, A. (2003). Contributory factors to political xenophobia in a multicultural society: The case of Israel. *International Journal of Intercultural Relations, 27,* 307–333.

Carballo, M. (1994). *Scientific consultation on the social and health impact of migration: Priorities for research. Final report.* Geneva, Switzerland: International Organization Migration.

Chataway, C., & Berry, J. W. (1989). Acculturation experiences, appraisal, coping and adaptation: A comparison of Hong Kong Chinese, French and English students in Canada. *Canadian Journal of Behavioural Science, 21,* 295–309.

Chiang, Y. S. D., & Schmida, M. (1999). *Language identity and language ownership: Linguistic conflicts of first-year university writing students.* Mahwah, NJ: Lawrence Erlbaum Associates.

Child, I. (1943). *Italian or American? The second generation in conflict.* New Haven, CT: Yale University Press.

Christopher, K. A. (2000). Determinants of psychological well-being in Irish immigrants. *Western Journal of Nursing Research, 22,* 123–143.

Chun, K., & Akutsu, P. (2003). Acculturation among ethnic minority families. In K. Chun, P. Balls-Organista, & G. Marin (Eds.), *Acculturation: Advances in theory, measurement, and applied research* (pp. 95–119). Washington, DC: American Psychological Association.

Chung, R. C., & Okazaki, S. (1991). Counseling Americans of Southeast Asian descent: The impact of the refugee experience. In C. C. Lee & B. L. Richardson (Eds.), *Multicultural issues in counseling: New approaches to diversity* (pp. 107–126). Alexandria, VA: American Association for Counseling and Development.

Cohen, J. (1988). *Statistical power analysis for the behavioral sciences* (2nd ed.). Hillsdale, NJ: Lawrence Erlbaum Associates.

Cohon, J. D. (1981). Psychological adaptation and dysfunction among refugees. *International Migration Review, 15,* 255–275.

Cozzarelli, C., & Karafa, J. A. (1998). Cultural estrangement and terror management theory. *Personality and Social Psychology Bulletin, 24,* 253–267.

Crocker, J., Cornwell, B., & Major, B. (1993). The stigma of overweight: Affective consequences of attributional ambiguity. *Journal of Personality and Social Psychology, 64,* 60–70.

Crocker, J., Voelkl, K., Testa, M., & Major, B. (1991). Social stigma: The effective consequences of attributional ambiguity. *Journal of Personality and Social Psychology, 60,* 218–228.

Crocket, L. J., & Silbereisen, R. (Eds.). (2000). *Negotiating adolescence in times of social change.* Cambridge, England: Cambridge University Press.

Crul, M. (2000). *De sleutel tot succes* [The key to success]. Amsterdam: Het Spinhuis.

Crul, M., & Doomernik, J. (2003). The Turkish and Moroccan second generation in the Netherlands: Divergent trends between and polarization within the two groups. *International Migration Review, 37,* 1039–1064.

Crul, M., & Vermeulen, H. (2003). The second generation in Europe. *International Migration Review, 37,* 965–986.

Cuellar, I., Arnold, B., & Maldonado, R. (1995). Acculturation rating scale for Mexican Americans-II: A revision of the original ARSMA scale. *Hispanic Journal of Behavioral Sciences, 17,* 275–304.

Cummins, R. A. (1995). On the trail of the golden standard for subjective well-being. *Social Indicators Research, 35,* 179–200.

Cummins, R. A. (1998). The second approximation to international standard for life satisfaction. *Social Indicators Research, 43,* 307–334.

Dacyl, J., & Westin, C. (Eds.). (2000). *Governance of cultural diversity.* Stockholm, Sweden: CEIFO, Stockholm University.

Dasen, P. R. (2000). Rapid social change and the turmoil of adolescence: A cross-cultural perspective. *International Journal of Group Tensions, 29,* 17–49.

Deaux, K. (1996). Social identification. In E. T. Higgins & A. W. Kruglanski (Eds.), *Social psychology: Handbook of basic principles* (pp. 777–798). New York: Guilford.

Deaux, K. (2000). Surveying the landscape of immigration: Social-psychological perspectives. *Journal of Community and Applied Psychology, 10,* 421–431.

Dekovic, M. (1999). Parent–adolescent conflict: Possible determinants and consequences. *International Journal of Behavioral Development, 23,* 997–1000.

Demir, A., & Tarhan, N. (2001). Loneliness and social dissatisfaction in Turkish adolescents. *Journal of Psychology, 135,* 113–123.

DeVos, G., & Romanucci-Ross, L. (Eds.). (1982). *Ethnic identity: Cultural continuities and change.* Chicago: University of Chicago Press.

Diener, E. (2000). Subjective well-being: The science of happiness and a proposal for a national index. *American Psychologist, 55,* 34–43.

Diener, E., Emmons, R. A., Larsen, R. J., & Griffin, A. (1985). The Satisfaction with Life Scale. *Journal of Personality Assessment, 49,* 71–75.

Diener, E., Scollon, C. K. N., Oishi, S., Dzokoto, V., & Suh, H. M. (2000). Positivity and the construction of life satisfaction judgments: Global happiness is not the sum of its parts. *Journal of Happiness Studies, 1,* 159–176.

Dona, G., & Berry, J. W. (1994). Acculturation attitudes and acculturative stress among Latin American refugees in Canada. *International Journal of Psychology, 29,* 57–70.

DuBois, D., & Hirsch, B. (1990). School and neighborhood friendship patterns of Blacks and Whites in early adolescence. *Child Development, 61,* 524–536.

Dunn, K. (2003, April). *Attitudes toward immigration and immigrants in Australia.* Paper presented at New Directions, New Settlers, New Challenges—Building and Enhancing Communities End-users Seminar. Wellington, New Zealand.

Economic Intelligence Unit. (2001). *Country profile: Turkey.* London: Author.

Edwards, J. (1992). Language in group and individual identity. In G. M. Breakwell (Ed.), *Social psychology of identity and the self concept* (pp. 129–146). London: Academic Press.

Eisikovits, R. A. (2000). Gender differences in cross-cultural adaptation styles of immigrant youths from the former USSR in Israel. *Youth and Society, 31,* 310–331.

Erikson, E. H. (1968). *Identity: Youth and crisis.* New York: Norton.

Eskin, M. (2003). Self-reported assertiveness in Swedish and Turkish adolescents: A cross-cultural comparison. *Scandinavian Journal of Psychology, 44,* 7–12.

Eurobarometer. (2000). Attitudes toward minority groups in the European Union. Eurobarometer Opinion Poll. Available at http://europa.eu.int/comm/public_opinion/index_en.htm

Eyou, M. L., Adair, V., & Dixon, R. (2000). Cultural identity and psychological adjustment of adolescent Chinese immigrants in New Zealand. *Journal of Adolescence, 23,* 531–543.

Ferdman, B. M., & Horenczyk, G. (2000). Cultural identity and immigration: Reconstructing the group during cultural transition. In E. Ohlshtain & G. Horenczyk (Eds.), *Language, identity, and immigration* (pp. 81–100). Jerusalem, Israel: Magnes.

Fishman, J. (1989). *Language and ethnicity in minority sociolinguistic perspective.* Clevedon, UK: Multilingual Matters.

Fishman, J. (1996). What do you lose when you lose your language? In G. Cantoni (Ed.), *Stabilizing indigenous languages* (pp. 80–91). Flagstaff: Center for Excellence in Education, Northern Arizona University.

Foner, N. (1997). The immigrant family: Cultural legacies and cultural changes. *International Migration Review, 31,* 961–974.

Fuligni, A. (1997). The academic achievement of adolescents from immigrant families: The role of family background, attitudes and behaviour. *Child Development, 68,* 351–363.

Fuligni, A. (1998a). The adjustment of children from immigrant families. *Current Directions in Psychological Science, 7,* 99–103.

Fuligni, A. (1998b). Authority, autonomy, and parent–adolescent relationships: A study of adolescents from Mexican, Chinese, Filipino, and European backgrounds. *Developmental Psychology, 34,* 782–792.

Fuligni, A. (2001). A comparative longitudinal approach to acculturation among children from immigrant families. *Harvard Educational Review, 71,* 566–578.

Fuligni, A., & Tseng, V. (1999). Family obligations and achievement motivation of children from immigrant and American-born families. In T. Urdan (Ed.), *Advances in motivation and achievement* (pp. 159–184). Stanford, CT: JAI Press.

Fuligni, A., Tseng, V., & Lam, M. (1999). Attitudes towards family obligations among American adolescents with Asian, Latin American, and European backgrounds. *Child Development, 70,* 1030–1044.

Furnham, A., & Bochner, S. (1982). Social difficulty in a foreign culture: An empirical analysis of culture shock. In S. Bochner (Ed.), *Cultures in contact: Studies in cross-cultural interaction* (pp. 161–198). Oxford, England: Pergamon.

Garcia Coll, C. (2005, April). *The immigrant paradox: Critical factors in Cambodian students' success.* Paper presented at the 2005 biennial meeting of the Society for Research in Child Development, Atlanta, GA.

Garcia Coll, C., & Magnusson, K. (1997). The psychological experience of immigration: A developmental perspective. In A. Booth, A. Crouter, & N. Landale (Eds.), *Immigration and the family: Research and policy on U.S. immigrants* (pp. 91–131). Mahwah, NJ: Lawrence Erlbaum Associates.

Gelfand, M. (2005, May). *The system of cultural tightness–looseness: Understanding the sources of intercultural conflict.* Keynote paper presented at the 4 biennial congress on intercultural research, Kent, OH.

Genesee, F. (1987). *Learning through two languages.* Cambridge, England: Newbury House.

Georgas, J. (1989). Changing family values in Greece: From collectivist to individualism. *Journal of Cross-Cultural Psychology, 20,* 80–91.

Georgas, J., Berry, J., Shaw, A., Christakopoulou, S., & Mylonas, S. (1996). Acculturation of Greek family values. *Journal of Cross-Cultural Psychology, 27,* 329–338.

Georgas, D., Berry, J. W., van de Vijver, F. J. R. Kagitcibasi, C., & Poortinga, Y. H. (in press). *Families across cultures: A 30 nation psychological study.* Cambridge: Cambridge University Press.

Ghuman, P. (1994). *Coping with two cultures: British Asian and Indo Canadian adolescents.* Clevedon UK: Multilingual Matters.

Ghuman, P. (2003). *Double loyalties: South Asian adolescents in the west.* Cardiff: University of Wales Press.

Gibson, M. (1988). *Accommodation without assimilation.* Ithaca, NY: Cornell University Press.

Gibson, M. (1991). Minorities and schooling: Some implications. In M. A. Gibson & J. U. Ogbu (Eds.), *Minority status and schooling: A comparative study of immigrant and involuntary minorities* (pp. 357–381). New York: Garland.

Gibson, M. (1995). Additive acculturation as a strategy for school improvement. In R. Rumbaut & W. Cornelius (Eds.), *California's immigrant children: Theory, research, and implications for educational policy.* San Diego, CA: Center for U.S.-Mexican Studies, University of California.

Gil, A., Vega, W., & Dimas, J. (1994). Acculturative stress and personal adjustment among Hispanic adolescent boys. *American Journal of Community Psychology, 22,* 43–54.

Giles, H., Bourhis, R., & Taylor, D. (1977). Toward a theory of language in ethnic group relations. In H. Giles (Ed.), *Language, ethnicity, and intergroup relations* (pp. 32–65). London: Academic Press.

Giles, H., & Robinson, W. E. (Eds.). (1990). *Handbook of language and social psychology.* Chichester, England: Wiley.

Glenn, C., & De Jong, E. (1996). *Educating immigrant children: Schools and language minorities in twelve nations.* New York: Garland.

Gold, S. (1992). *Refugee communities. A comparative field study.* Newbury Park, CA: Sage.

Gordon, M. (1964). *Assimilation in American life.* New York: Oxford University Press.

Graves, T. (1967). Psychological acculturation in a tri-ethnic community. *South-Western Journal of Anthropology, 23,* 337–350.

Greenfield, P. (1994). Independence and interdependence as developmental scripts: Implications for theory, research, and practice. In P. Greenfield & R. Cocking (Eds.), *Cross-cultural roots of minority child development* (pp. 1–37). Hillsdale, NJ: Lawrence Erlbaum Associates.

Grosfoguel, R. (1997). Colonial Caribbean migrations to France, the Netherlands, Great Britain, and the United States. *Ethnic and Racial Studies, 20,* 594–612.

Gudykunst, W. B., & Ting-Toomey, S. (1990). Ethnic identity, language and communication breakdowns. In H. Giles & W. P. Robinson, (Eds.), *Handbook of language and social psychology* (pp. 309–327). New York: Wiley.

Hamm, J. (2000). Do birds of a feather flock together? The variable bases for African American, Asian American, and European American adolescents' selection of similar friends. *Developmental Psychology, 36,* 209–219.

Hammer, M. R., Gudykunst, W. B., & Wiseman, R. L. (1978). Dimensions of intercultural effectiveness: An exploratory study. *International Journal of Intercultural Relations, 2,* 383–393.

Harris, K. M. (1999). The health status and risk behavior of adolescents in immigrant families. In D. J. Hernandez (Ed.), *Children of immigrants: health, adjustment and public assistance* (pp. 286–315). Washington, DC: National Academy Press.

Hayes-Bautista, D. (2004). *LA Nueva California: Latinos in the Golden State.* Los Angeles: University of California Press.

Heath, A., & Cheung, S.-Y. (Eds.). (in press). *Ethnic minority disadvantage in the labour market: Cross-national perspectives.* Oxford: Oxford University Press.

Heider, F. (1958). *The psychology of interpersonal relations.* New York: Wiley.

Heller, K., & Swindle, R. W. (1983). The effects of social support: Prevention and treatment implications. In R. D. Felner, L. A. Jason, J. N. Moritsugn, & S. S. Farber (Eds.), *Preventive psychology: Theory, research and practice* (pp. 87–103). New York: Pergamon.

Hensley, W. E. (1977). Differences between males and females on Rosenberg's Scale of Self-Esteem. *Psychological Reports, 41,* 829–830.

Henze, R., & Davis, K. A. (1999). Authenticity and identity: Lessons from indigenous language education. *Anthropology and Education Quarterly, 30,* 3–21.

Henderson, V. L., & Dweck, C. S. (1990). Motivation and achievement. In S. S. Feldman & G. R. Elliot (Eds.), *At the threshold: The developing adolescent* (pp. 308–329). Cambridge, MA: Harvard University Press.

Herz, L., & Gullone, E. (1999). The relationship between self-esteem and parenting style: A cross-cultural comparison of Australian and Vietnamese Australian adolescents. *Journal of Cross-Cultural Psychology, 30,* 742–761.

Hocoy, D. (1993). *Ethnic identity among Chinese in Canada.* Unpublished thesis, Queen's University, Canada.

Hofer, H., & Tham, H. (1991). *Foreign citizens and crime: The Swedish case.* Stockholm, Sweden: Statistical Reports of the Nordic Countries.

Hofstede, G. (2001). *Culture's consequences* (2nd ed.). Thousand Oaks, CA: Sage.

Horenczyk, G., & Ben-Shalom, U. (2001). Multicultural identities and adaptation of young immigrants in Israel. In N. K. Shimahara, I. Holowinsky, & S. Tomlinson-Clarke (Eds.), *Ethnicity, race, and nationality in education: A global perspective* (pp. 57–80). Mahwah, NJ: Lawrence Erlbaum Associates.

Howard, R. (1998). Being Canadian: Citizenship in Canada. *Citizenship Studies, 2,* 133–152.

Hurtado, A., & Gurin, P. (1995). Ethnic identity and bilingualism attitudes. In A. Padilla (Ed.), *Hispanic psychology* (pp. 89–103). Thousand Oaks, CA: Sage.

Hutnik, N. (1991). *Ethnic minority identity: A social psychological perspective.* Oxford, England: Clarendon.

Icduygu, A. (1996). Becoming a new citizen in an immigration country: Turks in Australia and Sweden and some comparative implications. *International Migration, 34,* 257–272.

Igoa, C. (1995). *The inner world of the immigrant child.* New York: St. Martin's Press.

Inglehart, R. (1997). *Modernization and postmodernization.* Princeton, NJ: Princeton University Press.

Inglehart, R., & Rabier, J. C. (1986). Aspirations adapt to situations—but why are the Belgians so much happier than the French? In F. M. Andrews (Ed.), *Research on the quality of life* (pp. 1–56). Ann Arbor: Survey Research Center, Institute for Research, University of Michigan.

Janssen, M. M. M., Verhulst, F. C., Bengi-Arslan, L., Erol, N., Salter, C. J., & Crijnen, A. A. M. (2004). Comparison of self-reported emotional and behavioural problems in Turkish immigrant, Dutch and Turkish adolescents. *Social Psychiatry and Psychiatric Epidemiology, 39,* 133–140.

Jasinskaja-Lahti, I., Liebkind, K., Horenczyk, G., & Schmitz, P. (2003). The interactive nature of acculturation: Perceived discrimination, acculturation attitudes and stress among young ethnic repatriates in Finland, Israel and Germany. *International Journal of Intercultural Relations, 27,* 79–97.

Jasinskaja-Lahti, J., Liebkind, K., Jaakkola, M., & Reuter, A. (in press). Perceived discrimination, social support networks and psychological well-being among three immigrant groups. *Journal of Cross-Cultural Psychology.*

Jasinskaja-Lahti, I., Liebkind, K., & Vesala, T. (2002). *Rasismi ja syrjintä Suomessa. Maahanmuuttajien kokemukset* [Racism and discrimination in Finland. The experiences of immigrants]. Helsinki, Finland: Gaudeamus.

Jasso, G., Massey, D. S., Rosenzweig, M. E., & Smith, J. P. (2004). Immigrant health: Selectivity and acculturation. In N. B. Anderson, R. A. Bulatao, & B. Cohen (Eds.), *Critical perspectives on racial and ethnic differences in health in late life* (pp. 227–266). Washington, DC: The National Academy Press.

Junger, M., & Polder, W. (1992): Some explanations of crime among four ethnic groups in the Netherlands. *Journal of Quantitative Criminology 8,* 51–78.

Junger-Tas, J., Terlouw, G., & Klein, M. (1994). *Delinquent behavior among young people in the Western world. First results of the international self-report study of delinquency.* Amsterdam: Kluwer.

Kagitcibasi, C. (1996). *Family and human development across cultures: A view from the other side.* Mahwah, NJ: Lawrence Erlbaum Associates.

Kalin, R., & Berry. J. W. (1982). Social ecology of ethnic attitudes in Canada. *Canadian Journal of Behavioural Science, 14,* 97–109.

Kalin, R., & Berry, J. W. (1996). Interethnic attitudes in Canada: Ethnocentrism, hierarchy and reciprocity. *Canadian Journal of Behavioral Science, 28,* 253–261.

Kao, G. (2000). Psychological well-being and educational achievement among immigrant youth. In D. J. Hernandez (Ed.), *Children of immigrants: Health, adjustment and public assistance* (pp. 410–477). Washington, DC: National Academy Press.

Kaplan, M. S., & Marks, G. (1990). Adverse effects of acculturation: Psychological distress among Mexican American young adults. *Social Science and Medicine, 31,* 1313–1319.

REFERENCES

Keaton, T. (1999). Muslim girls and the "other France": An examination of identity construction. *Social Identities, 5,* 47–64.

Kennedy, A. (1999). *Singaporean sojourners: Meeting the demands of cross-cultural transitions.* Unpublished doctoral thesis, National University of Singapore.

Kinzie, J. D., Manson, S. M., Vinh, D. T., Tolan, N. T., Anh, B., & Pho, T. N. (1982). Development and validation of a Vietnamese-language depression rating scale. *American Journal of Psychiatry, 139,* 1276–1281.

Koray, S. (1997). Dynamics of demography and development in Turkey. *Nufusbilim Dergisi, 19,* 37–55. (Paper in Turkish with English abstract)

Kovacs, M. (1980/1981). Rating scales to assess depression in school-aged children. *Acta Paedopsychiatry, 46,* 305–315.

Krause, N., Bennett, J., & Tran, T. V. (1989). Age differences in the acculturation process. *Psychology and Aging, 4,* 321–332.

Kurian, G. (1986). Intergenerational integration with special reference to Indian families. *Indian Journal of Social Work, 47,* 39–49.

Kurian, G. T. (Ed.). (2001). *The illustrated book of world rankings* (5th ed.). Armonk, ME: Sharpe Reference.

Kwak, K. (1991). *Second language learning in a multicultural society: A comparison between the learning of a dominant language and a heritage language.* Unpublished doctoral dissertation, Queen's University, Kingston, Canada.

Kwak, K. (2003). Adolescents and their parents: A review of intergenerational family relations for immigrant and non-immigrant families. *Human Development, 46,* 115–136.

Kymlicka, W. (1995). *Multicultural citizenship.* Oxford, England: Oxford University Press.

LaFromboise, T., Coleman, H., & Gerton, J. (1993). Psychological impact of biculturalism: Evidence and theory. *Psychological Bulletin, 114,* 395–412.

Lalonde, R. N., Taylor, D. M., & Moghaddam, F. H. (1992). The process of social identification for visible immigrant women in a multicultural context. *Journal of Cross-Cultural Psychology, 23,* 25–39.

Landry, R., & Bourhis, R. Y. (1997). Linguistic landscape and ethnolinguistic vitality: An empirical study. *Journal of Language and Social Psychology, 16,* 23–49.

Lay, C., & Nguyen, T. (1998). The role of acculturation-related and acculturation non-related daily hassles: Vietnamese-Canadian students and psychological distress. *Canadian Journal of Behavioural Science, 30,* 5–14.

Lazarus, R. S. (1997). Acculturation isn't everything. *Applied Psychology: An International Review, 46,* 39–43.

Lazarus, A., & Folkman, S. (1984). *Stress, coping and appraisal.* New York: Springer.

Lebedeva, N., & Tatarko, A. (2004). Socio-psychological factors of ethnic intolerance in Russia's multicultural regions. In B. Setiadi, A. Supratiknya, W. Lonner, & Y. Poortinga (Eds.), *Ongoing themes in psychology and culture. Selected papers from the Sixteenth International Congress of IACCP* (pp. 507–532). Jakarta: Indonesian Universities Press.

Leman, J. (1991). The education of immigrant children in Belgium. *Anthropology and Education Quarterly, 63,* 25–39.

Leondari, A. (2001). The impact of acculturation on immigrant children's self-perceptions, feelings of loneliness and social status. *Educational and Child Psychology, 18,* 35–46.

Leung, C. (2001). The sociocultural and psychological adaptation of Chinese migrant adolescents in Australia and Canada. *International Journal of Psychology, 36,* 8–19.

Liebkind, K. (1992a). Ethnic identity: Challenging the boundaries of social psychology. In G. Breakwell (Ed.), *Social psychology of identity and the self-concept* (pp. 147–148). London: Academic Press.

Liebkind, K. (1992b). Refugee mental health and cultural identity. *Psychiatria Fennica, 23,* 47–58.

Liebkind, K. (1993). Self-reported ethnic identity, depression and anxiety among young Vietnamese refugees and their parents. *Journal of Refugee Studies, 6,* 25–39.

Liebkind, K. (1996a). Acculturation and stress—Vietnamese refugees in Finland. *Journal of Cross-Cultural Psychology, 27,* 161–180.

Liebkind, K. (1996b). Social psychology and contact linguistics. In H. Goebl, P. H. Nelde, Z. Stary, & W. Wölck (Eds.), *Contact linguistics. International handbook of contemporary research, Vol. 1* (pp. 41–18). Berlin, NY: Walter de Gruyter.

Liebkind, K. (1999). Social psychology. In J. Fishman (Ed.), *Handbook of language and ethnic identity* (pp. 140–151). New York: Oxford University Press.

Liebkind, K. (2001). Acculturation. In R. Brown & S. Gaetner (Eds.), *Blackwell handbook of social psychology. Vol. 3: Intergroup processes* (pp. 386–406). Oxford, England: Blackwell.

Liebkind, K., & Jasinskaja-Lahti, I. (2000a). Acculturation and psychological well-being among immigrant adolescents in Finland: A comparative study of adolescents from different cultural backgrounds. *Journal of Adolescent Research, 15,* 446–469.

Liebkind, K., & Jasinskaja-Lahti, I. (2000b). The influence of experiences of discrimination on psychological stress: A comparison of seven immigrant groups. *Journal of Community & Applied Social Psychology, 10,* 1–16.

Liebkind, K., Jasinskaja-Lahti, I., & Solheim, E. (2004). Cultural identity, perceived discrimination and parental support as determinants of immigrants' school adjustment: Vietnamese youth in Finland. *Journal of Adolescent Research, 19,* 635–656.

Littlewood, R., & Lipsedge, M. (1989). *Aliens and alienists: Ethnic minority and psychiatry.* London: Unwin Hyman.

Malzberg, B., & Lee., E. S. (1956). *Migration and mental disease.* New York: Social Science Research Council.

Mann, J. W. (1958). Group relations and the marginal personality. *Human Relations, 1,* 77–91.

Mann, J. W. (1965). Adolescent marginality. *Journal of Genetic Psychology, 106,* 221–235.

Marcia, J. (1994). The empirical study of ego identity. In H. Bosma, T. Graafsma, H. Grotevant, & D. de Levita (Eds.), *Identity and development: An interdisciplinary approach* (pp. 67–80). Thousand Oaks, CA: Sage.

Marcia, J., Waterman, A., Matteson, D., Archer, S., & Orlofsky, J. (1993). *Ego identity: A handbook of psychosocial research.* New York: Springer-Verlag.

Markus, H., & Lin, L. (1999). Conflictways: Cultural diversity in the meanings and practices of conflict. In D. Prentice & D. Miller (Eds.), *Cultural divides: Understanding and overcoming group conflict* (pp. 302–333). New York: Russell Sage Foundation.

Martin, D. S., Craft, A. R., & Tillema, H. (2002). International collaboration: Challenges for researchers. *The Educational Forum, 66,* 365–371.

Masgoret, A.-M., & Ward, C. (2006). The cultural learning approach to acculturation. In D. L. Sam & J. W. Berry (Eds.), *Cambridge handbook of acculturation psychology* (pp. 58–77). Cambridge, England: Cambridge University Press.

Matsuoka, J. K. (1990). Differential acculturation among Vietnamese refugees. *Social Work, 35,* 341–345.

Matute-Bianchi, M. (1986). Ethnic identities and patterns of school success and failure among Mexican-descent and Japanese-American students in a California high school. *American Journal of Education, 95,* 233–255.

Mays, J. B. (Ed.). (1972). *Juvenile delinquency: The family and the social group: A reader.* London: Longmans.

McCord, J. (1990). Problem behaviors. In S. S. Feldman & G. R. Elliot (Eds.), *At the threshold: The developing adolescent* (pp. 414–439). Cambridge, MA: Harvard University Press.

McLatchie, R. (1997). Psychological adjustment and school performance in immigrant children. *Journal of Psychological Practice, 3,* 34–46.

McRae, K. D. (1997). *Conflict and compromise in multilingual societies: Finland.* Waterloo, Canada: Wilfrid Laurier University Press.

Mendenhall, M., & Oddou, G. (1985). The dimensions of expatriate acculturation. *Academy of Management Review, 10,* 39–47.

Merton, R. K. (1938). Social structure and anomie. *American Sociological Review, 3,* 672–682.

Moffitt, T. (1993). Adolescence-limited and life-course persistent antisocial behaviour: A developmental taxonomy. *Psychological Review, 100,* 674–701.

Mollenkopf, J. (2000). Assimilating immigrants in Amsterdam: A perspective from New York. *Netherlands Journal of Social Sciences, 36*(2), 126–145.

Mollica, R., Wyshak, G., deMarneffe, D., Khuon, F., & Lavelle, J. (1987). Indochinese versions of the Hopkins Symptom Checklist–25: A screening instrument for the psychiatric care of refugees. *American Journal of Psychiatry, 144,* 497–500.

Moos, R. H. (1979). *Evaluating educational environments: Procedures, measures, findings and policy implications.* San Francisco: Jossey-Bass.

Moos, R. (1989). *Evaluating educational environments.* San Francisco: Jossey-Bass.

Murphy, H. B. M. (1965). Migration and the major mental disorders. In M. B. Kantor (Ed.), *Mobility and mental health* (pp. 221–249). Springfield, IL: Thomas.

Nesdale, D., Rooney, R., & Smith, L. (1997). Migrant ethnic identity and psychological distress. *Journal of Cross-Cultural Psychology, 28,* 569–588.

Nguyen, H., Messe, L. A., & Stollak, G. E. (1999). Toward a more complex understanding of acculturation and adjustment: Cultural involvement and psychological functioning in Vietnamese youth. *Journal of Cross-Cultural Psychology, 30,* 5–31.

Nguyen, N., & Williams, H. (1989). Transition from East to West: Vietnamese adolescents and their parents. *Journal of the American Academy of Child and Adolescent Psychiatry, 28,* 505–515.

Nixon, J., & Dugdale, A. (1984). A primary health care for Indochinese in Australia. *Australian Paediatric Journal, 20,* 57–58.

Noh, S., Beiser, M., Kaspar, V., Hou, F., & Rummens, J. (1999). Perceived racial discrimination, depression and coping. *Journal of Health and Social Behavior, 40,* 193–207.

Noh, S., & Kaspar, V. (2003). Perceived discrimination and depression: Moderating effects of coping, acculturation, and ethnic support. *American Journal of Public Health, 93,* 232–238.

Ødegaard, O. (1932). Emigration and insanity. *Acta Psyciatrica et Neurological,* Supplement 4.

OECD. (2003). *Employment outlook: Toward more and better jobs.* Paris: Author.

Ogbu, J. (1991). Immigrant and involuntary minorities in comparative perspective. In M. Gibson & J. Ogbu (Eds.), *Minorities status and schooling: A comparative study of immigrant and involuntary minorities* (pp. 3–33). New York: Garland.

Ogbu, J. U. (1995). Understanding cultural diversity and learning. In J. A. Banks & C. A. M. Banks (Eds.), *Handbook of research on multicultural education* (pp. 582–593). New York: Macmillan.

Ogbu, J. U. (1997). Understanding the school performance of urban Blacks: Some essential background knowledge. In H. J. Walberg (Ed.), *Children and youth: Interdisciplinary perspectives* (pp. 190–222). Thousand Oaks, CA: Sage.

Olneck, M. R. (1995). Immigrants and education. In J. A. Banks & C. A. M. Banks (Eds.), *Handbook of research on multicultural education* (pp. 310–327). New York: Macmillan.

Olweus, D. (1989). Prevalence and incidence in the study of antisocial behaviour: Definition and measurement. In M. W. Klein (Ed.), *Cross-national research in self-reported crime and delinquency* (pp. 187–201). Dordrecht, Holland: Kluwer Academic.

Olweus, D. (1994). *The revised Olweus Bully/Victim Questionnaire.* Bergen, Norway: Research Center for Health Promotion, University of Bergen.

Oppedal, B., Røysamb, E., & Sam, D. L. (2004). The effect of acculturation and social support on change in mental health among young immigrants. *International Journal of Behavioral Development, 28,* 481–494.

Oriol, M. (1989). Modeles ideologiques et modeles culturels dans la reproduction des identities collectives en situation d'emigration [Ideological and cultural models for the reproduction of a sense of collective identity in the emigration situation]. *Revue Internationale d'Action Communautaire, 21,* 117–123.

Østergaard-Nielsen, E. K. (2001). Transnational political practices and the receiving state: Turks and Kurds in Germany and the Netherlands. *Global Networks: A Journal of Transnational Affairs, 1,* 261–282.

Padolsky, E. (1994). Canadian ethnic minority literature. In J. W. Berry & J. Laponce (Eds.), *Ethnicity and culture in Canada: The research landscape* (pp. 361–386). Toronto, Canada: University of Toronto Press.

Pandharipande, R. (1992). Language shift in India: Issues and implications. In W. Fase, K. Jaspaert, & S. Kroon (Eds.), *Maintenance and loss of minority languages* (pp. 253–276). Amsterdam: John Benjamins.

Pettigrew, T., & Tropp, L. (2000). Does intergroup contact reduce prejudice? Recent meta-analytic findings. In S. Oskamp (Ed.), *Reducing prejudice and discrimination* (pp. 93–114). Mahwah, NJ: Lawrence Erlbaum Associates.

Pew Research Center. (2005). *Islamic extremism: Common concern for Muslim and Western Public.* Retrieved July 18, 2005, from (http://pewglobal.org/reports/pdf/248.pdf)

Phalet, K., & Kosic, A. (2006). Acculturation in an enlarged European context. In D. Sam & J. W. Berry (Eds.), *The Cambridge handbook of acculturation psychology* (pp. 331–348). Cambridge, England: Cambridge University Press.

Phalet, K., & Schönpflug, U. (2001). Intergenerational transmission of collectivism and achievement values in two acculturation contexts: The case of Turkish families in Germany and Turkish and Moroccan families in the Netherlands. *Journal of Cross-Cultural Psychology, 32,* 186–201.

Phalet, K., & Swyngedouw, M. (2003). Measuring immigrant integration: The case of Belgium. *Migration Studies, 40,* 773–803.

Phinney, J. (1989). Stages of ethnic identity development in minority group adolescents. *Journal of Early Adolescence, 9,* 34–49.

Phinney, J. (1990). Ethnic identity in adolescents and adults: A review of research. *Psychological Bulletin, 108,* 499–514.

Phinney, J. (1992). The Multigroup Ethnic Identity Measure: A new scale for use with diverse groups. *Journal of Adolescent Research, 7,* 156–176.

Phinney, J. (1993). A three-stage model of ethnic identity development. In M. Bernal & G. Knight (Eds.), *Ethnic identity: Formation and transmission among Hispanics and other minorities* (pp. 61–79). Albany: State University of New York Press.

Phinney, J. (2003). Ethnic identity and acculturation. In K. Chun, P. Organista, & G. Marin (Eds.), *Acculturation: Advances in theory, measurement, and applied research* (pp. 63–81). Washington, DC: American Psychological Association.

Phinney, J., Cantu, C., & Kurtz, D. (1997). Ethnic and American identity as predictors of self-esteem among African American, Latino, and White adolescents. *Journal of Youth and Adolescence, 26,* 165–185.

Phinney, J., & Devich-Navarro, M. (1997). Variations in bicultural identification among African American and Mexican American adolescents. *Journal of Research on Adolescence, 7,* 3–32.

Phinney, J., Dupont, S., Espinosa, C., Revill, J., & Sanders, K. (1994). Ethnic identity and American identification among ethnic minority youths. In A. Bouvy, F. van de Vijver, P. Boski, & P. Schmitz (Eds.), *Journeys into cross-cultural psychology* (pp. 167–183). Amsterdam: Swets & Zeitlinger.

Phinney, J., Ferguson, D., & Tate, J. (1997). Intergroup attitudes among ethnic minority adolescents: A causal model. *Child Development, 68,* 955–969.

Phinney, J., Horenczyk, G., Liebkind, K., & Vedder, P. (2001). Ethnic identity, immigration, and well-being: An interactional perspective. *Journal of Social Issues, 57,* 493–510.

Phinney, J., Kim-Jo, T., Osorio, S., & Vilhjalmsdottir, P. (2005) Autonomy and relatedness in adolescent–parent disagreements: Ethnic and developmental factors. *Journal of Adolescent Research, 20,* 8–39.

Phinney, J., Madden, T., & Santos, L. (1998). Psychological variables as predictors of perceived ethnic discrimination among minority and immigrant adolescents. *Journal of Applied Social Psychology, 28,* 937–953.

Phinney, J., & Ong, A. (2002). Adolescent–parent disagreements and life satisfaction in families from Vietnamese- and European-American backgrounds. *International Journal of Behavioral Development, 26,* 556–561.

Phinney, J., Ong, A., & Madden, T. (2000). Cultural values and intergenerational value discrepancies in immigrant and non-immigrant families. *Child Development, 71,* 528–539.

Phinney, J., Romero, I., Nava, M., & Huang, D. (2001). The role of language, parents and peers in ethnic identity among adolescents in immigrant families. *Journal of Youth and Adolescence, 30,* 135–153.

Plato. (1969). Laws XII (A. E. Taylor, Trans). In E. Hamilton & H. Cairns (Eds.), *The collected dialogues of Plato* (pp. 1488–1513). Princeton, NJ: Princeton University Press.

Portes, A. (Ed.). (1995). *The economic sociology of immigration.* New York: Russell Sage Foundation.

Portes, A. (1997). Immigration theory for a new century: Some problems and opportunities. *International Migration Review, 31,* 799–825.

Portes, A., & Rumbaut, R. (2001). *Legacies: The story of the immigrant second generation.* Berkeley, CA: University of California Press.

Portes, A., & Schauffler, R. (1994). Language and the second generation: Bilingualism yesterday and today. *International Migration Review, 28,* 640–661.

Portes, A., & Zhou, M. (1993). The new second generation: Segmented assimilation and its variants. *Annals AAPSS, 530,* 74–96.

Portes, P. R. (1999). Social and psychological factors in the academic achievement of children of immigrants: A cultural history puzzle. *American Educational Research Journal, 36,* 489–507.

Rack, P. (1982). *Race, culture and mental disorder.* London: Tavistock.

Redfield, R., Linton, R., & Herskovits, M. (1936). Memorandum on the study of acculturation. *American Anthropologist, 38,* 149–152.

Reicher, S., & Hopkins, N. (2001). *Self and nation: Categorisation, contestation and mobilisation.* London: Sage.

Reynolds, C. R., & Richmond, B. O. (1985). *Revised Children's Manifest Anxiety Scale (RCMAS): Manual.* Los Angeles, CA: Western Psychological Services.

Roberts, R., Phinney, J., Masse, L., Chen, Y., Roberts, C., & Romero, A. (1999). The structure of ethnic identity in young adolescents from diverse ethnocultural groups. *Journal of Early Adolescence, 19,* 301–322.

Robinson, J. P., Shaver, P. R., & Wrightsman, L. S. (Eds.). (1991). *Measures of personality and social psychological attitudes: Vol 1.* San Diego, CA: Academic Press.

Rogler, L. H., Cortes, D. E., & Malgady, L. G. (1991). Acculturation and mental health status among Hispanics: Convergence and new directions for research. *American Psychologist, 46,* 585–597.

Romero, A., & Roberts, R. (1998). Perception of discrimination and ethnocultural variables in a diverse group of adolescents. *Journal of Adolescence, 21,* 641–656.

Rosenberg, M. (1965). *Society and the adolescent self-image.* Princeton, NJ: Princeton University Press.

Rosenthal, D., Ranieri, N., & Klimidis, S. (1996). Vietnamese adolescents in Australia: Relationships between perceptions of self and parental values, intergenerational conflict, and gender dissatisfaction. *International Journal of Psychology, 31,* 81–91.

Rothbaum, F., Pott, M., Azuma, H., Miyake, K., & Weisz, J. (2000). The development of close relationships in Japan and the United States: Paths of symbiotic harmony and generative tension. *Child Development, 71,* 1121–1476.

Rudmin, F. (2003). Critical history of the acculturation psychology of assimilation, integration, separation and marginalization. *Review of General Psychology, 7,* 3–37.

Rumbaut, R. (1994). The crucible within: Ethnic identity, self-esteem, and segmented assimilation among children of immigrants. *International Migration Review, 28,* 748–794.

Rumbaut, R. (1997). *Passages to adulthood: The adaptation of children of immigrants in Southern California.* New York: Russell Sage Foundation.

Rumbaut, R. (1999). Assimilation and its discontents: Ironies and paradoxes. In C. Hirschman, P. Kasinitz, & J. DeWind (Eds.), *The handbook of international migration: The American experience* (pp. 172–195). New York: Russell Sage Foundation.

Rumbaut, R. G. (2000). Passages to adulthood: The adaptation of children of immigrants in Southern California. In D. J. Hernandez (Ed.), *Children of immigrants: Health, adjustment and public assistance* (pp. 478–535). Washington, DC: National Academy Press.

Rumbaut, R., & Portes, A. (Eds.). (2001). *Ethnicities: Children of immigrants in America.* Berkeley: University of California Press.

Rutter, M. (1995). *Psychosocial disturbances in young people: Challenges and prevention.* Cambridge, England: Cambridge University Press.

Rutter, M., & Giller, H. (1983). *Juvenile delinquency: Trends and perspectives.* Hammondsworth, UK: Penguin.

Rutter, M., Giller, H., & Hagell, A. (1998). *Antisocial behaviour by young people.* Cambridge, England: Cambridge University Press.

Rutter, M., Yule, B., Norton, J., & Bagley, C. (1974). Children of West Indian immigrants—I. Rates of behavioural deviance and psychiatric disorders. *Journal of Child Psychology and Psychiatry, 15,* 241–262.

Rutter, M., Yule, B., Norton, J., & Bagley, C. (1975). Children of West Indian immigrants–III. Home circumstances and family pattern. *Journal of Child Psychology and Psychiatry, 16,* 105–123.

Ryder, A., Alden, L., & Paulhus, D. (2000). Is acculturation unidimensional or bidimensional? *Journal of Personality and Social Psychology, 79,* 49–65.

Sabogal, F., Marin, G., Otero-Sabogal, R., Marin, B., & Perez-Stable, E. (1987). Hispanic familism and acculturation: What changes and what doesn't? *Hispanic Journal of Behavioral Sciences, 9,* 397–412.

Safdar, S., Lay, C., & Struthers, W. (2003). The acculturation process and basic goals: Testing a multidimensional individual difference acculturation model with Iranian immigrants in Canada. *Applied Psychology: An International Review, 52,* 555–579.

Sam, D. L. (1994). School adaptation of young Vietnamese refugees in Norway. *Migration: European Journal of International Migration and Ethnic Relations, 24,* 219–242.

Sam, D. L. (1995). Acculturation attitudes among young immigrants as a function of perceived parental attitudes to cultural change. *Journal of Early Adolescence, 15,* 238–258.

Sam, D. L., & Berry, J. W. (2006). Introduction to psychology of acculturation. In D. L. Sam & J. W. Berry (Eds.), *Cambridge handbook of acculturation psychology* (pp. 1–7). Cambridge, England: Cambridge University Press.

Samdal, O. (1998). *The school environment as a risk or resource for students' health-related behaviour and subjective well-being.* Unpublished doctoral dissertation, University of Bergen.

Schalk-Soekar, S., van de Vijver, F. J. R., & Hoogsteder, M. (in press). Migrants' and majority members' orientations toward multiculturalism in the Netherlands. *International Journal of Intercultural Relations.*

Schlegel, A. (2003). Modernisation and changes in adolescent social life. In T. S. Saraswathi (Ed.), *Cross-cultural perspectives on human development* (pp. 236–257) New Delhi, India: Sage.

Schmitt, M. T., & Branscombe, N. R. (2002). The meaning and consequences of perceived discrimination in disadvantaged and privileged social groups. In W. Stroebe & M. Hewstone (Eds.), *European review of social psychology. Vol. 12* (pp. 167–199). Chichester, England: Wiley.

Schmitt, M. T., Branscombe, N. R., Kobrynowicz, D., & Owen, S. (2002). Perceiving discrimination against one's gender group has different implications for well-being in women and men. *Personality and Social Psychology Bulletin, 28,* 197–210.

Schnittker, J. (2002). Acculturation in context: The self-esteem of Chinese immigrants. *Social Psychology Quarterly, 65,* 56–76.

Schofield, J., & Whitley, B. (1983). Peer nomination vs. rating scale measurement of children's peer preferences. *Social Psychology Quarterly, 46,* 242–251.

Schönpflug, U. (1997). Acculturation: Adaptation or development? *Applied Psychology: An International Review, 46,* 52–55.

Scott, R. & Scott, W. A. (1998). *Adjustment of adolescents: Cross-cultural similarities and differences.* London: Routledge.

Scott, W. A., & Scott, R. (1989). *Adaptation of immigrants: Individual differences and determinants.* Oxford, England: Pergamon.

Searle, W., & Ward, C. (1990). The prediction of psychological and sociocultural adjustment during cross-cultural transitions. *International Journal of Intercultural Relations, 14,* 449–464.

Segall, M. H., Dasen, P. R., Berry, J. W., & Poortinga, Y. H. (1999). *Human behaviour in a global perspective: An introduction to cross-cultural psychology* (2nd ed.). Boston: Allyn & Bacon.

Sellers, R., & Shelton, J. (2003). The role of racial identity in perceived racial discrimination. *Journal of Personality and Social Psychology, 84,* 1079–1092.

Semons, M. (1991). Ethnicity in the urban high school: A naturalistic study of student experiences. *The Urban Review, 23,* 137–158.

Sever, R. (1999). Patterns of coping with the task at schools. In T. Horowitz (Ed.), *Children of perestroika in Israel* (pp. 178–189). Lanham, MD: University Press of America.

Shen, B.-J., & Takeuchi, D. T. (2001). A structural model of acculturation and mental health status among Chinese Americans. *American Journal of Community Psychology, 29,* 387–418.

Shin, D., & Johnson, D. (1987). Avowed happiness as an overall assessment of quality of life. *Social Indicators Research, 5,* 474–492.

Shrake, E., & Rhee, S. (2004). Ethnic identity as a predictor of problem behaviours among Korean American adolescents. *Adolescence, 39,* 601–622.

Simon, R., & Lynch, J. (1999). A comparative assessment of public opinion toward immigrants and immigration policy. *International Migration Review, 33,* 455–467.

Simpson, C. K., & Boyal, D. (1975). Esteem construct and generality and academic performance. *Educational and Psychological Measurement, 35,* 897–907.

Skutnabb-Kangas, T. (1999). Education of minorities. In J. A. Fishman (Ed.), *Handbook of language and ethnic identity* (pp. 42–59). New York: Oxford University Press.

Slonim-Nevo, V., & Sharaga, Y. (2000). Psychological and social adjustment of Russian-born and Israeli-born Jewish adolescents. *Child and Adolescent Social Work Journal, 17,* 455–475.

Smetana, J. (1995). Conflict and coordination in adolescent–parent relationships. In S. Shulman (Ed.), *Close relationships and socioemotional development* (pp. 155–184). Norwood, NJ: Ablex.

Smetana, J., & Asquith, P. (1994). Adolescents' and parents' conceptions of parental authority and personal autonomy. *Child Development, 65,* 1147–1162.

Snauwaert, B., Soenens, B., Vanbeselaere, N., & Boen, F. (2003). When integration does not necessarily imply integration: Different conceptualizations of acculturation orientations lead to different classifications. *Journal of Cross-Cultural Psychology, 34,* 231–239.

Steinberg, L. (1990). Autonomy, conflict, and harmony in the family relationship. In S. Feldman & G. Elliot (Eds.), *At the threshold: The developing adolescent* (pp. 255–276). Cambridge, MA: Harvard University Press.

Sterling, R. W. (1974). *Macropolitics: International relations in a global society.* New York: Knopf.

Stewart, S. M., Bond, M. H., McBride-Chang, C., Fielding, R., Deeds, O., & Westrick, J. (1998). Parent and adolescent contributors to teenage misconduct in Western and Asian high school students in Hong Kong. *International Journal of Behavioral Development, 22,* 847–869.

Stiles, D. A., Gibbons, J. L., Lie, S., Sand, T., & Krull, J. (1998). "Now I am living in Norway": Immigrant girls describe themselves. *Cross Cultural Research: The Journal of Comparative Social Science, 32,* 279–298.

Stonequist, E. V. (1937). *The marginal man.* New York: Scribners.

Suarez-Orozco, M. M. (1989). *Central American refugees and U.S. high schools: A psychosocial study of motivation and achievement.* Stanford, CA: Stanford University Press.

Suarez-Orozco, C., & Suarez-Orozco, M. M. (2002). *Children of immigrants.* Cambridge, MA: Harvard University Press.

Suinn, R., Ahuna, C., & Khoo, G. (1992). The Suinn–Lew Asian Self-identity Acculturation Scale: Concurrent and factorial validation. *Educational & Psychological Measurement, 52,* 1041–1046.

Szapocznik, J., & Kurtines, W. (1993). Family psychology and cultural diversity. *American Psychologist, 48,* 400–407.

Tajfel, H. (1978). *The social psychology of minorities.* London: Minority Rights Group.

Tajfel, H., & Turner, J. (1986). The social identity theory of intergroup behavior. In S. Worchel & W. Austin (Eds.), *Psychology of intergroup relations* (pp. 7–24). Chicago: Nelson-Hall.

Tanaka-Matsumi, J., & Draguns, J. (1997) Culture and psychopathology. In J. W. Berry, M. H. Segall, & C. Kagitcibasi (Eds.), *Handbook of cross-cultural psychology: Vol. 3. Social behaviors and applications* (2nd ed., pp. 413–448). Boston: Allyn & Bacon.

Tang, T. N., & Dion, K. L. (1999). Gender and acculturation in relation to traditionalism: Perceptions of self and parents among Chinese students. *Sex Roles, 41,* 17–29.

Taylor, C. L., & Jodice, D. A. (1983). *World handbook of political and social indicators.* New Haven: Yale University Press.

Ten Berge, J. M. F. (1986). Rotatie naar perfecte congruentie en de Multipele Groep Methode. [Rotation towards perfect congruence and the Multiple Group Method] *Nederlands Tijdschrift voor de Psychologie, 41,* 218–225.

Thai, N. D. (2003). Vietnamese youth gangs in Honolulu. *Journal of Prevention and Intervention in the Community, 25,* 47–64.

Tomlinson, S. (1989). Ethnicity and educational attainment in England. In L. Eldering & J. Kloprogge (Eds.), *Different cultures same school: Ethnic minority children in Europe* (pp. 15–38). Lisse, the Netherlands: Swets & Zeitlinger.

Torgersen, L. (2001). Patterns of self-reported delinquency in children with one immigrant parent, two immigrant parents and Norwegian-born parents. *Journal of Scandinavian Studies in Criminology and Crime Prevention, 2,* 213–227.

Tran, T. V. (1987). Ethnic community supports and psychological well-being of Vietnamese refugees. *International Migration Review, 21,* 833–844.

Tseng, W.-S. (2001). *Handbook of cultural psychiatry.* San Diego, CA: Academic Press.

Tucker, L. R. (1951). *A method for synthesis of factor analysis studies.* In Personnel Research Section Report No. 984. Washington, DC: Department of the Army.

Ullman, C., & Tatar, M. (2001). Psychological adjustment among Israeli adolescent immigrants: A report on life satisfaction, self-concept, and self-esteem. *Journal of Youth and Adolescence, 30,* 449–463.

United Nations Population Division. (2002). *World Immigration Report.* New York: Author.

Van de Vijver, F., Helms-Lorenz, M., & Feltzer, M. (1999). Acculturation and cognitive performance of migrant children in the Netherlands. *International Journal of Psychology, 34,* 149–162.

Van de Vijver, F. J. R., & Leung, K. (1997). *Methods and data analysis for cross-cultural research.* Newbury Park, CA: Sage.

Van de Vijver, F. J. R., & Poortinga, Y. H. (2002). Structural equivalence in multilevel research. *Journal of Cross-Cultural Psychology, 33,* 141–156.

Vedder, P. (2004). Turkish immigrant adolescents' adaptation in the Netherlands: The impact of the language context. *Estudios de Sociolingüística, 5,* 331–352.

Vedder, P., & O'Dowd, M. (1999). Swedish primary school pupils' interethnic relationships. *Scandinavian Journal of Psychology, 40,* 221–228.

Verkuyten, M. (1994). Self-esteem among ethnic minority youth in Western countries. *Social Indicators Research, 32,* 21–47.

Verkuyten, M. (2001). Global self-esteem, ethnic self-esteem, and family integrity: Turkish and Dutch early adolescents in The Netherlands. *International Journal of Behavioral Development, 25,* 357–366.

Verkuyten, M. (2005). The social psychology of ethnic identity. In *European Monographs in Social Psychology.* New York: Psychology Press.

Verkuyten, M., & Thijs, J. (2002). Racist victimization among children in the Netherlands: The effect of ethnic group and school. *Ethnic and Racial Studies, 25,* 310–331.

Viegas, T. (1997). *Timor-Leste.* Lisboa, Portugal: Universidade Aberta.

Virta, E., Sam, D. L., & Westin, C. (2004) Adolescents with Turkish background in Norway and Sweden: A comparative study of their psychological adaptation. *Scandinavian Journal of Psychology, 45,* 15–25.

Wall, J. A., Power, T. G., & Arbona, C. (1993). Susceptibility to antisocial peer pressure and its relation to acculturation in Mexican-American adolescents. *Journal of Adolescent Research, 8,* 403–418.

Ward, C. (1996). Acculturation. In D. Landis & R. Bhagat (Eds.), *Handbook of intercultural training* (2nd ed., pp. 124–147). Thousand Oaks, CA: Sage.

Ward, C. (2001). The A, B, Cs of acculturation. In D. Matsumoto (Ed.), *The handbook of culture and psychology* (pp. 411–445). Oxford, England: Oxford University Press.

Ward, C. (2004, May). *Identity, acculturation and adaptation among dual heritage youth.* Paper presented at the 4th biennial International Conference of the International Academy of Intercultural Research, Taipei, Taiwan.

Ward, C., Bochner, S., & Furnham, A. (2001) *The psychology of culture shock.* Hove, England: Routledge.

Ward, C., & Kennedy, A. (1996). Crossing cultures. The relationship between psychological and sociocultural dimensions of cross-cultural adjustment. In J. Pandey, D. Sinha, & D. P. S. Bhawuk (Eds.), *Asian contributions to cross-cultural psychology* (pp. 289–306): New Delhi, India: Sage.

Ward, C., & Kennedy, A. (1999). The measurement of sociocultural adaptation. *International Journal of Intercultural Relations, 23,* 1–19.

Ward, C., & Leong, C.-H. (2004). Chinese sojourners, Chinese hosts: A study of cultural identity and perceived discrimination in Singapore. In Y. Kashima, Y. Endo, E. Kashima, C. Leung, & J. McClure (Eds.), *Progress in Asian social psychology* (pp. 125–138). Seoul, Korea: Kyoyook-Kwahak Sa Publishing.

Ward, C., & Masgoret, A.-M. (2004, April). *New Zealanders' attitudes toward immigrants and immigration.* Paper presented at New Directions, New Settlers, New Challenges— Building and Enhancing Communities End-users Seminar. Wellington, New Zealand.

Ward, C., Okura, Y., Kennedy, A., & Kojima, T. (1998). The U-curve on trial: A longitudinal study of psychological and sociocultural adjustment during cross-cultural transition. *International Journal of Intercultural Relations, 22,* 277–291.

Ward, C., & Rana-Deuba, A. (1999). Acculturation and adaptation revisited. *Journal of Cross-Cultural Psychology, 30,* 272–292.

Waters, M. (1990). *Ethnic options: Choosing identities in America.* Berkeley, CA: University of California Press.

Waters, M. (1999). *Black identities.* Cambridge, MA: Harvard University Press.

Waters, M. (2000). Multiple ethnicities and identity in the United States. In P. Spickard & W. J. Burroughs (Eds.), *We are a people: Narrative and multiplicity in constructing ethnic identity* (pp. 23–40). Philadelphia: Temple University Press.

Westin, C. (2003). Young people of migrant origin in Sweden. *International Migration Review, 37,* 987–1010.

Whiting, B., & Whiting, J. (1975). *Children of six cultures: A psychocultural analysis.* Cambridge, MA: Harvard University Press.

Wold, B. (1995). *Health behaviour in school-aged children: A WHO cross-national survey (HSCB). Resource package of questions, 1993–94.* Bergen, Norway: Research Center for Health Promotion, University of Bergen.

Worbs, S. (2003). The second generation in Germany: Between school and labor market. *International Migration Review, 37,* 1011–1038.

Yau, J., & Smetana, J. (1996). Adolescent–parent conflict among Chinese adolescents in Hong Kong. *Child Development, 67,* 1262–1275.

Yildirim, I. (1997). *Ursachen und Folgen der Diskriminierung und Ausgrenzung von ethnischen Minderheiten in Deutschland.* [Discrimination and exclusion of ethnic minorities in Germany: Causes and consequences] Retrieved January 27, 2004, from http://www.aric-nrw.de/de/docs/pdf/ausgrenzung.pdf

Ying, Y. W. (1996). Immigration satisfaction of Chinese Americans: An empirical examination. *Journal of Community Psychology, 24,* 3–16.

Zegers de Beijl, R. (1999). *Documenting discrimination against migrant workers in the labour market: A comparative study of four European countries.* Geneva, Switzerland: International Labour Office.

Zentella, A. C. (1997). *Growing up bilingual: Puerto Rican children in New York.* Malden, MA: Blackwell.

Zetter, R. (1999). Reconceptualizing the myth of return: Continuity and transition amongst the Greek-Cypriot refugees of 1974. *Journal of Refugee Studies, 12,* 1–22.

Zhou, M. (1997a). Growing up American: The challenge confronting immigrant children and children of immigrants. *Annual Review of Sociology, 23,* 63–95.

Zhou, M. (1997b). Segmented assimilation: Issues controversies and recent research on the new second generation. *International Migration Review, 31,* 975–1008.

Zhou, M., & Bankston, C. (1994). Social capital and the adaptation of the second generation: The case of Vietnamese youth in New Orleans. *International Migration Review, 28,* 821–845.

Zhou, M., & Bankston, C. L. (1998). *Growing up American: How Vietnamese children adapt to life in the United States.* New York: Russell Sage Foundation.

Appendix A

Immigrant Adolescent Questionnaire

You can answer almost all the questions by making a check in the bracket [X] beside the answer that applies best. In some cases you are asked to write your answer. Try to answer each question quickly without stopping to think too long. If you wish, you may also write your own comments in the questionnaire.

A. **First, here are some questions about yourself and your background. Fill in the blank or check the answer that applies best.**

1. How old are you? _____ years

2. What is your gender?
   [ ] Female/Girl
   [ ] Male/Boy

3. In what grade are you in school? _____ grade

4. In what country were you born?
   [ ] [Host country]
   [ ] Another country What country? _____

5. If born in another country, how old were you when you came to [host country]?
   _____ years

6. Are you a [host country] citizen?
   [ ] Yes
   [ ] No
   [ ] Don't know

7. Are you a citizen of another country?
[ ] Yes
[ ] No
[ ] Don't know
If yes, of what other country are you a citizen? _____

8. What is your religion?
[ ] No religion   [ ] Jewish
[ ] Protestant   [ ] Muslim
[ ] Roman Catholic   [ ] Buddhist
[ ] Greek Orthodox   [ ] Hindu
[ ] Other (write in) _____

9. What is your ethnic background? *[This list was adapted for each group.]*
[ ] [Xxx]
[ ] [Xxx]
[ ] Other (write in) _____

10. What is your mother's ethnic background? *[This list was adapted for each group.]*
[ ] [Xxx]
[ ] [Xxx]
[ ] Other (write in) _____
[ ] Don't know

11. What is your father's ethnic background? *[This list was adapted for each group.]*
[ ] [Xxx]
[ ] [Xxx]
[ ] Other (write in) _____
[ ] Don't know

12. Where was your mother born?
[ ] [Host country]
[ ] Another country What country? _____
[ ] Don't know

13. Where was your father born?
[ ] [Host country]
[ ] Another country What country? _____
[ ] Don't know

14. What is the current occupation of your mother and father?

Mother	Father
[ ] Unskilled: farm labor, food service, janitor, house cleaner, factory work	[ ] Unskilled: farm labor, food service janitor, house cleaner, factory work
[ ] skilled work, such as technician, carpenter, hairdresser, seamstress	[ ] Skilled work, such as technician, carpenter, hairdresser, seamstress
[ ] White collar (office) work, such as clerk, salesperson, secretary, small business	[ ] White collar (office) work, such as clerk, salesperson, secretary, small business
[ ] Professional: doctor, lawyer, teacher business executive	[ ] Professional: doctor, lawyer, teacher, business executive
[ ] Not currently working: unemployed, retired, homemaker, student	[ ] Not currently working: unemployed, retired, homemaker, student
[ ] Other (specify:) _____	[ ] Other (specify:) _____
[ ] Don't know	[ ] Don't know

15. Which statement is most true about the neighborhood where you live?
    [ ] Almost all people are from a different ethnic group than mine
    [ ] A majority of the people is from a different ethnic group than mine
    [ ] There is about an equal mix of people from my ethnic group and other groups
    [ ] A majority of the people is from my ethnic group
    [ ] Almost all people are from my ethnic group

B. **Here are some questions about languages. Please answer by checking the answer that applies best.**

1. What language do you speak at home?
   With parents

	Not at all	A little	Half the time	A lot	All the time
a. I speak [ethnic language] with my parents	[ ]	[ ]	[ ]	[ ]	[ ]
b. I speak [national language] with my parents	[ ]	[ ]	[ ]	[ ]	[ ]

Answer the following if you have brothers or sisters.
If not, check here:

c. [ ] I have no brothers or sisters
   With brothers and sisters

	Not at all	A little	Half the time	A lot	All the time
d. I speak [ethnic language] with my brothers and sisters	[ ]	[ ]	[ ]	[ ]	[ ]
e. I speak [national language] with my brothers and sisters	[ ]	[ ]	[ ]	[ ]	[ ]

The following questions concern your knowledge of [ethnic language].

	Not at all	A little	Some-what	Fairly well	Very well
2. How well do you					
(a) understand [ethnic language]?	[ ]	[ ]	[ ]	[ ]	[ ]
(b) speak [ethnic language]?	[ ]	[ ]	[ ]	[ ]	[ ]
(c) read [ethnic language]?	[ ]	[ ]	[ ]	[ ]	[ ]
(d) write [ethnic language]?	[ ]	[ ]	[ ]	[ ]	[ ]

The following questions concern your knowledge of [national language].

	Not at all	A little	Some-what	Fairly well	Very well
3. How well do you					
(a) understand [national language]?	[ ]	[ ]	[ ]	[ ]	[ ]
(b) speak [national language]?	[ ]	[ ]	[ ]	[ ]	[ ]
(c) read [national language]?	[ ]	[ ]	[ ]	[ ]	[ ]
(d) write [national language]?	[ ]	[ ]	[ ]	[ ]	[ ]

4. Do you speak any other language at home than [national language] or [ethnic language]?

[ ] Yes   What language? _____

[ ] No

C. The following statements are about school. How well do you think they apply to you? Please check the answer that corresponds best to your own opinions and experiences.

	Strongly disagree	Somewhat disagree	Not sure /neutral	Somewhat agree	Strongly agree
1. At present I like school.	[ ]	[ ]	[ ]	[ ]	[ ]
2. I have problems concentrating during classes.	[ ]	[ ]	[ ]	[ ]	[ ]
3. I feel uneasy about going to school in the morning.	[ ]	[ ]	[ ]	[ ]	[ ]
4. I have problems concentrating when doing homework.	[ ]	[ ]	[ ]	[ ]	[ ]
5. I wish I could quit school for good.	[ ]	[ ]	[ ]	[ ]	[ ]
6. I feel lonely at school.	[ ]	[ ]	[ ]	[ ]	[ ]

7. I believe my teacher thinks my school performance is:

[ ] Poor

[ ] Below average

[ ] Average

[ ] Above average

[ ] Good

8. My present average grade is: ___

9. I have been absent from school all day or part of the day without a valid reason.
[ ] Never   [ ] Almost never   [ ] A few times a year
[ ] A few times a month   [ ] A few times a week

D. **People can think of themselves in various ways. For example, they may feel that they are members of various ethnic groups, such as Vietnamese (etc.), and that they are part of the larger society, [host society]. These questions are about how you think of yourself in this respect.**

	Not at all	A little	Some-what	Fairly well	Very well
1. How do you think of yourself?					
a. I think of myself as [ethnic].	[ ]	[ ]	[ ]	[ ]	[ ]
b. I think of myself as [national].	[ ]	[ ]	[ ]	[ ]	[ ]
c. I think of myself as part of another ethnic group.					
What group? _____	[ ]	[ ]	[ ]	[ ]	[ ]

	Strongly disagree	Somewhat disagree	Not sure /neutral	Somewhat agree	Strongly agree
2. I feel that I am part of [ethic] culture.	[ ]	[ ]	[ ]	[ ]	[ ]
3. I am proud of being [ethnic].	[ ]	[ ]	[ ]	[ ]	[ ]
4. I am happy to be [ethnic].	[ ]	[ ]	[ ]	[ ]	[ ]
5. I feel that I am part of [national] culture.	[ ]	[ ]	[ ]	[ ]	[ ]
6. I am proud of being [national].	[ ]	[ ]	[ ]	[ ]	[ ]
7. I am happy to be [national].	[ ]	[ ]	[ ]	[ ]	[ ]
8. Being part of [ethnic] culture is embarrassing to me.	[ ]	[ ]	[ ]	[ ]	[ ]
9. Being [ethnic] is uncomfortable for me.	[ ]	[ ]	[ ]	[ ]	[ ]
10. Being part of [ethnic] culture makes me feel happy.	[ ]	[ ]	[ ]	[ ]	[ ]
11. Being [ethnic] makes me feel good.	[ ]	[ ]	[ ]	[ ]	[ ]

People differ in how important they consider aspects of themselves to be. How important are the following aspects of yourself to you?

	Not at all	A little	Some-what	Important	Very important
12. That I am [national]	[ ]	[ ]	[ ]	[ ]	[ ]
13. That I am [ethnic]	[ ]	[ ]	[ ]	[ ]	[ ]
14. That I am a person/human being	[ ]	[ ]	[ ]	[ ]	[ ]

15. That I have a religion	[ ]	[ ]	[ ]	[ ]	[ ]
16. That I am male or female (boy or girl)	[ ]	[ ]	[ ]	[ ]	[ ]

E. **Here are some statements about language, cultural traditions, friends etc. Please indicate how much you agree or disagree with each statement by checking the answer that applies best to you.**

	Strongly disagree	Somewhat disagree	Not sure /neutral	Somewhat agree	Strongly agree
1. I feel that [ethnic group] should adapt to [national] cultural traditions and not maintain those of their own.	[ ]	[ ]	[ ]	[ ]	[ ]
2. I would rather marry a [ethnic] than a [national].	[ ]	[ ]	[ ]	[ ]	[ ]
3. I feel that [ethnic group] should maintain their own cultural traditions but also adapt to those of [national].	[ ]	[ ]	[ ]	[ ]	[ ]
4. I would rather marry a [national] than a [ethnic].	[ ]	[ ]	[ ]	[ ]	[ ]
5. I would be just as willing to marry a [national] as a [ethnic].	[ ]	[ ]	[ ]	[ ]	[ ]
6. I feel that it is not important for [ethnic group] either to maintain their own cultural traditions or to adapt to those of [national].	[ ]	[ ]	[ ]	[ ]	[ ]
7. I feel that [ethnic group] should maintain their own cultural traditions and not adapt to those of [national].	[ ]	[ ]	[ ]	[ ]	[ ]
8. I would not like to marry either a [national] or a [ethnic].	[ ]	[ ]	[ ]	[ ]	[ ]
9. It is more important to me to be fluent in [ethnic] than in [national language].	[ ]	[ ]	[ ]	[ ]	[ ]
10. It is more important to me to be fluent in [national language] than in [ethnic language].	[ ]	[ ]	[ ]	[ ]	[ ]
11. It is important to me to be fluent in both [national language] and in [ethnic language].	[ ]	[ ]	[ ]	[ ]	[ ]
12. It is not important to me to be fluent either in [ethnic language] or [national language].	[ ]	[ ]	[ ]	[ ]	[ ]
13. I prefer social activities that involve both [national members] and [ethnic members].	[ ]	[ ]	[ ]	[ ]	[ ]
14. I prefer to have only [national] friends.	[ ]	[ ]	[ ]	[ ]	[ ]
15. I prefer to have only [ethnic] friends.	[ ]	[ ]	[ ]	[ ]	[ ]
16. I prefer social activities that involve [nationals] only.	[ ]	[ ]	[ ]	[ ]	[ ]

17. I prefer to have both [ethnic] and
    [national] friends.   [ ]   [ ]   [ ]   [ ]   [ ]
18. I don't want to attend either [national] or
    [ethnic] social activities.   [ ]   [ ]   [ ]   [ ]   [ ]
19. I prefer social activities that involve
    [ethnic group members] only. [ ]   [ ]   [ ]   [ ]   [ ]
20. I don't want to have either [national]
    or [ethnic] friends.   [ ]   [ ]   [ ]   [ ]   [ ]

F. **Here are some questions about your friends and people you know. Indicate
    the answer that applies best.**

1. How many close [ethnic], [national], and [other ethnic] friends do you have?

	None	Only one	A few	Some	Many
(a) Close [ethnic] friends	[ ]	[ ]	[ ]	[ ]	[ ]
(b) Close [national] friends	[ ]	[ ]	[ ]	[ ]	[ ]
(c) Close [other ethnic] friends	[ ]	[ ]	[ ]	[ ]	[ ]

2. How often do you spend free time in school with …

	Almost never	Seldom	Some-times	Often	Almost always
(a) [Ethnic members]?	[ ]	[ ]	[ ]	[ ]	[ ]
(b) [National members]?	[ ]	[ ]	[ ]	[ ]	[ ]
(c) [Other ethnic members]?	[ ]	[ ]	[ ]	[ ]	[ ]

3. How often do you spend free time out of school with:

	Almost never	Seldom	Some-times	Often	Almost always
(a) [Ethnic members]?	[ ]	[ ]	[ ]	[ ]	[ ]
(b) [National members]?	[ ]	[ ]	[ ]	[ ]	[ ]
(c) [Other ethnic members]?	[ ]	[ ]	[ ]	[ ]	[ ]

4. How often do you play sports with:

	Almost never	Seldom	Some-times	Often	Almost always
(a) [Ethnic members]?	[ ]	[ ]	[ ]	[ ]	[ ]
(b) [National members]?	[ ]	[ ]	[ ]	[ ]	[ ]
(c) [Other ethnic members]?	[ ]	[ ]	[ ]	[ ]	[ ]

	Never	Almost never	A few times a year	A few times a month	Weekly
5. How often do you participate in traditional [ethnic] activities or customs?	[ ]	[ ]	[ ]	[ ]	[ ]
6. How often do you participate in traditional [national] activities or customs?	[ ]	[ ]	[ ]	[ ]	[ ]

G. Here are some statements dealing with relationships within the family. How well do the statements apply to your own opinions?

	Strongly disagree	Somewhat disagree	Not sure /neutral	Somewhat agree	Strongly agree
1. There should be a clear line of authority within the family and no doubt about who decides.	[ ]	[ ]	[ ]	[ ]	[ ]
2. It is all right for boys over the age of 18 to decide when to marry and whom to marry.	[ ]	[ ]	[ ]	[ ]	[ ]
3. Children should obey their parents	[ ]	[ ]	[ ]	[ ]	[ ]
4. Parents should teach their children to behave properly.	[ ]	[ ]	[ ]	[ ]	[ ]
5. When a boy reaches the age of 16, it is all right for him to decide whom to date and when to date.	[ ]	[ ]	[ ]	[ ]	[ ]
6. Children should not talk back to their parents.	[ ]	[ ]	[ ]	[ ]	[ ]
7. It is all right for girls over the age of 18 to decide when to marry and whom to marry.	[ ]	[ ]	[ ]	[ ]	[ ]
8. It is a child's responsibility to look after the parents when they need help.	[ ]	[ ]	[ ]	[ ]	[ ]
9. Girls should share in the work at home without payment.	[ ]	[ ]	[ ]	[ ]	[ ]
10. Parents always know what is best.	[ ]	[ ]	[ ]	[ ]	[ ]
11. When a girl reaches the age of 16, it is all right for her to decide whom to date and when to date.	[ ]	[ ]	[ ]	[ ]	[ ]
12. Boys should share in the work at home without payment.	[ ]	[ ]	[ ]	[ ]	[ ]
13. Girls should live at home until they marry.	[ ]	[ ]	[ ]	[ ]	[ ]
14. Boys should live at home until they marry.	[ ]	[ ]	[ ]	[ ]	[ ]

H. When people with different backgrounds are together, one may sometimes feel unfairly treated. The following questions are about these kinds of experiences.

	Strongly disagree	Somewhat disagree	Not sure /neutral	Somewhat agree	Strongly agree
1. I think that others have behaved in an unfair or negative way towards my ethnic group.	[ ]	[ ]	[ ]	[ ]	[ ]
2. I don't feel accepted by [national group].	[ ]	[ ]	[ ]	[ ]	[ ]
3. I feel [national group] has something against me.	[ ]	[ ]	[ ]	[ ]	[ ]

4. I have been teased or insulted because
   of my ethnic background.   [ ]   [ ]   [ ]   [ ]   [ ]
5. I have been threatened or attacked because
   of my ethnic background.   [ ]   [ ]   [ ]   [ ]   [ ]

How often do the following people treat you unfairly or negatively because of your ethnic background?

	Never	Rarely	Some-times	Often	Very often
6. Teachers	[ ]	[ ]	[ ]	[ ]	[ ]
7. Other adults outside school	[ ]	[ ]	[ ]	[ ]	[ ]
8. Other students	[ ]	[ ]	[ ]	[ ]	[ ]
9. Other kids/teens outside school	[ ]	[ ]	[ ]	[ ]	[ ]

I.   How much do you agree or disagree with the following statements about yourself?[1]

	Strongly disagree	Somewhat disagree	Not sure/neutral	Somewhat agree	Strongly agree
1. I am able to protect my personal interests.	[ ]	[ ]	[ ]	[ ]	[ ]
2. What happens to me in the future depends on me.	[ ]	[ ]	[ ]	[ ]	[ ]
3. I can do anything I really set my mind to do.	[ ]	[ ]	[ ]	[ ]	[ ]
4. When I get what I want, it is because of my own effort.	[ ]	[ ]	[ ]	[ ]	[ ]
5. I can determine what will happen in my life.	[ ]	[ ]	[ ]	[ ]	[ ]
6. When I make plans, I feel certain that I can make them work.	[ ]	[ ]	[ ]	[ ]	[ ]

J.   How do the following statements apply to how you think about yourself and your life?

	Strongly disagree	Somewhat disagree	Not sure/neutral	Somewhat agree	Strongly agree
1. On the whole, I am satisfied with myself.	[ ]	[ ]	[ ]	[ ]	[ ]
2. At times I think I am no good at all.	[ ]	[ ]	[ ]	[ ]	[ ]
3. I feel that I have a number of good qualities.	[ ]	[ ]	[ ]	[ ]	[ ]
4. I am able to do things as well as most other people.	[ ]	[ ]	[ ]	[ ]	[ ]

[1]This scale for mastery was not used in the analyses and presentation of findings.

5. I feel I have not much to be
proud of. [ ] [ ] [ ] [ ] [ ]
6. I certainly feel useless at times. [ ] [ ] [ ] [ ] [ ]
7. I feel that I am a person of worth, at least
on an equal plane with others. [ ] [ ] [ ] [ ] [ ]
8. I wish I could have more respect for myself.
[ ] [ ] [ ] [ ] [ ]
9. All in all, I am inclined to feel that I am
a failure. [ ] [ ] [ ] [ ] [ ]
10. I take a positive attitude to
myself. [ ] [ ] [ ] [ ] [ ]
11. In most ways my life is close
to my ideal. [ ] [ ] [ ] [ ] [ ]
12. The conditions of my life are
excellent. [ ] [ ] [ ] [ ] [ ]
13. I am satisfied with my life. [ ] [ ] [ ] [ ] [ ]
14. So far I have got the important things
I want in life. [ ] [ ] [ ] [ ] [ ]
15. If I could live my life over, I would
change almost nothing. [ ] [ ] [ ] [ ] [ ]

K. How often do you experience the following?

	Strongly disagree	Somewhat disagree	Not sure /neutral	Somewhat agree	Strongly agree
1. I feel tired.	[ ]	[ ]	[ ]	[ ]	[ ]
2. I feel sick in the stomach.	[ ]	[ ]	[ ]	[ ]	[ ]
3. I feel dizzy and faint.	[ ]	[ ]	[ ]	[ ]	[ ]
4. I feel short of breath even when not exerting myself.	[ ]	[ ]	[ ]	[ ]	[ ]
5. I feel weak all over.	[ ]	[ ]	[ ]	[ ]	[ ]
6. I feel tense or keyed up	[ ]	[ ]	[ ]	[ ]	[ ]
7. I feel nervous and shaky inside.	[ ]	[ ]	[ ]	[ ]	[ ]
8. I feel restless.	[ ]	[ ]	[ ]	[ ]	[ ]
9. I feel annoyed or irritated.	[ ]	[ ]	[ ]	[ ]	[ ]
10. I am worried about something bad happening to me.	[ ]	[ ]	[ ]	[ ]	[ ]
11. I feel unhappy and sad.	[ ]	[ ]	[ ]	[ ]	[ ]
12. My thoughts seem to be mixed up.	[ ]	[ ]	[ ]	[ ]	[ ]
13. I worry a lot of the time.	[ ]	[ ]	[ ]	[ ]	[ ]
14. I feel lonely even with other people.	[ ]	[ ]	[ ]	[ ]	[ ]
15. I lose interest and pleasure in things which I usually enjoy.	[ ]	[ ]	[ ]	[ ]	[ ]

L. Many students have at some time engaged in negative activities. We are interested in how frequently these activities occur, not who does them. Remember that no one will know how you respond. Have you been involved in any of the following, and in that case how often?

	Never	Yes, but not during the past 12 months	Once during the past 12 months	A few times during the past 12 months	Many times during the past 12 months
1. Had a serious quarrel with a teacher.	[ ]	[ ]	[ ]	[ ]	[ ]
2. Been kicked out of classroom because of something you did.	[ ]	[ ]	[ ]	[ ]	[ ]
3. Stolen money or something else from members of your family	[ ]	[ ]	[ ]	[ ]	[ ]
4. Taken things from a shop without paying.	[ ]	[ ]	[ ]	[ ]	[ ]
5. Purposely destroyed seats on a bus, at the cinema or other places.	[ ]	[ ]	[ ]	[ ]	[ ]
6. Purposely destroyed or broken windows, benches, telephone booths, or something similar.	[ ]	[ ]	[ ]	[ ]	[ ]
7. Cursed at a teacher.	[ ]	[ ]	[ ]	[ ]	[ ]
8. Been called to the principal for something wrong you had done.	[ ]	[ ]	[ ]	[ ]	[ ]
9. Avoided paying for such things as movies, bus or train rides.	[ ]	[ ]	[ ]	[ ]	[ ]
10. Bullied another kid.	[ ]	[ ]	[ ]	[ ]	[ ]

Appendix B

**Standard Treatment: Factor Loadings in the Pooled Sample
of Immigrant Adolescents Specified for Each Scale**

TABLE B.1

Factor Loadings in the Pooled Sample of Immigrant Adolescents: Integration

Item	Loading
Traditions	.52
Marriage	.44
Language	.54
Friends	.67
Social activities	.67

Note. Eigenvalues = 1.67, .97, .88, .79, .69; first factor explains 33.4%.

TABLE B.2

Factor Loadings in the Pooled Sample of Immigrant Adolescents: Separation

Item	Loading
Traditions	.61
Marriage	.56
Language	.59
Friends	.73
Social activities	.75

Note. Eigenvalues = 2.12, .89, .77, .74, .48; first factor explains 42.5%.

TABLE B.3

Factor Loadings in the Pooled Sample of Immigrant Adolescents: Assimilation

Item	Loading
Traditions	.51
Marriage	.59
Language	.46
Friends	.77
Social activities	.76

Note. Eigenvalues = 1.99, .94, .86, .77, .44; first factor explains 39.8%.

TABLE B.4

Factor Loadings in the Pooled Sample of Immigrant Adolescents: Marginalization

Item	Loading
Traditions	.52
Marriage	.44
Language	.54
Friends	.67
Social activities	.67

Note. Eigenvalues = 1.67, .97, .88, .79, .69; first factor explains 33.4%.

TABLE B.5

Factor Loadings in the Pooled Sample of Immigrant Adolescents: Ethnic Identity

Item	Loading
Part of ethnic culture	.68
Pride in ethnic culture	.84
Happy to be ethnic	.85
Embarrassing to be ethnic*	.47
Uncomfortable being ethnic*	.48
Feels happy about ethnic culture	.77
Feels good about ethnic culture	.83
Important being ethnic	.64

Note. Eigenvalues = 4.02, 1.21, .63, .61, .56, .48, .29, .20; first factor explains 50.3%. Items with an asterisk were reverse scored.

TABLE B.6

Factor Loadings in the Pooled Sample of Immigrant Adolescents:
National Identity

Item	Loading
Feels part of national society	.79
Proud to be national	.91
Happy to be national	.89
Important being national	.73

Note. Eigenvalues = 2.77, .58, .47, .18; first factor explains 69.2%.

TABLE B.7

Factor Loadings in the Pooled Sample of Immigrant Adolescents:
Proficiency in Ethnic Language

Item	Loading
Understands ethnic language	.79
Speaks ethnic language	.85
Reads ethnic language	.88
Writes ethnic language	.86

Note. Eigenvalues = 2.86, .74, .26, .15; first factor explains 71.4%.

TABLE B.8

Factor Loadings in the Pooled Sample of Immigrant Adolescents:
Proficiency in National Language

Item	Loading
Understands national language	.87
Speaks national language	.90
Reads national language	.90
Writes national language	.88

Note. Eigenvalues = 3.14, .45, .21, .20; first factor explains 78.6%.

TABLE B.9
Factor Loadings in the Pooled Sample of Immigrant Adolescents: National Language Use

Item	Loading
Speaks ethnic language with parents*	.79
Speaks national language with parents	.76
Speaks ethnic language with siblings*	.78
Speaks national language with siblings	.78

Note. Eigenvalues = 2.42, .69, .66, .24; first factor explains 60.5%. Items with an asterisk were reverse scored.

TABLE B.10
Factor Loadings in the Pooled Sample of Immigrant Adolescents: Ethnic Peer contacts

Item	Loading
Number of friends of own ethnic group	.74
With friends in school of own ethnic group	.79
With friends outside school of own ethnic group	.86
Sports with friends of own ethnic group	.75

Note. Eigenvalues = 2.48, .63, .52, .38; first factor explains 61.9%.

TABLE B.11
Factor Loadings in the Pooled Sample of Immigrant Adolescents: National Peer Contacts

Item	Loading
Number of nonethnic friends/national friends	.76
With nonethnic/national friends in school	.81
With nonethnic/national friends outside school	.85
Sports with nonethnic/national friends	.73

Note. Eigenvalues = 2.49, .63, .51, .38; first factor explains 62.1%.

TABLE B.12

Factor Loadings in the Pooled Sample of Immigrant Adolescents: Adolescents' Rights

Item	Loading
Boy's right to choose marriage partner	.72
Boy's right to date	.79
Girl's right to choose marriage partner	.80
Girl's right to date	.79

Note. Eigenvalues = 2.42, .78, .49, .32; first factor explains 60.5%.

TABLE B.13

Factor Loadings in the Pooled Sample of Immigrant Adolescents: Family Obligations

Item	Loading
Authority at home	.39
Obedience to parents	.64
Parental training	.54
Speaking back to parents	.58
Children's responsibility to parents	.49
Working at home—girls	.60
Parents know best	.60
Working at home—boys	.46
Living at home until marriage—girls	.63
Living at home until marriage—boys	.57

Note. Eigenvalues = 3.09, 1.47, 1.18, .90, .79, .76, .62, .51, .48, .22; first factor explains 30.9%.

TABLE B.14

**Factor Loadings in the Pooled Sample of Immigrant Adolescents:
Perceived Discrimination**

Item	Loading
Negative behavior to ethnic group	.52
Not accepted by majority members	.67
Majority members have something against me	.70
Teased and insulted	.72
Threatened and attacked	.65
Negative behavior from teachers	.57
Negative behavior from adults	.70
Negative behavior from students	.75
Negative behavior from kids outside school	.72

Note. Eigenvalues = 4.04, 1.21, .86, .75, .65, .46, .43, .32, .29; first factor explains 34.9%.

TABLE B.15

**Factor Loadings in the Pooled Sample of Immigrant Adolescents:
Life Satisfaction**

Item	Loading
Ideal life	.69
Excellent living conditions	.81
Satisfied with life	.82
Gotten important things in life	.73
Won't make changes in life	.62

Note. Eigenvalues = 2.72, .75, .64, .53, .37; first factor explains 54.4%.

TABLE B.16
Factor Loadings in the Pooled Sample of Immigrant Adolescents:
Self-Esteem

Item	Loading
Satisfied with self	.55
Think I am not good*	.56
Have good qualities	.61
Do things as good as others	.58
Have nothing to be proud of*	.59
Feel useless at times*	.62
Have equal worth as others	.52
Need more self-respect*	.38
Feel like a failure*	.64
Positive self-attitude	.61

Note. Eigenvalues = 3.26, 1.61, .85, .72, .71, .68, .61, .58; first factor explains 32.6%. Items with an asterisk were reverse scored.

TABLE B.17
Factor Loadings in the Pooled Sample of Immigrant Adolescents:
Psychological Problems

Item	Loading
Tiredness	.54
Sick in the stomach	.52
Dizziness	.59
Short of breath	.55
Powerlessness	.66
Tensed	.63
Nervousness	.66
Restlessness	.61
Irritation	.67
Worried	.60
Unhappiness	.72
Mixed thoughts	.72
Worry a lot	.70
Loneliness	.65
Loss of interest	.62

Note. Eigenvalues = 6.00, 1.30, 1.02, .87, .69, .62, .60, .59, .53, .52, .50, .49, .46, .44, .38; first factor explains 39.8%.

TABLE B.18

Factor Loadings in the Pooled Sample of Immigrant Adolescents: School Adjustment

Item	Loading
Likes school presently	.29
Concentration problems during classes*	.73
Feels uneasy about school*	.54
Concentration problems during homework*	.75
Wishes to quit school*	.46
Feels lonely at school*	.36
School attendance*	.42

Note. Eigenvalues = 1.99, 1.44, 1.07, .98, .79, .41, .34; first factor explains 28.4%. Items with an asterisk were reverse scored.

TABLE B.19

Factor Loadings in the Pooled Sample of Immigrant Adolescents: Behavior Problems

Item	Loading
Serious argument with teacher	.59
Sent out of classroom	.65
Stolen from family member	.52
Shoplifting	.66
Purposely destroyed seats etc.	.69
Purposely destroyed windows etc.	.71
Cursed at a teacher	.64
Called to headmaster for wrong doing	.69
Avoided paying on buses etc.	.59
Bullied another kid	.62

Note. Eigenvalues = 4.09, 1.16, .79, .74, .68, .61, .56, .52, .49, .36; first factor explains 40.9%.

TABLE B.20

**Factor Loadings in the Pooled Sample of National Adolescents:
Acculturation Attitudes**

Item	Loading
E1: assimilation-traditions	.62
E2: separation-marriage	.30
E3: integration-traditions	−.61
E4: assimilation-marriage	.19
E5: integration-marriage	−.69
E6: marginalization-traditions	.40
E7: separation-traditions	.16

Note. Eigenvalues = 1.54, 1.32, 1.26, .93, .84, .59, .52; first factor explains 22.0%.

TABLE B.21

**Factor Loadings in the Pooled Sample of National Adolescents:
National Identity**

Item	Loading
Feels part of national society	.72
Proud to be national	.87
Happy to be national	.84
Important being national	.70

Note. Eigenvalues = 2.43, .68, .59, .29; first factor explains 60.8%.

TABLE B.22

**Factor Loadings in the Pooled Sample of National Adolescents:
Ethnic Peer Contacts**

Item	Loading
Number of ethnic friends	.74
With ethnic friends in school	.85
With ethnic friends outside school	.87
Sports with ethnic friends	.77

Note. Eigenvalues = 2.61, .62, .46, .32; first factor explains 65.2%.

TABLE B.23
Factor Loadings in the Pooled Sample of National Adolescents: National Peer Contacts

Item	Loading
Number of nonethnic friends/national friends	.68
With nonethnic/national friends in school	.83
With nonethnic/national friends outside school	.85
Sports with nonethnic/national friends	.66

Note. Eigenvalues = 2.31, .75, .57, .36; first factor explains 57.8%.

TABLE B.24
Factor Loadings in the Pooled Sample of National Adolescents: Family Obligations

Item	Loading
Authority at home	.52
Obedience to parents	.62
Parental training	.41
Speaking back to parents	.62
Children's responsibility to parents	.35
Working at home—girls	.48
Parents know best	.68
Working at home—boys	.38
Living at home until marriage—girls	.64
Living at home until marriage—boys	.64

Note. Eigenvalues = 2.97, 1.57, 1.29, .92, .89, .71, .59, .48, .45, .14; first factor explains 29.7%.

TABLE B.25
Factor Loadings in the Pooled Sample of National Adolescents: Adolescents' Rights

Item	Loading
Boy's right to choose marriage partner	.67
Boy's right to date	.79
Girl's right to choose marriage partner	.76
Girl's right to date	.80

Note. Eigenvalues = 2.29, .97, .45, .29; first factor explains 57.2%.

TABLE B.26
Factor Loadings in the Pooled Sample of National Adolescents:
Life Satisfaction

Item	Loading
Ideal life	.77
Excellent living conditions	.77
Satisfied with life	.84
Gotten important things in life	.75
Won't make changes in life	.70

Note. Eigenvalues = 2.95, .67, .54, .48, .37; first factor explains 58.9%.

TABLE B.27
Factor Loadings in the Pooled Sample of National Adolescents:
Self-Esteem

Item	Loading
Satisfied with self	.68
Think I am not good*	.60
Have good qualities	.68
Do things as good as others	.62
Have nothing to be proud of*	.62
Feel useless at times*	.62
Have equal worth as others	.58
Need more self-respect*	.53
Feel like a failure*	.70
Positive self-attitude	.75

Note. Eigenvalues = 4.11, 1.41, .74, .71, .64, .59, .54, .44, .43, .39; first factor explains 41.1%. Items with an asterisk were reverse scored.

TABLE B.28

Factor Loadings in the Pooled Sample of National Adolescents: Psychological Problems

Item	Loading
Tiredness	.54
Sick in the stomach	.57
Dizziness	.59
Short of breath	.56
Powerlessness	.68
Tensed	.61
Nervousness	.70
Restlessness	.58
Irritation	.63
Worried	.57
Unhappiness	.71
Mixed thoughts	.71
Worry a lot	.70
Loneliness	.66
Loss of interest	.62

Note. Eigenvalues = 5.98, 1.20, 1.04, .83, .73, .68, .64, .61, .56, .54, .49, .48, .44, .42, .37; first factor explains 40.0%.

TABLE B.29

Factor Loadings in the Pooled Sample of National Adolescents: School Adjustment

Item	Loading
Likes school presently	.26
Concentration problems during classes*	.56
Feels uneasy about school*	.68
Concentration problems during homework*	.52
Wishes to quit school*	.36
Feels lonely at school*	.30
School attendance*	.44

Note. Eigenvalues = 1.52, 1.31, 1.03, .96, .81, .75, .62; first factor explains 21.8%. Items with an asterisk were reverse scored.

TABLE B.30

Factor Loadings in the Pooled Sample of National Adolescents: Behavior Problems

Item	Loading
Serious argument with teacher	.64
Sent out of classroom	.64
Stolen from family member	.54
Shoplifting	.70
Purposely destroyed seats, etc.	.68
Purposely destroyed windows, etc.	.70
Cursed at a teacher	.66
Called to headmaster for wrongdoing	.67
Avoided paying on buses, etc.	.62
Bullied another kid	.58

Note. Eigenvalues = 4.14, 1.18, .81, .75, .68, .63, .53, .49, .44, .36; first factor explains 41.4%.

Appendix C

Estimated Values, Corrected for Age, Gender, and Proportion of Time Spent in New Country

	Assimilation				Integration				Separation				Marginalization				Ethnic Identity				National Identity			
	N	M	SD	Cohen's d	N	M	SD	Cohen's d	N	M	SD	Cohen's d	N	M	SD	Cohen's d	N	M	SD	Cohen's d	N	M	SD	Cohen's d
Grand mean	7363	2.34	0.23		7221	3.85	0.14		7367	2.51	0.14		7353	1.95	0.26		4755	4.27	0.21		7358	3.45	0.40	
All immigrants	4,748	2.20	0.15	-0.70	4,745	3.93	0.08	0.72	4,747	2.59	0.11	0.58	4,736	1.78	0.10	-0.90	4,755	4.27	0.21	0.00	4,739	3.15	0.06	-1.03
All hosts	2615	2.59	0.11	1.38	2476	3.69	0.08	-1.38	2620	2.37	0.07	-1.20	2617	2.28	0.10	1.62					2619	3.98	0.01	1.89
Australia Immigrants	304	2.19	0.14	-0.80	304	3.94	0.08	0.77	304	2.58	0.11	0.56	304	1.78	0.10	-0.90	304	4.34	0.08	0.44	304	3.16	0.06	-1.02
Australia Nationals	155	2.57	0.11	1.29	155	3.71	0.08	-1.28	155	2.38	0.07	-1.21	155	2.28	0.10	1.64					155	3.98	0.01	1.89
Canada Immigrants	256	2.19	0.16	-0.73	256	3.94	0.08	0.84	256	2.57	0.12	0.46	254	1.75	0.10	-1.04	257	4.45	0.10	1.07	257	3.15	0.07	-1.05
Canada Nationals	137	2.58	0.11	1.29	137	3.69	0.08	-1.28	138	2.36	0.07	-1.32	139	2.26	0.09	1.56					139	3.98	0.01	1.89
Finland Immigrants	419	2.32	0.16	-0.13	418	3.94	0.08	0.84	418	2.69	0.12	1.32	417	1.81	0.11	-0.72	415	3.91	0.09	-2.22	411	3.10	0.06	-1.24
Finland Nationals	346	2.61	0.11	1.49	346	3.68	0.08	-1.51	346	2.39	0.07	-1.06	346	2.30	0.09	1.77					346	3.98	0.01	1.89
France Immigrants	505	2.13	0.12	-1.15	505	3.93	0.08	0.73	505	2.52	0.08	0.05	505	1.74	0.10	-1.08	506	4.35	0.05	0.48	506	3.19	0.03	-0.92
France Nationals	150	2.57	0.12	1.24	150	3.71	0.09	-1.21	150	2.36	0.09	-1.28	150	2.25	0.12	1.48					150	3.98	0.01	1.89
Germany Immigrants	250	2.20	0.12	-0.75	250	3.94	0.08	0.78	250	2.56	0.11	0.34	250	1.73	0.10	-1.13	250	4.01	0.07	-1.61	246	3.15	0.05	-1.05
Germany Nationals	248	2.56	0.11	1.18	248	3.72	0.08	-1.12	248	2.32	0.07	-1.67	248	2.20	0.10	1.25					244	3.97	0.01	1.87
Israel Immigrants	454	2.33	0.15	-0.05	454	3.94	0.08	0.85	454	2.67	0.11	1.27	452	1.78	0.09	-0.90	456	4.14	0.07	-0.83	456	3.08	0.05	-1.29
Israel Nationals	214	2.59	0.11	1.40	213	3.69	0.08	-1.38	214	2.34	0.06	-1.53	213	2.23	0.08	1.45					214	3.97	0.01	1.87
Netherlands Immigrants	348	2.16	0.13	-0.95	348	3.91	0.08	0.55	348	2.56	0.09	0.39	348	1.79	0.11	-0.83	349	4.54	0.06	1.74	348	3.19	0.04	-0.93
Netherlands Nationals	101	2.58	0.11	1.30	101	3.70	0.08	-1.30	101	2.39	0.07	-1.10	101	2.29	0.10	1.69					101	3.98	0.01	1.90
New Zealand Immigrants	159	2.13	0.11	-1.16	158	3.92	0.08	0.60	159	2.52	0.06	0.05	157	1.76	0.09	-1.03	163	4.33	0.03	0.40	163	3.20	0.05	-0.90
New Zealand Nationals	241	2.63	0.10	1.61	241	3.67	0.07	-1.65	241	2.40	0.06	-1.03	242	2.31	0.08	1.83					243	3.98	0.01	1.89
Norway Immigrants	462	2.19	0.14	-0.80	460	3.92	0.08	0.65	461	2.57	0.10	0.50	459	1.78	0.10	-0.89	463	4.28	0.07	0.07	459	3.17	0.05	-0.99
Norway Nationals	202	2.60	0.11	1.42	201	3.69	0.08	-1.42	205	2.38	0.07	-1.12	203	2.29	0.10	1.69					204	3.98	0.01	1.89
Portugal Immigrants	190	2.29	0.13	-0.29	191	3.96	0.08	0.97	191	2.68	0.10	1.38	191	1.81	0.10	-0.75	191	4.46	0.07	1.18	191	3.10	0.05	-1.23
Portugal Nationals	353	2.61	0.11	1.49	353	3.68	0.08	-1.53	353	2.41	0.06	-0.92	353	2.32	0.09	1.90					354	3.98	0.01	1.90
Sweden Immigrants	815	2.17	0.14	-0.89	815	3.92	0.08	0.62	815	2.56	0.10	0.42	813	1.78	0.10	-0.88	816	4.42	0.07	0.92	813	3.18	0.05	-0.96
Sweden Nationals	213	2.58	0.11	1.30	213	3.71	0.08	-1.28	214	2.35	0.07	-1.40	212	2.24	0.10	1.47					213	3.98	0.01	1.88
United Kingdom Immigrants	120	2.16	0.12	-1.00	120	3.91	0.08	0.50	120	2.54	0.09	0.24	120	1.78	0.11	-0.88	120	4.58	0.05	2.01	120	3.19	0.03	-0.91
United Kingdom Nationals	120	2.59	0.11	1.35	120	3.70	0.08	-1.34	120	2.37	0.08	-1.24	120	2.27	0.11	1.56					120	3.98	0.01	1.88
United States Immigrants	466	2.18	0.14	-0.84	466	3.93	0.08	0.71	466	2.59	0.10	0.65	466	1.80	0.09	-0.79	465	3.99	0.07	-1.79	465	3.17	0.05	-0.99
United States Nationals	135	2.57	0.10	1.27	135	3.71	0.07	-1.27	135	2.39	0.07	-1.10	135	2.29	0.09	1.73					136	3.98	0.01	1.90

		Ethnic Language				National Language				Language Use				Ethnic Peer Contacts				National Peer Contacts			
		N	M	SD	Cohen's d	N	M	SD	Cohen's d	N	M	SD	Cohen's d	N	M	SD	Cohen's d	N	M	SD	Cohen's d
Grand mean		4,714	3.67	0.46		4,574	4.45	0.37		4,175	-0.21	0.60		6,555	3.35	0.42		7,263	3.60	0.48	
All immigrants	Immigrants	4,714	3.67	0.46	0.00	4,574	4.45	0.37	0.00	4,175	-0.21	0.60	0.00	4,661	3.61	0.13	0.82	4,646	3.25	0.15	-0.32
All nationals	Nationals													1,894	2.73	0.12	-2.02	2,617	4.22	0.05	2.92
Australia	Immigrants	302	3.21	0.38	-1.10	304	4.57	0.28	0.36	221	0.38	0.37	1.17	301	3.61	0.13	0.83	301	3.25	0.14	-0.33
	Nationals													155	2.72	0.11	-2.06	154	4.21	0.05	2.87
Canada	Immigrants	257	3.51	0.42	-0.37	257	4.61	0.32	0.48	249	0.29	0.44	0.95	257	3.57	0.13	0.71	255	3.25	0.15	-0.32
	Nationals																	139	4.22	0.05	2.92
Finland	Immigrants	415	4.10	0.44	0.93	416	3.89	0.32	-1.61	371	-0.84	0.44	-1.21	416	3.68	0.14	1.05	416	3.10	0.16	-0.80
	Nationals													190	2.78	0.10	-1.90	345	4.22	0.05	2.91
France	Immigrants	505	3.25	0.20	-1.19	505	4.80	0.15	1.26	465	0.51	0.19	1.61	450	3.54	0.13	0.61	452	3.35	0.08	-0.02
	Nationals													150	2.69	0.15	-2.11	150	4.22	0.05	2.92
Germany	Immigrants	235	3.85	0.37	0.42	236	4.42	0.27	-0.07	213	-0.23	0.37	-0.06	246	3.55	0.12	0.62	250	3.28	0.14	-0.23
	Nationals													247	2.62	0.12	-2.39	248	4.25	0.05	3.01
Israel	Immigrants	454	4.06	0.35	0.94	456	4.31	0.26	-0.43	420	-0.44	0.36	-0.48	446	3.63	0.11	0.91	446	3.12	0.13	-0.76
	Nationals																	213	4.26	0.05	3.04
Netherlands	Immigrants	337	3.48	0.26	-0.51	351	4.60	0.18	0.54	307	0.13	0.25	0.74	347	3.61	0.13	0.82	349	3.32	0.10	-0.11
	Nationals													99	2.74	0.13	-1.98	101	4.20	0.05	2.85
New Zealand	Immigrants	157	3.16	0.06	-1.56	120	4.27	0.25	-0.58					152	3.56	0.10	0.67	152	3.37	0.05	0.04
	Nationals													241	2.75	0.09	-1.99	241	4.23	0.05	2.94
Norway	Immigrants	465	3.70	0.34	0.07	462	4.08	0.25	-1.18	426	-0.55	0.33	-0.71	460	3.60	0.12	0.81	455	3.29	0.13	-0.22
	Nationals													204	2.73	0.12	-2.02	204	4.22	0.05	2.91
Portugal	Immigrants	191	3.15	0.35	-1.27	191	4.37	0.23	-0.27	185	0.47	0.34	1.39	190	3.68	0.13	1.05	190	3.09	0.13	-0.84
	Nationals													354	2.78	0.10	-1.89	354	4.21	0.04	2.86
Sweden	Immigrants	810	3.93	0.32	0.64	814	4.94	0.14	1.77	776	-0.76	0.31	-1.17	812	3.60	0.13	0.80	811	3.30	0.12	-0.16
	Nationals																	214	4.24	0.05	2.95
United Kingdom	Immigrants	120	3.35	0.20	-0.91	120	4.77	0.25	1.02	116	0.58	0.20	1.78	120	3.59	0.13	0.75	119	3.35	0.08	-0.02
	Nationals													120	2.70	0.13	-2.10	120	4.23	0.05	2.93
United States	Immigrants	466	3.82	0.34	0.36	462	4.77	0.25	1.02	426	-0.18	0.33	0.06	464	3.64	0.11	0.92	450	3.26	0.13	-0.31
	Nationals													134	2.75	0.11	-1.97	134	4.20	0.05	2.82

		Family Obligations				Adolescents' Rights				Perceived Discrimination			
		N	M	SD	Cohen's d	N	M	SD	Cohen's d	N	M	SD	Cohen's d
Grand mean		7342	3.44	0.30		7334	3.38	0.07		4699	2.07	0.22	
All immigrants		4726	3.65	0.07	1.00	4722	3.35	0.06	-0.50	4699	2.07	0.22	0.00
All nationals		2,616	3.05	0.05	-1.83	2,612	3.43	0.04	1.01				
Australia	Immigrants	303	3.65	0.07	1.00	303	3.36	0.05	-0.36	303	2.04	0.08	-0.20
	Nationals	155	3.05	0.05	-1.81	155	3.44	0.04	1.20				
Canada	Immigrants	255	3.64	0.07	0.93	255	3.34	0.06	-0.57	254	2.00	0.09	-0.42
	Nationals	138	3.04	0.05	-1.87	138	3.44	0.04	1.07				
Finland	Immigrants	417	3.71	0.08	1.26	415	3.31	0.06	-1.07	417	2.18	0.09	0.66
	Nationals	346	3.06	0.05	-1.77	346	3.43	0.04	1.01				
France	Immigrants	505	3.61	0.06	0.82	505	3.37	0.04	-0.18	506	1.90	0.07	-1.07
	Nationals	150	3.04	0.06	-1.86	150	3.44	0.04	1.11				
Germany	Immigrants	250	3.62	0.07	0.87	250	3.33	0.05	-0.80	236	1.90	0.08	-1.06
	Nationals	248	3.00	0.05	-2.03	248	3.42	0.04	0.82				
Israel	Immigrants	454	3.69	0.06	1.17	454	3.29	0.05	-1.55	455	2.50	0.08	2.52
	Nationals	214	3.02	0.04	-1.98	214	3.41	0.04	0.66				
Netherlands	Immigrants	345	3.64	0.06	0.95	344	3.37	0.05	-0.15	342	1.92	0.07	-0.95
	Nationals	101	3.06	0.06	-1.76	101	3.45	0.04	1.29				
New Zealand	Immigrants	151	3.61	0.04	0.83	151	3.37	0.04	-0.15	150	2.49	0.06	2.55
	Nationals	239	3.06	0.04	-1.77	239	3.42	0.04	0.87				
Norway	Immigrants	457	3.65	0.06	0.97	456	3.35	0.05	-0.39	455	2.18	0.08	0.63
	Nationals	201	3.05	0.05	-1.79	201	3.43	0.04	1.03				
Portugal	Immigrants	190	3.71	0.06	1.26	190	3.32	0.05	-0.90	188	2.28	0.07	1.23
	Nationals	354	3.08	0.04	-1.70	354	3.44	0.04	1.20				
Sweden	Immigrants	813	3.64	0.06	0.95	813	3.36	0.05	-0.27	807	1.83	0.07	-1.46
	Nationals	214	3.03	0.05	-1.91	214	3.43	0.04	0.91				
United Kingdom	Immigrants	120	3.63	0.06	0.89	120	3.37	0.04	-0.21	120	2.21	0.06	0.81
	Nationals	120	3.04	0.06	-1.85	120	3.43	0.04	0.99				
United States	Immigrants	466	3.66	0.06	1.06	466	3.37	0.05	-0.16	466	2.09	0.08	0.08
	Nationals	136	3.06	0.05	-1.75	132	3.45	0.04	1.39				

Country	Group	Self Esteem N	M	SD	Cohen's d	Life Satisfaction N	M	SD	Cohen's d	Psychological Problems N	M	SD	Cohen's d	School Adjustment N	M	SD	Cohen's d	Behavior Problems N	M	SD	Cohen's d
Grand mean		7,327	3.75	0.07		7,310	3.53	0.11		7,299	2.35	0.10		7,374	3.84	0.13		7,293	1.59	0.15	
All immigrants		4,710	3.75	0.08	0.02	4,699	3.52	0.13	-0.09	4,699	2.32	0.09	-0.34	4,751	3.89	0.11	0.45	4,686	1.53	0.12	-0.45
All nationals		2,617	3.74	0.07	-0.87	2,611	3.55	0.08	0.21	2,600	2.41	0.09	0.62	2,623	3.74	0.10	-0.84	2,607	1.70	0.12	0.81
Australia	Immigrants	303	3.74	0.08	-0.91	303	3.53	0.13	-0.04	303	2.32	0.09	-0.32	303	3.91	0.11	0.61	303	1.52	0.12	-0.57
	Nationals	153	3.73	0.07	-1.04	153	3.55	0.07	0.22	154	2.42	0.08	0.71	155	3.76	0.10	-0.65	153	1.67	0.12	0.61
Canada	Immigrants	251	3.75	0.07	-0.77	249	3.49	0.14	-0.35	251	2.35	0.09	-0.07	257	3.86	0.12	0.19	247	1.53	0.12	-0.50
	Nationals	138	3.74	0.07	-0.92	138	3.54	0.07	0.09	138	2.43	0.08	0.79	139	3.73	0.09	-0.94	134	1.69	0.12	0.72
Finland	Immigrants	416	3.71	0.08	-1.17	416	3.43	0.13	-0.89	416	2.34	0.09	-0.16	419	3.86	0.11	0.20	417	1.50	0.12	-0.68
	Nationals	346	3.74	0.07	-0.89	345	3.57	0.07	0.42	345	2.39	0.08	0.41	346	3.74	0.10	-0.80	345	1.71	0.12	0.89
France	Immigrants	504	3.77	0.07	-0.60	501	3.57	0.09	0.31	502	2.32	0.09	-0.31	504	3.90	0.10	0.55	497	1.54	0.12	-0.36
	Nationals	150	3.74	0.06	-0.94	150	3.54	0.09	0.05	150	2.43	0.10	0.76	150	3.74	0.05	-0.98	150	1.68	0.11	0.70
Germany	Immigrants	250	3.78	0.08	-0.52	250	3.49	0.11	-0.41	247	2.35	0.09	-0.06	250	3.82	0.09	-0.14	250	1.56	0.12	-0.25
	Nationals	248	3.77	0.07	-0.65	248	3.50	0.07	-0.38	237	2.47	0.09	1.18	248	3.67	0.09	-1.47	248	1.70	0.12	0.84
Israel	Immigrants	453	3.74	0.07	-0.91	449	3.39	0.09	-1.41	447	2.36	0.08	0.06	456	3.79	0.08	-0.42	451	1.53	0.12	-0.44
	Nationals	214	3.78	0.06	-0.52	214	3.52	0.06	-0.15	214	2.44	0.08	0.91	213	3.66	0.07	-1.67	214	1.74	0.12	1.12
Netherlands	Immigrants	343	3.76	0.07	-0.72	346	3.59	0.10	0.56	343	2.29	0.09	-0.66	347	3.93	0.10	0.81	344	1.55	0.12	-0.33
	Nationals	101	3.72	0.07	-1.13	100	3.57	0.08	0.33	100	2.41	0.09	0.58	101	3.78	0.11	-0.46	100	1.67	0.12	0.56
New Zealand	Immigrants	149	3.78	0.07	-0.52	147	3.59	0.06	0.63	148	2.31	0.08	-0.52	163	3.90	0.09	0.57	146	1.56	0.12	-0.23
	Nationals	238	3.76	0.06	-0.77	237	3.58	0.06	0.47	234	2.38	0.08	0.33	243	3.73	0.09	-0.93	235	1.73	0.11	1.07
Norway	Immigrants	457	3.76	0.08	-0.74	452	3.55	0.11	0.12	457	2.31	0.09	-0.46	465	3.90	0.11	0.53	453	1.54	0.12	-0.38
	Nationals	205	3.74	0.07	-0.91	204	3.56	0.07	0.32	205	2.40	0.09	0.52	205	3.74	0.10	-0.82	205	1.70	0.12	0.81
Portugal	Immigrants	189	3.69	0.08	-1.36	189	3.43	0.12	-0.90	189	2.35	0.09	-0.07	191	3.89	0.11	0.45	188	1.47	0.12	-0.91
	Nationals	354	3.72	0.06	-1.07	354	3.59	0.06	0.63	353	2.38	0.08	0.27	354	3.78	0.08	-0.51	354	1.69	0.12	0.77
Sweden	Immigrants	809	3.76	0.08	-0.72	811	3.57	0.11	0.31	810	2.30	0.09	-0.53	817	3.91	0.11	0.61	808	1.54	0.12	-0.36
	Nationals	214	3.75	0.07	-0.76	212	3.53	0.07	-0.03	214	2.43	0.09	0.86	214	3.70	0.11	-1.12	213	1.70	0.12	0.83
Unit. Kingdom	Immigrants	120	3.78	0.07	-0.55	120	3.60	0.10	0.59	120	2.29	0.10	-0.63	120	3.91	0.11	0.61	120	1.57	0.12	-0.19
	Nationals	120	3.75	0.07	-0.84	120	3.55	0.08	0.13	120	2.42	0.09	0.68	120	3.73	0.11	-0.89	120	1.70	0.12	0.83
United States	Immigrants	466	3.73	0.07	-1.03	466	3.56	0.11	0.24	466	2.30	0.09	-0.54	466	3.95	0.10	0.98	462	1.51	0.12	-0.63
	Nationals	136	3.71	0.07	-1.24	136	3.57	0.07	0.39	136	2.41	0.08	0.59	135	3.80	0.10	-0.30	136	1.65	0.12	0.46

Country	Group	Assimilation				Integration				Separation				Marginalization				Ethnic Identity				National Identity			
		N	M	SD	Cohen's d	N	M	SD	Cohen's d	N	M	SD	Cohen's d	N	M	SD	Cohen's d	N	M	SD	Cohen's d	N	M	SD	Cohen's d
Australia	Vietnamese	112	2.16	0.13	-0.96	112	3.95	0.08	0.92	112	2.57	0.10	0.44	112	1.76	0.11	-1.00	112	4.35	0.08	0.48	112	3.16	0.05	-1.01
	Chinese	83	2.22	0.16	-0.61	83	3.92	0.08	0.63	83	2.60	0.12	0.68	83	1.79	0.10	-0.81	83	4.33	0.09	0.37	83	3.15	0.06	-1.04
	Filipino	109	2.19	0.14	-0.79	109	3.93	0.08	0.74	109	2.59	0.11	0.61	109	1.79	0.10	-0.86	109	4.35	0.08	0.46	109	3.16	0.06	-1.01
Canada	Vietnamese	84	2.23	0.17	-0.52	84	3.94	0.08	0.80	84	2.59	0.12	0.62	83	1.75	0.10	-1.02	84	4.42	0.10	0.90	84	3.13	0.07	-1.11
	Koreans	81	2.22	0.16	-0.61	81	3.95	0.08	0.92	81	2.60	0.11	0.64	81	1.75	0.10	-1.04	81	4.43	0.10	0.93	81	3.13	0.07	-1.11
	Indo-Canadian	91	2.14	0.14	-1.06	91	3.94	0.08	0.81	91	2.53	0.11	0.15	90	1.74	0.11	-1.05	92	4.49	0.07	1.37	92	3.18	0.05	-0.96
Finland	Vietnamese	203	2.27	0.14	-0.35	202	3.94	0.08	0.81	203	2.65	0.10	1.13	202	1.79	0.12	-0.82	202	4.49	0.09	-2.08	201	3.11	0.06	-1.17
	Turks	57	2.18	0.18	-0.76	57	3.95	0.08	0.90	57	2.57	0.15	0.40	57	1.75	0.12	-1.01	57	3.93	0.09	-1.81	56	3.15	0.06	-1.04
	Russians	159	2.42	0.11	0.41	159	3.94	0.08	0.86	158	2.78	0.07	2.40	158	1.86	0.09	-0.49	156	3.85	0.05	-2.71	154	3.05	0.02	-1.41
France	Vietnamese	82	2.14	0.14	-1.05	82	3.94	0.08	0.85	82	2.51	0.09	-0.02	82	1.71	0.10	-1.27	82	4.31	0.07	0.26	82	3.17	0.05	-0.98
	Turks	61	2.13	0.12	-1.14	61	3.92	0.08	0.60	61	2.52	0.08	0.11	61	1.76	0.11	-0.96	61	4.36	0.04	0.57	61	3.20	0.01	-0.90
	Algerians	110	2.11	0.13	-1.23	110	3.94	0.08	0.80	110	2.51	0.09	-0.02	110	1.73	0.11	-1.12	111	4.35	0.05	0.52	111	3.19	0.03	-0.92
	Moroccan	133	2.12	0.11	-1.23	133	3.93	0.08	0.71	133	2.52	0.08	0.04	133	1.75	0.09	-1.04	133	4.36	0.04	0.58	133	3.19	0.01	-0.90
Germany	Portugese	119	2.14	0.12	-1.08	119	3.93	0.08	0.68	119	2.53	0.09	0.12	119	1.75	0.10	-1.05	119	4.34	0.06	0.46	119	3.19	0.03	-0.93
	Turks	95	2.15	0.13	-0.99	95	3.93	0.08	0.68	95	2.51	0.08	0.03	95	1.72	0.10	-1.18	95	4.04	0.06	-1.44	92	3.17	0.04	-0.97
	Portugese/Spaniards	70	2.16	0.12	-0.95	70	3.94	0.08	0.78	70	2.53	0.09	0.13	70	1.72	0.09	-1.22	70	4.03	0.06	-1.52	69	3.16	0.05	-1.00
	Aussiedler	85	2.27	0.15	-0.36	85	3.95	0.08	0.88	85	2.62	0.11	0.87	85	1.76	0.09	-1.00	85	3.96	0.07	-1.93	85	3.11	0.07	-1.20
Israel	Russians	296	2.38	0.12	0.24	296	3.94	0.08	0.82	296	2.72	0.07	1.85	294	1.81	0.08	-0.76	296	4.11	0.05	-1.02	296	3.06	0.03	-1.37
	Ethiopians	158	2.23	0.15	-0.56	158	3.95	0.07	0.91	158	2.58	0.10	0.56	158	1.73	0.09	-1.17	160	4.19	0.07	-0.52	160	3.12	0.05	-1.14
Netherlands	Turks	165	2.15	0.12	-1.03	165	3.94	0.08	0.46	165	2.60	0.08	0.65	164	1.80	0.11	-0.79	164	4.56	0.04	1.88	164	3.20	0.01	-0.89
	Antilleans (Dutch)	87	2.20	0.16	-1.19	87	3.94	0.08	0.77	87	2.54	0.08	0.23	88	1.79	0.11	-0.85	88	4.50	0.08	1.44	87	3.15	0.06	-1.04
	Suramese/Hindu	96	2.15	0.11	-0.84	96	3.91	0.08	0.50	96	2.52	0.07	0.06	96	1.78	0.11	-0.88	97	4.55	0.04	1.83	97	3.20	0.02	-0.90
New Zealand	Chinese	37	2.17	0.11	-1.06	37	3.90	0.08	0.47	37	2.52	0.07	0.05	37	1.76	0.11	-1.01	37	4.32	0.04	0.32	37	3.19	0.01	-0.91
	Pacific Islander	122	2.12	0.11	-0.71	121	3.92	0.08	0.64	122	2.57	0.06	0.50	120	1.76	0.08	-1.04	126	4.33	0.03	0.42	126	3.20	0.01	-0.89
Norway	Vietnamese	137	2.18	0.14	-1.06	137	3.93	0.08	0.74	137	2.59	0.10	0.62	136	1.77	0.10	-0.94	137	4.28	0.08	0.04	137	3.16	0.05	-1.01
	Turks	103	2.20	0.14	-0.71	103	3.92	0.08	0.60	103	2.55	0.10	0.35	103	1.79	0.10	-0.83	104	4.28	0.04	0.04	102	3.16	0.04	-1.01
Portugal	Pakistanis	175	2.17	0.13	-0.90	174	3.92	0.08	0.62	175	2.61	0.10	0.81	173	1.77	0.10	-0.94	176	4.29	0.07	0.14	174	3.18	0.04	-0.96
	Chilean	47	2.22	0.15	-0.59	46	3.92	0.08	0.65	46	2.64	0.13	0.98	47	1.80	0.11	-0.76	46	4.27	0.07	-0.03	46	3.15	0.05	-1.05
	Cape Verdeans	20	2.21	0.14	-0.67	20	3.99	0.05	1.39	20	2.68	0.09	1.45	20	1.77	0.10	-0.92	20	4.49	0.07	1.37	20	3.11	0.05	-1.18
	Angolans	44	2.29	0.12	-0.25	44	3.96	0.08	0.95	44	2.64	0.08	1.12	44	1.77	0.09	-0.76	44	4.45	0.07	1.15	44	3.10	0.05	-1.24
	Indians	30	2.24	0.12	-0.56	30	3.93	0.08	0.77	30	2.63	0.14	0.87	30	1.82	0.10	-0.69	30	4.51	0.07	1.54	30	3.14	0.04	-1.09
	Mozambicans	11	2.22	0.16	-0.61	12	3.95	0.07	0.97	12	2.71	0.09	1.66	12	1.79	0.10	-0.83	12	4.50	0.07	1.42	12	3.13	0.05	-1.13
Sweden	Timorese	85	2.33	0.12	-0.07	85	3.96	0.08	0.97	85	2.59	0.10	0.55	85	1.81	0.10	-0.72	85	4.43	0.06	1.02	85	3.08	0.04	-1.30
	Vietnamese	100	2.22	0.16	-0.63	100	3.93	0.08	0.72	100	2.56	0.10	0.40	99	1.76	0.11	-0.95	101	4.37	0.07	0.60	101	3.14	0.06	-1.07
	Turks	277	2.17	0.13	-0.92	277	3.91	0.08	0.58	277	2.60	0.10	0.40	276	1.79	0.10	-0.85	277	4.43	0.07	0.98	277	3.18	0.04	-0.94
	Kurds	64	2.19	0.16	-0.75	64	3.94	0.07	0.84	64	2.55	0.09	0.31	64	1.78	0.09	-0.88	64	4.39	0.09	0.75	64	3.15	0.06	-1.04
United Kingdom	C. L. and S. America	179	2.17	0.13	-0.92	179	3.92	0.08	0.60	179	2.54	0.09	0.24	179	1.78	0.10	-0.89	179	4.42	0.07	0.92	179	3.10	0.04	-0.95
	Finns	195	2.15	0.12	-1.02	195	3.91	0.08	0.56	195	2.56	0.09	0.45	195	1.78	0.11	-0.86	195	4.44	0.05	1.07	192	3.18	0.03	-0.91
	Indians	120	2.16	0.12	-1.00	120	3.91	0.07	0.50	120	2.54	0.09	0.24	120	1.78	0.11	-0.88	120	4.58	0.05	2.01	120	3.19	0.03	-0.91
United States	Vietnamese	103	2.16	0.14	-0.93	103	3.93	0.07	0.75	103	2.63	0.10	0.94	103	1.82	0.09	-0.90	102	3.99	0.05	-1.77	102	3.17	0.05	-0.97
	Armenians	193	2.21	0.14	-0.67	193	3.93	0.08	0.73	193	2.57	0.10	0.46	193	1.82	0.09	-0.70	193	3.97	0.08	-1.88	193	3.15	0.06	-1.04
	Mexican	170	2.15	0.12	-1.01	170	3.92	0.08	0.67	170	2.57	0.08	0.46	170	1.79	0.10	-0.83	170	4.00	0.06	-1.70	170	3.18	0.04	-0.94

Country	Group	Ethnic Language				National Language				Language Use				Ethnic Peer Contacts				National Peer Contacts			
		N	M	SD	Cohen's d	N	M	SD	Cohen's d	N	M	SD	Cohen's d	N	M	SD	Cohen's d	N	M	SD	Cohen's d
Australia	Vietnamese	111	3.19	0.33	-1.21	112	4.58	0.25	0.44	54	0.51	0.28	1.53	110	3.59	0.13	0.75	110	3.26	0.12	-0.32
	Chinese	83	3.23	0.41	-1.01	83	4.54	0.30	0.27	69	0.32	0.41	1.03	83	3.63	0.13	0.88	83	3.25	0.15	-0.33
	Filipino	108	3.21	0.41	-1.06	109	4.57	0.29	0.36	98	0.34	0.38	1.10	108	3.62	0.13	0.86	108	3.25	0.16	-0.33
Canada	Vietnamese	84	3.60	0.42	-0.18	84	4.54	0.32	0.26	79	0.20	0.44	0.77	84	3.58	0.13	0.73	82	3.23	0.15	-0.39
	Koreans	81	3.62	0.45	-0.11	81	4.53	0.34	0.23	80	0.17	0.46	0.71	81	3.59	0.12	0.75	81	3.21	0.16	-0.45
	Indo-Canadian	92	3.33	0.34	-0.84	92	4.75	0.25	0.97	90	0.48	0.35	1.40	92	3.56	0.14	0.65	92	3.31	0.13	-0.14
Finland	Vietnamese	202	3.94	0.39	0.63	202	4.00	0.29	-1.35	195	-0.72	0.38	-1.02	201	3.65	0.11	0.95	201	3.16	0.15	-0.63
	Turks	57	3.69	0.50	0.03	57	4.19	0.36	-0.71	53	-0.43	0.48	-0.42	57	3.58	0.17	0.69	56	3.25	0.18	-0.31
	Russians	156	4.44	0.14	2.22	157	3.65	0.10	-2.97	123	-1.21	0.14	-2.32	158	3.77	0.11	1.35	159	2.98	0.07	-1.27
France	Vietnamese	82	3.31	0.30	-0.92	82	4.73	0.22	0.94	71	0.43	0.29	1.36	80	3.50	0.11	0.49	82	3.33	0.11	-0.08
	Turks	61	3.21	0.08	-1.39	61	4.83	0.05	1.45	55	0.53	0.17	1.72	61	3.57	0.13	0.69	61	3.36	0.05	0.01
	Algerians	110	3.24	0.18	-1.24	110	4.81	0.13	1.32	99	0.53	0.17	1.69	100	3.54	0.12	0.58	100	3.34	0.08	-0.04
	Moroccan	133	3.22	0.10	-1.35	133	4.83	0.07	1.43	130	0.54	0.11	1.73	118	3.56	0.12	0.67	118	3.36	0.05	0.00
	Portugese	119	3.26	0.25	-1.11	119	4.79	0.17	1.18	110	0.50	0.22	1.56	91	3.54	0.12	0.62	91	3.36	0.08	0.00
Germany	Turks	94	3.66	0.24	-0.04	94	4.56	0.18	0.41	86	-0.04	0.25	0.36	94	3.52	0.12	0.53	95	3.35	0.09	-0.02
	Portugese/Spaniards	61	3.74	0.34	0.15	62	4.50	0.24	0.18	50	-0.11	0.32	0.19	68	3.52	0.11	0.55	70	3.32	0.14	-0.12
	Aussiedler	80	4.17	0.32	1.24	80	4.20	0.23	-0.80	77	-0.53	0.32	-0.68	84	3.60	0.13	0.78	85	3.18	0.13	-0.58
Israel	Russians	294	4.23	0.22	1.52	296	4.19	0.15	-0.90	268	-0.62	0.21	-0.93	290	3.68	0.08	1.08	290	3.06	0.09	-0.98
	Ethiopians	160	3.76	0.36	0.20	160	4.53	0.26	0.26	152	-0.13	0.36	0.15	156	3.55	0.11	0.63	156	3.23	0.13	-0.41
Netherlands	Turks	162	3.41	0.09	-0.80	165	4.66	0.06	0.80	158	0.20	0.36	0.94	163	3.61	0.13	0.84	165	3.35	0.05	-0.02
	Antilleans (Dutch)	85	3.72	0.40	0.09	89	4.45	0.29	0.00	69	-0.09	0.42	0.22	87	3.63	0.13	0.87	87	3.24	0.14	-0.38
	Suramese/Hindu	90	3.40	0.11	-0.82	97	4.66	0.06	0.80	80	0.20	0.10	0.95	97	3.59	0.13	0.76	97	3.35	0.06	0.00
New Zealand	Chinese	36	3.14	0.07	-1.61									37	3.55	0.11	0.64	37	3.38	0.05	0.09
	Pacific Islander	121	3.17	0.05	-1.54									115	3.56	0.09	0.67	115	3.36	0.05	0.03
Norway	Vietnamese	137	3.74	0.35	0.16	137	4.24	0.25	-0.65	127	-0.57	0.34	-0.76	137	3.60	0.12	0.79	137	3.27	0.13	-0.27
	Turks	104	3.73	0.36	0.14	104	4.24	0.26	-0.64	100	-0.59	0.36	-0.77	103	3.62	0.12	0.87	101	3.28	0.14	-0.25
	Pakistanis	177	3.62	0.30	-0.14	174	4.33	0.21	-0.41	162	-0.47	0.29	-0.57	173	3.59	0.13	0.75	171	3.32	0.12	-0.12
Portugal	Chilean	47	3.85	0.35	0.42	47	4.17	0.27	-0.88	37	-0.68	0.35	-0.96	47	3.65	0.12	0.95	46	3.23	0.12	-0.39
	Cape Verdeans	20	3.10	0.38	-1.35	20	4.14	0.27	-0.94	20	0.56	0.38	1.54	20	3.65	0.15	0.92	20	3.10	0.14	-0.82
	Angolans	44	3.17	0.37	-1.21	44	4.07	0.26	-1.19	44	0.45	0.35	1.34	44	3.68	0.11	1.07	44	3.09	0.14	-0.84
	Indians	30	2.91	0.30	-1.97	30	4.27	0.21	-0.61	29	0.71	0.29	1.95	30	3.68	0.11	1.06	30	3.18	0.11	-0.57
	Mozambicans	12	2.96	0.42	-1.62	12	4.22	0.29	-0.68	12	0.66	0.40	1.70	12	3.64	0.16	0.92	12	3.16	0.16	-0.60
	Timorese	85	3.28	0.27	-1.05	85	3.99	0.18	-1.59	80	0.34	0.25	1.18	84	3.69	0.13	1.10	84	3.05	0.11	-0.99
Sweden	Vietnamese	101	4.11	0.42	0.98	101	4.23	0.30	-0.66	93	-0.94	0.41	-1.43	101	3.59	0.14	0.75	101	3.25	0.15	-0.33
	Turks	278	3.90	0.30	0.57	277	4.39	0.22	-0.19	262	-0.73	0.36	-0.77	276	3.61	0.13	0.81	276	3.31	0.13	-0.13
	Kurds	64	4.12	0.38	1.04	62	4.24	0.29	-0.64	62	-0.94	0.40	-1.44	64	3.62	0.12	0.88	63	3.23	0.13	-0.40
	C., L., and S. America	172	3.91	0.27	0.63	179	4.38	0.20	-0.24	171	-0.74	0.26	-1.17	178	3.60	0.12	0.79	178	3.34	0.13	-0.14
	Finns	195	3.84	0.24	0.45	195	4.43	0.16	-0.05	188	-0.67	0.22	-1.04	193	3.60	0.12	0.79	193	3.34	0.14	-0.06
United Kingdom	Indians	120	3.35	0.20	-0.91	120	4.94	0.13	1.77	116	0.58	0.33	1.78	120	3.59	0.12	0.75	119	3.35	0.08	-0.02
United States	Vietnamese	103	3.76	0.32	0.21	102	4.81	0.24	1.16	96	-0.12	0.33	0.18	103	3.61	0.12	0.82	100	3.28	0.12	-0.23
	Armenians	193	3.95	0.37	0.65	192	4.68	0.27	0.72	171	-0.30	0.36	-0.19	192	3.67	0.12	1.04	188	3.21	0.12	-0.46
	Mexican	170	3.71	0.27	0.10	168	4.85	0.20	1.35	159	-0.08	0.26	0.28	169	3.62	0.11	0.86	162	3.30	0.11	-0.19

Country	Group	Family Obligations				Adolescents' Rights				Perceived Discrimination			
		N	M	SD	Cohen's d	N	M	SD	Cohen's d	N	M	SD	Cohen's d
Australia	Vietnamese	112	3.64	0.06	0.96	112	3.36	0.05	-0.24	112	2.03	0.07	-0.28
	Chinese	82	3.66	0.07	1.04	82	3.34	0.06	-0.54	82	2.06	0.09	-0.09
Canada	Filipino	109	3.66	0.07	1.02	109	3.36	0.06	-0.35	109	2.04	0.07	-0.20
	Vietnamese	84	3.65	0.07	0.98	84	3.32	0.06	-0.84	83	2.03	0.10	-0.27
	Koreans	81	3.65	0.07	0.99	81	3.33	0.06	-0.71	80	2.01	0.09	-0.35
Finland	Indo-Canadian	90	3.62	0.07	0.84	90	3.37	0.05	-0.20	91	1.97	0.08	-0.63
	Vietnamese	203	3.69	0.06	1.16	203	3.32	0.06	-0.90	202	2.17	0.08	0.55
	Turks	56	3.64	0.10	0.92	56	3.35	0.05	-0.47	56	2.12	0.09	0.27
France	Russians	158	3.77	0.05	1.54	156	3.28	0.04	-1.65	159	2.23	0.06	0.96
	Vietnamese	82	3.60	0.06	0.75	82	3.35	0.05	-0.51	82	1.92	0.07	-0.93
	Turks	61	3.62	0.06	0.85	61	3.37	0.04	-0.09	61	1.89	0.06	-1.09
	Algerians	110	3.61	0.06	0.80	110	3.37	0.04	-0.09	111	1.89	0.06	-1.12
	Moroccan	133	3.61	0.05	0.83	133	3.38	0.04	-0.02	133	1.89	0.06	-1.13
	Portugese	119	3.62	0.06	0.84	119	3.36	0.05	-0.24	119	1.90	0.07	-1.02
Germany	Turks	95	3.60	0.05	0.77	95	3.34	0.05	-0.59	94	1.87	0.07	-1.20
	Portugese/Spaniards	70	3.61	0.06	0.80	70	3.34	0.04	-0.67	62	1.88	0.07	-1.16
	Aussiedler	85	3.66	0.07	1.05	85	3.31	0.05	-1.19	80	1.93	0.08	-0.83
Israel	Russians	296	3.72	0.04	1.33	296	3.27	0.04	-1.88	296	2.52	0.06	2.72
	Ethiopians	158	3.63	0.06	0.92	158	3.31	0.05	-1.09	159	2.45	0.08	2.24
Netherlands	Turks	162	3.64	0.06	0.94	162	3.38	0.04	-0.03	163	1.91	0.06	-1.01
	Antilleans (Dutch)	87	3.66	0.07	1.04	86	3.35	0.06	-0.39	84	1.94	0.08	-0.80
	Surinamese/Hindu	96	3.63	0.06	0.89	96	3.37	0.04	-0.13	95	1.91	0.06	-1.00
New Zealand	Chinese	37	3.61	0.05	0.81	37	3.36	0.04	-0.37	37	2.51	0.06	2.65
	Pacific Islander	114	3.61	0.04	0.83	114	3.37	0.04	-0.08	113	2.49	0.06	2.52
Norway	Vietnamese	136	3.64	0.06	0.97	136	3.35	0.05	-0.39	136	2.18	0.07	0.63
	Turks	101	3.66	0.06	1.02	101	3.35	0.06	-0.46	100	2.19	0.08	0.67
	Pakistanis	173	3.63	0.06	0.92	172	3.36	0.05	-0.33	172	2.17	0.07	0.59
	Chilean	47	3.67	0.06	1.10	47	3.35	0.06	-0.48	47	2.19	0.09	0.71
Portugal	Cape Verdeans	20	3.69	0.08	1.18	20	3.35	0.04	-0.46	20	2.24	0.07	0.99
	Angolans	44	3.71	0.06	1.28	44	3.32	0.05	-0.99	44	2.29	0.07	1.28
	Indians	30	3.69	0.05	1.20	30	3.35	0.05	-0.46	30	2.25	0.06	1.03
	Mozambicans	11	3.88	0.06	1.10	11	3.35	0.05	-0.53	10	2.23	0.06	0.94
	Timorese	85	3.72	0.06	1.33	85	3.31	0.05	-1.21	84	2.30	0.07	1.39
Sweden	Vietnamese	101	3.65	0.07	0.97	101	3.33	0.05	-0.73	99	1.86	0.08	-1.25
	Turks	275	3.64	0.06	0.95	275	3.37	0.05	-0.20	275	1.82	0.07	-1.50
	Kurds	64	3.66	0.06	1.05	64	3.36	0.06	-0.32	63	1.84	0.09	-1.37
	C.L. and S. America	179	3.64	0.06	0.94	179	3.36	0.05	-0.28	179	1.83	0.07	-1.47
United Kingdom	Indians	194	3.64	0.06	0.93	194	3.37	0.04	-0.11	191	1.81	0.07	-1.57
	Finns	120	3.63	0.06	0.89	120	3.37	0.04	-0.21	120	2.21	0.06	0.81
United States	Vietnamese	103	3.65	0.06	0.98	103	3.37	0.05	-0.16	103	2.08	0.08	0.06
	Armenians	193	3.68	0.05	1.16	193	3.36	0.05	-0.29	193	2.10	0.08	0.17
	Mexican	170	3.65	0.05	0.99	170	3.38	0.05	-0.02	170	2.07	0.07	0.00

Country	Group	Self Esteem				Life Satisfaction				Psychological Problems				School Adjustment				Behavior Problems			
		N	M	SD	Cohen's d	N	M	SD	Cohen's d	N	M	SD	Cohen's d	N	M	SD	Cohen's d	N	M	SD	Cohen's d
Australia	Vietnamese	111	3.73	0.07	-1.00	111	3.52	0.13	-0.11	111	2.34	0.10	-0.14	112	4.00	0.10	1.37	112	1.49	0.11	18.99
	Chinese	83	3.75	0.08	-0.80	83	3.53	0.12	-0.02	83	2.31	0.08	-0.49	83	3.97	0.11	1.15	83	1.54	0.12	17.73
	Filippino	109	3.74	0.08	-0.90	109	3.54	0.13	0.02	109	2.32	0.09	-0.38	108	4.00	0.11	1.35	108	1.52	0.13	16.72
Canada	Vietnamese	82	3.76	0.07	-0.72	82	3.46	0.13	-0.59	82	2.35	0.09	-0.03	84	3.91	0.11	0.59	79	1.54	0.11	19.27
	Koreans	79	3.74	0.08	-0.88	77	3.45	0.15	-0.61	78	2.36	0.09	0.07	81	3.93	0.10	0.81	78	1.51	0.12	17.62
	Indo-Canadian	90	3.76	0.07	-0.73	90	3.55	0.11	0.10	91	2.33	0.09	-0.21	92	3.96	0.10	1.07	90	1.53	0.11	18.76
Finland	Vietnamese	203	3.72	0.08	-1.03	201	3.45	0.14	-0.62	203	2.34	0.09	-0.17	203	3.78	0.08	-0.53	203	1.51	0.13	16.88
	Turks	56	3.75	0.09	-0.80	56	3.50	0.12	-0.30	55	2.35	0.09	-0.07	57	3.78	0.08	-0.53	56	1.52	0.12	17.84
	Russians	157	3.67	0.07	-1.56	159	3.37	0.08	-1.73	158	2.34	0.08	-0.17	159	3.79	0.06	-0.45	158	1.48	0.12	17.20
France	Vietnamese	82	3.79	0.06	-0.48	82	3.51	0.11	-0.21	82	2.36	0.09	0.03	82	3.89	0.06	0.55	82	1.55	0.12	18.91
	Turks	60	3.77	0.06	-0.61	59	3.59	0.08	0.61	60	2.30	0.09	-0.50	59	3.96	0.11	1.01	58	1.55	0.12	18.87
	Algerians	111	3.77	0.06	-0.68	110	3.56	0.09	0.29	111	2.33	0.09	-0.23	111	3.95	0.10	0.96	109	1.53	0.11	19.50
	Moroccan	132	3.77	0.07	-0.66	131	3.59	0.07	0.55	130	2.31	0.09	-0.43	133	3.96	0.08	1.13	129	1.54	0.12	18.69
	Portugese	119	3.77	0.08	-0.56	119	3.57	0.09	0.34	119	2.32	0.09	-0.40	119	3.94	0.09	0.89	119	1.55	0.12	17.71
Germany	Turks	95	3.80	0.07	-0.34	95	3.53	0.10	-0.01	94	2.34	0.09	-0.18	95	3.79	0.08	-0.45	95	1.58	0.12	18.93
	Portugese/Spaniards	70	3.79	0.08	-0.43	70	3.51	0.11	-0.25	69	2.35	0.08	-0.06	70	3.79	0.10	-0.41	70	1.56	0.13	16.74
	Aussiedler	85	3.75	0.07	-0.82	85	3.42	0.10	-1.03	84	2.36	0.09	0.08	85	3.79	0.06	-0.48	85	1.53	0.12	18.32
Israel	Russians	294	3.72	0.06	-1.07	292	3.37	0.07	-1.76	292	2.35	0.07	-0.01	296	3.74	0.05	-0.94	296	1.53	0.12	18.63
	Ethiopians	159	3.77	0.07	-0.64	157	3.43	0.10	-0.94	155	2.37	0.08	0.19	160	3.73	0.06	-1.01	155	1.54	0.12	18.17
Netherlands	Antilleans (Dutch)	161	3.77	0.07	-0.67	164	3.62	0.08	0.89	161	2.28	0.09	-0.80	164	4.01	0.06	1.69	162	1.56	0.12	18.79
	Suramese/Hindu	85	3.73	0.07	-0.98	85	3.52	0.12	-0.08	86	2.32	0.09	-0.38	87	3.98	0.07	1.47	86	1.52	0.12	18.01
New Zealand	Chinese	97	3.77	0.07	-0.59	97	3.61	0.09	0.72	96	2.29	0.09	-0.67	96	3.98	0.06	1.45	96	1.56	0.12	18.44
	Pacific Islander	37	3.77	0.07	-0.30	37	3.59	0.07	0.61	37	2.30	0.08	-0.61	37	3.61	0.06	-2.16	37	1.59	0.12	18.70
Norway	Vietnamese	112	3.77	0.07	-0.60	110	3.59	0.06	0.64	111	2.31	0.08	-0.49	126	3.65	0.05	-1.84	109	1.55	0.12	18.36
	Turks	136	3.75	0.07	-0.82	135	3.53	0.12	0.01	136	2.32	0.09	-0.32	137	3.89	0.07	0.53	136	1.53	0.12	17.83
	Pakistanis	101	3.75	0.08	-0.74	100	3.55	0.12	0.11	101	2.30	0.08	-0.53	104	3.88	0.08	0.44	101	1.54	0.13	17.08
	Chilean	173	3.77	0.08	-0.63	170	3.56	0.10	0.29	173	2.31	0.08	-0.51	177	3.89	0.07	0.52	169	1.55	0.12	17.63
Portugal	Cape Verdeans	47	3.73	0.07	-0.96	47	3.53	0.12	-0.04	47	2.31	0.09	-0.49	47	3.90	0.08	0.62	47	1.52	0.12	18.19
	Angolans	20	3.66	0.06	-1.68	20	3.43	0.13	-1.01	20	2.38	0.07	0.27	20	3.85	0.06	0.15	19	1.41	0.08	26.04
	Indians	44	3.69	0.08	-1.33	44	3.42	0.13	-0.90	44	2.35	0.09	-0.06	44	3.80	0.07	-0.32	44	1.47	0.13	16.28
	Mozambicans	30	3.70	0.08	-1.22	30	3.52	0.11	-0.16	30	2.31	0.09	-0.45	30	3.84	0.07	0.01	30	1.49	0.12	16.92
	Timorese	11	3.70	0.09	-1.20	11	3.46	0.08	-0.76	11	2.35	0.07	0.01	12	3.82	0.07	-0.19	11	1.46	0.12	16.83
Sweden	Vietnamese	84	3.69	0.08	-1.38	84	3.40	0.11	-1.22	84	2.35	0.09	-0.02	85	3.79	0.07	-0.42	84	1.47	0.13	16.55
	Turks	100	3.76	0.07	-0.70	100	3.50	0.13	-0.30	100	2.33	0.10	-0.21	101	3.81	0.07	-0.25	99	1.55	0.12	18.41
	Chilean	275	3.76	0.07	-0.73	275	3.58	0.11	0.44	274	2.30	0.09	-0.60	278	3.86	0.07	0.23	274	1.54	0.12	18.06
	Kurds	63	3.72	0.08	-1.03	64	3.52	0.12	-0.10	64	2.32	0.08	-0.33	64	3.87	0.09	0.32	64	1.50	0.12	18.03
United Kingdom	C., L., and S. America Indians	178	3.76	0.08	-0.68	179	3.57	0.11	0.33	179	2.30	0.08	-0.53	179	3.85	0.08	0.12	179	1.55	0.12	17.70
	Finns	193	3.76	0.08	-0.66	193	3.60	0.09	0.65	193	2.29	0.09	-0.67	195	3.86	0.06	0.27	192	1.55	0.12	17.73
United States	Vietnamese	120	3.78	0.07	-0.55	120	3.60	0.10	0.59	120	2.29	0.10	-0.63	120	3.79	0.06	-0.43	120	1.57	0.12	18.60
	Vietnamese	103	3.74	0.08	-0.89	103	3.56	0.10	0.25	103	2.31	0.08	-0.47	103	4.12	0.11	2.35	102	1.52	0.12	17.91
	Armenians	193	3.71	0.07	-1.21	193	3.54	0.13	0.06	193	2.30	0.08	-0.53	193	4.15	0.09	2.79	192	1.49	0.12	17.88
	Mexican	170	3.74	0.07	-0.93	170	3.59	0.10	0.48	170	2.30	0.09	-0.59	170	4.14	0.09	2.67	168	1.52	0.12	18.15

Appendix D

**Eigenvalues and Percentages of Variance Explained of Factors
for Acculturation Processes and Adaptation Outcomes**

	Eigenvalue	% explained variance
Ethnic orientation	1.422	47.39
National orientation	1.199	59.94
Integration	1.277	63.85
Ethnic behaviors	1.537	38.43
Psychological adaptation	1.747	58.23
Sociocultural adaptation	1.357	67.86

Author Index

Subject Index